THE WIND ENSEMBLE AND ITS REPERTOIRE

DEDICATION

To Fred, and to all the composers, conductors, and performers who have supported and nurtured the Wind Ensemble concept.

Funding towards the production of this work was generously provided by the H. Earle Johnson Foundation of the Sonneck Society for American Music.

THE
WIND ENSEMBLE
AND ITS
REPERTOIRE

*Essays on the Fortieth Anniversary of the
Eastman Wind Ensemble*

EDITED BY
FRANK J. CIPOLLA & DONALD HUNSBERGER

UNIVERSITY OF ROCHESTER PRESS

First published 1994

University of Rochester Press
34–36 Administration Building, University of Rochester
Rochester, New York, 14627, USA
and at PO Box 9, Woodbridge, Suffolk IP12 3DF, UK

ISBN 1 878822 46 2

Library of Congress Cataloging-in-Publication Data

The wind ensemble and its repertoire : essays on the 40th anniversary
  of the Eastman Wind Ensemble / edited by Frank J. Cipolla and Donald
  R. Hunsberger.
        p.   cm.
    Includes bibliographical references.
    Discography: p.
    ISBN 1–878822–46–2 :
    1. Band music—History and criticism.   2. Wind ensembles—History
  and criticism.   3. Eastman Wind Ensemble.   I. Cipolla, Frank.
  II. Hunsberger, Donald.   III. Eastman Wind Ensemble.
  ML1300.W58   1994
  784.8—dc20   94-29156

British Library Cataloguing-in-Publication Data

A catalogue record for this book is available from the British Library

This publication is printed on acid-free paper
Printed in the United States of America

Contents

THE INTERNATIONAL SPREAD OF THE WIND ENSEMBLE

APPENDICES

Introduction

FRANK CIPOLLA

"THE first Eastman Wind Ensemble rehearsal callsheet posted by Frederick Fennell on September 20, 1952 became a kind of emancipation proclamation—a declaration of freedom for composers, conductors, players, and audiences." So stated Kenneth Neidig, editor of *BD Guide,* in introducing the fortieth-anniversary gala Prism Concert presented by the Eastman Wind Ensemble as part of a celebratory weekend of concerts, conducting workshops, and analytical and historical research papers. (The complete schedule of events is listed as Appendix B.) If Neidig's comments seem overly forceful, one need only compare the state of the American band and its literature in the early 1950s with what is available today. The sheer number of wind ensembles functioning world-wide and the quality of music being written and performed by them is ample proof of the influence that the Eastman Wind Ensemble has wielded for the past forty-plus years. Today it would be a rarity to find wind conductors and ensembles who have not garnered encouragement and motivation from Frederick Fennell's initial Mercury recordings with the Eastman Wind Ensemble or from Clyde Roller's exceptionally fine interpretation of Vittorio Giannini's Symphony No. 3 on that same label. The *Homespun America* album and many others recorded by Donald Hunsberger complete a legacy of forty years of notable performances that was celebrated, with justifiable pride, at the Eastman School of Music, 7–9 February 1992.

Incorporated into the Eastman festivities was a series of presentations by the Conductors' Guild and the Sonneck Society for American Music. The Conductors' Guild held several workshop sessions with the Eastman Wind Ensemble in which young conductors were critiqued by Frederick Fennell, Clyde Roller, and Donald Hunsberger. The Sonneck Society, a scholarly organization for the promotion and dissemination of information on all aspects of American music and music in America, sponsored the reading of research papers. This volume testifies to the spirit and wealth of information that flowed through that extraordinary weekend and is presented here not only to chronicle the Ensemble's past, but to provide musicians everywhere a glimpse of the tremendous growth in the quality and quantity of material relating to wind bands in this second half of the twentieth century.

Central for many who peruse these pages will be Donald Hunsberger's account of the evolution of the Eastman Wind Ensemble (EWE). Hunsberger was a student member of the EWE at its inception and has continued that association through his long tenure as its conductor. His insight and perspective is extremely valuable, and his detailed description of events is documented for the first time here. The historical viewpoint of the EWE that emerges is fascinating in itself, but intertwined with it is the gradual growth of repertoire and the increasingly global involvement of composers and conductors. The development of repertoire and composer interest is also obvious in a reading of Appendix A, for it offers a comprehensive catalog of repertoire, programs, and recordings of the EWE and its predecessor, the Eastman Symphony Band. In fact, Appendix A can serve as a voluminous resource for the study of contemporary wind literature.

The section "Studies on the Repertoire" presents analytical points of view on specific composers by Robert Wason, Michael Votta, and Frank Byrne, in articles on Stravinsky's *Symphonies of Wind Instruments*, Wagner's *Trauermusik*, and Sousa's marches, respectively. Each of these subjects is closely associated with the EWE, for the composers discussed were an important part of the recorded output of the Ensemble's early years. For example, forty years ago one would be hard pressed to find a work such as the Stravinsky *Symphonies* being programmed other than for an orchestral concert. Frederick Fennell, however, performed and recorded it with the EWE, thus bringing that composition (and similarly the music of Andrea and Giovanni Gabrieli, as well as Mozart, Richard Strauss, and other "orchestral" composers) to the attention of the "band" fraternity—to the point that the Stravinsky *Symphonies* is now a staple of the wind repertoire. Wind conductors contemplating performing the work will find Robert Wason's penetrating analysis most enlightening. Likewise, performing the marches of John Philip Sousa will be a different experience for many after encountering Frank Byrne's in-depth study of that genre.

Richard Wagner's original score of *Trauermusik* was written to be performed out of doors, and calls for a large wind band with multiple players to a part, including seven oboes and ten bassoons. Such a scoring has precluded frequent programming of the piece in its original form, but in the 1940s Eric Leidzen revised the score to match the instrumentation of the Goldman Band; it is in that transformation that the work is performed most often. Michael Votta has examined Wagner's original scoring, Leidzen's revision, and one other version of *Trauermusik*, and formulates his own theories on resolving the instrumental problems of multiple players. Votta proposes a new version that replicates Wagner's original outdoor sound structure for performance within the confines of the concert hall.

An extensive history of bands, or even the history of bands in the United States, is beyond the scope of this book. However, aspects of that history are pertinent for an understanding of how we have arrived at the present state of wind bands and, more especially, the wind ensemble concept. Raoul Camus speaks to the development of early American wind bands and their small but mixed brass/woodwind instrumental combinations. Since European musical customs and traditions arrived with the colonists, most of the music performed by these groups was of English, French, or German derivation, and much of it was in the form of the march. Camus presents a thorough discussion of the subject with suggestions on how best to interpret this music, with special regard to tempos, since none were indicated.

The development of the keyed bugle in the first part of the nineteenth century further helped to shape the future of American bands and American band music.

Early virtuosos who helped popularize that instrument were Richard Willis, leader of the West Point Academy Band, Edward (Ned) Kendall of Boston, eventual leader of the Boston Brass Band, and Francis Johnson, the great African-American composer/performer and leader of the Washington Guards Band of Philadelphia. The adaptation of the key principle to larger brass instruments—ophicleides and bass horns—led to the formation of all-brass bands, ushering in an era which dates from the mid 1830s to the turn of the century. Jon Newsom's perceptive article focuses on the 1850s, the "golden age" of the brass band. Newsom quotes liberally from John Sullivan Dwight, editor of *Dwight's Journal of Music* and pillar of mid-nineteenth-century New England "cultured" musical thought. Newson characterizes Dwight as "promoting, guiding, and frequently condemning popular musical fashions in the course of reporting and polemicizing on the brass band movement in America before, during, and after the Civil War."

Brass instruments and their use in an ensemble context before the era of the brass band is the subject of Robert Sheldon's essay. The "trumpet corps" which functioned within the domain of aristocratic European court life can be construed as the forerunner of the brass band. Each instrumentalist sounded only one or two notes, so a great number of players were required for ensemble playing, and split-second coordination was necessary. It was, as Sheldon says, "the hornistic version of hand bell ringing." Two interesting examples are cited with suggestions as to how they may be adapted for modern performance.

The international spread of the wind ensemble movement was confirmed in the 1980s with the establishment of the World Association of Symphonic Bands and Ensembles (WASBE) and a corollary group in England, the British Association of Symphonic Bands and Wind Ensembles (BASBWE). Both of these organizations are dedicated to fostering growth in band repertoire by engaging composers to write for winds—one of Frederick Fennell's original goals in establishing the EWE. As one might expect, numerous individuals in these organizations look to the Eastman Wind Ensemble for leadership and have established wind groups in that same mold. Repertoire development, particularly in the United Kingdom, has been significant. Timothy Reynish, a staunch advocate of contemporary wind literature, cites a large number of compositions that should be of interest to all conductors and performers of wind music. These works document Reynish's assertion that the writing of wind music in the U.K. appears to have regained the attention of serious composers after a long period of neglect since the medium first captured the interest of Gustav Holst and Ralph Vaughan Williams in the first part of the century. Factors involved in bringing the wind compositions of Holst and Vaughan Williams to fruition are discussed in Jon Mitchell's article. As Mitchell indicates, much of the credit belongs to Col. John A. C. Sommerville, Commandant of the Royal Military School of Music at Kneller Hall, Twickenham, England. Premiere performances of both composers' works were given either at the school or in concerts in London by the school's personnel. Mitchell also discusses the development of military music in the United Kingdom and the establishment of the Royal Military School of Music.

Leon Bly's report on the status of wind bands in continental Europe suggests that while band activities there are not as attuned to the Eastman concept as in the U.K., bands and bandsmen alike have been influenced by the EWE recordings. Continental European bands are community or adult-oriented amateur organizations. The instrumentation of these groups varies greatly between countries, making it difficult for composers to have their works played outside of their own borders. However, as the concept of flexible instrumentation takes hold, much of that problem will cease to exist. Bly further suggests that a growing number of European ensembles are beginning to bridge the gap that has traditionally existed between band music and wind chamber music, as players in each type of organization come to expect a more refined and inclusive repertoire.

Another area of the globe in which the Eastman Wind Ensemble concept has been openly embraced is Japan. Many of today's leaders in Japanese wind music have been influenced by the Eastman School of Music (some actually having attended there) and emulate the ensemble experience they received from that institution. The EWE, under Donald Hunsberger, first toured Japan in 1978, and it has returned several times in recent years. The influence of the EWE is also evident in the concerts, television appearances, recordings, and tours by the Tokyo Kosei Wind Orchestra, whose resident conductor since 1984 has been Frederick Fennell. Toshio Akiyama's article traces the historical development of bands in Japan, beginning in the mid-nineteenth century with the first influences of Western culture, through the enormous growth in bands and band music that has taken place in that country since the mid-1940s.

*   *   *   *   *

The Eastman Wind Ensemble's fortieth anniversary celebration weekend included additional papers that could not be a part of this volume but deserve acknowledgement. Frederick Williams of Philadelphia, Pennsylvania, presented a program combining graphic illustrations and early band recordings from his vast personal collection. Williams, a leading exponent of recorded band music, traced its history from the late 1880s to a 1928 recording of *The Stars and Stripes Forever* by the band of John Philip Sousa. A paper on the high school wind ensemble was given by James Croft, Director of Bands, Florida State University, Tallahassee, Florida, one of the first band directors to use the wind ensemble concept at the secondary school level. Donald Hunsberger's account of the history of the EWE incorporates some of this material. Likewise, the remarks by David Whitwell, Director of Bands, California State University at Northridge, on aspects of band traditions in Europe, are covered in the paper by Leon Bly, *Wind Bands in Continental Europe*.

*   *   *   *   *

The editors would like to acknowledge and thank Ralph Locke, Professor of Musicology, Eastman School of Music, for his perceptive criticisms and valuable suggestions, which greatly contributed to the final form of the volume. Kenneth Neidig, editor of *BD Guide*, and Charles Staley, Arts Coordinator and Wind Ensemble Director, Waubonsie Valley High School, Aurora, Illinois, also gave generously of their time in critiquing several of the articles. A further debt is due Ruth Watanabe, Librarian Emeritus, Eastman School; Frank Battisti, Conductor, New England Conservatory; and Mark Scatterday, Director of Bands, Cornell University, for their comments and assistance.

Compilation of the programs, repertoire, and discography that comprise Appendix A was initiated by Jeffrey Renshaw, Director of Bands, University of Connecticut, with meticulous reading and editing by Robert Rumbelow, John Clanton, and Donald Hunsberger from the Conducting and Ensembles Department of the Eastman School, and Wilma Reid Cipolla, Librarian Emeritus, State University of New York at Buffalo. Suzanne Stover from the Recording Arts and Services Department, Eastman School, assisted generously by providing information on the recordings.

The task of formatting and copyediting the diverse contributions to transform them into a unified whole was accomplished by Michael Dodds of the Eastman School. His interest and attention to the myriad details represented in the various articles is gratefully appreciated.

Finally, we offer sincere thanks to Robert Easton, Managing Editor, University of Rochester Press, for his professional expertise and encouragement in support of this project, and to Dr. Robert Freeman, Director of the Eastman School of Music, for his continued advocacy of the Eastman Wind Ensemble.

FRANK J. CIPOLLA
Professor Emeritus, Department of Music
State University of New York at Buffalo

The Wind Ensemble Concept

DONALD HUNSBERGER

DURING the past forty-two years, the music world has witnessed the development of a new approach to the wind band, an approach that has drawn attention to an emerging original repertoire and to new performance possibilities for concerted wind music. An increasing number of conductors, composers and performers have moved away from the popular-culture aspects of the traditional concert or military band toward a classical performance medium. Much of this may be attributed directly to the achievements of the musicians involved in what is now known as the "Wind Ensemble Concept."

The growth of this concept may be traced through several stages, each approximately a decade in length:

1. 1952–62: Innovations.
2. 1962–72: Transitions and expansions.
3. 1972–82: National development.
4. 1982–present: Repertoire development and international relations.

The primary innovator in the founding and early development of this movement was Frederick Fennell, who established the Eastman Wind Ensemble at the Eastman School of Music of the University of Rochester in the fall of 1952. Fennell described this initiative in an article entitled "The Wind Ensemble":

> In the winter of 1951, an unusual concert of music for wind instruments was performed at the Eastman School of Music under the writer's direction. This evening of music began with a *Ricercare* for wind instruments by Adrian Willaert (1480–1562) and ended ten compositions later with the *Symphonies for Wind Instruments* by Igor Stravinsky. This program, which was almost twenty years in the building, had significance far beyond the beauties of the music played and the excellence of the performance given by students from our Instrumental Ensemble Department. The wonderful effect this concert had upon the discriminating audience and the press is a pleasure to recall, as is the reaction of the players which was positive, articulate and enthusiastic in the extreme.
>
> The direct result of this evening of original music for wind instruments was the establishment in the Fall of 1952 of the Eastman Wind Ensemble. Prior to opening of school this year, I sent a mimeographed letter to approximately four hundred composers in all parts of the world telling them of our plan to establish an ensemble of the following instrumentation:

REEDS

Two flutes and piccolo and/or Alto flute
Two oboes and English horn
One E flat clarinet
Eight B flat clarinets, or A clarinets divided in any manner desired or fewer in
  number if so desired
One E flat alto clarinet
One B flat bass clarinet
Choir of saxophones—Two alto E flat, tenor B flat, baritone E flat

BRASS

Three cornets in B flat
Two trumpets in B flat or Five trumpets
Four horns
Two euphoniums (Bass clef)
Three trombones
One E flat tuba
One BB flat tuba or two BB flat tubas if desired
One string bass

OTHER INSTRUMENTS

Percussion, harp, celeste, piano, organ, harpsichord, solo string instruments,
  and choral forces as desired.

My letter stated in part that it was our hope that composers would look upon this instrumental establishment as the basic instrumentation from which they could deviate should a particular score require more or less instruments than were listed. It was further stated that they might consider this in the same manner as one does the *tutti* orchestra, the full organ, or the complete seven-plus octave range of the piano keyboard—a sonority to be utilized *only* when desired. My correspondents were informed that the Eastman School would have one annual symposium for the reading of all new music written for the Wind Ensemble, and that there would be no "commissions" save those of a performance that was prepared with skill and devotion.[1]

In an interview with *New York Times* critic Howard Taubman, Fennell further discussed the core instrumentation he had selected:

[the new group] consists of the reed-brass-percussion combination of the orchestra which Wagner assembled for Bayreuth plus a section of saxophones. All of the perhaps less pleasant reactions one customarily associates with a band I do not think you will find present here. From the standpoint of texture it is not bloated, is clear and at the same time intense, in tune, flexible, virtuosic—contains a magnificent range of dynamics plus a beautiful tone quality.[2]

With these opening statements, Frederick Fennell set the course for a movement that would inaugurate changes in all forms of the wind band, including the development of original, indigenous repertoire and performance practices for varying sizes of collected wind and percussion ensembles. Fennell explained further the rationale behind his decision:

One factor which is of constantly increasing concern to some educators is the problem of the ever-enlarging personnel which is the fashion with the college concert band. In spite of this large participation, and whether we like it or not, there is an ever-increasing number of our student wind players who are not interested in the band. The individual who is weary of being the fifteenth cornet or the twenty-fourth clarinet may be noncommittal on the subject, but unless he is lucky and good enough to get a chair in the orchestra, he winds up in the big band. The average student in our schools desires and needs more training, more individual responsibility, than these conditions can offer. In the limited repertory which most concert bands play in a season, a student's contact with the music of the sixteenth, seventeenth, and eighteenth centuries is practically nil, as are his experiences with much of the best music of the twentieth century. Most of this music does not fit the personnel of the concert band, and since the performance of most music for winds, aside from chamber music, is the strict province of the band director, it rarely gets performed in our schools. . . .

The primary concern of the professional conductors, professional educators, instrument manufacturers, and music publishers who are responsible for the development of the concert band in the last forty years has been, and continues to be, the problem of a standardized instrumentation. Art by manifest seldom succeeds. In establishing "standard instrumentations" approved by prominent and influential associations, the composer has been told for what instruments he must write, not in so many words perhaps, but the implication is usually quite clear. Is it any wonder, therefore, that the wind band medium has been approached, if at all, with the caution of the skeptic? The history of musical composition *is* the history of music; and it proves without question that the composer has always shaped the development of those instrumental ensembles which have survived. The orchestra, the opera, the string quartet, and the marching-military band, for instance, all have a distinguished literature to which the composers of every occidental culture have contributed endlessly and without persuasion for over three hundred years.[3]

This philosophy, in opposition to entrenched practices at that time, placed a primary emphasis upon the enlistment of composers on behalf of the wind band. Since the early days of the century, the quality and quantity of substantial original works was sparse compared to the vast amount of music transcribed for band from orchestral, operatic and keyboard sources. This imbalance between transcribed and original music originated in the middle of the previous century when military band journals were beginning to be published in both the United States and England. The arranger and the transcriber held a position of importance in the eyes of band directors, especially during the first half of this century.

The large doubled-instrumentation band was indeed the model for many band directors. In actuality, Fennell had modeled the Eastman Symphony Band (the precursor of the Eastman Wind Ensemble) on Albert Austin Harding's University of Illinois Band (Fennell had worked and performed with Harding at the National Music Camp at Interlochen, Michigan in the 1930s). For Fennell to turn away from this widely popular instrumentation ideal and embrace a different set of principles was indeed a bold step—one that would be misunderstood by symphonic band directors for many years.

Instrumentation

Fennell's manifesto put forth two main principles: (1) the development of an original repertoire, as opposed to a borrowed, arranged, or transcribed one, and (2) the idea of flexible instrumentation and personnel assignments for each work—established, whenever possible, by the composer. While many band directors may have shared his desire for an original repertoire, the second of his proposals directly conflicted with the then-common standardized instrumentation in which all players performed every composition, with a great deal of doubling between instruments. Fennell proposed in *The American Music Teacher* that:

> The Wind Ensemble's "Instrumentation" is not a further attempt at standardization. It is presented simply as a point of departure. With it, however, one can perform, with but few exceptions, all the great music written for wind instruments dating from the sixteenth century to today. From this imposing amount of music I chose three works for the debut concert of the Eastman Wind Ensemble which took place on February 8, 1953: Mozart's 10th Serenade in B-Flat for thirteen winds, Wallingford Riegger's Nonet for Brass, and Paul Hindemith's Symphony in B-Flat for Concert Band. This program argues strongly against the old complaint leveled against wind instruments that there is no music written for them which is of sufficient interest to make anyone care to hear it performed. In an article for the September, 1952 issue of *Music Journal,* I wrote that "the time has come for the wind instruments to own a home of their own, unmortgaged by the limitations and traditions of other properties in which they have resided for so long. We are providing one such home in Rochester." The future developments of literature for this attractive music medium once again rests squarely in the hands of the composer.[4]

It is necessary to examine the years surrounding 1952 when Fennell formally inaugurated the Eastman Wind Ensemble (EWE) program to accurately assess his analysis of the status of concert bands and their programs at that time. It would be a decade before the wind ensemble movement would spread beyond a small number of conservatory-oriented colleges and universities and selected secondary schools. Much tacit and overt opposition to the movement was apparent, especially among older-generation leaders of the large, standard-instrumentation symphonic bands.

Why did Fennell feel it necessary to create a new and different performing ensemble with its own agenda for the development of a new repertoire and performing style? Why did it literally take years following the issue of the first recordings in the Mercury series (1953) for many band conductors to recognize the value and importance of this new concept of flexibility and originality? What avenues developed over the next forty years to spread the concept throughout the United States, and indeed, the entire world? What is the current status of the concept and what is the future for continued development? These questions and similar concerns will be subjects for discussion among wind musicians for many years to come.

Programming and Repertoire

The most important key to the success of any performing ensemble lies in the quality of its repertoire. The literature for the string quartet speaks for the development of that ensemble over the past two centuries, and the vast repertoire for the chamber orchestra and symphony orchestra attests to the validity of each of these performing media, as do the repertoires for choral and operatic ensembles.

Fennell's claim, that during the decades prior to the founding of the Eastman Wind Ensemble, concert and military band directors failed to encourage and develop their own original repertoire, rather preferring to exist on a borrowed literature, is certainly true when one examines the small number of original works for band composed prior to 1950. This listing includes:

Samuel Barber	*Commando March* (1943)
Robert Russell Bennett	*Suite of Old American Dances* (1947)
Percy Grainger	*Lincolnshire Posy* (1936)
	Lads of Wamphray (1935)
Gustav Holst	Suite in E-flat (1910)
	Suite in F (1922)
	Hammersmith (1931)
Gordon Jacob	*William Byrd Suite* (1924)
	An Original Suite (1924)
Nikolai Miaskovsky	Symphony No. 19 in E-flat (1939)
Darius Milhaud	*Suite Française* (1944)
Vincent Persichetti	*Divertimento* (1950)
Ottorino Respighi	*Huntingtower Ballad* (1932)
Florent Schmitt	*Dionysiaques* (1913)
Arnold Schoenberg	Theme and Variations, op. 43a (1943)
William Schuman	*George Washington Bridge* (1950)
Virgil Thomson	*A Solemn Music* (1949)
Ralph Vaughan Williams	*Folk Song Suite* (1922)
	Toccata Marziale (1924)

Interestingly, a spate of works composed between 1950 and 1952 signaled the impetus for a new surge of original composition for band by established American composers. This activity provided much of the repertoire for the first two recordings of the Ensemble.

Numerous educational institutions were working to build large ensembles with high performance capabilities and complete instrumentations. Yet, one element was still missing that would provide acceptability of the band within the general community of professional music organizations: the presence of a growing repertoire created specifically for the band by composers who functioned freely in all other forms of performance ensemble media. To understand this paucity of original works, examine the following programs of Mark Hindsley (University of Illinois) and William Revelli (University of Michigan), who were models of then-contemporary programming:

University of Illinois Concert Band
Mark Hindsley, Conductor
Sixty-first Anniversary Concert, March 20 and 21, 1951
University Auditorium

Overture to *Tannhäuser*	Richard Wagner
Second Movement from Symphony No. 1, "Nordic"	Howard Hanson
Salome's Dance from *Salome*	Richard Strauss
Masquerade Suite	Aram Khatchaturian

Intermission

"Tap Roots," from the motion picture	Frank Skinner
Suite for Concert Band	Gerald Kechley
Les Preludes	Franz Liszt

Mark H. Hindsley, conducting

Unveiling of a portrait of Albert Austin Harding, Director *Emeritus*, University of Illinois Bands

Finale from *Death and Transfiguration*	Richard Strauss
University of Illinois March	John Philip Sousa

Albert Austin Harding, conducting

University of Michigan Symphony Band
William D. Revelli, Conductor
Hill Auditorium, February 26, 1952
Sigurd Rascher, Saxophonist

Homage March	Wagner
Symphonic Poem—*The Universal Judgment*	De Nardis
"Meditation" from the Opera *Thaïs*	Massenet
Featuring the Flute Choir	
Concert March—*A Step Ahead*	Alford
Aria from *Bachianas Brasilieras* No. 2	Villa Lobos
"Carnival" from *La Fiesta Mexicana*	Reed

Intermission

Toccata and Fugue in D minor	Bach
Introduction and Samba	Whitney
Sigurd Rascher, saxophone soloist	
Overture to the Opera *Colas Breugnon*	Kabalevsky
Trumpet and Drum	Land
Barbara McGoey, drum soloist	
Paul Willerth, trumpet soloist	
"Rag" from *Suite of Old American Dances*	Bennett
Michigan Rhapsody	Arr. by Werle

Since Fennell's early programs in the 1930s and 1940s were basically following the examples of the Illinois and Michigan Bands, it is interesting to search for clues in his programming in 1951–52 which might forecast his 1952 innovations with the EWE:

Eastman Symphony Band
Frederick Fennell, Conductor
Eastman Theatre, March 14, 1951

Overture to the opera *The Barber of Seville*	Rossini (Duthoit)
Chorale—"Christ lay in the Bonds of Death"	Bach (Mairs)
Fugue a la gigue	Bach (Holst)
Slavonic Dance No. 2	Dvorak (Ertl)
Theme and Variations from Suite No. 3	Tchaikovsky (Winterbottom)

Intermission

Zigeunerweisen	De Sarasate (Cailliet)
Richard Barnett, marimba soloist	
Woodland Sketches	MacDowell (F. Winterbottom)
Circus Polka	Stravinsky
Pieces of Eight—March	Jenkins and Neff
Manhattan Beach—March	Sousa

*   *   *   *   *

Eastman Symphony Band
Frederick Fennell, Conductor
Eastman Theatre, December 17, 1952

March—*Bugles and Drums*	Goldman
English Folk Song Suite	Vaughan Williams
Elegy Before Dawn	Cazden
A Celtic Set	Cowell
Suite from the film *Things To Come*	Bliss
The Moldau	Smetana (Winterbottom)
The Rifle Regiment	Sousa
Old Comrades March	Tieke

While there was an increasing number of original works appearing on the programs, it was only in the 1951 special concert, described in Fennell's *The American Music Teacher* article, that the breadth of repertoire and future style of programming made an appearance:

Concert Music for Wind Instruments
(Orchestral Department)
Frederick Fennell, Conductor
Kilbourn Hall, February 5, 1951

Ricercare for Wind Instruments (1559)	Willaert
Canzon XXVI (Bergamasca) for Five Instruments	Scheidt
Motet: *Tui Sunt Coeli* for Eight-voice Double Brass Choir	Di Lasso
Sonata pian e forte	Gabrieli
Canzon Noni Toni a 12 from *Sacrae Symphonie* (1597)	Gabrieli
Suite No. 2 for Brass Instruments (*Turmmusik*) (1685)	Pezel
Three Equali for Four Trombones (1812)	Beethoven

Intermission

Serenade No. 10 in B-flat major for Wind Instruments (1781)	Mozart

Intermission

Serenade in E-flat major, op. 7, for Thirteen Wind Instruments	Strauss
"Angels," from *Men and Angels* (1921) for Multiple Brass Choir	Ruggles
Symphonies for Wind Instruments	Stravinsky
In Memory of Claude Debussy (1920)	

(Consult Appendix A at the back of this volume for a complete listing of the repertories of the Eastman Symphony Band and the Eastman Wind Ensemble.)

Fennell made a particularly illuminating statement in programming technique in the works selected for the 8 February 1953 premiere concert of the Eastman Wind Ensemble, by dividing the program into one-third woodwind music (Mozart's Serenade No. 10 in B-flat, K. 370a [formerly K. 361]), one-third brass music (Riegger's Nonet for Brass), and one-third music for full ensemble (Hindemith's Symphony in B-flat for Concert Band). He did not appear to continue this approach in actual usage, but it created a striking inauguration for his new program. It was such a major departure from current practices that the premiere program could easily have been overlooked by many band directors because the three works were not then part of the accepted concept of literature or programming. Was the traditional band not so serious a subject to them as this new flexible group was to Fennell? Definitely, the welfare of each individual band was a most important subject to its conductor, but unfortunately, the musical literature selected for public statements of their craft frequently did not match their level of desire for technical and performance perfection.

It is possible to draw an imaginary line through the middle of the twentieth century, dividing creative activity for winds into two separate and distinct groupings. This is due primarily to the minute size of the original wind repertoire prior to 1950, and particularly, to the beginnings of compositional efforts which would provide a basis for Fennell to begin his new program. The hard work of many conductors and composers during the second half of the century has produced amazing results in the development of original literature for all forms of the wind band. If the literature of an ensemble is an indication of its intent, then a careful examination of the complete concert and recorded repertoire of the Eastman Wind Ensemble will illustrate the principles and standards of the wind ensemble concept as practiced at the Eastman School of Music.

There were several reasons for the success of the Eastman Wind Ensemble during its first decade:

1. Fennell's concept of woodwind and brass ensemble performance coupled with his years of experience as an orchestral conductor carried over into carefully rehearsed works with meticulous editings, especially in music such as Sousa marches.

2. His interpretive style of performance had a unique consistency, as evidenced by the quality of performance of the EWE on Mercury Records and in concerts in the Eastman Theatre between 1952 and 1962, a standard that many conductors sought to emulate.

3. The quality of the individual performers at Eastman and especially the quality of their private instruction meant that the Ensemble director did not have to teach anyone how to play his or her instrument. The studio teachers were all in the latter part of their professional careers, and each was either still performing as a principal chair in the Rochester Philharmonic Orchestra (Erich Leinsdorf was conductor of the RPO in 1952), or had recently retired after decades of orchestral performance. Those teachers included:

> Joseph Mariano   flute
> Robert Sprenkle   oboe
> Rufus Arey   clarinet
> Vincent Pezzi   bassoon
> William Osseck   saxophone
> Arkady Yegudkin   horn
> Sidney Mear   trumpet
> Emory Remington   trombone
> William Whybrew   tuba
> William Street   percussion

The conductor's relationship with the students has always been an interpretive collaboration, and one expects the same variety of tone qualities and individual performance techniques in the Wind Ensemble as in the Eastman Philharmonia or the Rochester Philharmonic. There has always been an orchestral approach to wind playing at Eastman in my recollection, and in fact, the students today rotate freely between the orchestras, wind ensembles and contemporary music ensembles.

4. The national and international image of the Ensemble might never have been created had it not been for the contractual collaboration between Mercury and the Eastman School. This venture had been established by Howard Hanson in 1952 to record the Eastman-Rochester Orchestra in a series of compositions by American composers. For Hanson, this was another step in the continuation of the American Composers Concerts, which he initiated in 1925, and the Festival of American Music, which began under his direction in 1930.

Eastman and Mercury

The Mercury project was especially important because Mercury was a principal leader in the development of recording techniques during the 1950s and 1960s, and thus attracted worldwide attention for its innovations. C. Robert Fine of Fine Sound recorded the Mercury Living Presence Series in Rochester, Chicago, Minneapolis, and Detroit, among other cities, and led the way in binaural sound, stereo, and the use of 35 mm. film for recording. The Mercury Living Presence techniques were well suited to the EWE's approach to performance and the Ensemble was part of every stage of development of the LP record. In addition, David Hall, Harold Lawrence, and Wilma Cozart were highly imaginative producers who worked closely with Fennell in developing not only the Ensemble's recorded sound, but also the flow of selected repertoire. The Eastman-Mercury collaboration continued until the middle 1960s after Howard Hanson retired from the Directorship of the School. Mercury Records was purchased by Phillips Records and ceased live recording in the United States within the next few years.

The EWE has continued this progressive stance in recording techniques through the succeeding decades with innovative participation in quadraphonic recording, direct-to-disc and digital recording, on the Deutsche Gramophone, Phillips, CBS Masterworks (now Sony Classical), Toshiba EMI, Tioch (now KEF), Vox, Centaur, and Desto labels.

The first recording made by the EWE, in 1953, focussed upon what Fennell considered to be the best of the new compositions for winds, all written within the span of a few years years prior to 1953. Although these were exemplary compositions by legitimate, classical, contemporary composers, each used the standardized concert band instrumentation; Fennell, in his approach, employed single players except for the B-flat clarinet section which had two to a part.

Within the first group of albums, one finds two recordings of American composers (the Eastman American Composers Series), an English album of Holst and Vaughan Williams, and two sets each of marches and ceremonial music for fife and drums, and trumpets and drums. The first album to contain major repertoire (not to be found on traditional band programs) brought together Hindemith's Symphony in B-flat, Schoenberg's Theme and Variations, op. 43a, and Stravinsky's *Symphonies of Wind Instruments*. Both the Hindemith and the Schoenberg works had been available for quite some time, but were not considered for most conductor's repertoire due to the difficulty of the compositional craft in each. One would not have expected the average band director to even be aware of the Stravinsky, as it was considered to be an orchestral wind section work, rather than a composition for band.

Recording no. 10 (see Discography in Appendix), which included Grainger's *Lincolnshire Posy*, Milhaud's *Suite Française*, Rogers's *Three Japanese Dances,* and the thirteen-voice Serenade in E-flat, op. 7, of Richard Strauss, further demonstrated innovative compositional and scoring practices not found in most traditional band works. The release of recording no. 11, with Mozart's monumental Serenade No. 10 in B-flat, K. 370a (formerly K. 361), allowed the rest of the wind world to experience the breadth and depth of repertoire that Fennell had already been performing within the confines of the Rochester community.

Although many band directors may have admired the performance skills of the Ensemble's Mercury recordings, it was not unreasonable for them to have missed the true purpose of the wind ensemble concept, for what they saw and heard during these first years appeared to them to be merely a small concert band with a set standardized instrumentation. National band organizations were attempting to establish standardized instrumentations (even on an international level) while Fennell was advocating a flexible instrumentation approach. The first recordings, which contained concert band compositions and marches, helped to reinforce their theories. Although Fennell did not play transcriptions (at least until he recorded the *Ballet for Band* album and the Wagner album), a primary difference between the average band director's approach and their perception of Fennell's approach lay primarily in his use of a reduced clarinet section. The large clarinet section, "the violins of the band," had become such an integral part of the standard band instrumentation that any effort to reduce the size or importance of this section was tantamount to heresy. The confusion many felt concerning the wind ensemble concept remained unclarified until the late 1960s, when national efforts were undertaken to publicize the concept's principles.

Upon beginning the recording project with Mercury, the Ensemble was confronted with two unique situations common to the professional recording industry: first, the heavy financial requirement dictated by the American Federation of Musicians (AFM); and second, the time constraints in which each composition was recorded. It must be understood that Fennell's first recording session was sandwiched in between several Eastman-Rochester Orchestra recording sessions (conducted by Howard Hanson), so the Rochester Musicians Association, AFM Local 66, took the position that this was all union recording on the same level. Thus, the fledgling EWE (although all students) became a union recording ensemble overnight! These financial conditions under which the Eastman Wind Ensemble began recording in 1953 continue to this day, with the musicians receiving symphonic-recording-scale wages for each recording session.

The EWE has never had the luxury of the "prestige type" recording so much in vogue throughout the U.S. today, in which college, university, and high school ensembles can make recordings without constraints of time or the enormous AFM union financial costs. Little wonder that EWE recordings have been sporadic at best during the past three decades since the Eastman School/Mercury connection ceased to exist in the mid 1960s. The positive side of these professional level recording engagements over the years lies in the experience gained by the Eastman student performers, who quickly learn how to adjust to the rigors and demands of professional life as they exist outside the walls of an educational institution.

The general acceptance of the Ensemble's Mercury recordings during the 1950s and early 1960s frequently offset a need for the group to be heard in live performance outside of Rochester. During Fennell's tenure, the Ensemble performed for the Eastern Division of the College Band Directors National Association (CBDNA) at Eastman in 1954, in Orchestra Hall, Chicago in 1955 for the CBDNA at its national conference, for the Music Educators National Association in Atlantic City in 1959, and in a Carnegie Hall concert in 1961.

Frederick Fennell left the Eastman School in May 1962 to become Associate Conductor of the Minneapolis Symphony Orchestra, and Howard Hanson appointed A. Clyde Roller Conductor of the Eastman Wind Ensemble and Co-Conductor of the Eastman Philharmonia and the School Orchestra. Roller, an oboist and 1941 graduate of Eastman, was Music Director of the Amarillo, Texas, Symphony Orchestra and a frequent conductor at the National Music Camp at Interlochen, where Hanson visited each summer. At that same time, I was appointed Conductor of the Eastman Symphony Band and Coordinator of the Instrumental Ensemble Program.

Clyde Roller's years at Eastman provided a solidity of purpose and concern for the development of the student body as demonstrated through the inauguration of a rotation assignment system in the Wind Ensemble and Philharmonia (previously, personnel for each ensemble was fixed for the academic year). This rotation system has since developed into a program now considered to be one of Eastman's most positive educational trademarks. The individual student benefits from the opportunity to perform in every ensemble in the school and to perform on every part, from principal through doubling assignments.

During his three years' tenure at Eastman, Roller made the final recording of the EWE for Mercury, pairing the Symphony No. 3 by Giannini with Hovhaness's Symphony No. 4. Roller's programming style mixed new and older original works with transcriptions of orchestral compositions; a particular highlight was his premiere performance of Warren Benson's *The Leaves Are Falling* in 1963. Clyde Roller left Eastman in 1965 to become Associate Conductor of the Houston Symphony Orchestra.

The American Wind Symphony Orchestra

In 1957, a parallel approach to the Eastman Wind Ensemble, named the American Wind Symphony Orchestra (AWSO)—also known as the American Waterways Wind Orchestra—was established in Pittsburgh, Pennsylvania, by Robert Austin Boudreau. The American Wind Symphony Orchestra may well be called the purest of all wind ensembles as it has no function other than to develop original repertoire for its varied instrumentations and to perform this music for interested audiences. Boudreau initiated the commissioning of an entire repertoire of more than three hundred and fifty compositions for his ensemble. Certain of these compositions, one hundred fifty-nine in number, have become part of the American Wind Symphony editions, available through the C. F. Peters Corporation in various instrumentations ranging from chamber works through large scale ensembles. All parts are performed with single players to each voice.[4] Whereas Fennell proposed the resources of the then-current concert band plus any instrumentation the composer might desire, Boudreau offered single or multiple instruments of each orchestra wind section. No saxophones or euphoniums are used in the AWSO series.

The instrumentation for this ensemble initially began with a double orchestra wind section: six flutes, two piccolos, six oboes, two English horns, six clarinets, two bass clarinets, six bassoons, two contra bassoons, six horns, six trumpets, six trombones, two tubas, percussion, harp, keyboards and string bass. This large instrumentation was soon replaced by more accessible instrumentations using various forms of the orchestra wind section. Boudreau's venue for public performance has been the waterways of America, the Caribbean, and Europe, with the AWSO performing on various barges equipped with suitable concert stages. The ensemble performs primarily from May through September, with its personnel selected by audition of college and university students.

The American Wind Symphony Editions have largely been ignored by the majority of the wind band world, due partly to misconceptions concerning the instrumentation of the works, partly because of many unfamiliar composers in the series (Boudreau has made a goal of seeking composers from Europe, Central and South America who are unknown by name to many in the United States), and also because of the fact that the performance parts are all on rental.[5] The fact that music on rental has failed to find a strong place in wind programming until recently has also severely restricted circulation of this catalog, as well as those of other contemporary music projects. Selected scores are available for purchase; however, recordings exist for only a few of the compositions.

While these theories may explain a lack of attention to the AWSO project and minuscule use of the repertoire over its first decade, they do not explain similar circumstances remaining into the present day. Contemporary music utilizes compositional and orchestration techniques involving new harmonic and rhythmic procedures, set theory, minimalist techniques, aleatoric improvisation, proportional notation, jazz techniques, and electronic media, all which require abilities not frequently taught in many traditional undergraduate and graduate music school programs. Thus, it has become possible for an entire musically progressive, flexible instrumentation program to wither on the vine, unnoticed by mainstream symphonic band directors.

The Second Decade

An important change occurred in the Eastman School through the retirement of Howard Hanson from the Directorship in 1964, a post to which he had been appointed in 1924 by George Eastman and Rush Rhees, President of the University of Rochester. Hanson's successor was conductor Walter Hendl, who was currently serving as Associate Conductor of the Chicago Symphony (Fritz Reiner, conductor). Hendl infused the school and its programs with a new national image and open approach to the international music scene, in direct contrast to the more nationalistic American music direction espoused by Hanson. Hendl remained Director until the spring of 1972.

In 1965, following Clyde Roller's departure, Walter Hendl offered me an appointment as Conductor of the Eastman Wind Ensemble and the Eastman Symphony Band in addition to continuation of the position of Coordinator of

Ensembles. I had conducted the EWE frequently during the previous years, especially during the 1964–65 season, when Roller assumed major Eastman Philharmonia conducting responsibilities following Howard Hanson's retirement.

One of Hendl's greatest initiatives that opened the Eastman School to more international attention occurred through residencies of such composers as Dimitri Kabalevsky, Aram Khatchaturian, and Igor Stravinsky. In 1971–72 Hendl staged a year-long celebration of the fiftieth anniversary of Eastman, affording faculty and students the opportunity to meet and hear many composers, critics, musicologists and educators. (A particular high point for me occurred in March 1967, when Igor Stravinsky and Robert Craft were invited to Eastman for a week of rehearsals and performances. During one of the public programs I conducted the Wind Ensemble in the *Symphonies of Wind Instruments* with Stravinsky sitting on the edge of the stage of the Eastman Theatre. The magnitude of that moment remains with me to this day!)

Transitions and Expansions

If the first decade of the wind ensemble concept may be termed the decade of innovation, the next decade became a time of transition, trial and error, of new beginnings, and a time of reaching out through publications, new recordings and conferences. Many conductors and performers were utilizing elements of the wind ensemble concept on both the secondary school level and in colleges and universities. However, the basic tenets of the concept were frequently misunderstood, especially among traditional symphonic band conductors. Four guiding principles were paramount and essential to the successful operation of the concept:

1. *Freedom of programming in size of ensemble and instrumentation.* This involves the use of flexible instrumentation, as opposed to the traditional fixed-instrumentation approach, and includes chamber music and smaller instrumentations within the concert band or orchestra wind section.

2. *Attention focused upon the composer rather than the arranger or transcriber.* In addition to more serious concert literature, an original repertoire for educational use gradually developed. The use of transcriptions began to wane as composers including Gunther Schuller, Ingolf Dahl, Karel Husa, Olivier Messiaen and Krzysztof Penderecki created a new arena for compositional and programming techniques. Much of this new music was difficult to perform, to understand, and to approach.

3. *Development of timbres unique to each individual composition.* In a fixed instrumentation ensemble with its doubled sections, tonal tendencies remain somewhat constant from work to work as the same number of performers are involved in each composition; similar timbre orchestration devices are frequently employed. Since all performers in the band played each composition, the balance of musical line was frequently created more by the size of each section than through the importance or function of the line. In a consideration of the *instrumentation versus personnel assignment* philosophy, the flexible instrumentation approach begins with single voices which are coupled with one another to achieve weight of line, whereas the fixed instrumentation approach starts with a constant level of thickness which is reduced to achieve a desired lightness.

4. *Flexible seating arrangements*. No longer was it necessary for the wind band to remain in its initial seating plot regardless of the requirements of the composition being performed. New philosophies were developed offering these flexible approaches to seating based upon the ability of performers to hear and communicate with each other, and also to be heard most effectively by the audience.

The Eastman Wind Ensemble functions to this day with these principles serving as basic operating procedures. It is felt that this approach offers all involved—performer, composer, audience—the most positive opportunities for maximum musical expression. Efforts were initiated in the late 1960s to create widespread communication within the wind world concerning the basic principles and those procedures essential for their inclusion into traditional band programs.

The MCA Symphonic Editions

In 1967, I began a collaboration with MCA Music, Inc. to publish the *MCA Symphonic Wind Ensemble Editions*. The basic premise underlying this collaboration included three sources of professional level activity: (1) *the finder and performer of new works*-the Eastman Wind Ensemble and its conductor; (2) *the publisher*—MCA Music, with Lewis Roth, Director of Publications and Arthur Cohn, Director of the Serious Music Rental Section; and (3) *the recording company*—Decca Records (a subsidiary of MCA) with Israel Horowitz, Decca recording producer. A publication and rental process would produce new compositions for all types of wind ensembles, and a series of Decca recordings performed by the EWE, featuring publications in the Editions, was projected to complete the triangle. I was to produce and serve as editor for a newsletter, *The Wind Ensemble*, in which we would discuss all aspects of the wind ensemble concept. The project continued for a period of three years during which a series of printed scores and parts (additional works were on rental) were made available by MCA Music. These releases included:

J. S. Bach	Passacaglia and Fugue in C minor (scored by Donald Hunsberger)
Warren Benson	*The Solitary Dancer*
	Aeolian Song for Saxophone and Wind Ensemble
	Concertino for Alto Saxophone and Wind Ensemble
	Helix for Tuba and Wind Ensemble
	Juniperus Suite
	The Mask of Night
	Recuerdo for Oboe and Wind Ensemble
	Shadow Wood for Soprano and Wind Ensemble
	Star Edge for Alto Saxophone and Wind Ensemble
Henry Brant	*Verticals Ascending*
Ingolf Dahl	Concerto for Saxophone and Wind Ensemble
Walter Hartley	*Sinfonia* No. 4
Oscar Morawetz	*Sinfonietta* for Winds and Percussion
Bernard Rogers	"Apparitions, Scenes" from *The Temptation of St. Anthony* (after Flaubert)

Robert Starer	Concerto for Piano and Winds
John Weinzweig	*Divertimento* No. 5 for Solo Trumpet, Trombone and Wind Orchestra
John T. Williams	*Sinfonietta* for Wind Ensemble

The Hartley *Sinfonia* No. 4 was included on the first Decca recordings, the Williams *Sinfonietta* was later recorded by Eastman on Deutsche Gramophone, and the Bach Passacaglia and Fugue in C minor was recorded by the EWE for a Toshiba-EMI LP during the 1978 Japan/Far East tour.

MCA published three newsletters, called *The Wind Ensemble*, that contained valuable information regarding the status of the wind band and the hopes of MCA Editions to further concerted wind music. A partial listing of articles includes:

Warren Benson	"Inertia and the Wind Ensemble"
Henry Brant	"Space as an Essential Aspect of Musical Composition"
Brian Fairfax	"The Wind Ensemble in Britain"
Donald Hunsberger	"Basic Principles of the Symphonic Wind Ensemble Concept"
	"Beecham Did It First!"
	"Scoring for the Wind Ensemble"

Description of New Publications:

Ingolf Dahl	Concerto for Saxophone and Wind Ensemble
Walter Hartley	*Sinfonia* No. 4
Oskar Morawetz	*Sinfonietta* for Winds and Percussion
John T. Williams	*Sinfonietta* for Wind Ensemble

In the first newsletter, I wrote an introductory article describing the wind ensemble concept as I perceived it. Wind ensembles of various sizes and instrumentations were springing up throughout the country, many of them capitalizing on the success of the EWE and its recordings but not following any standards or precepts, since there had been no definitive writings or other materials to assist conductors in preparing performances. Frederick Fennell's *Time and the Winds*, published in 1954, introduced his concept of instrumentation and composer development, but did not delve into actual performance techniques.

Thus, I undertook the task of attempting to enumerate and discuss the various principles guiding the concept (additional articles, speeches and presentations would be made over the following twenty-five years to continue this developmental process). The following excerpt is from that introductory article, entitled "Basic Principles of the Wind Ensemble Concept," contained in the first issue of *The Wind Ensemble* (January 1968):

Each work in the EDITIONS contains elements of the basic principles of the symphonic wind ensemble concept:

specified instrumentation
orchestral concept of performance
single performer approach
development of individual tone colors

These precepts are developed in composition and performance through the hypothesis that concerted wind music possesses the same artistic potential for the composer, the performer and the listener as offered by other concert media. The eventual goal of the *symphonic wind ensemble* movement *is an unqualified acceptance of concerted wind music on the same level as all other forms of instrumental or vocal composition. To achieve this goal an ensemble is required which will provide these functions:*

1. Offer the composer an artistic medium which will provide faithful performances of his music in the manner written: i.e., instrumental tone colors to be employed as specified (without substitution or addition of doubling voices) and with all the instrumental weights and balances to be reproduced as originally conceived.

2. Offer the woodwind, brass and percussion performer the opportunity to express himself on the highest musical plane through employment of the single performer concept.

3. Offer the concert-goer the experience of hearing concerted wind music composed and performed on the same artistic level as found in the string ensemble and the full symphony orchestra; this experience to be a pure aesthetic one without the detracting elements of commercialism which currently surround the relatively short concert season of the American symphonic band.

The symphonic wind ensemble is a concert organization, devoted to granting the composer and his audience the most faithful performances of his music. It is an ensemble which calls upon the strictest disciplines possible, for the *composer*--in establishing his wants and needs; for the *conductor*—in placing the composer and his music above personal promotion and peripheral activity interference; for the *performer*—to assume his rightful position as a legitimate symphonic musician dedicated to the furtherance of wind performance; and, for the *audience*—to discard past prejudices regarding wind music and wind performers as second class musical citizens.[6]

The third issue of *The Wind Ensemble* (January 1970) contained a timely article by Warren Benson, who by this time had written numerous significant wind works, including his Symphony for Drums and Wind Orchestra (published in 1963 by the American Wind Symphony Editions), *The Leaves Are Falling,* and *The Solitary Dancer.* In his article "Inertia and the Wind Ensemble" Benson addressed several issues relevant to the wind ensemble concept as it began its third decade:

The wind ensemble concept has been with us for several years and yet the medium has not encompassed the great potential it offers. In the first place, while much music from earlier times is available for various sized wind ensembles, we seldom hear this great literature in performance. . . .
    Why is it that the present world of the wind band is mainly dedicated to the new, in a kind of "hit parade" fever? Is there no interest in the great heritage from the past?
    Conductors have failed to utilize the wealth of older wind material for several reasons:

1. The lack of commitment to a broad base of literature that demonstrates the worthwhile benefits accruing from the performance of good music.

2. The lack of time or interest to do sufficient research to discover the wealth of small wind ensemble music of significance, be it past or present.

3. The lack of organizational ability to accomplish the division of large resources into smaller ensembles in a manner beneficial to the performers involved.

4. The preference for music that keeps everyone in the organization busy. (Bear in mind that much music from the Classical period calls for chamber-size ensembles.)

5. The weight of *inertia*—that which makes it so much easier to continue as one has, rather than implement a varied and stimulating musical experience.

Another problem involving *inertia* centers about the difficulty of much modern wind ensemble music, especially for those whose theoretical training has been limited, and whose conducting experience has been developed primarily through contact with inferior wind music. It takes a great deal of energy, time and commitment to study a difficult contemporary score and then to carry it off effectively in performance. It is no secret that college training in music has made little progress during the past twenty-five years in developing a student who can make qualitative judgments about music.[7]

The MCA project came to a close because of a decision on the part of the MCA administration that it was financially unfeasible to publish works with a then-limited buying market. I had warned the management of MCA that there would be little hope for financial remuneration or stabilization within an initial five-year start-up period, due to the fact that we were operating with musical material located outside of mainstream band activity, all of which required education of the band world toward our processes and procedures. The "bottom line" finally prevailed, and our contract was aborted by MCA in 1970. Lewis Roth, Arthur Cohn, Israel Horowitz and I were deeply disappointed by this action, but felt that the progress achieved thus far had been well worth the effort.

The Music Educators National Conference, Seattle

A major step forward for the Eastman Wind Ensemble occurred in 1968 when the University of Rochester Alumni Office sponsored a cross-country tour of the EWE and the Eastman Jazz Ensemble (all members of the EWE!) to the West Coast. On 17 March, following tour concerts in the Chicago area, Denver, Los Angeles, Redlands, Palo Alto, and Seattle, we performed a concert for the General Session of the National MENC in the Seattle Opera House before a standing room only audience. It had been almost ten years since the EWE had appeared at a national conference and this became a most special occasion, both for repertoire development and for a public projection of the Ensemble's current performance practices. (Although much of my experience occurred under Frederick Fennell's baton, we each had our own approach to the wind band. This was the first public demonstration to the traditional—and skeptical—band institution that the EWE and its concept were still alive and "on course.")

Several programs of music were selected for the cross-country portion of the tour. The MENC concert featured the Ingolf Dahl *Sinfonietta* (1964), Aaron Copland's *Emblems* (1964), and Norman Dinerstein's *The Answered Question* (1967), a work chosen from compositions written for the Ford Foundation Contemporary Music Project. Following the Ensemble's return from the tour, two recordings were made in the Eastman Theatre for the new Decca/MCA project.

Two additional recordings, made in 1969 and 1970, were released on Deutsche Gramophone and Phillips respectively. The repertoire ranged from all contemporary literature on the first—*Pittsburgh Overture* by Krzysztof Penderecki, *Music With Sculpture* by Toshiro Mayuzumi, and John T. Williams's *Sinfonietta*—to an album of early John Philip Sousa marches on the Phillips LP. Continuing efforts to secure a long-term relationship with a major recording company remained unsuccessful, primarily due to what the recording companies felt were insufficient sales possibilities for wind band recordings, especially in the educational market—an area they did not understand or pursue!

The Third Decade—National Development

Dissemination of the wind ensemble concept received a major impetus in 1970 when Frank Battisti, conductor of the Wind Ensemble at the New England Conservatory of Music (NEC) in Boston, organized a national meeting under the simple title: *A Wind Ensemble Conference*. This would soon grow into a series of eight such gatherings to be held in various locations throughout the country. The first conference, 12–14 February 1970, featured repertory-rehearsal sessions with composers Leslie Bassett, Karel Husa, Warren Benson, and Gunther Schuller, along with conductors Frederick Fennell, Donald Hunsberger, Robert Boudreau, James Neilson, and Willis Traphagan. Several panel discussion sessions featuring the composers and conductors were also presented. Performing ensembles from Lowell State University, Massachusetts, and the NEC provided performance readings. Robert Moog, inventor of the Moog Synthesizer, presented a special session on the use of electronic instruments, and James Neilson and Arnold Broido were presented on a panel discussion.

This conference provided a gathering place for conductors, composers, and performers interested in the *flexible personnel and instrumentation* approach. Future meetings were to provide valuable discussion grounds for the next several years, until it was felt by the organizers that the basic values and principles of the symphonic wind ensemble concept had been sufficiently absorbed into other professional wind organizations such as the College Band Directors National Association and the National Band Association.

Frederick Fennell later described his impression of this first meeting in an Address of Greetings to the Eighth National Wind Ensemble Conference, held at Northern Illinois University in January 1977:

As the Eastman group was actually born, some who had read my initial letter to composers were urging me to establish a formal association, in the image, I presume, of those alphabetically lettered organizations that so dominate all educational musical life in this country. But this was never my need in what I grew to know at Rochester. In 1954 we had a one-day gathering like this and in the Hanson tradition of that school, it was called a symposium. But I resisted all moves at organizing.

I like the loose, unstructured, non-political format established at the start by Frank Battisti in the first of these at New England, and which all who have hosted since have continued. I like it because it is simply and purely dedicated to the recreation of musical ideas and their unfettered performance for the scrutiny of musicians and listeners.[8]

At each of these meetings an exposure to specific repertoire being performing on a regular basis by leading wind ensembles became one of the primary attractions; while this repertoire was readily available to all conductors, only a small percentage of them were aware of its existence or suitability to their own ensembles. The conferences offered a unique opportunity for conductors, composers, and performers to discuss music, and to freely associate in a relaxed environment.

The repertoire and participating artists included in the first conference are listed below; programs for succeeding conferences are reproduced in Addendum A following this chapter.

First Conference, February 12–14, 1971, New England Conservatory

Conductors:
  Frank Battisti
  Warren Benson
  Robert Boudreau
  Frederick Fennell
  Donald Hunsberger
  Karel Husa
  James Neilsen
  Richard Pittman
  Gunther Schuller
  Willis Traphagan

Composers:
  Leslie Bassett
  Warren Benson
  Donald Harris
  Karel Husa
  Donald Martino
  Gunther Schuller

Panelists/Presenters:
  Arnold Broido
  Robert Moog

Performance Repertoire:
  Bach, J.S./Hunsberger   Passacaglia and Fugue in C minor
  Bassett, Leslie   *Designs, Images and Textures*
                      Nonet (two movements for Winds, Brass and Piano)
  Benson, Warren   *The Leaves Are Falling*
                                                        Mask of Night
                                                       Solitary Dancer
  Gross, Charles   *Alle Psallite*
  Husa, Karel   *Music for Prague 1968*
                                    Music for Brass Quintet and Strings

Hovhaness, Alan — *Symphony No. 4*
Mayuzumi, Toshiro — Concerto for Percussion and Wind Orchestra
Penderecki, Krzysztof — *Pittsburgh Overture*
Russell, Armand — *Symphony in Three Images*
Schuller, Gunther — *Meditation*
Dyptich for Brass Quintet and Band
Shostakovitch, Dmitri/Hunsberger — *Festive Overture*, op. 96
Traphagan, Willis — *Patterns for Wind Orchestra*

Successive annual conferences were:

No. 2, 1971: New England Conservatory (Frank Battisti)
No. 3, 1972: Eastman School of Music (Donald Hunsberger)
No. 4, 1973: University of Wisconsin (H. Robert Reynolds)
No. 5, 1974: University of Illinois (Robert Gray)
No. 6, 1975: California State University, Northridge (David Whitwell)
No. 7, 1976: Yale University (Keith Brion)
No. 8, 1977: Northern Illinois University (Larry Livingston)

Subtle changes in repertoire and conference format occurred in succeeding years. At the first conference, a number of high quality concert band works were included to encourage attendance by concert band directors not active in wind ensemble type activities. In later years, the repertoire became more specifically oriented toward flexible instrumentation compositions.

The eight national conferences were directed primarily toward college-university level conductors and performers, but attempts were made to create interest in the wind ensemble concept on the high school level. Portions of the programs were directed toward secondary school directors in most of the national conferences, but direct involvement on their part did not come easily. In 1974 a pilot high school conference was presented at Hewlett High School, Hewlett, Long Island, New York under the auspices of The National Wind Ensemble Conference and the National Center for the Symphonic Wind Ensemble (at Eastman). Stephen B. Work, conductor of the Hewlett High School Wind Ensemble, was the conference chairman.

Ensembles performing at the conference, in addition to Hewlett, were:

Cherry Hill High School Wind Ensemble, Cherry Hill, New Jersey
    Max Culpepper, Conductor
East Meadow High School Wind Ensemble, East Meadow, New York
    William Katz, Conductor
Hicksville High School Wind Ensemble, Hicksville, New York
    David Abt, Conductor
New Rochelle High School Wind Ensemble, New Rochelle, New York
    James D. Wayne, Conductor
Rockville High School Wind Ensemble, Vernon, Connecticut
    Edwin C. DeGroat and Samuel Goldfarb, Conductors

Guest Artists/Clinicians:

David Amram
Frank Battisti
Warren Benson
Mario DiBonaventura
Frederick Fennell
Donald Hunsberger
Martin Mailman
James Petercsak

The entire schedule is presented in Addendum B following this article to illus-trate the all-inclusive breadth and depth of the program and especially the quality repertoire selected for these high school performers.

The Hewlett conference focussed on interpretation, analysis, and performance problem-solving, with each conductor treating the selected repertoire in a highly personal manner. A wide array of historical compositional interest was presented, including works ranging from Gabrieli through compositions involving aleatoric techniques and/or prerecorded tape. Ensembles ranged in size from small chamber groups through the fully instrumented wind band.

While the repertoire was, in effect, a microcosm of the available literature for all forms of the flexible wind band, no composition presented surpassed the capabili-ties of the high school players gathered for the weekend. This fact, in itself, answered many questions in the minds of those present, especially for those conductors not actively engaged in flexible instrumentation programming and personnel assignment.

A primary factor in this conference's success lay in the manner in which each of the high school conductors had trained his ensemble. Each organization had realized its responsibilities in the interpretive development of musical line and phrasing and the desire to listen to one's fellow performers in ensemble; each worked freely with the guest conductors and their repertoire.

A second National High School Wind Ensemble Conference was held on 8–10 April 1976 at Williamsville East High School in Williamsville, New York, a suburb of Buffalo, New York. The program was greatly reduced from that of the Hewlett conference and focused primarily upon the areas of conducting techniques, con-temporary compositional practices, analytical techniques, and the development of chamber ensembles within the large band instrumentation. Conductor/lecturers included Frederick Fennell, Donald Hunsberger, Frank Battisti, and composer Sydney Hodkinson. Performing ensembles included the Grand Island High School Wind Ensemble (Sherman Lyke, conductor), the Clarence High School Wind Ensemble (Ronald Sutherland, conductor), the Eastman Wind Ensemble (Donald Hunsberger, conductor), the Niagara-Wheatfield High School Band (Wallace Goodman, conductor), and chamber ensembles selected from wind ensembles from Williamsville North, Williamsville South, and Williamsville East High Schools.

In analytical sessions following this conference, it was decided that it would be more beneficial to infuse the various principles of the wind ensemble concept into larger established organizations, such as national school band organizations, state music educators associations, and MENC, rather than attempting to separate the concept from such mainstream activity through meetings devoted solely to the wind ensemble approach.

In 1970 the New York State School Music Association (NYSSMA) presented its first All-State High School Wind Ensemble at its fall conference; I was invited to be the ensemble's first conductor. The final concert results were positive and encouraging, although the preparation for the concert was quite difficult to achieve as few of the high school participants had sufficient experience playing a one-on-a-part type performance. (This was one of the major deficiencies in many high school level wind ensemble programs at the time.) Even in the clarinet section, where the performers were all solo first-chair players in their own high school ensembles, and thus somewhat accustomed to individual leadership roles, initial reactions were slow in developing.

Ten years later, I conducted yet another New York All-State Wind Ensemble with entirely different results. Directors of many school programs had become aware of the positive aspects of the wind ensemble concept, both in performance skills as well as in use of more suitable repertoire, and this All-State ensemble was a much happier and more successful situation. The New York All-State Wind Ensemble continues through this day, and is probably the oldest and most continuous ensemble of its type in the country. NYSSMA also presents an All-State Symphonic Band along with several orchestras and choruses at its annual conferences.

The National Center for the Symphonic Wind Ensemble

In 1973, following the Third National Wind Ensemble Conference, a Center for the Symphonic Wind Ensemble was established at Eastman. I served as Executive Secretary, and the primary purpose of the Center focussed upon providing formal assistance throughout the country to conductors working on wind development projects. Born with a minuscule staff and budget, the Center helped to coordinate the later National Wind Ensemble Conferences, beginning with the conference held at the University of Illinois in 1974. The Center also collected scores and recordings, many of which were made available in score study rooms at the National Conferences.

In the public announcement of 7 May 1973 about the founding of the Center, Robert Freeman, Director of the Eastman School, stated:

> A performance leader since 1953, when the Eastman Wind Ensemble was founded by Frederick Fennell, the Eastman School now will coordinate the collection of music, the dissemination of information, and the documentation of activity for symphonic bands and wind ensembles. Through this Center, Eastman will serve as a focal point for both performance and scholarship for wind instruments.

The Advisory Council to the Center appointed by Freeman included:

Frank Battisti, New England Conservatory
Warren Benson, Eastman School of Music
Richard Franko Goldman, Goldman Band and Peabody Conservatory of Music
Vincent Persichetti, Juilliard School and Elkan Vogel Music Publishers
Ruth Watanabe, Librarian, Sibley Music Library of the Eastman School of Music
Edward Waters, Chief, Music Division, Library of Congress

The National Center, through its coordination, support, and information dissemination, furnished invaluable assistance to many conductors, providing a focus to disparate activities and offering an office to turn to in time of need. Still a part of the Eastman School, its activities have been somewhat limited in recent years due to the assimilation of the wind ensemble concept into national organizations such as the College Band Directors National Association.

As one of the activities of the Center, the EWE participated in a historical restoration project involving music for the American brass band (1854–1864) found in part-books discovered in Manchester, New Hampshire. In the same manner as Fennell had researched and recorded music of both northern and southern military bands from the Civil War era, the EWE performed and recorded music found in several part-books used by the Manchester Cornet Band in the 1850s. (The Manchester Cornet Band became the New Hampshire 3rd Regiment Band during the Civil War.) This brass band music, plus vocal music from the original Hutchinson Family Singers (who lived outside Manchester during the period) and social orchestra compositions, was recorded by Vox Records and released in a three-record set entitled *Homespun America*. The National Association of State and Local Historians presented me with an Award of Merit, its highest accolade, for the research, performance restoration, and recording of an entire community's music activities during a specific period of time.

An infusion of the wind ensemble concept into a traditionally oriented organization began with the 1977 biannual national conference of the College Band Directors National Association (CBDNA), held at the University of Maryland. David Whitwell, National President of CBDNA 1975–77, established a format which broke from previous traditional-style conferences, and in essence, provided a natural continuation of the National Wind Ensemble Conferences. Of seven performing organizations at Maryland, all were wind ensembles! This extreme swing of the pendulum created much consternation among many in the organization (once again frequently along generational divisions). However, the next decade saw an even stronger move toward original repertoire development and the flexible ensemble approach, with the election of Frank Battisti as National President (1979–81), H. Robert Reynolds (1983–85), and Donald Hunsberger (1985–87).

An important event occurred during the 1977 CBDNA Conference at Maryland when the Eastman Wind Ensemble performed the national premiere of Joseph Schwantner's "*. . . and the mountains rising nowhere,*" a compositional high point of the decade. Following Karel Husa's concept of composition and orchestration as demonstrated in *Music For Prague 1968*, *Apotheosis of this Earth* (1971), and Concerto for Percussion and Wind Ensemble (1971), Schwantner's inventiveness issued a call to all composers to take an active role in the development of a contemporary wind repertoire. Wind composition would never be the same after the works of Husa

and Schwantner, a position amply demonstrated through the quality of compositions selected over the past fifteen years for the Sudler Award, the American
Bandmasters Association Composition Award, the National Band Association
Composition Awards, and the Barlow Prize. These compositions, and many others
spawned through their creation, are now staples of the repertoire Fennell so
fervently sought in his 1952 letter to composers. The EWE recorded ". . . *and the
mountains rising nowhere*" in 1977 for Mercury Records, coupled with Copland's
Emblems and Howard Hanson's *Young Person's Guide to the Six-Tone Scale*, a set of
variations for solo piano and wind ensemble.

The development of the wind ensemble concept in college and university music
programs was becoming more firmly established as a new generation of conductors, many with advanced degrees, appeared upon the scene. Previously, numerous conductors had been operating independently within their own institutions
and spheres of influence, but now the concept was being spread throughout
CBDNA, the National Band Association (NBA), and the American School Band
Directors Association (ASBDA). Within the next decade it would continue its
dissemination worldwide through the World Association of Symphonic Bands and
Ensembles (WASBE). In England, a large and active movement was established
through the efforts of Timothy Reynish at the Royal Northern College of Music,
Manchester, who was instrumental in founding the British Association of Sym-
phonic Bands and Wind Ensembles (BASBWE).

In 1978, the EWE performed eighteen concerts in Japan organized and sponsored by the Kambara Arts Office, Tokyo. This three-week tour was followed by a
second three-week segment performing in the capital cities of Hong Kong, the
Philippines, Indonesia, Malaysia, Singapore, and Korea under the sponsorship of
the United States Department of State. These concerts were of utmost importance
to the local musicians and audiences, for although they may not have had the
wherewithal to achieve similar levels of performance, an example of the wind
ensemble concept, performed by the premiere ensemble from America, had been
provided for all to hear. Subsequent tours to Japan, under the sponsorship of Sony
Music Communications, Inc. and Eastman Kodak Japan, have taken place in 1990,
1992, and 1994.

In 1981, National Public Radio (NPR) inaugurated a thirteen-week broadcast
series entitled *Windworks*. Organized during Frank Battisti's term as President of
CBDNA, the programs were described to NPR member stations as follows:

> This is a series of 13 one-hour programs devoted to the band and wind ensemble
> tradition in the United States. The music is performed primarily by college and
> university wind groups. Included are interviews with composers and conductors,
> features on the history and sociology of the American wind band movement, a weekly
> quiz, plus a few surprises. . . . Frederick Fennell is commentator and Fred Calland is
> the host.

The repertoire ranged from the Gabrieli *Aria della Battaglia* performed by the
University of Illinois Wind Ensemble, through *Skating on the Sheyenne* by Ross Lee
Finney, performed by the Brooklyn College Symphonic Band, to Olivier Messiaen's

Les Oiseaux exotiques, performed by the Oberlin Wind Ensemble. In all, forty major compositions performed by twenty different bands and wind ensembles were broadcast.

The Fourth Decade

A major international project involving the EWE occurred in 1986 when CBS Masterworks (now Sony Classical) approached me to create musical accompaniments for a collection of turn-of-the-century cornet solos that would be recorded by Wynton Marsalis. This involved research into solo material acceptable to Marsalis and the creation of new accompaniments and cadenzas for each solo. This collaboration between Marsalis and the Ensemble resulted in the *Carnaval* CD, which was recorded in September 1986. This recording was nominated for a National Academy of Recording Arts and Sciences (NARAS) Grammy Award in 1987 in the category of Best Solo Performance with Orchestra!

During the next year this recording was followed by a tour with the EWE and Marsalis which established yet another milestone by the Ensemble for performances heard outside of Rochester. These performances focused attention on the wind band movement itself, as few concert-goers in these major performance sites may actually have heard serious all-wind programs, especially in the style of programming espoused by the EWE. The tour included Montreal (Place des Arts), Toronto (Roy Thomson Hall), London, Ontario (University of Western Ontario), Boston (Symphony Hall), Philadelphia (Academy of Music), Washington, D.C. (Kennedy Center), New York (Carnegie Hall) and Rochester (Eastman Theatre), plus several concerts in smaller cities.

In addition to accompanying Marsalis in several solos, the Ensemble performed numerous works including ". . . *and the mountains rising nowhere*" by Schwantner, which received its first performance in each of the above concert halls. Analysis of the complete repertoires contained in the Appendices at the back of this volume will reveal that Schwantner's ". . . *and the mountains rising nowhere*" has been programmed numerous times on EWE tours. Each of these occasions was for a different constituency, a different audience. The EWE has become so identified with this work that it is almost a signature piece signifying the standards of what we are attempting to develop and influence through our daily activities. More so than any other work, this composition has probably provided the major impetus for the development of the wind band and its current repertoire during the last two decades.

Invitations to perform on tour in the United States and Canada were frequently offered but, unfortunately, were sometimes declined due to financial constraints, especially if the Ensemble was undertaking a recording during that season. The importance of the live audience experience had to be weighed and balanced against the longevity of a recording, this being a most delicate decision when one measures the number of people who have actually heard the EWE live outside Rochester versus the international audience the Ensemble has enjoyed through its recordings.

The most recent American tour to the National MENC Conference in Indianapolis, Indiana in 1988, illustrated yet another insight into the EWE's programming style. The program, selected for the available performance time, included a new version of a Vaughan Williams brass band work, a composition by Richard Rodney Bennett for orchestral wind section plus saxophones recently commissioned by BASBWE and premiered the previous year at WASBE in Manchester, England, a 1927 work for German military band by Paul Hindemith, and Husa's *Music for Prague 1968*. Just as Fennell's repertoire for his CBDNA, MENC, and Carnegie Hall programs represented the state of the repertoire in each of those years, this program represented the position of the Ensemble in then-contemporary terms.

MENC Indianapolis: General Session
Thursday, April 21, 1988, 1:15 p.m.
Indiana Convention Center, Hall E

Variations for Wind Band (1957)	Ralph Vaughan Williams
Morning Music (1986)	Richard Rodney Bennett
Konzertmusik für Blasorchester, op. 41 (1927)	Paul Hindemith
Music for Prague 1968	Karel Husa

As on numerous previous occasions, the repertoire was then recorded, becoming the Sony Classics *Quiet City* CD, named for the setting for wind ensemble of Copland's *Quiet City*, with soloists Wynton Marsalis, trumpet, and Philip Koch, English horn. (The Bennett composition was also recorded by Sony Classics at that time, awaiting future release.)

The EWE and Japan

The three tours of Japan, sponsored by Sony Music Communications, Inc. and Eastman Kodak Japan, have required different programming considerations from those employed for the 1988 MENC Conference. Japanese bands do not perform a very high percentage of original works, especially those of a contemporary nature. Their typical band program contains some serious music (usually orchestral music in transcription) on the first half, and much lighter popular music on the second half.

The Japanese National Band Contests require a compulsory selection, which frequently has been a four-minute work with "tricky" technical problems, plus a selection of the band's own choosing. Few original works are used for this latter category. Therefore, one of the underlying philosophical reasons for the EWE's tours of Japan has been to demonstrate Eastman performance techniques and styles and to showcase original works in its repertoire. Extremely contemporary music is frowned upon in Japan, so a selection of conservative major works of the past forty years have been performed, in addition to special orchestrations of motion picture scores, marches, and short selections.

The tours have covered much of the Japanese main island with concerts in small, remote venues as well as in major performance centers such as Suntory Hall and Orchard Hall in Tokyo, Symphony Hall in Osaka, and in all three major auditoria in Hiroshima. Concerts in Tokyo and Osaka have been recorded for broadcast by NHK Radio, and performances in Hiroshima have been televised for the monthly *Winds Video Magazine*. The Sony Classics CD *Live in Osaka* was recorded in Symphony Hall, Osaka, in June 1990.

Coda

These years of growth have produced many positive wind band activities. It is highly gratifying that America's wind bands have become more free and flexible in programming, and more often place primary emphasis upon works originally conceived for winds. The quarterly *CBDNA Report*, published by the College Band Directors National Association, contains programs submitted by members which illustrate these elements of advanced programming.

In 1981, when Frank Battisti organized an international meeting of conductors, composers, and publishers at the Royal Northern College of Music in Manchester, England, he led the way to the official organization of WASBE and BASBWE. Since that time, numerous English conductors and performers have become involved in BASBWE activities, aided by the presence of visiting American conductors, including Battisti, H. Robert Reynolds, John Paynter, James Croft, and myself, among others, who have encouraged the movement's growth in England through lectures, conducting workshops, and repertoire sessions.

In 1988, I wrote the following words for *Winds* magazine, then the official journal of both organizations, to explain the Eastman concept of the wind ensemble. In many ways, this article was a two-decade update of my 1968 piece in the MCA newsletter, *The Wind Ensemble*:

> The wind band today currently stands at a level of development which reflects tremendous growth over the past four decades and promises a highly encouraging future as a concert performance medium. We have witnessed innumerable commissions of new works, we have been part of the creation of new international associations and partnerships, we have felt the fresh breath of innovative performance techniques, and yet, many conductors remain outside this forward progress with eyes and ears turned only toward the past. It is my feeling that such restricted adherence to traditional concert band activities only—though they serve positive developmental purposes in many ways—is no longer sufficient to project serious wind activity into the future on increasingly higher musical levels. *The primary way in which serious musicians and concert audiences may be expected to accept the wind band as a serious art medium is through the same quality approaches to performance and repertoire practiced by the orchestra, opera, choral and chamber ensembles.*
>
> What I envision for today's wind activities is a broad, more comprehensive approach to the multiple facets of the contemporary wind band. This approach is called *the umbrella concept,* or more simply *the family of ensembles.* . . all which fall under the general title THE WIND BAND. Each individual ensemble has strong positive attributes, and each possesses certain negative aspects if utilized to the exclusion of the

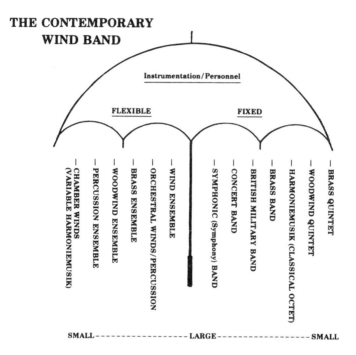

other constituent groups. Arguments of nomenclature regarding the individual ensembles are of much less consequence than the principles underlying the operation of each.

The umbrella, which serves as a gathering area for all types of wind activity is divided into two basic philosophies: FLEXIBLE INSTRUMENTATION and FIXED INSTRUMENTATION. Added to these approaches is the most important element of PERSONNEL ASSIGNMENT AND DISTRIBUTION, i.e., the exact number of players per musical line / per part.[9]

A Personal Philosophy

The past forty-two years have witnessed one of the greatest and fastest-moving periods of development in compositional practices in recent history; wind ensemble conductors were among those encouraging these developments. As a result, the wind band moved far ahead of other types of performing ensembles in contemporary repertoire. In doing this, it has sometimes surpassed its audiences' ability to comprehend contemporary music trends. Many band traditionalists were quick to condemn those active in the wind ensemble movement as being responsible for these steps in musical progress. This in itself was indeed shortsighted and foolish. What has been necessary since the 1960s is the realization that there are many forms, shapes, and sizes of the wind band under the all-encompassing umbrella, some new, some old, but each possessing unique advantages and limitations.

Some institutions use their large symphonic band as their umbrella, holding onto the support of their faithful alumni and followers through repertoire for the traditional, massed ensemble, while creating flexible-personnel ensembles to play more varied types of literature. I have never really understood why more large symphonic band programs do not use their instrumental sections in chamber ensembles to increase interest levels on the part of the individual performers. It is true that the ability to perform effectively in small ensembles can be difficult to develop, especially if one's performance experience has been limited to large wind groups where mass playing tends to overshadow individual participation. But in such massed ensembles errors are more difficult to detect and correct, personal expression is frequently repressed, and the individual personality becomes anonymous.

The one-on-a-part performance philosophy entails an important new responsibility—*the direct relationship of the conductor to each performer in the ensemble.* Today's conductor must be responsible for eliciting and developing highly personalized musical ideas from each player, who, in turn, is individually responsible for creating the musical statements. As chamber music has become more frequent in wind band programs, the conductor has also become a chamber music coach. I have always found it interesting to observe how performers' attitudes change and their personal application increases when the conductor steps off the podium to coach: for younger players, the conductor's sustained involvement is often invaluable in helping them develop attitudes of leadership and cooperation, so essential among chamber music performers.

As an exponent of the philosophy "you are what you program and perform," I firmly support the tenet that each conductor must stand for what he or she believes to be the true and right course to follow: a course that will guide the ensemble you conduct, the students you teach, and the audience that supports you, in a positive artistic direction. Today, each conductor must decide upon a course of activity that is conducive to forward thinking and leadership. One must not be merely a bystander, willing to stand by and reject the movement of time and effort, confident that the successes of the past will return to regain their former, self-proclaimed stature. The pendulum swings slowly, but it continues to swing, and it is better to be on the cutting edge of the swath than to be dragging behind it.

An analogy to the desired contemporary wind band program lies in the professional opera company, consisting of a group of soloists and secondary singers, a ballet corps, large orchestral resources, and supporting staff. If the opera selected for performance is *The Magic Flute* by Mozart, then a suitable roster of soloists, with an appropriately sized chorus and orchestra, is needed, while if the opera is *Aida* or *Carmen*, much larger and different forces are needed for a musically effective performance.

Several new directions in educational procedures and policies are necessary to achieve these standards and goals and to cement a healthy relationship between conductor, composer, performer, and audience:

1. *a commitment to teaching the skills and knowledge* needed by individual performers within the ensemble if they are to meet any challenge placed before them by the "emerging wind repertoire";

2. *creation of instructional programs in conducting* to develop those analytical, interpretive, communication, and physical skills needed to perform the newly found repertoire;

3. *encouragement of historical and analytical research* on works from all periods for ensembles of all sizes and instrumentations that are part of the wind ensemble's heritage;

4. *continued fostering of intercommunication* through international conferences to introduce repertoire and cultivate performance skills; and

5. *leadership in worldwide development of original composition for wind band* and development of performance practices that incorporate those qualities deemed essential for the continued growth of all forms of the wind band.

I believe that the primary strengths of the wind ensemble concept lie in its unique awareness of the potential of wind instruments in a rich variety of ensembles. Today the *composer*, as the creator of the colors, weights, and balances of his compositions, has been awakened to these possibilities; the *conductor* has truly become the representative or advocate of the composer; and the *ensemble* has become a medium of broader expression and communication. Compositions created during the past four decades have become the foundation for a new repertoire of quality and character. Having planted the seeds of the wind ensemble movement and enjoyed its first fruits, our task for the future lies in the continued cultivation of wind band music that will stand on its own merits.

NOTES

1. Frederick Fennell, "The Wind Ensemble," *The American Music Teacher*, vol. 2, no. 4 (March-April 1953): 12–13, 16–17.
2. *The New York Times*, 26 July 1953.
3. Fennell, pp. 13 and 16.
4. For complete instrumentations, see Jeffrey H. Renshaw, *The American Wind Symphony Commissioning Project: A Descriptive Catalogue of Published Editions, 1957–1991* (New York: Greenwood Press, 1991).
5. See Renshaw.
6. Donald Hunsberger, "Basic Principles of the Symphonic Wind Ensemble Concept," *The Wind Ensemble* 1, no. 1 (January 1968): 1–4.
7. Warren Benson, "Inertia and the Wind Ensemble," *The Wind Ensemble* 2 (January 1970): 1–2.
8. Frederick Fennell, "An Address of Greetings," Eighth National Wind Ensemble Conference, Northern Illinois University, January 1977.
9. "The Contemporary Wind Band: A Personal View," *Winds*, vol. 3, no. 1 (Spring 1988): 12, 14–16.

PHOTO CREDITS

Plates 2, 4, 6, 7, 8, 9, 10, 13 – courtesy of Louis Ouzer
Plates 3 and 14 – courtesy of Eastman Kodak
Plate 12 – courtesy of Phil Matt

ADDENDUM A

National Wind Ensemble Conferences

Second Conference
March 4–6, 1971
New England Conservatory

Conductors and composers:
Frank Battisti
Frank Ceely
Norman Dinerstein
Frederick Fennell
John Heiss
Donald Hunsberger
Donald Martino
Harvey Phillips
Daniel Pinkham
Gunther Schuller
Alec Wilder

Performing ensembles:
New England Conservatory Wind Ensemble
Greater Boston Youth Wind Ensemble

Repertoire performed and discussed:
Original music for wind ensemble:
Adler, Samuel
If Causality is Impossible—Genesis is Recurrent
Amram, David   *King Lear Variations*
Beethoven, Ludwig van   Sextet in E-flat, op. 71
March in B-flat
Polonaise and Ecossaise in D
Military March in C
Boyd, John   *Variations on a Sea Chanty*
Dinerstein, Norman   *The Answered Question*
Fabrizio, W.   *Statement* for Trumpet
Gabrieli, Giovanni
Canzon noni toni a 12 (among others)
Grainger, Percy   *Hill Song* No. 2
Hartley, Walter   Concerto for Trumpet

Hovhaness, Alan
Return and Rebuild the Desolate Places
Husa, Karel
Divertimento for Brass and Percussion
Ives, Charles   *From the Steeples and the Mountains*
McKay, Neil   *Evocations*
Milhaud, Darius   *Suite Française*
Mozart, W. A.   Serenade in B-flat, No. 10
Riegger, Wallingford
Music for Brass Choir and Percussion
Schiller, Steven
Elegy for Solo Trumpet with Brass Quartet
Schoenberg, Arnold
Theme and Variations, op. 43a
Schuller, Gunther   *Study in Textures*
Vaughan Williams, Ralph   *Scherzo Alla Marcia*
(Symphony No. 8)
Welcher, Dan   *Walls and Fences*
Wilder, Alec   *An Entertainment* (I)

Arrangements and transcriptions for wind ensemble:
Bach, J. S./D. Hunsberger   Prelude in E-flat
("St. Anne")
Berlioz, Hector/G. Schuller   *Le Corsair* Overture
Fischer, J. C. F./K. Wilson   *Le Journal du Printemps*
Gesualdo, Carlo/P. Phillips   *Io Pur Respiro*
Ginastera, Alberto/Johns   *Danza Final* (*Estancia*)
Vaughan Williams, R./R. Hare
Concerto for Tuba

Student works:
Downs, Lamont   *Sinfonia* for Wind Band
March
Peck, Russell   *Gothic Music*
Powell, Mel   *Capriccio*
Seyfrit, Michael   Symphony No. 2 ("Peace")

37

Third Conference
April 6–8, 1972
Eastman School of Music

(Concurrent with the Bi-Annual Meeting of the Eastern Division of the College Band Director National Association)

Conductors, composers, and lecturers:
Frank Battisti
Norbert Buskey
Frederick Fennell
Donald Hunsberger
Henry Romersa
David Whitwell

Performing ensembles:
Eastman Wind Ensemble
Members of the Eastman Symphony Band
Greater Rochester Youth Wind Ensemble

Repertoire performed and discussed:
Music for orchestral wind section or small wind ensemble:

Benson, Warren	*Shadow Wood*
Epstein, David	*Vent-Ures*
Kurka, Robert	
	Suite from *The Good Soldier Schweik*
Prokofiev, Sergei	*Ouverture*, op. 42
Schwartz, Elliot	*Voyage*
Stravinsky, Igor	Octet for Wind Instruments
Zielenski, Michael	*Magnificat*

Piano concertos with wind accompaniment:
Hindemith, Paul
Concert Music for Piano, Brass and Two Harps
Kennan, Kent
Concertino for Piano and Wind Ensemble

Starer, Robert	Concerto for Piano
Stravinsky, Igor	Concerto for Piano and Winds

Other repertoire:

Hanson, Howard	*Dies Natalis*
Husa, Karel	*The Apotheosis of This Earth*
Maschek, Paul	*The Battle of Leipzig*
Reynolds, Verne	*Scenes*
Schuller, Gunther	*Study in Textures*
Williams, John T.	*A Nostalgic Jazz Odyssey*

Panel discussions and lectures:
Panel:
    The Publisher's Dilemma (Or Art Versus the
                                    Accountant)
Panel:
    Musical and Administrative Considerations in
    Operating a Flexible Youth Wind Ensemble
                                    Program
Lecture:
    The Eighteenth-Century Wind Band: Repertoire
                    and Historical Importance

Fourth Conference
April 26–28, 1973
University of Wisconsin

Conductors, composers, and lecturers:
Frank Battisti
Frederick Fennell
Sydney Hodkinson
Donald Hunsberger
John Paynter
H. Robert Reynolds
Alan Stout
Les Thimmig
David Whitwell

Performing ensembles:
Northwestern University Wind Ensemble
University of Wisconsin Chamber Singers
University of Wisconsin Wind Ensemble

Repertoire performed and discussed:
Music for choir and wind ensemble:

Bach, J. S.	*O Jesu Christ, mein Lebens Licht*
Brahms, Johannes	*Begräbnißgesang*
Bruckner, Anton	"Gloria" from the Mass
Nelhybel, Vaclav	*Halleluiah*
Schubert, Franz	*Hymne*
Schumann, Robert	*Beim Abschiedzusingen*
Stravinsky, Igor	Mass

Music analysed and performed:

Berg, Alban	*Kammerkonzert*

New music for wind ensemble:
  Broege, Timothy   *Sinfonia* III
  Karlins, William
  Reflux—Concerto for Amplified Double Bass and
          Wind ensemble, piano and percussion
  Maros, M.   *Mutazoni*
  Maros, R.   *Eufonia* II
  Sallinen, Aulos   *Chorali*
  Snyder, Randall   *Six Sound Pieces*
  Tischenko, Boris   Cello Concerto

Other repertoire:
  Beethoven, Ludwig van   *Five Short Pieces*
  Donato, Anthony
          Nonet for Brass and Percussion
  Hindemith, Paul
          Concerto for Organ and Wind Orchestra
  Mahler, Gustav   *Um Mitternacht*
  Stout, Alan   *Pulsar*
  Toch, Ernst   *Valse*
  Tribensee, Joseph   *Concertino* for Piano
  Wagner, Richard   *Elizabeth's Prayer*
  Wolf, Hugo   *Auf ein altes Bild*

Lectures:
  Frank Battisti   The Music of Charles Ives
  Sydney Hodkinson
    Contemporary Music for Public School Ensembles
  Alan Stout   Contemporary European Wind Music
  Les Thimmig
          Understanding Contemporary Notation

Fifth Conference
April 18–20, 1974
University of Illinois

Conductors, composers, and lecturers:
  Frank Battisti
  Gordon Binkerd
  Frederick Fennell
  Robert Gray
  Donald Hunsberger
  John Paynter
  Soulima Stravinsky
  Jack Williamson
  Paul Zonn

Performing ensembles:
  Northwestern University Wind Ensemble
  University of Illinois Wind Ensemble

Repertoire performed and discussed (music in the Romantic tradition):
  Badings, Henk
      Concerto for Bassoon, Contrabassoon and Wind
                                        Orchestra
  Gounod, Charles   *Petite Symphonie* (1885)
  Husa, Karel
      Concerto for Alto Saxophone and Wind Ensemble
  Meulemans, Arthur   Symfonie Nr. 4 (1935)
  Spalding, Dan
  Concerto No. 2 for Percussion and Wind Ensemble
  Strauss, Richard *Vienna Philharmonic Fanfare* (1924)
  Surinach, Carlos   *Ritmo Jondo* (1952)
  Taillefaire, Germaine/J. Paynter   *Ouverture*
  Toch, Ernst   "Buffo" from *Spiel für Blasorchester*
  Otterloo, Willem van
          Sinfonietta for Wind Instruments (1943)

Sixth Conference
May 9–11, 1975
California State University, Northridge

Conductors, composers, and lecturers:
  John Alexander
  Randall Coleman
  Larry Curtis
  Frederick Fennell
  William Hill
  Donald Hunsberger
  Ronald Johnson
  Gerald Lawson
  Morrell Pfeifle
  H. Robert Reynolds
  David Whitwell
  Robert Wojciak

Performing ensembles:
  California State University, Northridge, Singers
      (John Alexander, conductor)
  California State University, Northridge, Wind
      Ensemble (Morrell Pfeifle, conductor)

California State University, Northridge, Wind
Orchestra (David Whitwell, conductor)
California State University, Long Beach,
Symphonic Wind Ensemble (Larry Curtis, conductor)
California State University, Los Angeles, Wind
Ensemble (William Hill, conductor)
Modesto College Wind Symphony (Ronald
Johnson, conductor)
University of Southern California Wind Orchestra
(Robert Wojciak, conductor)
Villa Park High School Wind Ensemble (Randall
Coleman, conductor)
Western States Junior College Honor Wind
Ensemble
Repertoire performed and discussed:
Wind band music of the French Revolution:
Gossec, Francois   *Hymne a la Liberté* (1793)
Le Triomphe de la Loi (The Triumph of the Law, 1792)
                         Te Deum (1790)
Jadin, Hyacinthe   *Ouverture* (1795)
LeFevre, Xavier   *Marche Militaire* (1794)
Mehul, Etienne   *Ouverture* (1793)

Works by CSUN composers:
Berkowitz, Leonard
          Divertimento for Symphonic Winds
Campo, Frank   *Agamemnon*
Kessner, Daniel   *Wind Sculptures*

Works from the Donemus Foundation:
Bonsel, Adriaan   *Folkloristische Suite*
Hemel, Oscar von   *Three Contrasts*
Ketting, Otto   *Interieur*

Other repertoire performed and discussed:
Batiste, Edouard   *Sinfonie* (1845)
Beethoven, Ludwig van   *Siegessinfonie* (1813)
Bennett, Robert Russell
           Suite of Old American Dances
Bruckner, Anton   Mass in E minor
Campo, Frank   *Capriccio* (premiere)
Chilese, Bastiano   *Canzon Trigesimaseconda*
Croley, Randell
         Concerto for flute and metal orchestra
Dalla Casa, Girolamo   *Alix Avoit*
Hill, William
Concertino for Alto Saxophone and Chamber Band
                Dances Sacred and Profane

Hindemith, Paul   *Konzertmusik*
Hindemith, Paul   Symphony in B-flat
Holbourne, Anthony   Suite
Holst, Gustav   Suite in F
                           Suite in E-flat
Husa, Karel   Concerto for Saxophone
Hutcheson, Jere   *Sensations*
Kelterborn, Rudolph   *Miroirs*
Linn, Robert   *Elevations*
Lopatnikoff, Nicholai
           Concerto for Wind Orchestra
Massaino, Tiburtio   *Canzon Trigesimaquarta*
                      Canzon Trigesimaquinta
McBeth, Francis   *Masque*
Mendelssohn, Felix
           Overture for Harmoniemusik
Mozart, W. A.   Serenade No. 10, K. 370a
Obersteiner, Johann   *Fest-Messe*
Ostreich, Carl   *Sinfonie* (1831)
Persichetti, Vincent   *Parable*
Reicha, Anton *Commemoration Symphony* (1815)
Rodrigo, Joaquin
Adagio para Orquestra de Instrumentos de Viento
Schoenberg, Arnold
           Theme and Variations, op. 43a
Slater, James
   Prelude and Variations on "Gone is my Mistris"
Sibelius, Jan   Suite for Wind Band
Stravinsky, Igor   *Circus Polka*
Vaughan Williams, Ralph *English Folk Song Suite*
Wagner, Richard
       Prelude, Act II, Scene 4 of *Lohengrin*
                          Trauersinfonie
Weiner, Lawrence   Third Symphony
Westin, Philip   *In Memoriam* ("to Ingolf Dahl")

Seventh Conference
February 26–28, 1976
Yale University

Conductors, composers, and lecturers:
Frank Battisti
Robert Bloom
Keith Brion
John Kirkpatrick
Robert Morris

Krystof Penderecki
James Sinclair
Arthur Weisberg
Keith Wilson

Performing ensembles:
New England Chamber Orchestra (James Sinclair, conductor)
New England Conservatory Wind Ensemble
Yale University Ensembles and Concert Band

Special guest ensemble:
Netherlands Wind Ensemble

Repertoire performed and discussed:

Dick, Robert	Concerto for Electronic Flute
Gershwin, George	
	Rhapsody in Blue (original version)
Grainger, Percy	*Colonial Song*
Heinrich, Anthony	Concerto for Kent Bugle
Hindemith, Paul	*Konzertmusik*, op. 41
	Septet for Winds
Kammermusik for Organ and Chamber Orchestra,	
	op. 46, no. 2
Holst, Gustav	*St. Paul's Suite*
Ives, Charles	Symphony No. 3
Krenek, Ernst	Symphony, op. 34
	Three Joyous Marches
Morris, Robert	*In Different Voices*
Mott, David	New work—untitled
Penderecki, Krystof	*Pittsburgh Overture*
	Prelude
Revueltas, Silvestre	*Ocho por Radio*
Ruggles, Carl	Prelude from *Cavalleria Rusticana*
Varèse, Edgar	*Octandre*
	Intégrales

Lectures:
Frank Battisti
Rehearsal-Discussion of the Music of Ernst Krenek and Edgar Varèse
Robert Bloom   Mozart's Serenade No. 12, K. 388
Keith Brion   Old and New Scores
John Kirkpatrick
The Music of Charles Ives and Carl Ruggles
Krystof Penderecki
Rehearsal-Discussion of His *Pittsburgh Overture* and *Prelude*

Arthur Weisberg
Contemporary Compositional Techniques and Performance Practice
Keith Wilson   A Personal View of Paul Hindemith

Eighth Conference
February 9–12, 1977
Northern Illinois University

Conductors, composers, lecturers, and panelists:
Frank Battisti
Eugene Corporon
Raphael Druian
Donald Erb
Ron Grun
Frederick Fennell
Donald Hunsberger
Larry Livingston
Frank McCarty
Peter Middleton
Russell Peck
H. Robert Reynolds
Elwood Smith
Jack Williamson

Performing ensembles:
Blackearth Percussion Group
Illinois Chamber Orchestra
Northwestern University Wind Octet
Northern Illinois University Concert Choir
Northern Illinois University Symphony Orchestra
Northern Illinois University Wind Ensemble
University of Wisconsin Wind Ensemble
Wheeling High School Wind Symphony

Repertoire performed and discussed:

Arnell, Richard	Serenade, op. 57
Bach, Jan	*The Eve of St. Agnes* (premiere)
Broege, Timothy	*Sinfonia* VII
Erb, Donald	*The Purple Roofed Ethical Suicide Parlor*
Gerard, Roberto	*Hymnody*
Jacob, Gordon	*Old Wine in New Bottles*
Linn, Robert	*Elevations*
Lutoslawski, Withold	*Trois Poemes d'Henri Michaux*
Mahler, Gustav	Symphony No. 4 in G Major
McCarty, Frank	*Timescapes* (premiere)
	Ludes and Dances

Messiaen, Olivier   *Le Merle Noir*
                Harawi (Chant D'Amour Et De Mort)
                            Oiseaux Exotiques
Milhaud, Darius   *Little Symphony* No. 5
Mozart, W. A.   Divertimento in F, K. 138
                          Divertimento No. 4, K. 186
                          Serenade in E-flat, K. 375
Peck, Russell   *Cave* (premiere)
Poulenc, Francis   *Suite Française*
Reynolds, Roger   *Only Now, and Again* (premiere)
Schein, Johann   *Verbum caro factum est*
Schoenberg, Arnold

                    Theme and Variations, op. 43a
Strauss, Richard   Serenade in E-flat, op. 7
Stravinsky, Igor   *Symphonies of Wind Instruments*
Varèse, Edgard   *Hyperprism*
                                    Intégrales
Xenakis, Iannis   *Akrata*
Yurko, Bruce   Concerto for Horn

Lectures:
Frank Battisti   The Wind Music of Varèse

Raphael Druian Mozart's Serenade in E-flat, K. 375
Ron Grun
        Performance Practices on Historical Wind
                                   Instruments
Donald Hunsberger
    Wind Ensemble Programming and Repertoire
Larry Livingston   Group Improvisation
Peter Middleton   Tuning and Pitch Perception
H. Robert Reynolds
        Analysis As It Influences Interpretation:
        Schoenberg, Theme and Variations, op. 43a
Elwood Smith   Music for Winds and Choirs
Frank McCarty
        The Composer and the High School Wind
                                    Ensemble

Panel on electronics and wind music:
    Donald Erb
    Frank McCarty
    Russell Peck

ADDENDUM B

Sessions were presented simultaneously, each with its own ensemble, in separate performance areas:

10:00–11:15
The Composer and His Music   Warren Benson
Symphony for Drums and Wind Orchestra
(1963)
Interpretation of the Score   Frederick Fennell
Gordon Jacobs, *Flag of Stars* (1956)
Interpretation of the Score   Donald Hunsberger
Clifton Williams, *Fanfare and Allegro* (1956)
Coaching Techniques for the Small
Chamber Ensemble   Martin Mailman
Repertoire to be announced.

11:30–12:45
Interpretation of the Score   Frederick Fennell
Percy Grainger, *Lincolnshire Posy* (1940)
Applying the Use of Form in the Rehearsal
Martin Mailman
John Barnes Chance, *Elegy* (1972) and Variations
on a Korean Folk Song (1967)
Contemporary Rehearsal Techniques
Donald Hunsberger
Darius Milhaud, *Suite Française*

1:00–2:15
The Composer and His Music   Martin Mailman
Geometrics No. I (1964)
Liturgical Music (1967)
New Music   Mario DiBonaventura
Randall Snyder, Variations for Wind Ensemble
(1973)

1:00–3:45
The Composer and His Music   David Amram
King Lear Variations (1967)

2:30–3:45
Adapting Transcriptions for the Wind Ensemble
Frederick Fennell
Sullivan/MacKerras/Duthoit, *Pineapple Pol* (1952)
Leonard Bernstein/Beeler, Overture to *Candide*
(1962)
The Composer and His Music   Warren Benson
The Solitary Dancer (1969)
Interpretation of the Score   Donald Hunsberger
Percy Grainger, *Hill Song* No. 2 (1930)
The Contemporary Percussion Sectional
James Petercsak

4:00–5:15
The Composer and His Music   Warren Benson
Symphony for Drums and Wind Orchestra
(1963)
Contemporary Rehearsal Techniques
Donald Hunsberger
Fischer Tull, *Terpsichore* (1972)
Edward Madden, Symphonic Variations on a
Theme by Purcell
Interpretation of the Score   Frederick Fennell
C. T. Griffes/Erickson, *The White Peacock*
F. Mendelssohn/Greissle, Overture in C for Wind
Band
Contemporary Brass Ensembles
Mario DiBonaventura
Knut Nystedt, *Pia Memoria*, op. 65 (1971)
Leon Kirchner, *Fanfare* (1965)
The Successful Percussion Sectional
James Petercsak
Selections to be announced.

7:00–8:15
Applying the Use of Form in the Rehearsal
Martin Mailman

John Barnes Chance, *Elegy* (1972) and Variations
on a Korean Folk Song (1967)
Preparing the High School Musician for
Contemporary Music   Donald Hunsberger
Rudolph Kelterborn, *Miroirs* (1966)
The Composer and His Music   Warren Benson
The Solitary Dancer (1969)
Coaching Techniques for Small Chamber Ensembles
Mario DiBonaventura
Selections to be announced.
Rehearsing the Larger Chamber Ensemble
Frederick Fennell
Mozart, Serenade No. 10 in B-flat, K. 361 (1781)

8:30–9:45
Interpretation of the Score   Frank Battisti
William Schuman, *Chester Overture* (1957)
Chris Dedrick, *Twilight*
Interpretation of the Score   Donald Hunsberger
Charles Ives/Rhoads, Variations on "America"
(1968)
Brass Ensembles—Then and Now
Frederick Fennell
Henk Badings, *Tower Music* for Brass and
Prerecorded Tape (1969)
Giovanni Gabrieli/King, *Canzon quarti toni* (1597)
Richard Wurz, *Morgen Musik* and *Abend Musik*

8:30–9:45
Rehearsing the Chorus and Wind Instruments
Frederick Fennell
Paul Hindemith, *Apparebit Repentina Dies* (1947)
Contemporary Rehearsal Techniques Frank Battisti
Paul Hindemith, March from *Symphonic
Metamorphosis*
Teaching Aleatoric Techniques
Donald Hunsberger
Sydney Hodkinson, *A Contemporary Primer* (1974)
Coaching Techniques for Small Chamber Ensembles
Martin Mailman
M. Corrette, *La Phenix* (ca. 1600)
P. DuBois, *Scherzo* (1963)
Sergei Prokofiev, *Humorous Scherzo*, op. 12, no. 9
(1953)
Brass Chamber Music   Mario DiBonaventura
Selections to be announced.
Discussion Hour: New Approaches to the High
School Percussion Ensemble   James Petercsak

10:00–11:15
Application of Aleatoric Techniques Frank Battisti
John Pennington, *Lines and Spaces* (1974)
Adapting the Symphonic Band Score for Wind
Ensemble   Donald Hunsberger
Robert Russell Bennett, *Suite of Old American
Dances* (1952)
Dmitri Shostakovitch/Hunsberger, *Galop* (arr.
1968)
Interpretation of the Score   Frederick Fennell
Vincent Persichetti, Symphony for Band (1957)
Rehearsal Techniques for Contemporary
Percussion Ensembles   James Petercsak
Fred Heim, Fanfare for Percussion (1967)
Michael Colgrass, *Concertino* for Timpani and
Brass (1965)
Coaching Techniques for the Small Chamber
Ensemble   Mario DiBonaventura
Malcolm Arnold, Divertimento for Flute, Oboe
and Clarinet
Discussion Hour: "Why Specified Instrumentation?"
Warren Benson

11:30–12:45
Rehearsing with Prerecorded Tape
Donald Hunsberger
H. Deutsch, Fantasia on Chorale "Es ist Genug"
Rehearsing the Contemporary Percussion
Ensemble   James Petercsak
Arthur Lauer, *No Two Crystals Alike* (1973)
Rehearsing Chamber Ensembles of Winds and
Strings   Frederick Fennell
Johannes Brahms, Serenade No. 2 in A (1875)
Antonin Dvorak, Serenade in D minor (1878)
Coaching Techniques for the Small Chamber
Ensemble   Frank Battisti
William Schuman, *Concertstück* for Four Horns
Interpretation of Early Brass Music
Martin Mailman
Giovanni Gabrieli, Canzonas 27 and 28 (ca. 1615)
Unifying the Woodwind Ensemble
Mario DiBonaventura
Selections to be announced.

1:30–2:45
Panel Discussion: The Wind Ensemble—Its Past,
Its Present, Its Future

All performing ensembles' conductors and guest
   conductor/lecturers

3:00–4:15

Contemporary Conducting Techniques
                           Frederick Fennell
  William Schuman, *Chester Overture* (1957)
    Geoffrey Richter, guest conductor
The Composer and His Music   Warren Benson
  Requerdo for Oboe and English horn (1966)
New Music   Mario DiBonaventura
  Gustav Holst/Boyd, *Capriccio* (1973)
Traditional Rehearsal Techniques for the
    Percussion Sectional   James Petercsak
  Selections to be announced.
Rehearsal Techniques for the Larger Chamber
    Ensemble   Frank Battisti
  Richard Strauss, Serenade in E-flat, op. 7 (1881)

4:30–5:45

The Application of Form and Analysis in the
    Rehearsal   Donald Hunsberger
  Darius Milhaud, *Suite Française* (1944)
Adapting Transcriptions for the Wind Ensemble
                           Frederick Fennell
  Leonard Bernstein/Beeler, Overture to *Candide*
   (1962)
The Composer and His Music   Martin Mailman
  Liturgical Music (1967)
Rehearsal Techniques for the Larger Chamber
    Ensemble   Frank Battisti
  L. van Beethoven, Rondino in E-flat (1830)
  Bernard Krol, *Konzertante* for Solo Viola and
    Wind Octet (1953)

7:00–

Jazz and the Wind Ensemble Program
                           James Petercsak
  Selections to be announced.

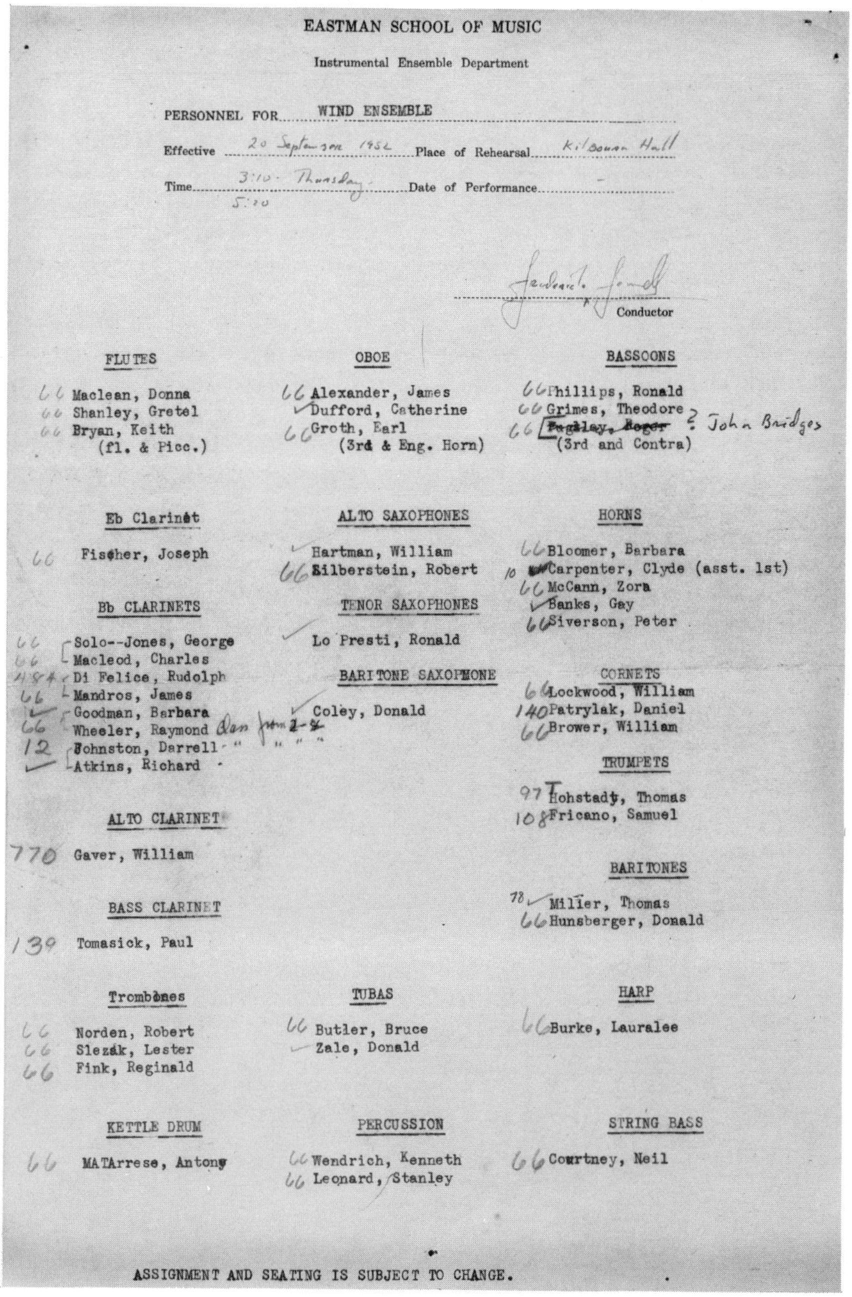

EASTMAN SCHOOL OF MUSIC

Instrumental Ensemble Department

PERSONNEL FOR _____ WIND ENSEMBLE _____

Effective _20 September 1952_ Place of Rehearsal _Kilbourn Hall_

Time _3:10 - Thursday_ Date of Performance _____
_5:00_

_____
Conductor

FLUTES
66 Maclean, Donna
66 Shanley, Gretel
66 Bryan, Keith
   (fl. & Picc.)

OBOE
66 Alexander, James
   Dufford, Catherine
66 Groth, Earl
   (3rd & Eng. Horn)

BASSOONS
66 Phillips, Ronald
66 Grimes, Theodore
66 Pugsley, Roger & John Bridges
   (3rd and Contra)

Eb Clarinet
66 Fischer, Joseph

ALTO SAXOPHONES
   Hartman, William
66 Silberstein, Robert

HORNS
66 Bloomer, Barbara
10 Carpenter, Clyde (asst. 1st)
66 McCann, Zora
   Banks, Gay
66 Siverson, Peter

Bb CLARINETS
66 Solo--Jones, George
66 Macleod, Charles
184 Di Felice, Rudolph
66 Mandros, James
   Goodman, Barbara
66 Wheeler, Raymond
12 Johnston, Darrell
   Atkins, Richard

TENOR SAXOPHONES
   Lo Presti, Ronald

BARITONE SAXOPHONE
   Coley, Donald

CORNETS
66 Lockwood, William
140 Patrylak, Daniel
66 Brower, William

TRUMPETS
97 Hohstadt, Thomas
108 Fricano, Samuel

ALTO CLARINET
770 Gaver, William

BARITONES
78 Miller, Thomas
66 Hunsberger, Donald

BASS CLARINET
139 Tomasick, Paul

Trombones
66 Norden, Robert
66 Slezak, Lester
66 Fink, Reginald

TUBAS
66 Butler, Bruce
   Zale, Donald

HARP
66 Burke, Lauralee

KETTLE DRUM
66 MATArrese, Antony

PERCUSSION
66 Wendrich, Kenneth
66 Leonard, Stanley

STRING BASS
66 Courtney, Neil

ASSIGNMENT AND SEATING IS SUBJECT TO CHANGE.

Plate 1: September 20, 1952. Original call-sheet posted on the Ensemble's bulletin-board announcing the first rehearsal of the EWE.

A STUDY IN DEVELOPMENT AND INSTRUMENTATION GROWTH

Plate 2: The first EWE.

Plate 3: The Modern EWE.

Plate 4: EWE in 1963–64 in Eastman Theatre conducted by A. Clyde Roller. *Inset*: A. Clyde Roller in rehearsal.

The Wind Ensemble

VOLUME 1/NUMBER 1   JANUARY 1968

BASIC PRINCIPLES OF THE SYMPHONIC WIND ENSEMBLE CONCEPT

By DONALD HUNSBERGER, General Editor

THE basic principles guiding the composer, conductor and performer in the *symphonic wind ensemble* concept may be stated as:

1. Specified instrumentation
2. Orchestral concept of performance
3. Single performer approach
4. Development of individual instrument tone colors

These precepts are developed in composition and performance through the hypothesis that concerted wind music possesses the same artistic potential for the composer, the performer and the listener as offered by other concert media.

The eventual goal of the *symphonic wind ensemble* movement is *an unqualified acceptance of concerted wind music on the same level as all other forms of instrumental or vocal composition.*

To achieve this goal an ensemble is required which will provide these functions:

1. Offer the composer an artistic medium which will provide faithful performances of his music in the manner as written: i.e. instrumental tone colors to be employed as specified (without substitution or addition of doubling voices) with all the instrumental weights and balances to be reproduced as originally conceived.

2. Offer the woodwind, brass and percussion performer the opportunity to express himself on the highest musical plane through employment of the single performer concept.

3. Offer the concert-goer the experience of hearing concerted wind music composed and performed on the same artistic level as found in the

Donald Hunsberger

string ensemble and the full symphony orchestra; this experience to be a pure aesthetic one without the detracting elements of commercialism which currently surround the relatively short concert season of the American symphonic band.

To organize and maintain ensembles which would provide these principles, while being capable of incorporating existing programs, would appear to be a most formidable task. Actually, the problem is not so difficult as one might expect, for models for various-sized *symphonic wind ensembles* have been in existence for some time. Before delving into the actual organizations and their constitution, a closer look at the basic principles might serve to establish more firmly the need for such ensembles and the reason why most extant wind programs throughout the United States currently fail to meet these needs.

1. SPECIFIED INSTRUMENTATION

During the past few decades numerous attempts have been made by organizations of professional and educational wind directors and the Music Publishers Association to establish an instrumentation for the American symphonic band. The purpose of formulating such an instrumentation would be to provide composers known entities for which to write while offering wind directors nationally acceptable models upon which to base their individual programs.

Unfortunately, most of these efforts have not attained the desired results: a primary deterrent to success has been the local wind director himself, he in turn being the victim of his own organizational endeavors. In many educational institutions, both on the secondary and the college-university level, financial support for concert activities of the music department is a direct result of successful peripheral activities—those activities which historically are the reason for the very existence of the band: ceremonial functions, parades, and today—the spectacular football half-time productions. Once a director has recruited the required mass of players for these peripheral functions, he frequently finds it difficult to release a percentage of them to conform to a set instrumentation established by the composer or the arranger. Coupled with the musical insecurity of the less experienced players, requiring additional support on their instrumental voice parts, these elements have led to an overgrowth of the symphonic band and a gradual lessening of its vast potential as a legitimate, serious concert medium.

(Continued on next page)

Plate 5: The first issue of *The Wind Ensemble*, MCA Symphonic Wind Ensemble Editions.

1972 3rd NATIONAL WIND ENSEMBLE CONFERENCE—EASTMAN SCHOOL OF MUSIC

Plate 6: Donald Hunsberger (*right*) and H. Robert Reynolds discuss a score.

Plate 7: David Whitwell conducting the EWE.

Plate 8: Frank Battisti and the EWE.

Plate 9: 1972 Dr. Howard Hanson greeting Donald Hunsberger following the premiere performance of *Dies Natalis* by EWE.

Plate 10: 1980 Alec Wilder and Donald Hunsberger share a light moment during a rehearsal prior to the premiere of Wilder's "*Serenade for Wind Ensemble*".

Plate 11: 1974 National Wind Ensemble Conference held at University of Wisconsin. John Paynter, Frank Battisti, Donald Hunsberger, H. Robert Reynolds, Frederick Fennell outside the Music Building.

Plate 12: September 1986 CBS Masterworks recording session EWE—Donald Hunsberger conducting, Wynton Marsalis cornet soloist, *Carnaval* CD.

Plate 13: 1988 Frederick Fennell and Donald Hunsberger at rehearsal of EWE on occasion of Fennell receiving an honorary doctorate from the University of Rochester.

Plate 14: May 1990 EWE prior to 1st Sony-Eastman Kodak Japan Tour.

EASTMAN KODAK presents

世界でいちばん美しい風

イーストマン ウインド アンサンブル

EASTMAN WIND ENSEMBLE

指揮：ドナルド・ハンスバーガー／協演：アレン・ヴィズッティ（トランペット）
Conductor: Donald Hunsberger/Guest Perf.: Allen Vizzutti (Trumpet)

6/22(月) 18:30開演
Bunkamura オーチャードホール

6/28(日)
サントリーホール 14:00開演

S席7,000/A席6,000/B席5,000/C席4,000（税込）
主催：ソニー・ミュージックコミュニケーションズ／招聘：(財)ソニー音楽芸術振興会

[6/22プログラム]
ディエス・ナタリス（降誕祭）、
　　イーストマン・ウインド・アンサンブルのために／ハンソン
吹奏楽のための仮面舞踏会／パーシケッティ
吹奏楽のための交響曲変ロ調／ヒンデミット
ダンス組曲よりマーチ・スザート
ガブリエリの木管と金管のためのカンツォーナ
エルザの大聖堂への行進／ワーグナー
アレン・ヴィズッティ・トランペット・ソロ
全日本吹奏楽コンクール本年度課題曲（予定）

[6/28プログラム]
キャニオンズ（楽団創立40周年記念
　委嘱作品・日本初演）／マクベアブル
プレリュードとフーガ ト勝長 作品550／バッハ
アレン・ヴィズッティ・トランペット・ソロ
エンブレムズ（全曲）／コープランド
マーチ ワシントン・グレイズ／グラフラ
ヴォカリーズ／ラフマニノフ
　～13楽器のためのセレナード／シュトラウス
ウエストサイド物語／ハイライト／バーンスタイン
全日本吹奏楽コンクール本年度課題曲（予定）

演奏曲目は、一部変更になる場合がございますのでご了承ください
お問い合わせ、お申し込みは、
公演事務局 03-5996-1761
チケットぴあ 03-5237-9990
チケットセゾン 03-5990-9990
CNプレイガイド 03-3258-9999
Bunkamuraチケットセンター 03-3477-9999(6/22のみ)
サントリーホール・チケットセンター 03-3584-9999(6/28のみ)

6月20日16:30開演
聖徳学園川並記念講堂（学内公演）主催：聖徳大学

●後援：アメリカ大使館／(社)全日本吹奏楽連盟 全日本マーチングバンド・バトントワリング連盟 ソニー・ミュージックエンタテインメント バンドジャーナル バンドピープル パイパーズ
●協賛：**Kodak**●協力：ヤマハ(株)●企画：ソニー・ミュージックコミュニケーションズ

The Early American Wind Band

Hautboys, Harmonies, and Janissaries

RAOUL F. CAMUS

TO understand the early American wind band, one must first understand European traditions. In Europe, as in America, the band, like the orchestra, went through many developmental phases. The earliest, brought to the New World by the settlers, were the hautboy, Harmoniemusik, and janissary stages. The challenge of this paper is to cover bands and their music in America from their beginnings to the brass band movement.

Bands and band music are still the most neglected fields of musicological research in America. One reason is that there is no clear definition of the word "band." In many countries the terms "band" and "orchestra" are still used interchangeably.[1] Another reason is prejudice against bands and their music that came hand in hand with the distinction between the cultivated and the vernacular, to use Wiley Hitchcock's categorizations.[2] Bands were functional, popular, often military, and therefore everything that is not cultivated. They had a vernacular appeal, were mobile, frequently gave free informal concerts, generally performed lighter forms of popular music as entertainment for a mass public, and had to provide appropriate music for every possible ceremonial or social occasion. When one combines the prejudices of art music audiences against things popular, indigenous, and military, one can see these are hard obstacles to overcome. Yet another reason for the lack of serious band scholarship is the nature of the band itself. While there are great differences in size and instrumentation in the orchestral works of Bach, Haydn, Berlioz, and Mahler, one can still use the general term "orchestra" for an ensemble in which strings are the basic component. A similar historical evolution can be seen in wind ensembles, but the variety of instrumental combinations has given each stage its own name, and so, instead of the general term "band," there are *Stadtpfeifer* and waits, hautboys and *Hautboisten*, Harmoniemusik, janissary music, brass, concert, marching, circus, and symphonic bands, wind ensembles and wind orchestras. Each term has its own implications and ramifications. While orchestral music has always been "downward compatible," to use computer terminology, in that later groups could still play the music of the earlier ensembles, band music was not. The changes in instrumentation and the lack of a basic family core caused band directors at later stages to neglect and frequently to discard earlier repertoires. The introduction of valves especially made older arrangements obsolete; new all-brass arrangements were in turn super-

57

seded by the reintroduction of mixed wind bands. The music was accordingly forgotten or ignored. Some problems involved in this earlier band music and its performance deserve exploration by interested scholars, conductors, and performers.

The origins of the band are lost in history. Wind instruments were often associated with military, courtly, and civic activities. The medieval practice of having men "pipe watch" on a musical instrument at stated hours, whether for changing the guard, sounding an alarm, or simply announcing the time, led to the establishment of the town waits or *Stadtpfeifer*. By the time of the Renaissance, the most common instrumental combinations included one or two cornetts and two or three sackbuts. If one considers this the first stage in the development of the band, or, if preferred, the wind ensemble, one can then look to significant original compositions by Josquin, Holborne, Locke, Pezel, Reiche, the Gabrielis, and many others. One also can assume that most of the dance music published by Susato, Gervaise, and Praetorius would have been performed by these musicians. Regrettably, there is no evidence that the *Stadtpfeifer* tradition carried over to America. Other than military signals, the earliest reference to wind instruments located to date is the statement that a "band of music" paraded in Philadelphia in 1755. By this time, bands were in the hautboy stage.

The term "hautboy" dates from 1663, when Louis XIV of France replaced the fifes in his military units with oboes. England soon followed, and the term was used to denote the musicians themselves as well as the combination of two to three soprano instruments and one bass. While there are many examples of this combination by Lully and others in Europe, the earliest located so far in America is a brief march published in the *Massachusetts Magazine* in 1791. Some early collections of music for this combination, many of them preceptors or tutors, are listed in the Bibliographical Supplement following this chapter. As may be expected, considering the military and ceremonial duties of bands, many of the compositions are marches.

When military troops first marched in cadence is lost in history, but Egyptian tomb paintings of the fourteenth century B.C.E. depict soldiers marching in step preceded by their trumpeters. Vegetius, writing in the second century C.E., distinguished between the common and the quick step, adding that "if they exceed this pace, they no longer march but run."[3] Britain and France used these two basic cadences in the eighteenth century. British drill manuals did not specify the length of the step, nor the tempo of the cadence, but in 1759 the Windham plan for the militia was published in London. It specified a 24–inch step at the rate of 60 steps per minute for the common, and 120 for the quick step.[4] By 1786 the common step had increased to 70 steps per minute, and in 1794 it was set at 75 steps per minute with a 30-inch step.[5] France, meanwhile, had a step of 24 inches, 70 per minute, for the *pas ordinaire,* and 120 per minute for the *pas redoublé.* In 1791 the common step was raised to 76, while the *pas accéléré* was reduced to 100.[6] Prussia had but one cadence, the *langsammer Marsch,* between 60 and 72 steps per minute.[7] The common or ordinary step, as its name implies, was normally used by troops when marching. The quick step, sometimes called the *pas de manœuvre* by the French, was used only for turning movements or changing positions. When the movement was completed, the men would revert to the common step. The regulations were very clear in explaining that "march" by itself always meant the common step, and if the quick march were meant, it would be so commanded.

Since America was influenced by European traditions, it is not surprising to find a mixture of French, German, and British marches in American tune books. Which cadence should a conductor then use in interpreting a march? Since there are rarely any tempo indications, and the time signature is not an accurate guide, one must turn to the regulations that directed military activities. There were four basic march tempi common in European armies: the common or slow march, the quick step, the double quick, and the funeral march. Table 1 summarizes the changes in the regulations used by American troops, regular and militia, from the colonial period through the nineteenth century.

In looking at the table, it becomes clear that any march—as distinct from a quick step—of the colonial period through 1779 should be performed at a cadence of 60 beats per minute, at a cadence of 75 in the Revolutionary through Federalist periods, and from 1815 through the Civil War to 1891 at a cadence of 90 beats per minute. Since one cannot count on the time signature as a dependable indication of tempo, the functional uses of the music must be considered. It is therefore proposed that for *any* composition originally intended as a common step march, whether the time signature is common or *alla breve*, the unit is the half note, two beats per measure, at the cadence indicated in the table. Such a proposition is difficult to prove, for it rests on traditions and performance practice.[8]

One of the very few pieces from this literature available on record is "Jolley's March," taken from Joseph Herrick's *Instrumental Preceptor* of 1807 (Ex. 1).[9] A major problem in performing compositions from the past is a lack of familiarity with the notation and forms. All too frequently musicians find this music dull or boring because they interpret the work too slowly. Looking at the time signature of C, most musicians would perform this work at quarter note equal to 120. If so, the music would indeed be dull and boring. The problem lies in assuming that the march is a quick step, rather than a common step march. "Jolley's March" is a common or grand march, and therefore, in consulting the Table, should be performed at half note equal to 75 steps per minute.

Several changes took place in the hautboy combination in the first quarter of the eighteenth century. First, the musicians separated themselves from the company drummers, beginning the distinction between the "field music" and the "band of music." Second, two French horns were added to reinforce the inner voices, and to add a new tone color. One or more trumpets appeared occasionally, normally for use in flourishes or signals, but not as yet an integral part of the band. Figure 1 shows the three oboes and bassoon, with the two natural horns being played in hunting style, and one trumpet in front (Prussian style).

The clarinet was introduced into the band around the middle of the eighteenth century, and the instrumentation became standardized in the Western world into what is now called *Harmoniemusik*. Until the end of the century the ideal band, or Harmoniemusik, had pairs of oboes, clarinets, bassoons, and horns, though less affluent regiments or noblemen might do without the oboes or clarinets. The music might therefore range from five to eight or more parts, with frequent doubling.

Figure 2, a print of the changing of the guard at St. James's Palace in 1753, illustrates how this band was used in military formations. A band of eight musicians precedes the grenadier company. There are no drums in the band, these signaling instruments remaining with the field music, or with their companies. One may infer from regulations that American practices followed the British pattern.

Military bandsmen in America as well as Europe were also expected to accompany religious ceremonies and to provide music for social occasions, especially at balls and in the officers' mess. Civic bands appeared in pleasure gardens, taverns, coffee houses, and theaters. Five-part compositions seem to have been the most common in America, at least in those collections listed in the Bibliographical Supplement following this chapter. Band performances were not normally recorded in the newspapers, so there is little definite information as to the specific compositions performed. It is known there were bands everywhere in America, and that the many serenades, nocturnes, cassations, parthias, sinfonias, and divertimenti composed by Handel, Karl Philip and Johann Christian Bach, Haydn, Mozart, Pleyel, Krommer, Schubert, and a host of others were the repertoire of the eighteenth-century wind band. So too were the many arrangements of popular opera arias and selections, such as the ones Mozart featured in his own *Don Giovanni*.

The end of the eighteenth century saw a widespread interest in the percussion instruments of the Turkish janissary bands, and the bass drum, cymbals, triangle, tambourine, crescent, and single kettledrum were added to the band. The snare drum remained with the fife in the field music, and the separation between the two groups was retained. A later print of the changing of the guard at St. James's palace, reproduced as Fig. 3, shows the new janissary instruments between the band of music and the field music. Samuel Holyoke included the "Turkish Quick Step in the Battle of Prague" in his *Instrumental Assistant* of 1807 (Ex. 2).[10] The music looks very simple, and yet it was one of the most popular pieces of the time. Suppose one were asked to put on a program of authentic early American music: how should this piece be interpreted? Returning to Table 1, note the changes in the quick step. The "Turkish Quick Step" should be performed at 120 steps per minute, and since it is a "Turkish" quick step, the addition of janissary instruments would be appropriate.

There are few early illustrations of bands, and those that are available, whether in Europe or in America, very rarely show musicians playing from actual sheet music. Musicians were expected to memorize the compositions, and to improvise and ornament the melodies, a tradition surviving in today's Dixieland bands. These were fully professional musicians, and so one should not assume that the level of difficulty of the music was any less than that of professionals today. What was published usually was a simplified version for amateurs, a skeleton of what was actually performed.

About the only other recorded example available from this period is "Washington's March." Example 3 shows it as found in a manuscript intended for publication in 1808. One of two dedicated to America's first president, the march was extremely popular. Like "Yankee Doodle," nothing is known of its provenance, but something very similar appears in a collection of marches published in London around 1771. It apparently was so popular with British musicians that it did not even need a title, just a number in the collection. Example 4 is a score made from the published parts. Though this publication was intended for an amateur audience, the arrangement is much more complex, especially in the horn parts. Although it has a 2/4 time signature, normally an indication of a quick step, it is a common step march. Played at the tempo of quarter note at 75, it can be a very effective march deserving its wide reputation.[11]

The nineteenth century saw many changes in the basic Harmoniemusik. The industrial revolution aided by providing new and improved instruments, and the bands grew ever larger with the addition of flutes, piccolos, bass clarinets, contrabassoons, trombones, and serpents. With the addition of the janissary instruments, however, one can well imagine that the percussionists frequently overpowered the winds in live performances, especially with amateur players. What was needed was an instrument more powerful than the clarinet or oboe, but the brasses were still limited to the open tones of the harmonic series. One answer came from Joseph Halliday of Dublin in 1810. Applying keys to the regulation bugle, he developed a fully chromatic brass instrument. Keyed bass horns and ophicleides soon followed. Valve mechanisms were developed and constantly improved, and the cornopean or cornet-à-pistons soon replaced the keyed bugle. Adolphe Sax developed the saxhorn family of conical-bored valved chromatic brass instruments ranging in size from the soprano to the contrabass. These developments brought about the next stage of band music, the brass band, bringing this overview to a close.

The band has a heritage with traditions as glorious and worthy of recognition as any other musical combination. When orchestras were few and far between, the ubiquitous bands served a most important and significant function in bringing serious as well as popular music to the general public. Each phase, whether hautboys, Harmoniemusik, janissaries, brass, full symphonic band, or wind ensemble, is distinctive and has its own literature. As one considers the orchestras of Corelli, Haydn, and Mahler to be one logical progression, so too one should consider the wind music of Pezel, Mozart, Beethoven, Grafulla, Holst, Hindemith, and Benson to represent the band in its many varied stages of development. Unfortunately, many directors believe that serious band music started in 1909 with Holst's First Suite and completely neglect earlier repertoires.[12] The Bibliographical Supplement can help the curious explore earlier repertoires for themselves. The anthology of wind and percussion music recently published by G. K. Hall includes at least one composition from each of the major historical sources so that interested musicians can see the scope of the work, its instrumentation, and level of difficulty.[13]

Is this music worthy of revival? Can one answer the question before the music is fully explored? Consider other long-neglected repertoires. To everyone's surprise, a movie about an obscure seventeenth-century performer became an unqualified success in France in 1992. Garnering seven Césars, the French equivalent of the Oscar, Tous Les Matins du monde dealt with the life of Monsieur de Sainte Colombe as seen through the eyes of Marin Marais. One of the awards was for best music, and the recording by Jordi Saval achieved a double gold record. It was in the top ten on the pop music charts for fifteen weeks, even beating out Michael Jackson.

The movie caused a renewed interest in French baroque music, especially as performed on the viola da gamba. When one remembers that before the arrival of long-playing records in 1948, baroque was considered "early music" and meant Bach and Handel. The music of Marais, along with that of Vivaldi, Corelli, Boccherini, and hundreds of other composers available today on LPs and CDs, was known only by scholars and specialists. A society had to be formed to promote performances of Berlioz' works, and Mahler was someone only read about in music history texts. Research revived their music, and recordings brought old forgotten pieces back to life. If such a revival is possible for orchestral and chamber compositions, why not also for wind music? More than twenty-five years ago David Whitwell spoke of a vast body of eighteenth- and nineteenth-century literature that exists for large wind ensemble or wind band and called on the College Band Directors National Association president to appoint a standing committee on the wind ensemble to explore this wealth of completely ignored early band music.[14] Can we honestly say there is nothing of value in these earlier wind repertoires, simply because they are unfamiliar? It is for the band directors and wind musicians of today to join in preserving that heritage with enthusiasm, pride, and dignity.

NOTES

1. For a discussion of band terminology and its problems, see "Bands," *The New Grove Dictionary of American Music*, 4 vols. (London: Macmillan, 1986), 2:127–37.

2. See H. Wiley Hitchcock, *Music in the United States*, 3rd ed. (Englewood Cliffs, New Jersey: Prentice Hall, 1988), p. 54.

3. *Military Institutions of Vegetius*, trans. John Clarke (London: [John Clarke], 1767), p. 18.

4. William Windham, *A Plan of Discipline Composed for the Use of the Militia of the County of Norfolk* (London: J. Schuckburgh, 1759), p. 23.

5. Adjutant General's Office, *General Regulations and Orders for His Majesty's Forces* (London: War Office, 1786), p. 5; idem, *Rules and Regulations for the Formations, Field Exercise, and Movements of His Majesty's Forces* (London: War Office, 1794), pp. 7, 16–17.

6. Ministère de la Guerre, *Instructions que le roi a fait expédier pour régler provisoirment l'exercise de ses troupes d'infanterie* (Versailles: L'Imprimerie du Roi, 1775), pp. 20, 22; idem, *Réglement concernant l'exercise et les manoeuvres de l'infanterie* (Paris: Laillet, 1792), pp. 17, 56.

7. Georg Kandler, *Deutsche Armeemärsche* (Bad Godesberg: Hohwacht-Verlag K. G., 1962), p. 13.

8. A discussion of this topic may be found in this writer's article, "On the Cadence of the March," *Journal of Band Research* 16 (spring 1981): 13–23.

9. Joseph Herrick, "Jolley's March," *The Instrumental Preceptor* (Exeter, N.H.: Ranlet & Norris, 1807). Recorded on *Music of the Federal Era*, New World 299.

10. Samuel Holyoke, "Turkish Quick Step in the Battle of Prague," *The Instrumental Assistant*, vol. 2 (Exeter, N.H.: Samuel Holyoke, 1807). Recorded on *Music of the Federal Era*, New World 299.

11. Job Plimpton, "Washington's March," *The Universal Repository of Music* (manuscript, 1808). See *The Birth of Liberty*, New World 276. The musicians at the recording session adjusted to each other, as competent musicians do, and corrected errors or omissions in the parts. The oboists, for example, adapted their parts to fit the horns' dotted-sixteenth/thirty-second-note rhythms in mm. 13 and 14.

12. I addressed this attitude in "The Heritage of the Band" (paper presented at the World Association for Symphonic Bands and Ensembles Conference, Manchester, England, July 1991).

13. Raoul F. Camus, ed., *American Wind and Percussion Music*, Three Centuries of American Music, 12 (Boston: G. K. Hall & Co., 1992).

14. David Whitwell, "Band Music from a Historical Perspective," 1967, *The College and University Band*, compiled by David Whitwell and Acton Ostling, Jr. (Reston: Music Educators National Conference, 1977), pp. 59–62.

BIBLIOGRAPHICAL SUPPLEMENT

Some Early American Collections of Wind Music
(In Chronological Order)

1. *Hautboys (Music for Two Soprano Instruments and One Bass)*

Gram, H., *of Boston. "America—A New March." Massachusetts Magazine* 3, 1791.
Commonplace book. Brown University, Providence, R.I., ca. 1797. National Tune Index (NTI)/1: A32.
Bellamy Band Book. "The Property of the Bellamy Band." [Hamden, Conn.], 1799. 82 pp. Library of Congress (DLC), m1200.B45c. NTI/1&2: A18.
Holyoke, Samuel. *The Instrumental Assistant.* Vol. 1. Exeter, N.H.: H. Ranlet, 1800. 79 pp. American Antiquarian Society (MWA). E37643. NTI/1&2: J18.
Herrick, Joseph. *The Instrumental Preceptor.* Exeter, N.H.: Ranlet & Norris, 1807. 82 pp. CtY. Wolfe 3675. NTI/2: D33.
Olmstead, Timothy. *Martial Music: A Collection of Marches Harmonized for Field Bands.* Albany, N.Y.: Daniel Steele, 1807. 44 pp. New York Public Library-Lincoln Center (NN-L). SS 13284. Wolfe 6660. NTI/1&2: A96.
Shaw, Oliver. *For the Gentlemen: Favorite Selections of Instrumental Music.* Dedham, Mass.: H. Mann, 1807. 52 pp. NN-L. Wolfe 7940. Warner 291. NTI/2: D27.
Whiteley, William. *The Instrumental Preceptor.* Utica, N.Y.: Seward & Williams, 1816. 72 pp. DLC, m1270(mf)/1816/w. Wolfe 9885. NTI/2: D1.
Moore, Henry E. *Merrimack Collection of Instrumental and Martial Music.* Vol. 1. Concord: Jacob B. Moore, 1833. 96 pp. DLC, mf music 1982. NTI/2: D32.

2. *Harmoniemusik (Early Mixed Wind Bands)*

Holyoke, Samuel. *The Instrumental Assistant.* Vol. 2. Exeter, N.H.: Samuel Holyoke, 1807. 104 pp. DLC, ml177.H6, case. Wolfe 3935. NTI/1&2: A131
Plimpton, Job. *The Universal Repository of Music.* 1808. NN-L.
National Martial Music and Songs. Philadelphia: W. McCulloch, 1809. 20 pp. MiU-C. Wolfe 6470. NTI/2: D2.
Southgate, C. "President Madison's March." *The Visitor.* Richmond, Va., 1809.
Morse, Samuel. A Manuscript Collection of Music. Newburyport, 1811. 84 pp. Library of Congress, mf music 1993. NTI/2: S20.
Beach, John, compiler. "A Selection of Airs, Marches, &c." [Gloucester, Mass., 1801–25]. 145 pp. Ku-s, ms e23. NTI/2: S13.
Michael, David Moritz. *Parthias.* Winston-Salem, N.C.: Moravian Music Foundation, ca. 1812.
Goodale, Ezekiel. *The Instrumental Director.* Hallowell: E. Goodale, 1819. Library of Congress, mf music 3141/185. Wolfe 3168. NTI/2: D23.
Kyle, Alexander. 1820–43. Miscellaneous manuscripts and prints, ca. 1820–1843. Library of Congress, ML96.K97 Case; MI.Ai218; MI.A13K (and T) Case.
Webb, William. *A Set of Grand Military Divertimentos.* Philadelphia: G. E. Blake, [ca. 1828]. NN-L. NTI/2: D21.
Webb, William. *Second Set of Grand Military Divertimentos.* Philadelphia: G. E. Blake, [ca. 1828]. Scala Collection, Library of Congress NTI/2: D22.
McDowell, Lt. Irvin. Letter to Bvt. Captain Phil Barbour, adjutant, 3rd Infantry, 4 March 1844. Hitchcock Papers, Library of Congress.

Some Publishers of Early Wind Music

Carl Fischer, Inc., 52 Cooper Square, New York, NY 10003.

Edition Compusic, Amsterdam; Route 2, Box 4440, Crawfordville, FL 32327.

Edwin F.Kalmus & Co., P.O. Box 5011, Boca Raton, FL 33031. Very extensive catalog of reprints of European and American editions.

Mark Rogers, Box 81402, Mobile, AL 36608. Has a number of transcriptions available in modern editions.

Molenaar's Muziekcentrale, Wormerveer, The Netherlands.

Musica Rara, 2 Great Marlborough Street, London W1, England. Very extensive catalog of wind music editions.

Paul Maybery Editions, 360 Emma Street, St. Paul, MN 55102. Large catalog of nineteenth-century American brass band music.

Robert King Music Sales, Inc., 28 Main Street, North Easton, MA 02356–1499. Very extensive collection of brass ensemble music.

Roger Dean Publishing Company, 324 West Jackson, Macomb, IL 61455. Brass ensemble music.

WINDS (Wind Instruments New Dawn Society), Box 513, Northridge, CA 91328. Large catalog of original band works including Beethoven, Berlioz, Bochsa, Meyerbeer, Ponchielli, Reicha, and Wieprecht, some in modern editions, from the seventeenth through the twentieth centuries.

Some Indexes and Bibliographies of Early Wind Music

Adkins, Cecil, and Alis Dickinson, *International Index of Dissertations and Musicological Works in Progress.* Philadelphia: American Musicological Society and International Musicological Society, 1977. 2nd series, 1990.

Band Music Guide. 9th ed. Northfield, Ill.: The Instrumentalist Company, 1989. 360 pp. Standard reference guide for band music in print.

Brass Players Guide. North Easton, Mass.: Robert King Music Sales, 1991. 162 pp. Extensive catalog of music for brass instruments and ensembles from European and American publishers.

Camus, Raoul F. "Early American Wind and Ceremonial Music 1636–1836." *The National Tune Index*, phase 2. New York: University Music Editions, 1989. Microfiche edition of computer-generated index of 20,733 citations taken from sheet music and collections found in the United States, Canada, United Kingdom, Ireland, Germany, Belgium, Sweden, and France.

——. *American Wind and Percussion Music.* Three Centuries of American Music, 12. Boston: G. K. Hall & Co., 1992.

Chapman, James, Sheldon Fine, and Mary Rasmussen. "Music for Wind Instruments in Historical Editions, Collected Works and Numbered Series: A Bibliography." *Brass and Woodwind Quarterly* 1 (1968): 115–49; 2 (1969): 17–58.

Cipolla, Frank J. "Annotated Guide for the Study and Performance of Nineteenth Century Band Music in the United States." *Journal of Band Research* 14, no. 1 (1978): 22–40.

——. "A Bibliography of Dissertations Relative to the Study of Bands and Band Music." *Journal of Band Research* 15, no. 1 (1979): 1–31; 16, no. 1 (1980): 29–36.

Dissertation Abstracts International. Ann Arbor, Mich.: University Microfilms International. Published serially.

Farrington, James, and Jon R. Piersol. "Index to the *Journal of Band Research* Vol. I, No. 1, through Vol. XIX, No. 2." *Journal of Band Research* 20, no. 1 (1984): 41–78.

Fred, Herbert W. "Band Literature: A Bibliography." *Journal of Band Research* 17, no. 2 (1982): 37–43.

Goldman, Richard Franko. *The Band's Music.* New York: Pitman Publishing Company, 1938. Dated but still interesting discussion and listing of early wind music.

Good, Michael. "A Selected Bibliography for Original Concert Band Music." *Journal of Band Research* 18, no. 2 (1983): 12–35; 19, no. 1 (1983): 26–51. Deals mainly with works by twentieth-century composers, but includes some earlier original works for band.

Gordon, Roderick D. "Doctoral Dissertations in Music and Music Education." *Journal of Research in Music Education* 16, no. 2 (1968); 20, no. 1 (1972); 26, no. 3 (1978).

Hauswirth, Felix. *1000 ausgewählte Werke für Blasorchester und Bläserensembles*. Adliswil, Switzerland: Emil Ruh, 1986.

Hitchcock, H. Wiley, and Stanley Sadie, eds. *The New Grove Dictionary of American Music*. 4 vols. London: Macmillan Press, 1986. See especially the articles "Band" and "Military Music."

Kurtz, S. James. *A Study and Catalog of Ensemble Music for Woodwinds Alone or with Brass from ca. 1700 to ca. 1825*. Ph.D. diss., University of Iowa, 1971. 243 pp. Abstract in *Dissertation Abstracts International* 32: 5269. University Microfilms 72–8273.

Mead, Rita H. *Doctoral Dissertations in American Music*. Brooklyn College: Institute for Studies in American Music, 1974.

Rasmussen, Mary, and Donald Mattran. *A Teacher's Guide to the Literature of Woodwind Instruments*. Durham, N.H.: Brass and Woodwind Quarterly, 1966.

Rehrig, William H. *The Heritage Encyclopedia of Band Music: Composers and Their Music*. Edited by Paul Bierley. 2 vols. Westerville, Ohio: Integrity Press, 1991.

Reynolds, H. Robert, et al. *Wind Ensemble Literature*. 2nd ed., rev. Madison, Wisc.: University of Wisconsin Bands, 1975.

Suppan, Armin. *Repertorium der Märsche für Blasorchester*. Teil 1, Alta Musica 6; Teil 2, Alta Musica 13. Tutzing: Hans Schneider, 1982, 1990.

Suppan, Wolfgang. *Das neue Lexikon des Blasmusikwesens*. 3rd ed. Freiburg-Tiengen: Blasmusikverlag Schulz, 1988. Includes worklists following each biographical entry.

Toeche-Mittler, Joachim. *Armeemärsche*. 3 vols. Neckargemünd: Kurt Vowinckel, 1966–75. Vol. 2 contains a listing of the traditional German army marches.

Whitwell, David. *Band Music of the French Revolution*. Alta Musica 5. Tutzing: Hans Schneider, 1979.

——. *The History and Literature of the Wind Band*. 11 vols. Northridge, Calif.: WINDS, 1982–90.

Wolfe, Richard J. *Secular Music in America 1801–1825*. 3 vols. New York: The New York Public Library, 1964.

A Selection of Articles, Books, and Dissertations
Relevant to the Performance of Original Wind Music

Adkins, H. E. *Treatise on the Military Band*. 2nd ed. London: Boosey & Co., 1958.

Altenburg, Johann Ernst. *Essay on an Introduction to the . . . Trumpeters' and Kettledrummers' Art. (Versuch einer Anleitung . . . Trompeter- und Pauker-Kunst.)* Halle: Joh. Christ. Hendel, 1795. English translation by Edward H. Tarr. Nashville, Tenn.: The Brass Press, 1974.

Battisti, Frank. "My View of the Wind Repertoire." *The Instrumentalist* (October 1989): 12–17, 105; (November 1989): 16–20, 88; (December 1989): 19–22, 36.

Blades, James. *Percussion Instruments and their History*. New York: Frederick A. Praeger, 1970.

Bly, Leon J. *The March in American Society*. Ph.D. diss., University of Miami, 1977. 323 pp. Abstract in *Dissertation Abstracts International* 38, no. 12: 7910A. University Microfilms 78–8235.

Bolen, Charles W. *Open-Air Music of the Baroque: A Study of Selected Examples of Wind Music*. Ph.D. diss., Indiana University, 1954. 276 pp. Abstract in *Dissertation Abstracts International* 14, no. 8: 1232. University Microfilms 8778.

Bowles, Edmund A. "Tower Musicians in the Middle Ages." *Brass Quarterly* 5, no. 3 (1962): 91–103.

Brixel, Eugen, Gunther Martin, and Gottfried Pils. *Das ist Österreichs Militärmusik*. Graz: Edition Kaleidoskop, 1982.

——, and Wolfgang Suppan. *Das Grosse Steirische Blasmusikbuch*. Wien: Fritz Molden, 1981.

Bufkin, William A. *Union Bands of the Civil War (1862–65): Instrumentation and Score Analysis*. Ph.D. diss., Louisiana State University, 1973. 440 pp. Abstract in *Dissertation Abstracts International* 35, no. 2: 1139. University Microfilms 74–18,319.

Camus, Raoul F. *Military Music of the American Revolution*. 1976. Reprint, Westerville, Ohio: Integrity Press, 1992.

——. "On the Cadence of the March." *Journal of Band Research* 16, no. 2 (1978): 13–23.

——. "Some Nineteenth-Century Band Journals." In *Festschrift zum 60. Geburtstag von Wolfgang Suppan*, edited by Bernhard Habla, pp. 335–48. Tutzing: Hans Schneider, 1993.

Clappé, Arthur A. *The Wind-Band and its Instruments*. New York: Henry Holt, 1911.

Cooper, Donald A. *An Historical Account, Criticism, and Modern Performance Edition of the* Grand Symphony for Band *by Hector Berlioz*. Ph.D. diss., University of Montana, 1967. 162 pp. Abstract in *Dissertation Abstracts International* 28, no. 12: 5087. University Microfilms 68–7263.

Deutsch, Walter. *Das Grosse Niederösterreichische Blasmusikbuch.* Vienna: Christian Brandstätter, 1982.

Downs, Anneliese. "The Tower Music of a Seventeenth-Century Stadtpfeifer: Johann Pezel's *Hora decima* and *Fünff-stimmigte blasende Music.*" *Brass Quarterly* 7, no. 1 (1963): 3–33.

Dudgeon, Ralph T. *The Keyed Bugle: Its History, Literature and Technique.* Ph.D. diss., University of California, 1980.

Dudley, W. Sherwood. *Orchestration in the* musique d'harmonie *of the French Revolution.* Ph.D. diss., University of California, 1968. 346 pp. Abstract in *Dissertation Abstracts International* 29, no. 9: 3168. University Microfilms 69–3593.

Evenson, Pattee. *A History of Brass Instruments, Their Usage, Music, and Performance Practices in Ensembles During the Baroque Era.* D.M.A. thesis, University of Southern California, 1960. 518 pp. Abstract in *Dissertation Abstracts International* 22, no. 9: 3219. University Microfilms 61–6282.

Fennell, Frederick. "The Civil War: Its Music and its Sounds." *Journal of Band Research* 4 (1968): 36–44; 5 (1968): 8–14; 5 (1969): 4–10; 6 (1969): 46–58.

———. *Time and the Winds.* Kenosha, Wisc.: G. Leblanc Company, 1954.

Fetter, David J. "Daniel Speer, Stadtpfeifer (1636–1707)." M.A. thesis, American University, 1969. MA 8, no. 1: 27. University Microfilms 13–1982.

Garofalo, Robert, and Mark Elrod. "*Heritage Americana:* Reflections on the Performance Practices of Mid-Nineteenth Century Brass Bands." *Journal of Band Research* 17, no. 1 (1981): 1–26. Includes annotated discography and selected bibliography. A collection of American Civil War brass band music, *Heritage Americana* has been published by Neil A. Kjos Music Company, 4380 Jutland Drive, San Diego, CA 92117.

Gibson, O. Lea. *The Serenades and Divertimenti of Mozart.* Ph.D. diss., North Texas State University, 1960. 394 pp. Abstract in *Dissertation Abstracts International* 21, no. 3: 638. University Microfilms 60–2791.

Habla, Bernhard. *Besetzung und Instrumentation des Blasorchesters seit der Erfindung der Ventile für Blechblaserinstrumente bis zum Zweiten Weltkrieg in Österreich und Deutschland.* 2 vols. Alta Musica 12. Tutzing: Hans Schneider, 1990.

———, ed. *Johann Joseph Fux und die Barocke Bläsertradition.* Alta Musica 9. Tutzing: Hans Schneider, 1987.

Hazen, Margaret Hindle and Robert M. Hazen. *The Music Men: An Illustrated History of Brass Bands in America, 1800–1920.* Washington, D.C.: Smithsonian Institution Press, 1987.

Hellyer, Roger. Harmoniemusik: *Music for Small Wind Band in the Late Eighteenth and Nineteenth Centuries.* Ph.D. diss., Oxford University, 1973. 406 pp.

Herbert, James W. *The Wind Band of Nineteenth-Century Italy: its Origins and Transformation from the Late 1700s to Mid-Century.* Ed.D. diss., Columbia University Teachers College, 1986. 186 pp. Abstract in *Dissertation Abstracts International* 47, no. 11: 4012. University Microfilms 87–4300.

Hoe, Robert, Jr. *Heritage of the March.* Two series of recordings of marches with biographical liner notes (records 1–90, A-PPPP).

Hofer, Achim. *Blasmusikforschung: Eine kritische Einführung.* Darmstadt: Wissenschaftliche Buchgesellschaft, 1992.

———. *Studien zur Geschichte des Militärmarsches.* 2 vols. Tutzing: Hans Schneider, 1988.

Horsley, Imogene. "Wind Techniques in the Sixteenth and Early Seventeenth Centuries." *Brass Quarterly* 4, no. 2 (1960): 49–63.

Ingalls, David M. "Francis Scala: Leader of the Marine Band from 1855–1871." M.M. thesis, Catholic University, 1957. Contains a complete listing of the 608 titles in the collection at the Library of Congress, most of which is available on microfilm.

Jacobs, Richard M. *The Chamber Ensembles of C.P.E.Bach Using Two or More Wind Instruments.* Ph.D. diss., University of Iowa, 1964. 293 pp. Abstract in *Dissertation Abstracts International* 25, no. 2: 1248. University Microfilms 64–7926.

Jones, William L. *Three Wind Divertimenti (Partitas) by Franz Asplmayr in Vienna circa 1760.* Ph.D. diss., University of Wisconsin, 1972. 101 pp. Abstract in *Dissertation Abstracts International* 33, no. 6: 2969. University Microfilms 72–23,316.

Kappey, J. A. *Military Music.* London: Boosey & Co., [1894].

Kastner, Georges. *Manuel général de musique militaire a l'usage des armées françaises.* Paris: Didot Frères, 1848. Reprinted Geneva: Minkoff, 1973.

Lee, William R. "Wind Music of the Baroque: J. G. C. Störl and his Tower Sonatas." *Journal of Band Research* 20, no. 1 (1984): 2–8.

Lewis, Edgar J., Jr. *The Use of Wind Instruments in Seventeenth-Century Instrumental Music.* Ph.D. diss., University of Wisconsin, 1964. 538 pp. Abstract in *Dissertation Abstracts International* 24, no. 10: 4223. University Microfilms 64–3928.

Lord, Francis A., and Arthur Wise. *Bands and Drummer Boys of the Civil War.* 1966. Reprint, New York: DaCapo, 1979.

MacDonald, Robert J. *François-Joseph Gossec and French Instrumental Music in the Second Half of the Eighteenth Century.* Ph.D. diss., University of Michigan, 1968. 879 pp. Abstract in *Dissertation Abstracts International* 30, no. 2: 752. University Microfilms 69–12,175.

Mayer, Francis N. *A History of Scoring for Band: The Evolution of Band Scoring in the United States.* Ph.D. diss., University of Minnesota, 1957. 607 pp. Abstract in *Dissertation Abstracts International* 29, no. 4: 830. University Microfilms 22,468.

Mitchell, Jon C. *From Kneller Hall to Hammersmith: The Band Works of Gustav Holst.* Alta Musica 11. Tutzing: Hans Schneider, 1990.

Newsom, Jon. "The American Brass Band Movement." *The Quarterly Journal of the Library of Congress* 36 (1979): 115–39.

Olson, Kenneth E. *Music and Musket: Bands and Bandsmen of the American Civil War.* Westport, Conn.: Greenwood Press, 1981.

Panoff, Peter. *Militärmusik in Geschichte und Gegenwart.* Berlin: Karl Siegismund, 1938.

Phelps, Russell L. "Uses of Wind Instruments in the Classical Period." M.M. thesis, Northwestern University, 1955.

Piersol, Jon R. *The Oettingen-Wallerstein Hofkapelle and its Wind Music.* Ph.D. diss., University of Iowa, 1972. 853 pp. Abstract in *Dissertation Abstracts International* 33, no. 12: 6954. University Microfilms 73–13,583.

Polk, Keith. *Flemish Wind Bands in the Late Middle Ages: A Study in Improvisatory Performance Practices.* Ph.D. diss., University of California, 1968. 297 pp. Abstract in *Dissertation Abstracts International* 29, no. 9: 3174. University Microfilms 69–3674. See also idem, "Wind Bands of Medieval Flemish Cities," *Brass and Woodwind Quarterly* 1 (1968): 93–113.

Rameis, Emil. *Die Österreichische Militärmusik von ihren Anfängen bis zum Jahre 1918.* Alta Musica 2. Tutzing: Hans Schneider, 1976.

Ramey, Michael. "The Baroque Suite." *Journal of Band Research* 18, no. 2 (1983): 36–47. Discussion of baroque dance music, with a listing of many original works available in modern editions.

Rasmussen, Mary. "Gottfried Reiche and his *Vier und zwantzig Neue Quatricinia* (Leipzig 1696)." *Brass Quarterly* 4, no. 1 (1960): 3–17.

Rocco, Emma S. *Italian Wind Bands: A Surviving Tradition in the Milltowns of Lawrence and Beaver Counties of Pennsylvania.* Ph.D. diss., University of Pittsburgh, 1986. 421 pp. Abstract in *Dissertation Abstracts International* 47, no. 10: 3606. University Microfilms 87–2020.

Rorick, David R. *The Nineteenth-Century American Cornet Band: Its Origins, Development, Instrumentation, and Literature.* D.M.A. thesis, The Catholic University of America, 1979.

Sandman, Susan G. *Wind Band Music under Louis XIV: The Philidor Collection, Music for the Military and the Court.* Ph.D. diss., Stanford University, 1974. 437 pp. Abstract in *Dissertation Abstracts International* 35, no. 6: 3798. University Microfilms 74–27,103.

Schwab, Heinrich W. "Stadtpfeifer." *The New Grove Dictionary of Music and Musicians.* Edited by Stanley Sadie. London: MacMillan, 1980. Includes good bibliography.

Schwarz, Boris. *French Instrumental Music between the Revolutions (1789–1830).* Ph.D. diss., Columbia University, 1950. 387 pp. Abstract in *Dissertation Abstracts International* 10, no. 4: 250. University Microfilms 1897.

Shive, Clyde S., Jr. "Programming Marches from the U.S., 1775–1825." *Journal of Band Research* 22, no. 1 (1986): 1–8.

———. "The Wind Band in the United States, 1800 to 1825." *Kongreßbericht Oberschützen/Burgenland 1988, Toblach/Südtirol 1990,* ed. Bernhard Habla. Alta Musica 14, pp.159–80. Tutzing: Hans Schneider, 1992.

———. "Wind Music in Philadelphia in the First Decades of the Nineteenth Century." *Kongreßbericht Oberschützen/Burgenland 1988, Toblach/Südtirol 1990,* ed. Bernhard Habla. Alta Musica 14, pp. 181–92. Tutzing: Hans Schneider, 1992.

Sirman, Mitchel N. *The Wind Sonatas in Daniel Speer's Musicalish-Türckischer Eulen-Spiegel of 1688.* Ph.D. diss., University of Wisconsin, 1972. 183 pp. Abstract in *Dissertation Abstracts International* 33, no. 8: 4462. University Microfilms 72–29,512.

Smialek, William. "Jósef Elsner and Military Band Music in Nineteenth-century Poland." *Journal of Band Research* 20, no. 2 (1985): 2–7.

Smith, Norman E. *March Music Notes.* Lake Charles, La.: Program Note Press, 1986.

Soyer, A. "De l'orchestration militaire et de son histoire." *Encyclopédie de la musique et Dictionnaire du Conservatoire*, vol. 2, pp. 2,135–2,214. Paris: Librairie Delagrove, 1929.

Sperry, Gale. "The State of Band Research." *Journal of Band Research* 10, no. 1 (1974): 1–2. A listing of 32 dissertations relevant to band research.

Steinquist, Eugene W. *Royal Prussian Wind-Band Music, 1740–1797.* Ed.D. thesis, George Peabody College, 1971. 424 pp. Abstract in *Dissertation Abstracts International* 32, no. 7: 4052. University Microfilms 72–3817.

Suppan, Wolfgang. *Blasmusik in Baden.* Freiburg: Fritz Schulz, 1983.

——. "Die Harmoniemusik." In *Festschrift zum 65. Geburtstag von Walter Salmen*, edited by Monika Fink, Rainer Gstrein and Günter Mössmer, pp. 151–65. Innsbruch: Helbling, 1991.

Swanzy, David P. *The Wind Ensemble and Its Music During the French Revolution (1789–1795).* Ph.D. diss., Michigan State University, 1966. 298 pp. Abstract in *Dissertation Abstracts International* 27, no. 5: 1398. University Microfilms 66–8495.

Thomas, Orlan E. *Music for Double-Reed Ensembles from the Seventeenth and Eighteenth Centuries: 'Collection Philidor.'* D.M.A. thesis, Eastman School of Music, 1973. 151 pp. Abstract in *Dissertation Abstracts International* 35, no. 3: 1691. University Microfilms 74–20,475.

Titcomb, Caldwell. *The Kettledrums in Western Europe: Their History outside the Orchestra.* Ph.D. diss., Harvard University, 1952. 575 pp.

Uber, David A. *The Brass Choir in Antiphonal Music.* Ed.D. thesis, Columbia University, 1965. 275 pp. Abstract in *Dissertation Abstracts International* 26, no. 5: 2797. University Microfilms 65–11,713.

Vernon, Ronald F. *The Marches for Wind Band by Joseph Franz Wagner in the Austrian National Library.* D.M.A. thesis, University of Texas, 1973. 151 pp. Abstract in *Dissertation Abstracts International* 35, no. 8: 5455. University Microfilms 75–4493.

Votta, Michael, Jr. "The Wind Music of W. A. Mozart: An Annotated Catalog and Complete Discography." *CBDNA Journal* 1, no. 1 (1984): 37–42; 2, no. 1 (1985): 30–35; 2, no. 2 (1986): 24–31; 5 (1988): 24–31.

Warner, Thomas E. *Indications of Performance Practice in Woodwind Instruction Books of the 17th and 18th Centuries.* Ph.D. diss., New York University, 1964. 469 pp. Abstract in *Dissertation Abstracts International* 25, no. 10: 5982. University Microfilms 65–1678.

Whitwell, David. *A Concise History of the Wind Band.* Northridge, Calif.: WINDS, 1985. 291 pp. Selected bibliographies follow each chapter.

Regulations	Common Step	Quick Step	Double Quick Step
1759 (Windham)	24"-60/min.	24"-120/min.	(none)
1775 (Pickering)	24"-60/min.	24"-120/min.	(none)
1779 (von Steuben)	24"-75/min.	24"-120/min.	(none)
1812 (Smyth)	24"-75/min.	24"-100/min.	(none)
1815 (Scott 1815)	28"-90/min.	28"-120/min.	(none)
1835 (Scott 1835)	28"-90/min.	28"-110/min.	(none)
1855 (Hardee)	28"-90/min.	28"-110/min.	33"-165-180/min.
1862 (Casey)	28"-90/min.	28"-110/min.	33"-165/min.
1867 (Upton)	28"·90/min.	28"-110/min.	33"-165-180/min.
1891 (Board)	(none)	30"-120/min.	36"-180/min.

Windham, William. *A Plan of Discipline Composed for the Use of the Militia of the County of Norfolk.* London: J. Schuckburgh, 1759.

Pickering, Timothy, Jr. *An Easy Plan of Discipline for a Militia.* Salem: Samuel & Ebenezer Hall, 1775. Based primarily on Windham.

[von Steuben, Baron Frederick William Augustus]. U.S. Inspector General's Office. *Regulations for the Order and Discipline of the Troops of the United States.* Philadelphia: Styner & Cist, 1779; reprint, Philadelphia: Ray Riling Arms Books Co., 1966.

Smyth, Col. Alexander. *Regulations for the Field Exercise, Manœuvres, and Conduct of the Infantry of the United States.* Philadelphia: Anthony Finley, 1812.

[Scott, Bvt. Maj. Gen. Winfield]. U.S. Adjutant General's Office. *Rules and Regulations for the Field Exercise and Manœuvres of Infantry.* Concord: Isaac Hill, 1817.

Scott, Maj. Gen. Winfield. *Infantry Tactics; or Rules for the Exercise and Manœuvres of the United States Infantry.* 3 vols. New York: George Dearborn, 1835.

Hardee, Bvt. Lt. Col. W. J. *Rifle and Light Infantry Tactics; for the Exercise and Manœuvres of Troops when acting as Light Infantrymen or Riflemen.* 2 vols. Philadelphia: Lippincott, Grambo & Co., 1855.

Casey, Brig. Gen. Silas. *Infantry Tactics, for the Instruction, Exercise, and Manœuvres of the Soldier, a Company, Line of Skirmishers, Battalion, Brigade, or Corps d'Armée.* New York: D. Van Nostrand, 1862; reprint, Dayton: Morningside, 1985.

Upton, Bvt. Maj. Gen. Emory. *A New System of Infantry Tactics.* New York: D. Appleton & Co., 1867.

U.S. Adjutant General's Office. *Infantry Drill Regulations.* Washington, D.C.: G.P.O., 1891.

Table 1. Regulations used by American troops

Example 1: "Jolley's March." Joseph Herrick, *The Instrumental Preceptor*, 1807

Example 2: "Turkish Quick Step in the Battle of Prague." Samuel Holyoke, *The Instrumental Assistant*, vol. 2, 1807.

Example 3: "Washington's March." Job Plimpton, *The Universal Repository of Music*, 1808.

Example 4: "March 16." *A Second Collection of XXIV Favourite Marches*. London: C. & S. Thompson, ca. 1771.

XXIV Favourite Marches, II, c.1771

Example 4: "March 16." *A Second Collection of XXIV Favourite Marches.* London: C. & S. Thompson, ca. 1771.

Figure 1: Christoph Weigel, *Hautboisten*, ca. 1720 (courtesy Österreichische Nationalbibliothek).

Figure 2: *A View of Royal Building for His Majestys Horse & Foot Guards with the Treasury in St. James's Park, London.* London: H. Parker, 1753 (author's collection).

Figure 3: *Guard Mounting at St. James's Palace*, ca. 1780 (author's collection).

The American Brass Band Movement
in the Mid-Nineteenth Century

JON NEWSOM

W E usually imagine the ornate Victorian gazebos that once were bandstands as belonging more in the fanciful and diminutive setting of toy
railroads than to the leviathan of the industrial age that spawned them.
Yet even when seen in an artificially serene context, those quaint nostalgic objects
remind us of real, instead of toy, engines that were used not for recreation but to
get to wherever there was a profit to be made as fast as possible. The bandstands,
too, were not simply conjurings of small-town dreamers.

By the 1850s music in America was becoming big business. Both amateur and
professional musical organizations were thriving. And the eminent Boston music
journalist, John Sullivan Dwight, together with numerous colleagues, was promoting, guiding, and frequently condemning popular music fashions in the course
of reporting and polemicizing on the brass band movement in America before,
during, and after the Civil War.

"When shall we have music for the People?" asks Dwight in 1852. "Music that all
who will may hear, without money and without price; free to all ears, as the
sparkling fountain on the [Boston] Common is, to all eyes."[1] But by the following
year he reports with a sense of growing horror on the development of a new kind
of popular music-making that threatens to fulfill his dream with a vengeance
nearly as cruel, one is led to suppose, as the curse on the sorcerer's apprentice. "All
at once," he writes, "the idea of a Brass Band shot forth: and from this prolific
germ sprang up a multitude of its kind in every part of the land, like the crop of
iron men from the infernal seed of the dragon's teeth. And, as if the invention of
new and deadlier implements of war, which came out about the same time, had
hardened mens' hearts, all the softer companions of the savage science [the wood-
winds] were banished."[2] And later in the same issue he asks rhetorically: "Are the
business and politics of the day so harsh, that the tones of our street music must, in
correspondence, renounce all their sincerity and gentleness, and become mere
bluster?"[3] Indeed they must have, for three months later he reports on the summer concerts on the common, with some chagrin: "The experiment succeeds
beyond doubt or cavil," adding that "the music might be better, with larger and
more especial organization, but under the circumstances it has been very good, and
has been drunk in with every sign of attention and delight by a continually
increasing crowd of listeners. There could not have been fewer than ten thousand

persons, of all ages and classes, on the common the two last times."[4] By the summer of 1857 Dwight is nearly beside himself. "How can we continue the discussion of Brass Bands," he complains, melting, we imagine, in the mid-August heat, "in such intensity of dog-days! It is aggravating to think of them. But the Promenade Concerts at the Music Hall go on, with more and more success, and prove what fine things might be done."[5] The next week he adds: "We want volumes of sound, but not folio volumes."[6]

If the all-brass bands grate on Dwight's nerves, in combination with artillery and fireworks they offend both his sense of economy and his sense of smell. "The most noisy, rowdy, pop-gun and cracker-firing style of free expenditure" is his characterization of Fourth of July celebrations.[7] And after announcing, apropos of Boston's annual anniversary celebration on 17 September, that "nothing looms in the immediate distance but Mr. Burditt's monster brass band and cannonade concert," he subsequently declines to review the event thus: "The windward position which we took, to avoid the smell of villainous saltpetre, had an unfortunate effect on the music, so that we borrow the account of the Courier."[8]

Nothing, however, offends Dwight's sensibilities so much as the introduction of brass bands at serious occasions such as this one sponsored by his Alma Mater: "Last week we had commencement—commencement at old Harvard—and as usual, a Boston band assisted at the exercises. But—Ichabod!—the glory has departed. Brass, brass, brass,—nothing but brass."[9]

The bands that Dwight sought so consistently to reform or to have relegated to what he considered their proper place—the street—were what he called military as opposed to civil. And he ascribed to them not only a penchant for music of a warlike nature but dependence on the support of the military. "It is the military employment," he writes in 1856, "which creates and supports all our bands."[10] In assessing Dwight's statement, we must remember that bands, whether made up of full-time professional musicians or amateurs, were not part of the U.S. militia before the Civil War, the years during which Dwight wrote, and that they could be and indeed were supported in many ways other than by military officers. Band concerts were supported by private subscription, public funds administered by local elected officials, and, even during the Civil War, by private industry. In 1862 band concerts in New York's Central Park were paid for by the railroads to increase fare income by transporting out-of-town concertgoers.[11] Indeed, the brass band movement in America warrants comparison, however cautious, with a parallel movement in Britain; for in America, as in industrial England, amateur bands were also formed by workingmen. Yet the differences, as will be seen, were great.

English Influence

In England employers enthusiastically encouraged their factory workers to participate in music-making, probably with the thought that they would then be less likely to become involved in potentially disruptive activities. And so, factories had their highly competitive bands, as modern schools and colleges have their football teams, which were good for morale and business and served a definite purpose in the minds of the practical businessmen who supported them. These bands even practiced regularly during working hours, and well-planned competitions among rival bands drew tremendous crowds. Music-making probably has never so closely resembled a commercially sponsored contact sport. And we may be reasonably sure that occasionally the contact between and among spectators and bandsmen induced even more pain physically than the most rustic musical participants induced acoustically. Nevertheless, there is also evidence that the best amateur bands equaled or even surpassed the outstanding British professional military bands of the time. It should be emphasized, however, that these professional bands were not all brass, a predominant role being played by woodwinds—just the kind of instrumentation so ardently called for by Dwight. In Britain, the brass band movement was, and still is, strictly an amateur one. But in America, it was a relatively short-lived phenomenon involving professional and amateur musicians alike. This British import was subjected to many Yankee innovations, for America in the 1850s, even in the more industrial centers of the northern states, had not achieved the intense social climate of the densely populated towns and cities in which the brass band movement thrived in England.

The spirit in which American brass bands were formed is captured in John C. Linehan's recollections of the Fisherville Cornet Band, established shortly before the Civil War:

> The band in its infancy occupied the room over the present Methodist Church, and it was interesting for those outside to note the evolution from [the tune] "Few Days" to the rendition of a first class quick-step. . . .
>
> The best tribute paid the band [in 1860] . . . was its selection to perform service for the Governor's Horse Guards, one of the most stylish military organizations ever recruited in New Hampshire. . . .
>
> Their engagement by the Horse Guards, although a matter of pride, was nevertheless an occasion of dismay, for the boys for the first time in their lives had to play on horseback. As nearly all of them were novices in this direction the outlook was serious, for it is a question if there were half a dozen of the number that had ever straddled a horse. When the proposition was first broached in the band room, one of the saddest looking men was the leader, Loren Currier. He said he would vote to accept on one condition, and that was if a horse could be secured large enough to have them all ride together and give him a place in the middle. The proposition was, however, accepted. . . . It was a moving sight (the moving was all towards the ground, however), and the bucking broncos of the Wild West Show furnished no more sport, while it lasted, than did the gallant equestrians of the Fisherville Band while trying to train their horses to march and wheel by fours.[12]

German, Italian, and Irish Influences

In American amateur brass bands the lines dividing social classes were not so sharply drawn as in British ones. Moreover, while Britons were expanding their empire abroad, they were not, as were their Anglo-American relatives, receiving foreigners at home. The immigration of the Germans, Italians, and Irish, among others, had a decisive influence on American popular culture in the 1850s.

While the all-brass band was predominant in America, it coexisted with some bands whose makeup was influenced by European immigrants with musical training. As early as 1852, the fashionable New York Seventh Regiment Band introduced woodwinds. Col. Emmons Clark reports the following:

> In January, 1852, the engagement of Adkins's Washington Brass Band with the Seventh Regiment expired, and was not renewed. As there was no band in the city entirely satisfactory to the Regiment, it was proposed to organize a new military band. . . . Fortunately, the very best material for the purpose was to be found among the professional musicians of the German Musical Society. . . . In April . . . the music committee was directed to make arrangements for a new band of forty-two musicians, and to contract for suitable uniforms and equipments. Thus originated the famous Seventh Regiment Band, the only band exclusively regimental at that period in the country. The leader and musical director was Noll, a distinguished musician, and the members were professional musicians carefully selected, and the new band used both brass and reed instruments in due proportion, and performed only modern and popular music of the highest order.[13]

We do not know why Adkins or his brass band fell out of favor, but along with him, the all-brass instrumentation of the New York Seventh Regiment Band was discarded.

Colonel Clark's reference to the German Musical Society and "both brass and reed instruments" immediately brings to mind the most important German bandmaster of the time: Friedrich Wilhelm Wieprecht. His seven-volume *Königliche Preussische Armee Marsche*, which contains full scores of his instrumentations "für die jetzige Stimmenbesetzung" ("for the present-day instrumentation") of selected works arranged in the chronological order of their composition from the mid eighteenth century to 1853, represents the ultimate in German military band instrumentation of that period. He was certainly known and respected in New York. And early in the war our Boston critic, Dwight, recommends him:

> In Prussia there is a band master general, who organizes and controls the entire music of the Prussian army. Every band in the whole kingdom must conform, in numbers, in the selection and proportion of various instruments, in the particular structure, compass, pitch, &c., of each kind of instrument, to his unitary standard. He is thoroughly master of his subject, and probably knows more of the capacities of wind instruments and the best ways of combining them, so as to obtain the most effect, for every kind of service, than any man in Europe. Wieprecht is his name. He is preparing a treatise on wind instruments, which will be invaluable. Liszt and Berlioz, whose work on "Instrumentation" is well known, have owed much to Wieprecht.[14]

There was also the Italian influence. Francis Scala, leader of the U.S. Marine Band, had been brought to America about 1840 by the navy. He was a Neapolitan and, true to the custom of his homeland, held the clarinet to be the principal band instrument. He himself was a virtuoso on the E-flat clarinet, the instrument that usually stole the show—though he did permit some lively brasswind solos, mostly on what he often called the "Hippocorno." The word "Hippocorno" is Scala's unique corruption of the term "Ebor Corno," probably established by a New York bandmaster, Allen Dodworth, who dubbed a brasswind of the E-flat tenor horn family to which he applied some modifications the "New York Horn"—in Latin, the "Novo Eboracii Corno."

Patrick Sarsfield Gilmore, who was born in Ireland and was to prove himself a true innovator in band instrumentation, is supposed to have introduced reeds into his brass band in 1859. It was not uncommon to use piccolos and clarinets to double the soprano brasses, so if this is all that Gilmore was doing, it was no innovation. However, we have an interesting account concerning Gilmore's band in 1862. A member of the 24th Massachusetts Volunteer Infantry is reported to have written home of Gilmore's band: "[He] used to give some of the fashionable concerts we had at home and we lack nothing but the stringed instruments now. In their place however we have five reed instruments, of which no other can boast."[15] This may suggest a family of reeds with the full range normally covered by the violin, viola, and cello. It is more likely, however, that strings in this context were thought of as purely melodic instruments. Yet it was probably Patrick Gilmore who made the most important contribution to the concert band in America before John Philip Sousa by eventually developing an instrumentation that enabled a large wind ensemble to produce effects comparable to a full orchestra at a time when American orchestras of high quality were scarce. Victor Herbert, Gilmore's successor, makes this interesting statement in an article published in 1895:

> From the old bands which depended on the loud brasses and drums, all forced to their utmost to make the most noise possible, to the bands of the present day which interpret the works of the greatest so as to satisfy even the most exacting musician, has been a hard but glorious struggle up the steeps of Parnassus, and to Patrick Sarsfield Gilmore belongs most of the glory. . . . As the repertories of bands have increased, the demand for new tone-colour effects has caused new instruments to be made, so that to-day the composer or adapter has a wide range in registering. The use of compositions originally written for orchestras has caused a great increase in the wood-wind section of the bands—flutes, oboes, clarinets, and saxophones of which every band should have a quartet—bassoons, and contrabassoons. These additions make the repertory of the band universal. The greater sustaining power of the wood-winds gives a beautiful richness of harmony, and relieves one from the torture of listening to the scratchiness of poorly played strings.[16]

Dwight himself, as early as 1868, confirms that Gilmore was doing something unique with the mixture of brass and woodwinds. In an issue of his *Journal* that year he prints a review of a concert from Chicago. It reads, in part: "The reed and wind effects of Gilmore's band were quite novel here, where it is so unusual to find more than the smallest possible assortment of instruments in the orchestra. So our people curiously enough 'went out to see' and hear 'reeds shaken in the wind.'"[17]

Band Instruments

The phenomenal rise of the brass band in mid-nineteenth-century America can be better understood if we trace its antecedents and some of the technical developments that produced the type of brasswind family from soprano to bass that was the staple of our bands in the Civil War era.

The aristocracy of colonial America supported the kind of ensemble for which Mozart and Haydn wrote their divertimenti, serenades, *Feldparthien*, and other open air music under royal patronage. Thomas Jefferson, for example, wished to establish such an ensemble at Monticello for the entertainment of his household and suggested instrumentation to improve the U.S. Marine Band. Clarinets and oboes carried the melodic line; natural horns and bassoons gave harmonic support. The same kind of band provided military music during the American Revolution and for at least three decades afterward. Thus in one sense, the wind band, once the privilege of the European aristocracy, was gradually acquired, unceremoniously but intact and in an orderly fashion, by the American people, for whom it became a symbol of their newly acquired social and political status as well as a source of entertainment. A reminiscence of one of the last vestiges of this tradition in America appears in an anonymous article entitled "The Boston Band" in the *Boston Musical Gazette* of 25 July 1838:

> Full well do I remember when I first heard the sound of a *Clarinet, French Horn* and *Bassoon*: it was at a regimental muster, where I went with my father, as a spectator. It was reported all around the country for weeks beforehand, that the *Boston Band* was to be at muster, being hired at great expense by *Capt. Taylor*, the liberal and noble-spirited commander of the new troop of Cavalry. This band was all the topic of conversation among the boys, and many a luckless urchin had to do penance for listening to the wonderful stories of its performances, instead of attending to his task. I recollect that I was sent to mill, two miles distance, a day or two before the parade. I went whistling the *Rogue's March* all the way, which a famous old revolutionary fifer in our neighborhood had learnt to me. The crusty miller took off my bags; but I kept on whistling. "What the deuse ails ye, John, heh?" said he. "Capt. Dusty, ye goin to muster to hear the moosic?" I replied, and kept on whistling. "Hang your music! go to grass with your whistling!" cried the miller, as he shouldered my meal bags and carried them to the hopper. . . .
>
> At length the wished-for day arrived, and a glorious day it was, most clear and bright. . . . we saw a brilliant company of high-horse prancing over the plain. When they had arrived within half a mile of the parade ground, they slackened pace, and the music struck up *Washington's March*. . . . The march was continued until the company came in front of the public house, when it halted, and Capt. Taylor gave orders for *Yankee Doodle*. This fairly bewitched the crowd, and they rent the air with huzzas. . . .
>
> Capt. Taylor directed the musicians to continue their music for some time, which they did, and gave us several different tunes, one of which I perfectly recollect was *St. Patrick's Day in the Morning*. This was very pleasant to every one, but there was one man in particular, in the very centre of a dense group, that, the very instant they commenced it, set to dancing like a *Dandy Jack*, and kept it up until the tune was ended, to the no small amusement of all around. I had a curiosity to get sight at him, and crowding into the ring, behold! it was none other than my old miller, who had scolded so much about my music a day or two before. Both this man's parents were natives of Sweet Erin, and brought him to this country while a nursing infant. Just by way of remembrance, I cried out to him,—"So Capt. Dusty, you like the moosic?" "Hah! young spalpeen!" he replied, and they ceased playing. . . .
>
> Taste in music, as well as in almost every thing else, will have a change. These men, who, in their day, were considered first rate performers, would now be called but indifferent. Their number was only four. *Belsted* upon the Hautboy, *Granger*, (father of the late violinist), upon the Clarinet; the famous *Peter Schminch*, the French Horn;

and old *Dr. Faegnol*, the Bassoon. It was said that Belsted played a fine violin. The first and two last belonged to Burgoyne's band, and were taken with him at Saratoga. I believe these musicians found constant employ in their vocation. They have gratified their thousands; they have had their day, and have gone down with the generations. Such was once the Boston Band.[18]

The melodic dependency of the band on the reed instruments was gradually undermined after 1810 when a Dubliner named Joseph Halliday introduced his keyed bugle. Like the chromatic woodwinds developed earlier, in which the length of the bore, and hence the fundamental with its possible harmonics, could be instantly changed by opening or closing one or more keys, Halliday's invention was nothing new in principle. The keyed trumpet, for example, was already known. Halliday simply cut holes in the side of a bugle and provided lever-operated padded keys for opening and closing them to get a full chromatic scale.[19] Without having any special claims to originality, he had produced a good instrument at the right time which found an immediate market. It was only a matter of time before a full family of such instruments was developed: the ophicleides.[20]

In America the chromatic horns had gained at least an equal footing with the woodwinds as principal instruments as far as bands were concerned by 1835; we now generally consider that year, in which the first all-brass bands are known to have been established, as the beginning of the so-called brass band era. Of course, not everyone greeted this development with enthusiasm. As the brasswinds became more homogeneous in sound, the loss of a band with highly individualized members was, as we have learned from reading Dwight, lamented by some. This is made more evident in the following excerpt from an 1893 article by William R. Bayley in the *Philadelphia Evening Star*. Bayley, who was an active bandsman from 1833 to the 1890s, recalls:

> The average bands [during the 1840s] consisted of fifteen pieces—two E-flat bugles, 1st and 2nd French horns (without valves), the post horn, and E-flat trumpet. We had the brilliant tone of the slide B-flat trombone and F-bass trombone for bass, ophecleide [*sic*] (brass), and the serpent (a wooden instrument with keys), cymbals, snare and bass drums. At the risk of being considered old fashioned I have protested against the summary banishment of many of these instruments. I have contended that all change is not improvement. These instruments, differing in the principle of their construction, had a different quality of tone, and therein is the strength of my plea. Band instruments of today are much better made and easier to learn, but from the E-flat cornet to the E-flat bass they are all constructed on the same principle, and have therefore the same kind of tone, only deeper, of course, as they descend.[21]

The fact that Bayley, writing in 1893, speaks of the homogeneous brasswind instrumentation indicates that the brass band was still predominant, at least in his mind.

In the 1840s a Frenchman, Adolphe Sax, inventor of the familiar saxophone, was one of several makers who developed a family of chromatic valved bugles— eventually called saxhorns—that combined the qualities of even timbre throughout their range, accurate intonation, effectiveness as ensemble instruments, and a degree of facility that made them playable without extraordinary technical ability, while at the same time having the capability of satisfying the demands of a virtuoso.

Sax was by no means the first to work on a chromatic horn. Inventors in Europe and the British Isles had been working with varying degrees of success in key- and valve-system chromatic brasswinds before the beginning of the nineteenth century. But Sax's success was remarkably complete, owing in no small part to the fact that he produced a good set of instruments at just the right time. As well as being a good inventor, Sax was an equally good promoter of his own interests. If he had been able, he would probably have banished all but wind instruments from the orchestras of the western world—preferably, all but those he invented. An amusing article by Sax found its way into *Dwight's Journal* by way of the London *Musical Times*. Originally printed in *La France Musicale*, it offers some of the following useful information under the headline "How Wind Instruments Affect the Health."

> Persons who practice wind instruments, are, in general, distinguished—and anybody can verify the statement—by a broad chest and shoulders, an unequivocal sign of vigor. In the travelling bands that pass through our cities, who has not seen women playing the horn, the cornet, the trumpet, and even the trombone and ophiclide, and noticed that they all enjoyed perfect health, and exhibited a considerable development of the thorax? In an orchestra a curious circumstance can be noticed; and that is the corpulence, the strength which the players of wind instruments exhibit, and the spare frames of the disciples of Paganini. The same may be said, with more reason, of pianists.[22]

There were other factors as well that favored the acceptance of the new chromatic brasswinds. For one, there was already a demand for them not so much among orchestral musicians as among military bandsmen and a large number of aspiring amateurs. Valve horns in the soprano register—the French *cornet à pistons* and the German soprano *Flügelhorn*—had already found a secure place in the bands of Europe, and an outstanding quintet of Englishmen, the Distins, was to publicize Sax's new family of horns through their widely successful public performances on the instruments. Thus, although families of saxhorns—and their German counterparts the Flügelhorns—were not destined to find a place in the orchestra, they were to become standard band instruments for years to come, and not least of all in Great Britain and America. In these countries, as we have noted, interest in the formation of amateur brass bands was growing at such a rate that by the mid 1850s it had reached the proportions of a significant popular movement.[23]

Moreover, the homogeneous quality of the Saxhorn-type band and its carrying power in the outdoors were significant advantages. One writer who had heard a Canadian regimental band of the British type compared it unfavorably with the new all-brass style and was quoted in *Dwight's Journal* under the editor's magnanimous introductory remark that "happily all the world does not think alike":

> In the afternoon there was a review of the 39th Regiment on the Champ de Mars, near the court house. Whether it was intended for a scientific display or not I am unable to say; but this much is due—it was a creditable exhibition. The music by the band was good, though not "putting the Boston bands to blush," as the correspondent of the *Courier* is pleased to say. On the contrary, the Brigade, or Brass, or Germania are, all three of them, quite as scientific and skillful. Last autumn, at the railroad jubilee ball, I heard this same band in contrast with Chandler's Portland Band; and

those of your readers who were present at Bonsecours at the time will, I think, join
with me in giving to Chandler's the highest encomiums. The 39th band is large, but it
has some dozen men blowing their breath away on clarinets, bassoons and flutes, to
but little purpose. In short, it is a great waste of wind. The band is modelled as our
Boston bands were fifteen years ago. Take away the inefficient reeds and give them
tubas instead, and this Crimean band would crash out a mighty march; but now it
wants body, as an Englishman would say of his beer. The melody is one grand squeak,
sounding like the sesquialtra [*sic*] of the organ, and about as well adapted for melody
as that stop would be with a swell accompaniment. There is a brilliance to the
American bands not yet attained by the English, if this is a fair specimen of their
proficiency.[24]

Earlier, Dwight himself had expressed the contrary view:

A certain peculiar and pleasing effect invests [brass band] music, at first, but it is of a
kind which lacks character and durability. For genuine enjoyment I would as soon
listen to a Choral Symphony performed with flutes and the voices of eunuchs.[25]

But Dwight was also constructive in his criticisms and often balanced his invective
with positive statements:

The more pathetic, the more human the music to be interpreted, the more cold and
inadequate do the tones of these instruments appear. With all their mellowness and
smoothness, with all their luscious commingling, they sound to us like soulless, watery,
Undine-like natures; and while we have the perfect shape of the melody we loved, it
still affects us somehow like its ghost. But when that "Hungarian March" was played,
so full of sad, determined, truly moral heroism, who did not feel the fitness of the
music to the organs that conveyed it, and a more real, although simpler, satisfaction.
The same criticism, or an analogous one, applies to this whole modern improvement
in the construction of brass instruments; to the whole Sax-horn family, the valve-
trumpet, &c., so softened down and made so smooth and flexible instead of the harsh,
spirited, crackling blast of the old straight trumpet. That had *character*, if it was
somewhat intractable; but these are somewhat emasculated in their gentleness.—But
this opens a whole field of discussion, which we may not enter now.[26]

Later he reviewed a concert and made this comment on what he considered an
appropriate type of music for brass: "The selections for the brass instruments were
better than usual. That solemn old Chorale was just the thing for them; and the
piece from Meyerbeer's 'Camp of Silesia' was quite stirring. Give us more Chorales,
if you wish to edify us."[27]

Dwight's appreciation of the technical advantages of the new valve brasswinds
was mitigated by his concern that the advantages could lead to abuse:

It certainly cannot be questioned that the employment of valves greatly facilitates the
performance of difficult passages in music. Of the truth of this we have sad evidence
in the readiness with which half-fledged artists essay the execution of compositions
wholly beyond their calibre of comprehension, on the one hand; and, on the other, in
the performance, by virtuosos, of parts unfitted and never intended for the particular
instruments they profess. But however much be gained in ease and rapidity of
execution, the full equivalent, and more, is lost in quality of intonation. Like dampers

upon vibrating strings, this multiplicity of valves and keys interferes with the free action of the metal and essentially dulls and deadens its tone. In confirmation of this, compare the unsatisfactory effect of the valve trombone with the richness of intonation that belongs to that noble instrument in its original form.[28]

Band Music

That there was a proliferation of brass bands with all the necessary hardware in mid-nineteenth-century America there is no doubt.[29] But what of the hundreds of thousands of pages of music composed, arranged, published, or otherwise distributed, from which the bands learned and played their parts? Unfortunately, little of the music—considered ephemeral in its time—has survived, and little that was not worn out was considered worth keeping. Faced with a paucity of documents, we offer a brief account of some of the most notable remnants in the collections of the Music Division of the Library of Congress which document that part of our musical past under consideration here.[30]

In 1844 Elias Howe published in Boston his *First Part of the Musician's Companion*. It contained a number of "new and popular pieces in 6 and 8 parts, for a brass band, viz.: E-flat bugle, B-flat bugle, B-flat post horn, B-flat cornopean, tenor trombone, bass trombone, first orphecleide [*sic*], second orphecleide, &c."[31] These are printed in full score with movable type in the oblong format common for collections of sacred and some secular vocal music of the time.

Two years later, E. K. Eaton published, in elegantly engraved parts, *Twelve Pieces of Harmony for Military Brass Bands*. The instrumentation is larger than Howe's, calling for "E-flat bugle, 2 B-flat bugles, 1 cornopeon [*sic*] or post horn, 2 E-flat trumpets, 2 French horns, 2 alto ophecleides [*sic*], 3 trombones, 2 bass ophecleides, and side drums."[32] The pieces are rather difficult and demand equally high standards of musicianship from the entire ensemble.

By 1849, Allen Dodworth was instructing readers of the New York music journal *Message Bird* on the formation of brass bands.[33] On 1 August of that year, in the first of several installments, he writes:

> What, in our opinion, would make the best arrangement for a Band of ten, would be as follows: Two E-flat Trebles, Two B-flat Altos, Two E-flat Tenores, One B-flat Baritone, One A[-flat] or B-flat Bass, Two E-flat Contra Bass. If more are required, add two Trumpets; then two Post-horns; then two Trombones; Drums, Cymbals, &c. Many different kinds of instruments are used to take the parts here mentioned, but most of the Bands of the present day give preference to what is called the Saxhorn, which is made in all the different keys mentioned above.[34]

In 1853 Dodworth published his *Brass Band School*, complete with scores for a number of pieces calling for the same instrumentation advocated in the *Message Bird*. Although he takes into account the variety of brasswinds available, including the keyed bugles and ophicleides, it is the saxhorns that get the highest recommendation. "I have always, in my own mind," he writes "classed Trumpets, Post Horns, Trombones and French Horns, as supernumeraries; for, since the introduction of [keyed] Bugles, Cornets, Ebor Cornos and Sax Horns, they are no longer depended on for the principal parts." In forming a band of up to fourteen players, he advises: "Let nothing but Sax Horns, Ebor Cornos and Cornets, or instruments of like character be used, that is, valve instruments of large calibre."[35] Here he also mentions the special invention of the over-the-shoulder style horn:

> In selecting the instruments, attention should be paid to the use intended; if for military purposes only, those with bells behind, over the shoulder, are preferable, as they throw all the tone to those who are marching to it, but for any other purpose are not so good. These were first introduced by the Dodworth family in the year 1838.[36]

The application of this style probably was restricted to the trombones at first, but its popularity continued through the 1880s, for we find such instruments advertised in dealers' catalogs, along with the bell upright and bell front models, as late as 1888.[37]

In 1853 Firth, Pond and Company of New York began the publication of its *Brass Band Journal*, probably the first American publication of saxhorn pieces. The longevity of these attractive compositions and arrangements by G. W. E. Friederich is attested to by the fact that they were still being offered for sale in the 1870s. A similar publication appeared in Cincinnati in 1859. It consisted, for the most part, of popular dances and quicksteps arranged from piano pieces for a band of from six to twelve players and was published by W. C. Peters & Sons as *Peters' Sax-Horn Journal*.

Yet, the most challenging band music of this period is found not in published form but in manuscript part books, one of the best examples being a set in the Library of Congress from the Third New Hampshire Volunteer Infantry band formed in Concord under the direction of Gustavus Ingalls at the outset of the Civil War.

Civil War Bands

If ever there was a hope or danger of the demise of brass bands, the outbreak of war decisively cancelled or at least postponed the possibility. Throughout the long period of hostilities—both musical and otherwise—Dwight, our well-bred Yankee critic, maintained an attitude of gentlemanly stoicism. And so, for further news of development in the brass band world we must turn to accounts, usually fleeting references, in regimental histories. Many are anecdotal and told, often for mere comic relief, years after the event. Those drawn from letters and diaries have the better claim to reliability as well as to that spontaneity that brings us closer to the participants in the events recalled. In drawing from these sources it is our intention to have the words of eyewitnesses convey a sense of how bands functioned during the Civil War at home, in camp, and in battle.

Ulysses S. Grant, in his *Memoirs*, concisely portrays the general situation at the very beginning of the war:

> Upon the firing on Sumter, President Lincoln issued a proclamation calling for troops and convening Congress in extra session. The call was for 75,000 volunteers for

ninety days' service. If the shot fired at Fort Sumter "was heard around the world," the call of the President for 75,000 men was heard throughout the Northern States. There was not a State in the North of a million of inhabitants that would not have furnished the entire number faster than arms could have been supplied to them, if it had been necessary.[38]

Nevertheless, according to the recollections of a musician printed in the *Boston Transcript*, "inducements were held out to quicken the enlistment of recruits by publicly announcing that a famous band would be attached to some particular regiment," as if such inducements were necessary.[39] Edward Everett, observing the excitement in Boston, guessed that Lincoln's call might bring half a million volunteers. It is more likely that the employment of bands, like the wearing of flamboyant costumes that passed for military uniforms early in the war, was regarded by many as an appropriately festive gesture in the face of preparations for what was assumed would be a glorious and speedy victory. But, unlike the bright costumes which, in most cases, gave way to regulation uniforms, bands and their music became a more sought-after commodity as the hostilities wore on. *Dwight's Journal*, in one of its few references to bands in the war, notes in September 1861 that

> Gilmore's celebrated band has been engaged to accompany Col. Stephenson's Regiment to the war. The band will consist of sixty-eight pieces, including twenty drummers and twelve buglers. Such a band was never enjoyed by a regiment before, and it will probably incite the men to heroic deeds if loyal men can need any new stimulus in such a time as this. The band will appear three times more before the Boston public at the Promenade Concerts.[40]

Gilmore's contract was with the Twenty-fourth Massachusetts Volunteer Infantry and seems to have involved enlistment and, hence, the duty not only of playing in camp but of following the regiment into the field—and even the heat of battle, where he and his men were put to work, as most bandsmen were, as hospital corpsmen.[41] On his return, a year later, Gilmore advertised a concert in which his band—less one member, presumably lost in action—would perform

> the gems of such music as have floated over the wild waves and mingled with the howling winds of Hatteras; such patriotic airs as fell upon the ears of three thousand rebel prisoners, and echoed through the dense woods of Roanoke; such strains as followed our victorious arms at Newbern, and vibrated through the deserted streets of that once fair city; and, more than all, such music as has revived the drooping spirits of many a weary soldier, or soothed the pain of many a wounded patriot.[42]

Regarding the cost of their service, the regimental historian speaks only "of Gilmore's Band, of whose presence everyone is justly proud, even if the same did cost the officers a pretty figure."[43] We do, however, know the cost of Boston bandmaster E. B. Flagg to the 44th Massachusetts Volunteer Militia: $3,000, and that for limited service in camp.[44] A letter dated 13 September 1863 by an officer of the regiment informs us that:

> Since the 44th went into barracks they have been favored with the services of the Boston Brass Band, under the lead of Mr. Flagg. It is said the expense is to be defrayed by an assessment upon the regiment. Considering that the mass of the

regiment have had no voice in the selection of a band, a number of persons are inclined to consider this a little "rough."[45]

Another interesting band that found its way into military service was Frank Rauscher's cornet band from Germantown, near Philadelphia. His book on the subject is most informative.[46] This regiment was the colorful Zoaves d'Afrique of Gen. Charles Collis, one of many such companies and regiments from the North and South who modeled themselves after the French fighting troops in Africa by adopting the uniform of "red pants, Zouave jacket, white leggings, blue sash around the waist, and white turban."[47] Unlike other such outfits, however, whose splendid uniforms could not be kept up, Collis's Zouaves had a fortunate association with Capt. F. A. Elliott, a successful wool merchant in Germantown. It was he, no doubt, who arranged the purchase of such a supply of fresh material for uniforms from France that throughout the war they never lacked the distinctive Zouave dress. He also took a great interest in procuring the band, about which Rauscher, the leader, writes:

> As instrumental musicians, they were amateurs and beginners, but with a fair knowledge of music as vocalists, by close application they made rapid progress. . . . When the band was started, [Captain Elliott] became a helpful friend of the project, subscribing liberally toward procuring the instruments, and afterward assisted in supplying the members with uniforms. It was mainly from this kindly and valued association with the band that it resolved to follow the fortunes of the regiment.[48]

Another way in which regimental bands were formed, by far the cheapest, was by drawing upon the resources available from among the men in each company. With ten companies to a regiment and two musicians allowed to each company—that is to say the fifers, buglers, and drummers—one could put together some kind of band of twenty men or more, if the officers agreed to detail to the regimental band musically qualified men who had not enlisted as musicians.

This practice became especially popular after the passage in Congress of a bill on 17 July 1862, sections of which ordered the mustering out of regimental bands. The bill was approved by the president and announced in the War Department's General Order 91 of 29 July 1862. Rauscher's observation is interesting, although his band was mustered in after the order of 29 July:

> At the beginning of the war every regiment . . . had full brass bands, some of them numbering as high as fifty pieces. When it is considered that in every brigade there were from four to five regiments, three brigades in one division and three divisions in each corps, an aggregate of from thirty-six to forty bands is shown for every corps. When a division was encamped in a small space, which was frequently the case when on the march, and the band of each regiment performing at the same time at Regimental Headquarters, the effect of the confusion of sounds produced can hardly be imagined. Whilst this was an unnecessary arrangement and very expensive to the government, it kept a host of noncombatants in the rear of the army. Congress, however, at an early day passed an act abolishing all regimental bands in the volunteer service, with the provision that each brigade should be entitled to a band at the headquarters. It so happened that when the order of disbandment reached the Army [of the Potomac], the bands had seen considerable and hard service on the Peninsula,

under General McClellan, and therefore the men gladly accepted their discharges and almost to a man went home. As a consequence the army was left with scarcely any music.[49]

A band of the size described by Rauscher would have been double the number of twenty-four musicians authorized by General Order 49 of the War Department, 3 August 1861. By October of the same year, the War Department had already begun to trim the number of regimental bands by forbidding their further enlistment.[50] Quite possibly, the order was in response to actual abuses of General Order 49 resulting not only in a proliferation of bands but in monster bands full of deadbeats or nonessential personnel. In any case, by 1862, as the Union faced its greatest crisis from Lee's imminent invasion of the North, the more drastic measure of dropping regimental bands became necessary. Before the order of 29 July, there were an estimated 28,428 enlisted musicians in the North. Of these, 14,832 were bandsmen.[51] Thereafter such men, if they were to continue with the regiments, had either to be supported entirely by the members of the regiment or drawn from the musicians authorized as company fifers, buglers, and drummers. Undoubtedly, many compromises were reached in order to maintain regimental bands. Notwithstanding Rauscher's comment that the disbanded musicians "almost to a man went home," bands proliferated and, throughout the war, were heard on all manner of occasions, even during the heat of battle. For example, we read of bands performing service in the trenches. Lieutenant Thompson of the 13th New Hampshire describes an incident occurring just after the battle of Cold Harbor, 8 June 1864:

This evening the Band of the Thirteenth goes into the trenches at the front, and indulges in a "competition concert" with a band that is playing over across in the enemy's trenches. The enemy's Band renders Dixie, Bonnie Blue Flag, My Maryland, and other airs dear to the Southerner's heart. Our Band replies with America, Star Spangled Banner, Old John Brown, etc. After a little time, the enemy's band introduces another class of music; only to be joined almost instantly by our Band with the same tune. All at once the band over there stops, and a rebel battery opens with grape. Very few of our men are exposed, so the enemy wastes his ammunition; while our band continues its playing, all the more earnestly until all their shelling is over.[52]

A similar account, of music played during the battle of Gettysburg, was recalled by J. A. Leinbach, a member of the 26th North Carolina Regiment band:

About 6 o'clock [in the morning, the bands of the 26th and 11th North Carolina regiments] played together for sometime, heavy firing going on meanwhile. . . . Our playing seemed to do the men good, for they cheered us lustily. . . . We learned some time afterwards, from Northern papers, that our playing had been heard by the enemy, amid the noise of the cannon.[53]

A British observer, J. L. Freemantle, poised in a tree near Lee's headquarters on Seminary Ridge, also heard the music:

When the cannonade was at its height a Confederate band of music between the cemetery and ourselves, began to play polkas and waltzes, which sounded very curious, accompanied by the hissing and bursting of shells.[54]

Post Civil War Bands

At the close of the war many of the Yankee bands went home, perhaps to regroup as "civic" bands, as brassy as ever (much to the annoyance of John Sullivan Dwight, who resumed his antibrass campaign with his customary vigor), some to participate in a final victory celebration by marching in Washington or some hometown, or joining in the playing of the *Star-Spangled Banner* for the flag-raising ceremony at Fort Sumter on 14 April 1865, hours before Lincoln's assassination.

During the war, the quality of military (brass) bands had improved, as Dwight himself acknowledged. "Everyone who walks our Boston streets," he wrote in 1862, "or who attends the war meetings, must have been struck with the great improvement in some of our Military Bands of late. . . . The wonder is where so many musicians come from in these war times, and that while so many go off to the war, more than ever before seem to have sprung up at home."[55] Moreover, with the end of the war there was for Patrick Gilmore, once Dwight's fair-haired boy, a golden opportunity to put his promotional genius to work. The specter of monster concerts, consisting of massed bands or instrumental forces impressive for their sheer number, had only peeked over the horizon when the war temporarily arrested its progress in the direction of full-scale looming. In Gilmore's famous "Peace Jubilee" concerts, where thousands of performers entertained simultaneously in a display of acoustic brute force before an audience almost as large as the legion of orchestral and choral talent that confronted it, Dwight found a newer and better target for his arsenal of invective. Gilmore, it seems, was intent on eclipsing the Dog Star of the brass band movement by the magnitude of his own monstrous novelty. Wrote Dwight in the 16 January 1869 issue of his *Journal*:

> Our city has been o'er-full of music since the new year came in. We pity the man who undertook to hear the whole of it; it may be some one did so, on a wager, as now and then a valiant toper seeks immortality in drinking till he burst, or some spread-eagle patriot wheels a barrow from Providence to Boston when his party loses the election,—but of his fate we have not heard. Better wait, if ye have such an appetite for quantity, and, drinking the whole sonorous ocean at a draught, "go up" all together, gloriously, from bandmaster Gilmore's millennial tabernacle, over which, by earthquake shocks of harmony, the heavens, it is presumed, will open right up into the Paradise of Fools, where ye may dwell immortal![56]

On this note, we might end the story of the heyday of the brass band movement in America—or begin any number of others. However, we feel that Dwight, who posthumously has been our virtual coauthor, should be given this opportunity to express the generous side of his nature more fairly:

> It is easy to sneer at popular music, and to exalt the education of the ear to be derived from listening to classical or intricate compositions. But while the common people are the listeners to the concerts on the Common, and the class who patronize the great organ, the opera and the oratorio are away at Swampscott and Mount Washington, the preferences of the popular heart have a right to be consulted.[57]

We have dwelt on matters of popular music, a subject in which Dwight took a keen interest not as an historian but as a critic. Inevitably, his high standards, together with his desire to raise the quality of popular music, led him to express himself in a style whose tone is often cantankerous. Yet few critics of art music today so vigorously devote themselves to the matter of popular, as opposed to genteel, taste as did Dwight. At the end of the nineteenth century, John Philip Sousa, following the great success of Patrick Gilmore, seemed to achieve a balance between art music and "the preferences of the popular heart," which Dwight would certainly have hailed as an important achievement.

Since the first publication of this essay in 1979,[58] valuable studies and editions of music have appeared which provide further information and documents about brass bands in America.[59] In the light of such continued interest in band history, it is fitting that we acknowledge with special appreciation Frederick Fennell's unique and original contributions. His Mercury recordings of 1960 and 1962 for the Civil War centennial were the first significant contribution towards our understanding of nineteenth-century American brass bands; and his subsequent recording for the Library of Congress expanded our knowledge of their repertory and its sound in performance on original instruments.[60]

The achievements of the American brass band movement, though less monumental than those of Sousa, nonetheless helped produce the culture in which he flourished. The brass band movement was also the foundation of the community bands that continue to thrive as an American tradition that has many facets, not only artistic but social. These facets still yield images in words, pictures and sounds that are part of our folklore and which have, for many, those numinous qualities that are at once the band tradition's most significant and least definable aspects.

NOTES

1. *Dwight's Journal of Music*, 29 May 1852, 63.
2. Ibid., 16 April 1853, 9.
3. Ibid., 13.
4. Ibid., 16 July 1853, 119.
5. Ibid., 15 August 1857, 159.
6. Ibid., 22 August 1857, 166.
7. Ibid., 25 June 1853, 94.
8. Ibid., 11 September 1858, 191; 2 October 1858, 215.
9. Ibid., 2 August 1856, 141.
10. Ibid., 21 June 1856, 93–94.
11. Ibid., 5 July 1862, 111.
12. D. Arthur Brown, *History of Penacook, N.H.* (Concord, N.H.: The Rumford Press, 1902), pp. 248–49.
13. Emmons Clark, *History of the Seventh Regiment of New York, 1806–1889*, 2 vols. (New York: The Seventh Regiment, 1890), 1:379.
14. *Dwight's Journal of Music*, 21 December 1861, 303.
15. Bell Irvin Wiley, *The Life of Billy Yank, the Common Soldier of the Union* (Indianapolis: Bobbs-Merrill, 1952), p. 158.
16. Victor Herbert, "Artistic Bands," in *Music of the Modern World*, ed. Anton Seidl (New York: D. Appleton & Co., 1895), p. 120.
17. *Dwight's Journal of Music*, 15 February 1868, 189.
18. "The Boston Band," *Boston Musical Gazette*, 25 July 1838, 51–52.

19. Specifically, he used a model that most closely resembled the French military bugle of the time, a wide conical-bore instrument. It should not be confused with the modern American military instrument commonly called a bugle, but more properly called a "field trumpet," which is, in fact, a trumpet without valves. (See n. 35 below for amplification onthe boring subject.)

20. The technical disadvantage of this construction (notwithstanding the charming sound produced by the instruments) is that, except when all holes are closed, much of the sound comes not from the bell of the horn but from the open hole. Since it is the bell of the horn and the shape of the last one-third of the bore that most influences its tone, it is easy to see why the valve system has been ultimately preferred for brasswinds. The long-established acceptability of the open-hole system for woodwinds may have given Sax the idea of recycling, if not saving, the keyed bugles and ophicleides—a species he helped endanger—by substituting for the brasswind mouthpiece a single reed, as is used on clarinets. Thus, he "invented" the saxophone.

21. Quoted in William Carpenter White, *A History of Military Music in America* (New York: Exposition Press, 1944), p. 63.

22. *Dwight's Journal of Music*, 15 November 1862, 259.

23. Only the bass, or tuba, of the kind first developed and introduced in Berlin in 1838 by Wilhelm Wieprecht, is now consistently used in orchestras; the baritone is occasionally used as well. His tuba was a contrabass flugelhorn. Orchestral use of the saxhorn ensemble is found in quite special cases, e.g., Berlioz's *Les Troyens* and Respighi's *The Pines of Rome*.

24. *Dwight's Journal of Music*, 29 August 1857, 175.

25. Ibid., 16 April 1853, 10.

26. Ibid., 19 June 1852, 86.

27. Ibid., 10 July 1852, 111.

28. Ibid., 16 April 1853, 9.

29. A most extensive study of brasswind manufacturing in the United States during this period is found in Robert E. Eliason, *Brass Instrument Key and Valve Mechanisms Made in America before 1875* (Ph.D. diss., University of Missouri, Kansas City, 1968; Ann Arbor, Michigan: University Microfilms, Inc., No. 69–7227).

30. A checklist of sources for original band music in the United States has been published by Frank J. Cipolla, "Annotated Guide for the Study and Performance of Nineteenth Century Band Music in the United States," *Journal of Band Research* 14, no. 1 (fall 1978): 22–40.

31. Elias Howe, Jr., *First Part of the Musician's Companion* (Boston: Elias Howe, Jr., 1844), title page.

32. E. K. Eaton, *Twelve Pieces of Harmony for Military Brass Band* (New York: Firth & Hall, 1846), title page.

33. Allen Dodworth (1822–1896) was the most prominent member of a family that contributed significantly to musical life in New York. He and his father, Thomas, became managers of a band in 1838; they succeeded in developing their business to include providing bands and orchestras, establishing a dancing school, composing and arranging music, publishing, and both developing and selling musical instruments.

34. Allen Dodworth, "The Formation of Bands," *Message Bird*, 1 August 1849, 9.

35. Allen Dodworth, *Brass Band School* (New York: H. B. Dodworth, 1853), pp. 11–12. Dodworth's grouping of saxhorns and cornets is appropriate, but his general description of them as being "of large calibre," by which he means a large bore, may have been a bit casual. The soprano valve instruments appeared first in Europe in the second quarter of the century. Both the French *cornet à pistons* and the German soprano *Flügelhorn* (a term later used interchangeably with "saxhorn") are essentially conical-bore instruments, as opposed to trumpets and trombones, which are essentially cylindrical. The cornets, however, are high soprano horns, small relatives of what we now call the French horn; the caliber of the cornet bore is smaller and more gradually flared than that of the soprano saxhorn or flugelhorn, which resembles the French military bugle of the early nineteenth century (see n. 20 above). Of course, the designations "cylindrical" or "conical" are not completely accurate, since the degree of flare, the points at which it is pronounced or gradual, and the shape of all functional parts of the instrument from its mouthpiece to its bell are complex, variable, and decisive inits pitch and tone quality. Moreover, few horns are entirely cylindrical or conical: all are conical at the bell, and all valved models require a cylindrical section where the valves are introduced into the main tubing.

36. Ibid.

37. J. Howard Foote, *Catalogue of Musical Instruments* (New York: J. Howard Foote, 1888), p. 36.

38. Ulysses S. Grant, *Personal Memoirs*, 2 vols. (New York: The Century Co., 1909), 1:183–84.

39. *Boston Transcript*, 9 August 1890.

40. *Dwight's Journal of Music*, 28 September 1861, 207.

41. See Alfred S. Roe, *The Twenty-fourth Regiment, Massachusetts Volunteers, 1861–1866* (Worcester, Mass.: Twenty-fourth Veteran Association, 1907), pp. 124 and 417.

42. *Dwight's Journal of Music*, 13 September 1862, 191.

43. Roe, *The Twenty-fourth Regiment*, p. 31.

44. See Albert W. Mann, comp., *History of the Forty-fifth Regiment Massachusetts Volunteer Militia: "The Cadet Regiment,"* (Jamaica Plain, Mass.: Brookside Print, 1908), p. 196.

45. *Record of the Service of the Forty-fourth Massachusetts Volunteer Militia in North Carolina, August 1862 to May 1863* (Boston: Privately printed, 1887), p. 31.

46. Frank Rauscher, *Music on the March, with the Army of the Potomac, 114th Regt. P. V., Collis' Zouaves* (Philadelphia: Wm. F. Fell & Co., 1892).

47. Ibid., p. 13.

48. Ibid., pp. 13–14.

49. Ibid., pp. 14–15.

50. See Daniel Eldredge, *The Third New Hampshire and All About It* (Boston: E. B. Stillings & Co., 1893), p. 993.

51. Mann, *History of the Forty-fifth Regiment*, p. 195.

52. S. Millett Thompson, *Thirteenth Regiment of New Hampshire Volunteer Infantry in the War of the Rebellion, 1861–1865: A Diary Covering Three Years and a Day* (Boston & New York: Houghton, Mifflin & Co., 1888), p. 369.

53. Harry H. Hall, *A Johnny Reb Band from Salem* (Raleigh, N.C.: The North Carolina Confederate Centennial Commission, 1963), pp. 49–50.

54. Lt. Col. A. J. L. Freemantle, *Three Months in the Southern States: April-June 1863* (Edinburgh & London: William Blackwood & Sons, 1863), p. 266.

55. *Dwight's Journal of Music*, 6 September 1862, 183.

56. Ibid., 16 January 1869.

57. Ibid., 28 August 1868, 301.

58. In *The Quarterly Journal of the Library of Congress* (spring 1979): 114–139.

59. See Raoul F. Camus, *American Wind and Percussion Music*, Three Centuries of American Music, vol. 12 (Boston: G. K. Hall & Co., 1992). Margaret Hindle Hazen and Robert M. Hazen, *The Music Men* (Washington, D.C.: Smithsonian Institution, 1987); and Kenneth Kreitner, *Discoursing Sweet Music: Brass Bands and Community Life in Turn-of-the-Century Pennsylvania* (Illinois, 1990).

60. *The Civil War: Its Music and Its Sounds*, Frederick Fennell conducting the Eastman Wind Ensemble, Mercury LPS2–501 and LPS2–902, two-record set (reissued 1990 in slightly abbreviated form on two compact disks, Mercury 432 591–2); and *Our Musical Past: A Concert for Brass Band, Voice, and Piano*, The Library of Congress, OMP 101–102, two-record set (reissued in its entirety on one compact disk with somewhat abbreviated notes).

Before the Brass Band

Trumpet Ensemble Works by Küffner and Lossau

ROBERT E. SHELDON

IN considering a concept of brass bands before they were designated as such, one should first try to establish what a "brass band" is in the most distinctive sense of the term. As in any aspect of art, the eye of the beholder is usually the last word, but we can perhaps establish a logical definition and starting point somewhere in the early nineteenth century.

Small wind ensembles from earlier times perhaps functioned as brass bands for the listener if they relied mostly on cupped mouthpiece instruments such as cornetts (usually of wood in a curved shape with finger holes, not to be confused with the modern cornet) and trombones (or "sacbutts," to cite one of the various spelling possibilities for old English trombone nomenclature). Such ensembles usually mixed those instruments into useful groupings including shawms and other available voices for the so-called loud music, but the average listener probably enjoyed it as simply the "band" in whatever language pertained, with no concern about its specific instrumentation. The term "brass band" really came into being in the nineteenth century when metal instruments could be manufactured liberally and efficiently enough to form reliable ensembles—ensembles that needed to be distinguished from earlier, mostly woodwind, wind groups. For our purposes "brass band" shall refer to any of those all-brass ensembles which developed in the second quarter of the century.

Most of today's connoisseurs will likely affirm that the term in its most traditional and best sense refers to the British brass band, a very structured and select assortment of cornets, trombones, and most sizes of saxhorns (the flugelhorn-tuba group), with percussion. It was headed towards the current make-up well over a century ago as is described in *The Brass Band Movement*[1] and *Brass Bands of the Twentieth Century.*[2] In the U.K. the brass band functioned more as organized recreation and discipline for members of various commercial and manufacturing establishments—so-called works bands. The Salvation Army also wisely adopted the same brass band style for its own very special uses. Depending on one's view point, several of the current Salvationist staff bands can be considered examples of the best state of the art, both in performance and expressive repertoire.

The next most structured forms of the brass band regarding a long-term phase might be the nineteenth-century American versions. While never attaining real uniformity of concept (i.e., instrumentation) as in the U.K., they were perhaps more active within the overall life-style of the community, at least until the end of the century. In America the brass band did serve numerous commercial and military unit concerns, but more often than not it was formed to provide entertainment for smaller communities. There were obvious community benefits in trying to involve all interested and talented residents in one organized ensemble with equipment that could serve for various functions, indoors and out. Both approaches, British and American, were gladly encouraged by instrument manufacturers and music publishers, who so fueled the movement that they sometimes had trouble balancing supply and demand.

In the U.K., the brass band has always been differentiated as such because the standard mixed-wind-and-brass (or "military") band remained the norm for the Armed Services and many municipalities. In America the brass band often retained a few clarinetists and flutists, but the emphasis on an all-brass instrumentation caused many mixed windbands to all but disappear until the early twentieth century. Like our shawm and cornett band listener mentioned earlier, the average American brass band audience also probably just regarded it as "the band" with no special awareness of its all- or mostly brass nature. For an interesting and well-illustrated study of that American band scene, the reader is recommended to *The Music Men: An Illustrated History of Brass Bands in America, 1800–1920*.[3] Also, "The American Brass Band Movement" offers a detailed account of the mid-nineteenth-century phase which, for nearly three decades, favored a fairly homogeneous saxhorn instrumentation.[4]

Earlier brass band attempts during the second quarter of the nineteenth century on either side of the Atlantic had to begin with already existing trombones and natural, but soon-to-be valved, horns and trumpets (true long-tube-length trumpets), plus the various mechanized conical brasswinds (keyed bugles and ophicleides) that really made it all work in the initial stages. The then newly devised cornets (or cornopeans, the English term) were involved almost from the beginning, and by the mid 1840s, reasonably good valved versions of all of the above instruments were available or at least on the drawing board. Compared to what will be discussed later, each bandsman in these valved-instrument brass bands was finally able to play a fairly complete role in the new scoring concepts.

So far, we have stressed activities in the U.K. and America. However, the history of European bands can show sporadic parallels to any of those brass band developments and the various reasons for creating similar ensembles. It must also be conceded that most of the important mechanical and manufacturing innovations had continental origins. Adolphe Sax can surely be a candidate to head a long list of names in that regard. Although no particular European country can be said to have had a brass band movement quite equivalent to that in the U.K., it was really the activities on the continent that we may consider brass bands before brass bands.

Russian Horn Bands

The second half of the eighteenth century and several decades of the nineteenth century offered brass bands of sorts which operated under a different identity and necessarily utilized personnel in a narrow and specific manner. Perhaps the first was formed in the early 1750s by the Bohemian hornist, J. A. Maresch, then attached to the court of Empress Elizabeth of Russia. His original concept was said to be a band of thirty-seven very conical horns (no two of the same size), which could be straight or somewhat curved. Each horn was assigned to a player who would sound only one pitch (usually the second partial), fading in and out of play as his note was needed, often on a split-second basis. It was rather the hornistic version of hand-bell ringing. Needless to say, the timing and accuracy required for such a staggered in-and-out contribution of each bandsmen's note or notes would have been quite tricky. Fairly complex music was arranged for such bands, which, in some cases, came to include as many as sixty players.

Touring Russian horn bands were a great novelty and were usually received well enough that they flourished into the nineteenth century. They even caused such rudimentary instruments to achieve a little development in design and playing technique, for, in addition to sounding both the fundamental and first overtone, certain players might also close the bell with the hand for an occasional semitone beneath the upper partial. Some instruments supposedly had a pivoted cap or cover fixed to the bell rim for basic tuning and/or to initiate the hand technique cited above.

The larger horns (or in some cases, all of the horns) often had a sort of L-shape (the elbow being at the mouthpiece end) to facilitate general manageability and possibly any bell-covering technique as well. These were stand-up ensembles meant for outdoor performance, and the largest horns often had two- or three-leg wooden supporting brackets. The player's part book was usually held in his free hand, which in some cases was not all that free. There was eventually a Russian horn model equipped with one key mounted near the end of the bell, which when open would raise the pitch by a semitone and increase the player's duties to a two- or four-note realm. It also would likely require the other hand to steady the instrument at the mouthpiece end.

The Music Division of the Library of Congress has an incomplete but representative set of ten manuscript books from an early-nineteenth-century German horn band which was equipped with instruments of the one-keyed model. Catalogued as Russian hunting music, they actually contain fifty-three short arrangements of marches, chorales, and diverse dance music.[5] Each part assigned the player two pitches and was written in standard rhythmic notation on one line with a sharp, flat, or natural added as necessary. One of the bandsmen, Otto Kruhse, who played middle C and C-sharp, decorated his book cover in water colors or colored ink with his name and images of his L-shaped horn clearly showing its key on the bell, his music pouch, his initials (O.K.), and (most importantly), his tobacco pipe.

The problem of member absence due to illness or other cause is, of course, serious for any ensemble—but especially so for horn bands. It calls to mind a cartoon showing an orchestra on stage ready to begin a performance: just before the conductor's entrance the concertmaster is standing and announcing to the audience that "as a protest regarding ongoing and unsatisfactory negotiations with management, the following notes will be omitted from this evening's performance: A, F-sharp, G, and C-sharp!"

The Trumpeters' and Kettledrummers' Art

Our main focus concerns a unique, transitional period in trumpet playing, which in the first quarter of the nineteenth century spawned a very special and most extraordinary form of brass band before the brass band. To better understand why it is important and how it developed, particularly from the point of view of equipment and performing techniques, one needs to be familiar with seventeenth- and eighteenth-century trumpet and kettledrum corps. These ensembles may be considered an early, but specialized, form of brass band before the brass band.

The German-speaking lands (and several adjacent to them) were politically rather segmented and controlled by various mini-monarchs of varying importance. As part of the expected trappings to signify their status, most usually maintained a select corps of trumpeters and kettledrummers. While in existence well before the seventeenth and eighteenth centuries, such activity reached its musical apex during that period. Depending on the budgets and musical interests of the trumpeters' patrons, some corps might be accomplished enough to perform only the least complex music from the repertoire. Others, however, might be composed of very capable trumpeters, including two or more excellent clarinists, the upper-range players who could perform elaborate repertoire and divisions such as one hears in many Baroque-period works by Bach and others calling for trumpets and kettledrums. The trumpeters and drummers were a recognized unit, and they were granted the privilege of forming guilds to insure that they would receive training and official employment on a level which would affiliate them with royal patrons for their mutual benefit. All such trumpeters used essentially the same standard natural (valveless and nearly tenor trombone tube-length) instrument of the period. The players differentiated themselves into two basic ranges, the lower or so-called *principale,* and the higher or *clarino,* and their mouthpiece size and instrument's bell flare profile reflected their respective duties. For the *principale* trumpeters it was a matter of duty. Their range centered mostly in the second and third octaves of harmonics, which include partials two through six—the notes used for bugle calls that were part of the military trumpeter's field pieces of the era. Before making music with the corps, the *principale* was first and foremost a *Feldtrompeter* and therefore a part of the court military signal corps establishment, including hazardous duty as assigned.

Performance Style

The clarinists often achieved full command of the instrument's third, fourth, and part of the fifth octaves of harmonics, where the growing sequence of available notes narrows down to wholetones and semitones—thus offering the capability for step-wise melodies. *Clarino* playing required great development and stamina plus a commitment to a specialized and cloistered apprenticeship period. That, plus the general style of the repertoire, might imply that *clarino* playing emerged in some extroverted or heroic manner. The effect was probably considered heroic at the time but would be fairly gentle by current standards. It was reported that clarinists could play very elegantly and, indeed, the long trumpets imposed a careful and finite approach in that range. This is rather the opposite of today's often forward and unabashed style, more easily extracted from the current, nearly quarter-tube-length "piccolo" instruments (which, historically speaking, are really cornets).

The current situation is stylistically somewhat upside-down in that it was the *principale* or low players, along with their flamboyant kettledrummers, who played, as Percy Grainger might well have described it, "to the fore." All of that was apparently somewhat based on the vocal techniques of the period which, unlike the present norm, emphasized a grand approach in the lower range and a simple search for beauty and delicacy when ascending.

Wonderful descriptions of the whole picture of Baroque trumpet playing have survived from one of the last actual practitioners, Johann Ernst Altenburg (1734–1801). In 1795, Altenburg published his book, *Versuch einer Anleitung zur heroisch-musikalischen Trompeter- und Pauker-Kunst (Essay on an Introduction to the Heroic and Musical Trumpeters' and Kettledrummers' Art)*. In it, for example, he fondly remembers his father, Johann Caspar Altenburg (1689–1761), a fine all-around trumpeter who was most comfortable in the *clarino* realm and able to deliver it so softly as to be scarcely heard. One might take that to imply that such an approach was considered good taste and the norm among the better players. An excellent annotated and illustrated English translation of the Altenburg *Versuch* was published in 1974 by a current practitioner of the art, Edward Tarr.[6] The reader is also directed to Mr. Tarr's book, *The Trumpet*.[7] Either or both will provide a very clear picture of Baroque trumpet playing and what it meant at that time.

For our purposes here it is most important to know that such a trumpet corps almost invariably made use of instruments all in one key (usually C or D). Regardless of how melodic or elaborate the *clarino* end might become, the *principale* and kettledrum end was restricted to their available notes, which were quite drone-like during the early stages of the corps' development. The resultant sound was very stylized and regal, perfect for extended fanfare-like pieces (even suites) extolling the grandeur of royalty and court life but harmonically limited to a feast of tonic and dominant, though perhaps occasionally implying one or two chord classifications further removed. In short, for the trumpet corps to continue into the early nineteenth century, an age of new, romantic trends in music, it would have to be updated and revised to maintain interest while still performing its former duties as a court and military ensemble.

This came about as wind instrument designers launched new innovations around the turn of the nineteenth century. The old trumpet managed to continue service into the period but in various revised forms. Shorter tube-length trumpets higher than D had previously existed but were never the norm. The new concept was to shorten nearly all of them to a basic corpus pitched in (six-foot) F or a tone higher in G, but then to provide a set of crooks for all keys back downward to C and below. At the same time the body was shortened in the tube-bending process to have two coils (four U-bends instead of the earlier two) and frequently to incorporate a tuning slide in addition to the traditional separate tuning bits. In some cases, the slide was also part of the crooking system, combined with the older form applied at the mouthpipe. The term *Inventionstrompete* was frequently assigned to trumpets having any of those renovations. The same was true of the horn which, slightly earlier, was frequently known as the *Inventionshorn* if equipped with any novel form of tuning slide or improved means to apply crooks.

In addition to general handling convenience, regardless of key and tube-length, the newly designed trumpets brought the bell closer to the embouchure. Several fingers of the player's free hand could then be inserted into the bell for tuning various partials (in particular the sharp eleventh partial) or for flatting others to obtain occasional chromatic alterations. This was already a fairly standard technique for the horn of the period, which, due to its over-all sound and mission, did not suffer in timbre as much as a martial-sounding treble instrument. However less satisfactory they may have been for the trumpet, the hand notes were still regarded by some as mild progress and a technique worth pursuing to a point.

The more compact doubly folded trumpet was further revised for hand use by shifting the bell tube somewhat downward in design and then holding it off to one side for easier reach. A popular crescent-shaped model consequently acquired the name *trompette demilune,* and it along with other even more-compressed models were frequently called *Stopftrompete* in the German-speaking areas. The main exception to this trend was the English slide trumpet, which had re-emerged in a newly mechanized form at about the time the *Stopftrompete* experiments were occurring on the continent.

Early-nineteenth-century compressed trumpet models even spawned another reappearance of trumpets in full circular form and usually incorporating a tuning slide in the center of the coil like the standard *cor d'orchestre* of the period. Such an instrument, by Hirsbrunner of Sumiswald, Switzerland, is in the collections of the Smithsonian Institution in Washington, D.C.[8] (see illustration). It is in G, with only an F crook remaining of whatever crooks it originally had. The circular model eventually took on a cornet-like taper at the mouthpiece end, with nomenclature sometimes reflecting that, such as *cornet de poste.* However, such instruments were perhaps occasionally applied to music-making for which the player's part specified "Trumpet," and all concerned simply considered the outcome as trumpet music. In a way, these early "cornetized" trumpets foreshadowed the present situation in which, historically speaking, the trumpet has become a cornet in terms of tube-length and, nearly so, in taper.

Considering the various hand-stopping possibilities, it is easy to see how the Baroque trumpet corps could re-tool for the new musical trends of the nineteenth century. For one thing, to partly fill in the overtone gaps with hand notes meant that the former *clarino* range and name could all but disappear by shifting the melodic role down to a more comfortable register. However, as we shall notice in an example below, the term *principal(e)* did sometimes remain a way of identifying lower-range trumpet parts. The names for the early-nineteenth-century revised and enlarged trumpet corps varied from place to place, such as *Militär Musik*, "fanfare," or maybe just *Trompeten*. "Fanfare" throughout the century could also refer to any form of military music from brass to full wind band, and it could also refer to musicians and/or instruments so involved. In fact, vestiges of that nomenclature still remain today.

The Napoleonic-era trumpet corps frequently included well over a half-dozen natural trumpets in several different keys. Somewhat like the earlier Russian horn bands, they would be arranged to swap thematic and harmonic material as needed to fill in each others' gaps and to take advantage of open notes or the better (i.e., stronger) hand notes. One does, however, find examples in which the arranger perhaps slightly failed in that regard, as will be discussed below (Ex. 1). In the early pre-valve era the trumpets in the tenor and bass register would be supplemented by one or several trombones and occasionally a serpent, the latter probably being one of the upright (bassoon-form) models. In its initial stages, the corps often included a rather large bass (natural) trumpet, such as one in fourteen-foot E-flat (E-flat tuba length but functioning higher in the partials where a horn of the same length would tend to play). All of these various parts would shift in and out of play according to their acoustical limitations, with only the trombones and serpent able to wander in nearly any harmonic direction.

Example 1 is from an early-nineteenth-century, fairly unmechanized trumpet corps work, a quick march from *Zehn Trompeten-Aufzüge für Militär Musik* by J. Küffner, ca. 1815. It is the example used in Anthony Baines's *Brass Instruments*, which contains an interesting account of trumpet corps development.[9] Baines offers a concert pitch schematic of the actual melody notes as they would sound from the interplay between the various trumpet parts. That example has also been expanded here to show all the material as the listener would hear it.

All of the trumpet parts in Ex. 1 are in old notation, as the players in that period would have needed to view them (essentially as a graph indicating which partials are to be played, regardless of sounding pitch). For modern musicians this means that they are written like current (or at least former) horn notation. Written c^1 (middle C) calls for the fourth partial (i.e., third overtone).[10] For example, the four trumpet parts *in Es* (E-flat) are for the period seven-foot instrument (sounding, as now, a minor-third higher), and they begin respectively (top to bottom) on the tenth, eighth, sixth and fourth partials, although the second part has an optional or extra written e^1 (fifth partial), perhaps indicating that some degree of doubling was expected.

The trio of B-flat (*in B*) parts will appear most confusing to modern viewers. The *Alt Tromp* in B-flat is an early valveless version of today's B-flat instrument (regarding tube-length), but since it is written an octave lower than the modern B-flat trumpet, it actually sounds a minor seventh above written pitch. It appears as it properly would be written for the modern B-flat piccolo instrument, although today's players do not require transposed music for it.

The two so-called B-flat bass trumpet parts (*Bass T. in B*) look and sound as they should to modern viewers, except that they were the standard double length (nine-foot or tenor-trombone length) instruments and not enlarged-bore bass models. Their parts, as in current practice, sound only a tone lower and do not function as bass or even tenor voices. In cases like this involving the then recent half-length (4½-foot) B-flat trumpet termed *Alt,* the others in B-flat are merely termed *Bass* to differentiate them as the standard long B-flat size. The latter would not likely have been termed *Bass* without the presence of the shorter one. It would otherwise simply have been captioned "Trumpet in B-flat"; such a standard nine-foot instrument would have been what Beethoven expected to hear play the Leonora call in that key, for example.

The bass trumpet *in Es* is the fourteen-foot E-flat natural instrument cited above, and it is written like a horn or *Althorn* part in E-flat, sounding a major sixth lower than written. Consequently it is more of a bassett than a bass. Two of the other three trumpet parts transpose as expected, the F part sounding a fourth higher and the *Des* (D-flat) part sounding a semitone higher. The *As* (A-flat) part sounds a minor sixth higher, it being, like the B-flat *Alt,* written an octave lower than expected. The designation "2 Posaunen" likely meant B-flat tenor and F bass, with the serpent doubling the bass.

Example 1a shows what would actually be played; it is obvious that this band of fourteen (or more) players rarely sounded more than a half-dozen notes simultaneously. A Russian horn band might require nearly three times as many players to perform similar music, and minus the lower bass range.

A few aspects of these twelve measures from the Küffner music may cause one to wonder how well he understood the equipment and the balance that might result. Measures 2 and 4, for example, show the band landing with vigor on the mediant in major, or III$^{\#5}$ chord, in root position. Only two instruments, the F and A-flat trumpets, are sounding the third of the chord (b^1), and each is having to use a hand-flatted semitone (sixth and fifth partials respectively) to do it. This leaves seven instruments playing the root (G) as open sounds below (in three octaves) plus the first E-flat trumpet sounding it above. The fifth of the chord (d^2) is sounding as open notes from two of the B-flat trumpets, and the over-all balance (especially outdoors) would have the effect of showing little or no third. There was little other option concerning all but one of the trumpets. Those in E-flat would have to close down a very unsatisfactory whole-step to sound a concert b^1. The B-flat bass would be able to take it as a flatted (closed) ninth partial (rather ineffective), and the B-flat *Alt* would not be able to make it at all. Perhaps Küffner wanted a fairly hollow or nearly thirdless sound in m. 4, but that seems unlikely. Texturally, it is a full-band tutti, and the arranger still has two more good options for a stronger third. The only trumpet capable of playing a strong and open b^1 there is the *Des* (D-flat) instrument (as a seventh partial, written a^1), and it curiously is tacet. Also, the tenor trombone could have moved easily to small octave b (b below middle C). (Is this an attempt at tone painting or just poor planning?) Such music might frequently have been dashed off in haste when needed or perhaps arranged by an unknown bandsman from a composer's keyboard score, or perhaps even just from a basic melody line.

A Little Treasure at the Library of Congress

The Küffner music is fairly early trumpet corps repertoire, but the Music Division at the Library of Congress has a fine example of a later work in the form of a neatly copied score. Its title page reads: *Ouverture für Trompeten / componirt und hochachtungsvoll zugeignet den Grafen von Redern I / von / F. C. von Lossau.*[11] The piece is likely from the early- to mid-second quarter of the nineteenth century; compared to Küffner's work, it is rather more "high-tech" with the addition of one valved and two keyed brasswinds, plus an expanded trombone choir. The serpent has been released unless, if available, it played along with the bass without needing to be specified.

The work is scored for seven natural trumpets including four in C and one each in D, *F Alt*, and *G Alt*, *Corno Kent I & II* (keyed bugles in C), *Tromba cromatica* (in C), four *Tromboni* including alto and *Tenore* (in those clefs) and *Basso I & II* which operate in octaves or at the unison. First, one notices an interesting mix of language in the band's nomenclature. Like the *tromboni*, six of eight trumpets are also specified in Italian—*Tromba*—and the other two are marked "Principal" (discussed below). However, with *Corno Kent*, Lossau was perhaps attempting to identify his keyed bugles in the early English manner, "Kent bugle." Numerous English keyed bugles, including one in the writer's collection, flaunt that name in the bell engraving, sometimes in preference to the actual maker's name.

The *Ouverture*'s first two *tromba* parts in C and sections of the D trumpet part include the closest thing to what might be considered *clarino*-style playing. The tessitura is not particularly high, and the twelfth partial (written g^2) is the basic limit. Only in five places does the first C trumpet go beyond it to a^2, which would have been made by forcefully raising the thirteenth partial by lip or lowering the fourteenth with the bell-closing technique.

The third and fourth C trumpet parts are marked *Principal* (without a terminal -*e*) and harken back to earlier times when the lowest (or a lower) voice in the trumpet corps was so captioned. The Lossau "principal" parts operate between the third partial (written small octave g) and the eighth (written c^2). The three other natural trumpet parts (in D, F, and G) are transposed as expected, and for a concert C major work those parts have proper key signatures for transposing instruments in those keys (two flats, one sharp, and one flat respectively). Between the three, they cover the range of the C trumpet parts plus a wholestep lower (sounding small octave f to a^2).

The F and G parts are each marked *Alt*, which is unnecessary in that any such parts at that time would sound a fourth and fifth above written pitch, respectively. However, in the earlier trumpet corps (in the first quarter of the nineteenth century), there may have been some use of other double-length (actually near quadruple-length by modern standards) bass natural trumpets in those keys (similar to the fourteen-foot E-flat instrument in the Küffner score). "Alt" was probably added to differentiate and affirm the use of the standard upper size(s).

The *tromba cromatica* part in C was most likely for an early two- or three-valve trumpet in G or F crooked down to eight-foot C; in fact, all eight trumpets would have shared that feature of having a G or F corpus with crooks as needed. The other possibility for the *tromba cromatica*, if the work is late enough, is that it was for one of the then very early three-valve short-tube-length models which became the norm ever after. It is unlikely that the *cromatica* was one of the keyed models, as they were rarely ever crooked down to eight-foot C, which would have combined poorly with the tone-hole placement. Furthermore, with efficient keyed bugles already in the band, the keyed trumpet would have been no special addition compared to a new valved model that might have been a very coveted new gadget at that time.

Both the bugle and the valved trumpet parts cover the same range as the parts for first and second C trumpets, but the valve part exceeds it by a semitone on the low end (small octave a). Between the four trombone parts a rather large range is covered: great octave C-flat (or CC-flat) to e².

All seven natural trumpet parts require hand-flatted notes throughout their respective ranges, both prepared and unprepared in that they are not at all limited to quick passing tones between open notes. As in horn playing, the lower-range partials, such as the third and fourth, were probably altered more by embouchure than by hand. However, the work is cleverly done so that constant interplay rarely leaves a closed note not doubled at the unison by an open one in another voice or two. The composer also seems to be looking ahead to a more mechanized future. The valve trumpet and especially the bugles stay quite busy: the second bugle has only nineteen measures of rest in a 239–bar composition. In addition to being featured duetists, the bugles seem to be regarded as the treble range "trouble-shooters," frequently doubling various trumpet passages as if to ensure security.

Unless based on some long-forgotten opera or other material, the Lossau *Ouverture für Trompeten* seems to be a serious attempt to provide original music for such a stand-up ensemble. As a 239–measure work it would have required music stands and likely at least one page turn for each bandsman. It is obviously music for abstract entertainment (or possibly equestrian show) as opposed to functional repertoire for military ceremonies such as any that the Küffner *Trompeten-Aufzüge* were principally meant to serve. It is interesting that Lossau composed such a dramatic work before either the British or American brass band movements even had the equipment with which to establish themselves.

The *Ouverture* opens with a stately twenty-measure Adagio (Ex. 2). The very first measure reveals that Lossau (or possibly an arranger) avoided any manual pitch alteration more extreme than a semitone. The G trumpet is tacet for the first three beats, entering on beat four with written b¹ going to c² (but sounding a fifth above) (Ex. 3). To participate in the theme from the beginning would have required flatting the sixth partial (written g¹) a whole step down to f¹. The semitone hand notes were considered ineffective enough without over-doing it for little good reason. Technically, the G trumpet could have sneaked in on beat three with its written a¹ using the convenient seventh partial lowered less than a semitone.

Bar 19 closes the Adagio with a grand dominant seventh gesture followed by a 219–measure, non-stop Allegro furioso in 6/8 (Ex. 4). Example 5 shows a detail of the opening Allegro measures and some typical interplay between upper voices. Staff 1 is the concert pitch effect (treble instruments) and staves 2, 3, and 4 show

how the D, F, and G trumpets utilize the most effective notes in their series. The work contains the expected soli and tutti sections, and the composer also uses a few cumulative terraced effects for built-in crescendi (Ex. 6, mm. 41–46). In a spectacular effect at bar 45, the upper trombones top off the ensemble by joining the bugles for a unison drive into an E major tutti section.

The constant shifting of parts and timbres in trumpet corps music of this sort makes one wish for a hearing with period instruments, for such a band would never have sounded uninteresting. Although the use of modern instruments, more uniform in timbre, would rather miss the point, the music itself has merit for current use. Rarely are there more than six individual pitches sounding at once: some of this repertoire might well be adapted for the modern brass quintet, although the varied colors and contrasts between tutti and soli would be less pronounced. Of greater concern is that the fatigue factor of an extended work with non-stop playing by a band of only five players would probably cause it to be programmed only rarely. A select brass choir can certainly play such works, however, and in the case of the Lossau *Ouverture*, a slight concession to the intended tone color scheme would be to use: (1) flugelhorns for the keyed bugle parts (they are valved bugles after all); (2) the smallest modern trombone equipment that can be mustered; and (3) no trumpets or cornets shorter (i.e., higher) than B-flat for any of the eight trumpet parts.

Depending on one's viewpoint, the short-lived era at the turn of the nineteenth century when natural and keyed trumpets coexisted may be considered the most unique period in the history of the trumpet family of instruments. While the hand notes were not nearly as effective as on the horn, they did carry trumpet-playing forward in several directions. Various early-nineteenth-century orchestral works, including operas, called for trumpets occasionally to play formerly unavailable pitches. Depending on time, place, and available equipment, they were perhaps negotiated as necessary on a *Stopftrompete*. For example, e² occurs a few times in the first trumpet part of Franz Schubert's Second Symphony, and many works at that time included the written top-line f² (eleventh partial) which, just as on the horn, could be tuned with *Stopftrompete* technique.

It is difficult to determine the playing styles employed by the early-nineteenth-century trumpet corps, for there was no practitioner from that period like Altenburg, who left such a detailed account of the eighteenth-century trumpeter's art. If Altenburg truly described the norm for the closing phase of the earlier trumpet and kettledrummer corps, it is perhaps rational to assume that the next generation included trumpeters who remembered it well and carried on in a similar manner with the new equipment. That, plus the newer trends in romantic music and the inclusion of hand notes, might indicate that the relatively gentle approach of the earlier clarinists was probably somewhat necessary for all of the trumpet parts, depending on complexity and chromaticism. The lower parts, whether or not marked *principale*, would not necessarily have been covered by personnel trained in that tradition. They simply had become inner voices in the new trumpet music. It was surely the inclusion of more valve instruments that propelled increasingly aggressive styles of brass playing ever onward toward today's norms.

The early-nineteenth-century trumpet corps was a unit prized as an accoutrement of power by royalty in what was left of European aristocratic court life. It was a remarkable ensemble, which should be reconsidered now for its musical merits. The music of Küffner, Lossau, and others enhanced the listening experiences of audiences, who, from our perspective, were simply and enthusiastically enjoying a *brass band,* alive and well, before it was so captioned.

NOTES

1. J. F. Russell and J. H. Elliot, *The Brass Band Movement* (London: J. M. Dent & Sons Ltd., 1936).

2. G. Brand and V. Brand, *Brass Bands of the Twentieth Century* (Letchworth, Herts: Egon Publishers Ltd., 1979).

3. Margaret Hazen and Robert Hazen, *The Music Men: An Illustrated History of Brass Bands in America, 1800–1920* (Washington, D.C.: Smithsonian Institution Press, 1987).

4. Jon Newsom, "The American Brass Band Movement," *The Quarterly Journal of the Library of Congress* (spring 1979): 114–139.

5. Library of Congress, Music Division, M1200.R97 Case.

6. J. E. Altenburg, *Trumpeters' and Kettledrummers' Art,* trans. Edward H. Tarr (Nashville, Tenn.: The Brass Press, 1974).

7. Edward Tarr, *The Trumpet* (Portland, Oregon: Amadeus Press, 1988).

8. Smithsonian Institution, Washington, D.C., catalogue No. 95,270.

9. Anthony Baines, *Brass Instruments: Their History and Development* (London: Faber & Faber, 1976), pp. 184–190.

10. Modern double-horn players may take that note on the short-tube side as a third partial (or second overtone).

11. Library of Congress, Music Division, M1204.L62S.

Example 1. Küffner, J., Trompeten-Aufzüge, Quick March or Fanfare Piece, ca. 1815.

c.1815 ~ J. Küffner, 10 Trompeten-Aufzüge für Militär Musik, Offenbach a/Main
Trumpet parts sharing melody notes shown in brackets above

Example 1A. The above realized in concert pitch.

Example 2. Lossau, F. C., *Ouverture für Trompeten*, mm 1–7, condensed score.

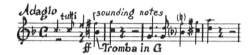

Example 3. Lossau, F. C., *Ouverture*, mm 1–4, g
trumpet part.

Example 4. Lossau, F. C., *Ouverture*, mm 18–25, condensed score.

Example 5. Lossau, F. C., *Ouverture*, measures 21–25, condensed score and transposition detail.

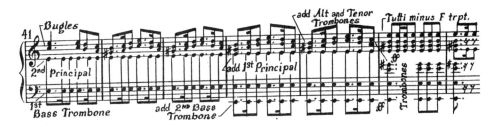

Example 6. Lossau, F. C., *Ouverture*, mm 41–46, condensed score.

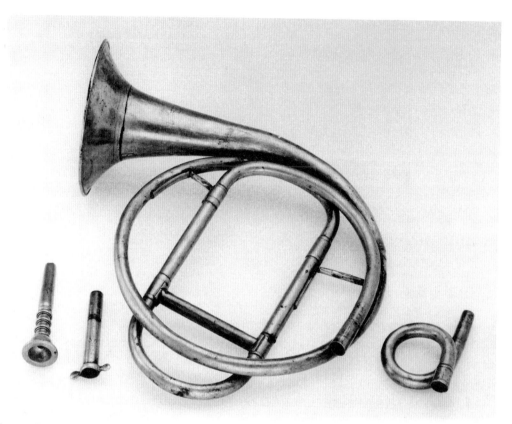

Plate 1: Trumpet in G with F crook: "Hirsbrunner a Sumiswald" ca. 1825 Smithsonian Institution, Washington, D.C., period mouthpiece and shank from the author's collection.
Photograph by Eric Long, Smithsonian Institution.

J. A. C. Sommerville and the British Band in the Era of Holst and Vaughan Williams

JON C. MITCHELL

AMONG the earliest recordings of the Eastman Wind Ensemble under Frederick Fennell's direction was a two-record series referred to as *British Band Classics*.[1] These recordings, which featured original compositions for winds by Gustav Holst, Ralph Vaughan Williams, Gordon Jacob, and Percy Grainger, as well as a William Walton work transcribed by Nathaniel Duthoit, have since become "classics" in themselves for their interpretation of British military band music.

The vast majority of these compositions owe their fame, if not their existence, to one person, Col. John A. C. Sommerville, Commandant at the Royal Military School of Music at Kneller Hall from 1920 to 1925. However, before discussing Sommerville and his involvement with the band's repertoire, it is appropriate that the development of the British military band and the history of the Royal Military School of Music be cursorily examined.

The British Military Band Tradition

The general history of British military bands before the founding of the Royal Military School of Music is not difficult to trace, although specifics are often difficult to verify. Unfortunately, many available sources, from historical tomes to stirring accounts of imperialist exploitation, are often undocumented, contradictory, and self-congratulatory. Nevertheless, while searching for verifications, one can obtain a feeling for pomp and circumstance as well as the zeal for honor and glory often associated with the proud past of British military bands.

One of the earliest references to British military music comes from Bartholmaeus in 1366:

> A trompe is properly an instrument ordeyned, for men that fighteth in battayle, to crye and to warn of the sygnes of battayle. Men in olde tyme usyd trompes in battayle to fere and affraye thyr enmyes, and to comforte their own knyghtes and fyghtynge men. For it is sometyme blowe to arraye battaylles, and sometyme for that battayles sholde smyte togyder.[2]

111

Trumpets were often accompanied by drums. Bagpipes were also used as military instruments in the later middle ages until the reign of Henry VIII (1509–1547) when they were largely supplanted by fifes. Additional woodwinds were subsequently borrowed from the continent. Oboes and bassoons were introduced about 1678, after Charles II heard the band at the court of Louis XIII of France. Clarinets were introduced to England by Johann Christian Bach in the early 1760s and by 1763, the British military band had achieved the same instrumentation of the *Harmoniemusik* ensembles extant in much of the rest of Europe: two oboes, two clarinets, two horns, and two bassoons. Sometimes four oboes or four clarinets were used instead of the "two-plus-two" combination as in J. L. Hoberecht's *Grand Military Piece*, composed in 1799.[3] Flutes, English bass horns, serpents, ophicleides, trumpets, trombones, and percussion were occasionally added to the *Harmoniemusik* combination during the early years of the nineteenth century.

Instrumentation varied greatly from one band to the next, since nearly all of the bandmasters were foreigners who emulated the bands of their home countries. This situation was alleviated somewhat with the introduction of various military band journals. These journals relied heavily on subscriptions from the bands. The music contained in them was of a light character and, although there were contributions from some English composers, the vast majority of the pieces were transcriptions of continental European works. The earliest of the journals, Wessel and Stapleton's *Military Journal*, was first published in 1845.[4] Other journals soon followed. Still, the problem of uniformity persisted, for instrumentation specifications varied between journals. Thus, by the middle of the nineteenth century, the entire British military band scene was in one glorious mess.

Nothing displayed the need for a revamping of the entire British military band system more than the mortification faced by British bandsmen during the Crimean War at the Queen's Birthday Parade, held at Scutari (Shkoder, Albania).[5] Farmer comments about this debacle:

> At Scutari in 1854, the British troops, comprising the army of the east destined for the Crimea, held a grand review on the birthday of Queen Victoria. There were some sixteen thousand men on parade, and while their appearance and marching were perfect, and the cheering deafening, our bands struck up "God Save the Queen," not only from different arrangements but in different keys! And all this before the staff of the Allied Army.[6]

Over the course of the war, the situation did not improve. Many of the overseas bands were dissolved and the bandsmen pressed into actual military service.

The Royal Military School of Music

His Royal Highness, George William Frederick Charles, the Duke of Cambridge and a cousin to Queen Victoria, was appointed Commander-in-Chief in 1856. He served in the Crimean War and may have witnessed the Scutari catastrophe. At the urging of British bandmasters Henry Schallehn, James Smyth and others, he proposed the establishment of a School of Music.[7] The Duke had seen and heard the fine results obtained by the French from their Ecole Militaire and advocated adapting the same type of system. Although the official reason given for the establishment of a School of Music was to provide uniform instruction for musicians in the service, an underlying motive was to eventually rid the British military of foreign bandmasters. The funding for the school was to come primarily from the regiments themselves.

The site for the school was to be Kneller Hall, located between Whitton and Twickenham in the far southwestern suburbs of London. The building is named for Godfrey Kneller (1648–1723), the German-English portrait artist, who purchased the property in 1709 and had a large edifice constructed upon it.[8] Originally called Whitton Hall, the building had become known as Kneller Hall by the middle of the nineteenth century. On 3 March 1857 the first military music class came into being at what was to be known as the Royal Military School of Music at Kneller Hall. Henry Schallehn, who had conducted the Crystal Palace Band from 1854 to 1856, became the first superintendent of the school. He was assisted by a visiting staff of four instructors.[9]

As would be expected, a number of changes took place over the next half century in regard to the operation of the school. In 1865 its administration was taken over by the government; in 1881 an examination requirement was added and, from 1890 onward, there would be a commissioned officer in charge.[10]

At the turn of the century the Commandant at the Royal Military School of Music was Col. F. Onslow Barrington Foote (1850–1911), who served in that capacity from 1900 until 1905.[11] He was also the president of the Royal Artillery Band Committee. The Director of Music was Quartermaster and Honorary Lieutenant Arthur J. Stretton (1863–1947), who held that post for a remarkable twenty-five years (1896–1921).

In 1902, The Worshipful Company of Musicians, a London-based organization promoting all aspects of the art and science of music, sponsored a contest for the best march written for the coronation of Edward VII. A similar contest was sponsored by the same group in 1911 for the coronation of George V. This was unusual for its time, for the music performed by the British military bands consisted largely of quickstep marches and orchestral transcriptions. A noteworthy original work of the era was *The Spirit of Pageantry*, a grand march by Percy Fletcher (1879–1932) that was published in 1901. It should also be mentioned that the *Lads of Wamphray March* by Percy Grainger (1882–1961) was played through in 1904 by the Band of the Coldstream Guards under the direction of the highly-decorated Lt. Col. John Mackenzie Rogan. This was a one-time occurrence, however, and the march was not published until much later.

Succeeding Foote as Commandant was Col. (later Brig. Gen.) Sir Alfred Granville Balfour (1858–1936), who served until 1910. Balfour was a distinguished musician who later served as a Vice President of the Royal Academy of Music. He was also an Honorable Freeman of The Worshipful Company of Musicians.[12] His connection with this organization could have had considerable bearing on their 1909 contest for original military band compositions "moulded in the higher forms." The winner of that contest was Fletcher's *Back to the Land*.[13] Also during Balfour's tenure, the Royal Military School of Music celebrated its jubilee (1907). Still, the most lasting testimonial to the Balfour years at Kneller Hall was the First Suite in E-Flat for Military Band, Op. 28, No. 1, composed in 1909 by Gustav Holst.[14] The exact origins of the suite are not known, although Holst lived nearby and frequented Kneller Hall whenever his works were rehearsed or performed there. This work, however, would not receive its first documented performance for more than another decade.

The First Somerville

In June of 1910 Col. Thomas Cameron FitzGerald Somerville (1860–1942) succeeded Col. Alfred Balfour as Commandant of the Royal Military School of Music. Somerville was from a distinguished Irish family, being the eldest son of Lt. Col. T. H. Somerville, the Deputy Lieutenant of Drishane, County Cork, and Adelaide, daughter of Admiral Sir Josiah Coghill and granddaughter of Charles Kendal Bushe, Chief Justice of Ireland.[15] His elder sister was Edith Somerville (1858–1949), an author and illustrator. Two younger brothers also had distinguished military careers: Hugh Gautier-Coghill Somerville (1873–1950) became a vice admiral, while Col. J. A. C. Somerville would succeed Cameron (as he was called) at Kneller Hall.

Cameron Somerville was educated at Clifton College and the Royal Military College at Sandhurst. Prior to his appointment at Kneller Hall he had served in The King's Own Royal Regiment, as an aide-de-camp in China and South Africa, and commanded The King's Own Lancaster Regiment. In 1911, during his tenure at Kneller Hall, he was selected to command the massed bands (numbering some 1600 bandsmen from forty-six British and Indian Army Bands) at the Delhi Durbar, a celebration of George V's coronation.

The year 1911 turned out to be quite important for military band composition. In that year Holst composed his Second Military Suite in F Minor, which was later revised and retitled Second Suite in F for Military Band, Op. 28 No. 2.[16] As in the case of his First Suite in E-Flat, the exact reason for its composition is not known, and it too would see more than a decade pass before its public premiere. 1911 also witnessed the enormous Festival of Empire Imperial Exhibition at the Crystal Palace in London. Most of the guards bands took part, although the bands of the Royal Military School of Music did not. The *Pageant of London*, an immense undertaking containing four parts and thirty-two scenes, was the center of attraction. Due to the fact that the pageant was outdoors, the medium of musical expression chosen for the accompanying incidental music was the military band. Many of England's finest composers—Gustav Holst, Ralph Vaughan Williams, Cecil Forsyth, Frank Bridge, Edward German, and Haydn Wood—each contributed incidental music.[17]

The normal tenure for a commandant had been four to five years, but the length of stay for Cameron Somerville was extended because of the outbreak of World War I. Binns comments about the effect of the war on the activities at Kneller Hall:

> Pupils and students over the age of eighteen were at once returned to their regiments—many of them to become stretcher bearers, the role assigned to bandsmen on mobilization. In their place came thirteen junior bandmasters, bringing with them all their band-boys. Thus, during a period when so much was to change or disappear forever, the function and continuity of Kneller Hall was assured.[18]

Fortunately for all, the work of the Royal Military School of Music continued in a more or less uninterrupted manner, thereby setting up what was to become the greatest period of British military band activity ever.

The Second Somerville

In 1920 Col. John Arthur Coghill Somerville (1872–1955) became Commandant of the Royal Military School of Music. J. A. C. Somerville, as he is often referred to, was educated at Bedford Grammar School and at the Royal Military College at Sandhurst. Prior to his arrival at Kneller Hall, he had served and ascended through the ranks in the Northumberland Fusiliers and the Royal Sussex Regiment. He was well travelled, having served in the following overseas locations: South Africa (1899–1901), Tokyo and Korea (1911–1914; 1915–1919), and Siberia (1919). In 1918 he was made a Companion of St. Michael and St. George (C.M.G.) and in the following year he became a Commander, Order of the British Empire (C.B.E.). After retiring from Kneller Hall in 1925, he served as Secretary of The Japan Society (1928–1937) and maintained a continuing interest in Oriental art. He was married twice: his first wife, Vera, died in 1937, and he remarried, in 1942, to Mildred McCheane.[19]

J. A. C. Somerville was indeed a fine musician. The improvement and dissemination of the British military band repertoire was of utmost importance to him. Gordon Jacob comments:

> But Col. Somerville was very keen on improving the repertoire and status of military bands, and interested Holst and Vaughan Williams in the idea of writing for them. He no doubt got to know Vaughan Williams as he sang in the London Bach Choir of which Vaughan Williams was conductor in the 20's and 30's. . . . Both Holst and Vaughan Williams were keen encouragers of amateur music making and had somewhat socialist political views which made them want to include the popular military and brass bands in their purview, but I think Vaughan Williams' contribution to the repertoire was slighter than Holst's.[20]

One of the first events of Somerville's tenure was the earliest documented performance of Holst's First Suite in E-Flat for Military Band. There may have been earlier performances of the work, for it was composed in 1909 and manuscript parts exist which identify the composer as "Gustav von Holst," the composer's full name until he had the "von" legally removed during World War I. Furthermore, there is correspondence concerning James Causley Windram (1886–1944), then Bandmaster of the 5th Northumberland Fusiliers, in which Holst hints at an earlier planned performance of at least one of the suites.[21] Still, the 23 June 1920 performance conducted by student D. W. Jones on the grounds of Kneller Hall must be remembered as "THE" performance which not only formally introduced the suite, but also opened up the door for the enormous amount of compositional activity for military band that followed.[22] Due in part to Windram's efforts, the First Suite in E-Flat for Military Band was published by Boosey and Hawkes in 1921.

That Holst's suite was published and being performed throughout the British Commonwealth was very encouraging to Somerville, who continued his campaign for original military band music from composers of stature. Yet the question of instrumentation continued to befuddle composers and the military alike. Even Holst listed many instruments in his suite as being "optional." Somerville solved this question in a very direct manner. He comments:

> One difficulty which has greatly hampered composers in the past has been the fact that, up to now, there has been no authoratative pronouncement as to what is the combination of instruments constituting a military band. This, fortunately, no longer remains. On the 7th December, 1921, a conference was held at Kneller Hall, attended by practically all the military Directors of Music and representatives of the Navy, Marines, and Air Force, at which the "minimum band" and its instrumentation, and the system on which it should be augmented, were definitely determined. For outdoor engagements, the number was fixed at 25, and for indoor at 20 performers.
>
> Recommendations were also made by the conference regarding the instrumentation, both of the two minimum bands and of others of larger numbers of performers up to fifty.[23]

Alto and bass clarinets were eliminated from standard instrumentation as was the B-flat baritone horn. This added a greater amount of responsibility to the saxophones, which were then relative newcomers to the military band. This fact caused Holst additional scoring difficulties with the Second Suite in F for Military Band, forcing him to alter its instrumentation significantly.[24]

The 1920s composition of the full Kneller Hall band, which normally rehearsed as four separate bands, was listed by Somerville:[25]

Flutes and Piccolos	10
Oboes	6
E-Flat Clarinets	7
Solo B-Flat Clarinets	13
Ripieno Clarinets	7
2nd B-Flat Clarinets	12
3rd B-Flat Clarinets	10
E-Flat Alto Saxophones	4
B-Flat Tenor Saxophones	4
1st Bassoons	7
2nd Bassoons	5
1st Horns	6
2nd Horns	6
3rd Horns	5
4th Horns	4
1st B-Flat Cornets	14
2nd B-Flat Cornets	10
1st Trombones	7
2nd Trombones	6
Bass Trombones	1
Euphoniums	12
Basses	12
Tympani	2
Total	165

This was the size of the Kneller Hall Band that gave the premiere performance of Holst's Second Suite in F for Military Band, Op. 28, No. 2, at Albert Hall on 30 June 1922. The British Music Society, Incorporated Society of Musicians, and Federation of British Music Industries jointly sponsored this auspicious concert, which was given to display the quality literature then available for the medium. Somerville was, of course, "at the throttle." He had hoped that the concert would mark the beginning of a new and better epoch for the military band.[26] In addition to the Second Suite in F, Holst's *Festival Choruses* (with military band accompaniment arranged by the composer), Dame Ethel Smythe's *The Wreckers Overture*, and *Three Humoresques* by Bertram Walton O'Donnell (1887–1939) were also premiered.[27] O'Donnell, who already had an important work (*Theme and Variations*) to his credit, would later achieve additional fame as conductor of the B.B.C. Military Band. He had two brothers, P(ercy) S. G. O'Donnell and R(upert) P. O'Donnell, who were also well-known band directors.

The band, for this auspicious Albert Hall concert, was conducted by Hector Earnest Adkins (1885–1945), Director of Music at the Royal Military School of

Music from 1921 to 1942. Adkins was quite a character (he taught conducting with a handkerchief), and a shrewd businessman. His system of fines was legendary: he often fined players for the smallest infraction of the rules. Although his book, *Adkin's Treatise on the Military Band*, was largely a compilation of student assignments, it remains unsurpassed as a military band instrumentation textbook.[28] Adkins was in the right place at the right time; he also conducted the world premieres of Vaughan Williams' *English Folk Song Suite* (4 July 1923) and *Toccata Marziale* (July 1924).

In addition to highly-publicized concerts, Somerville was deeply interested in the quality of the education being received by the pupils and students at Kneller Hall. He made arrangements with Sir Hugh Allen at the Royal College of Music (Holst and Vaughan Williams' alma mater) for many of the future bandmasters to gain experience performing in that college's orchestra.[29] Along with Holst and Vaughan Williams, Somerville also had many composers visit Kneller Hall to rehearse their own works, among them Ethel Smythe, Eugene Goosens, Henry Wood, and Walford Davies.[30]

The instructional staff at Kneller Hall was excellent. On the faculty were such men as Frank Winterbottom (1861–1930), who not only taught instrumentation, but also supplied the band world with more than three hundred excellent transcriptions, and the cornetist Charles Leggatt, who would conduct many fine electronic recordings of the Holst and Vaughan Williams military band suites in the not-too-distant future. A student, George Smith, who transcribed "Mars" and "Jupiter" from Holst's orchestral suite, *The Planets*, Op. 32, also deserves mention.

In 1923, the two Holst suites were recorded for the first time and the following year Vaughan Williams' *English Folk Song Suite* was recorded. Unfortunately, these acoustical 78 r.p.m. recordings, by the Coldstream Guards Band (conducted by R. G. Evans)[31] and the Life Guards Band (conducted by Lt. H. Eldridge),[32] are severely edited, and, at times, musically inept. Nonetheless, they brought these important military band works into people's homes throughout the United Kingdom.

The Royal Military School of Music supplied much of the music for the 1924 British Empire Exhibition held at Wembley Stadium. It was here that Vaughan Williams' *Quick March—"Sea Songs"* and *Toccata Marziale* were given their premieres. It was also here that Gordon Jacob saw his first works for military band performed. He comments:

> My own interest was aroused by (1) being commissioned to orchestrate Vaughan Williams' *Folk Song Suite* and (2) by the suggestion of Adrian Boult that I should arrange my orchestral *William Byrd Suite* to be played by massed bands in Wembley Stadium at the opening of the 1924 Festival of Britain. This led to my *Original Suite* and later on to *Music for a Festival* for the 1951 Festival of Britain and many other works for symphonic band and brass band.[33]

By the middle of the decade, a new medium, radio, had found its way into nearly every home and office building. As early as 23 March 1924, the Manchester Station Military Band, under the direction of Harry Mortimer, gave the first broadcast of

Holst's Second Suite in F.[34] The Grenadier Guards Band followed suit with the broadcast premiere of the First Suite in E-Flat on 7 May of that year.[35] Military bands transmitted quite well over the airwaves. The Manchester Station Military Band, just cited, was a predecessor to the B.B.C. Wireless Military Band formed in 1927. The Kneller Hall Band was not to be left out. On 8 July 1924, it made its first broadcast from the B.B.C. studios at Savoy Hill.[36]

On 31 January 1925, J. A. C. Somerville turned over the Commandant position of the Royal Military School of Music to Sir Francis Napier Horne-Elphinstone-Dalrymple, Bart., who served for the next four years. The Somerville era, which had been marked by a flourish of activity, had come to an end. J. A. C. Somerville, through encouraging composers, performing their pieces, and broadcasting them, had elevated the British military band into a significant art form. Although major composers such as Gordon Jacob and Haydn Wood would continue to compose for military band, there would never again be the same intensity of spirit that existed from 1920 to 1925. Whether one considers the Somerville era to begin with the tenure of Cameron Somerville in 1910 or of J. A. C. Somerville in 1920, the evidence is clear that by the end of that era in 1925 the British military band had won acceptance as an important musical medium.

NOTES

1. *Folksong Suites and Other British Band Classics*, Eastman Wind Ensemble conducted by Frederick Fennell, Mercury MG50088/SR90088, Mercury Golden Import Series SRI 75011, reissued on *Frederick Fennell Conducts*, Mercury MG50388/SR90388; *British Band Classics*, Vol. 2, Eastman Wind Ensemble conducted by Frederick Fennell, MG50197/SR90197, Mercury Golden Import Series SRI 75028, reissued on *British and American Band Classics*, Mercury Living Presence CD 432 009–2.

2. Quoted in J. A. C. Somerville, "Historical Sketch of the Evolution of the Military Band," in *Famous Bands of the British Empire*, ed. Alfred Zealley and J. Ord Hume (London: J. P. Hull, 1926), p. 11.

3. J. L. Hoberecht, *Grand Military Piece* (London: Goulding, Phipps, & D'Almaine, 1799).

4. Clarence Wiggins, *Editions for Modern Band of Selected Works from Early Nineteenth-Century English Military Band Music* (D.M.A. diss., University of Southern California, 1966), p. 43.

5. Somerville, "Historical Sketch," p. 12, cites Varna (in Bulgaria), not Scutari, as the scene of the fiasco.

6. Henry George Farmer, *The Rise and Development of Military Music* (London: William Reeves, 1912), p. 118.

7. P. L. Binns, *A Hundred Years of Military Music* (Gillingham, Dorset: The Blackmore Press, 1959), p. 31.

8. Ibid., p. 6.

9. *The New Grove Dictionary of Music and Musicians*, ed. Stanley Sadie (London: Macmillan, 1980), vol. 11, p. 212.

10. Ibid.

11. Binns, *Military Music*, pp. 118, 120.

12. *Who Was Who, III (1929–1940)* (London: Adam & Charles Black, 1941), p. 57.

13. Personal correspondence from W. R. I. Crewdson, Clerk, The Worshipful Company of Musicians, 10 March 1983. The second, third, and fourth place winners were, respectively, *A Lost Cause* by Walter Wesche, *Toujours Jouet* by Percy Fletcher, and *Ars Longa* by W. J. Cunningham Woods.

14. Gustav Holst, *List of Compositions*, London, British Library, Add. MS. 57863.

15. *Who Was Who, IV (1941–1950)* (London: Charles Black, 1952), p. 1086.

16. Holst, *List of Compositions*.

17. Sophie M. Lomas, *Festival of Empire: Book of the Pageant* (London and Derby: Bemrose & Sons, Ltd., 1911) p. xiii ff.

18. Binns, *Military Music*, p. 122.

19. *Who Was Who, V (1951–1960)* (London: Adam & Charles Black, 1961), p. 1024.

20. Personal correspondence from Gordon Jacob, 6 June 1983.

21. Correspondence from Gustav Holst to W. G. Whittaker, 30 March 1917, in Michael Short, ed., *Gustav Holst: Letters to W. G. Whittaker* (Glasgow: University of Glasgow Press, 1974).

22. Concert programme, Royal Military School of Music, Kneller Hall, Whitton, 23 June 1920.

23. Somerville, "Historical Sketch," p. 13.

24. Gustav Holst, Second Suite in F for Military Band, Op. 28, No. 2, British Library Add. MS 47825.

25. Somerville, "Historical Sketch," p. 13.

26. *The British Music Bulletin* 4, no. 7 (July 1922): 130.

27. Concert programme, Band of the Royal Military School of Music, Albert Hall, 30 June 1922.

28. Hector Adkins, *Adkins' Treatise on the Military Band* (London: Boosey & Co., 1931).

29. Binns, *Military Music*, p. 123.

30. Ibid., pp. 123–124.

31. Gustav Holst, First Suite in E Flat (Gramo. HMV C1115), and Second Suite in F (Gramo. HMV C1165/6).

32. Gustav Holst, Second Suite in F (Vocalion K05082), and Vaughan Williams, *English Folk Song Suite* (Vocalion K05086).

33. Jacob, loc. cit.

34. Kenneth Thompson, *A Dictionary of Twentieth Century Composers (1911–1971)* (London: Faber & Faber, 1973), p. 215.

35. Ibid., p. 214.

36. Binns, *Military Music*, p. 126.

Toward a Critical Edition of Stravinsky's
Symphonies of Wind Instruments

ROBERT W. WASON

SOME four years after Stravinsky made his *Symphonies of Wind Instruments* generally available for the first time by publishing a revised version, Frederick Fennell programmed the work on a concert at the Eastman School of Music in Kilbourn Hall on 5 February 1951. According to Fennell, *Symphonies* was the culminating score in a chronological survey of little-known and rarely played works. Certainly this and subsequent performances of the piece by Fennell helped to rescue *Symphonies* from the fate of being "little-known and rarely played." Indeed, the Mercury recording of a few years later by Fennell and the Eastman Wind Ensemble, which also included the Schoenberg *Variations*, op. 42a and Hindemith's Symphony in B-flat, did much to establish these three works as the major classics of wind-ensemble music from the first half of the twentieth century.

More recently, Donald Hunsberger has championed the 1920 version of *Symphonies*, the score of which finally became available in the early 80s. Through Hunsberger's efforts, it has become increasingly clear to American wind-ensemble directors that *Symphonies*, in its original incarnation, is quite a different piece than the 1947 version, and richly deserving of performance and study in its own right. But though it is certainly wonderful to have a score of the earlier version available, with it comes the obligation of presenting the piece in a historically correct manner, and this, unfortunately, is not easy. To begin with, the score that is now available is *not* equivalent to the one that served as the source of the first performances. Furthermore, study of this score cannot help but raise editorial questions, as is demonstrated by Keating Johnson's list of alleged "wrong notes" in the piece.[1] All of this points to the necessity of a critical edition of *Symphonies*, though alas, even if support for such a project were to emerge, it would remain a difficult undertaking, exacerbated by the lengthy and complex compositional history of the piece, as well as our primitive technical understanding of Stravinsky's musical language. Until very recently, the primary source materials for such an edition presented their own problems. Fortunately, these have abated somewhat, since the whereabouts of all source materials is now known, and the two most important documents—the autographs of the short score and full score of the 1920 version—have recently been published in facsimile.[2] Still, in attempting to establish an authoritative text for the piece, we must ask the crucial question: given the level of confusion that still exists, how is one to know right notes from wrong ones? As a first step towards providing some basis for editing the work, we shall review the present state of both historical and theoretical source materials dealing with *Symphonies*, since both bear on these problems. We shall then apply our newly attained knowledge in an attempt to solve the textual problems uncovered by Johnson. We shall conclude with brief remarks concerning possible implications of what we have learned for further work in analysis and interpretation of *Symphonies*.

The Chronology of Composition

According to Stravinsky's own testimony, the Chorale was composed on 20 June 1920 in Carentec, Brittany; Stravinsky goes on to say that the piece as a whole was completed by 2 July, but that he "returned to it a few days later to add the two adumbrative bits of chorale in the body of the piece."[3] For some time now, speculation has had it that he meant the two literal statements of the chorale's opening measures at rehearsals 25 and 34 in the 1920 score (rehearsals 42 and 56 in the 1947 score). The documents prove this speculation to be correct, for in looking at pages 11 and 13 of the autograph short score, we can see the erasures and the cramped appearance of the chorale segments. (See Fig. 1, which shows the first of these pages.) In fact, André Baltensperger and Felix Meyer were able to reconstruct the passages that were erased: these are shown in Ex. 1. The first of these (Ex. 1a) anticipates the "dance music" of the next section, while the second (Ex. 1b) provides a transition to the upcoming "pendulum motive" of the winds.[4] This finding also serves to clarify Stravinsky's statement: obviously, when he spoke of 2 July as the date of completion he referred to the short score. But we might also ask: why did he find it necessary to "return" to the piece to add these chorale fragments? We shall return to that problem shortly.

Though Eric Walter White lists the date of completion as 20 November 1920, this is apparently an error, since the autograph of the full score ends with the date 30 November 1920.[5] But much more important than discrepancies regarding the date of completion of the piece is the fact that Craft's 1983 study of sketch material sets a much earlier date for at least the initial stages of composition, and seems to show that some of the primary material of the piece may have been inspired directly by the news of Debussy's death, rather than by the well-known request for a contribution to *Revue Musicale*, of which we shall speak shortly. Example 2 shows a diplomatic transcription of the first sketch notation of what White has called the "Bell Motive."[6] Craft believes that Stravinsky wrote this in late March or early April 1918, upon hearing the news of Debussy's death (which had occurred on 26 March).[7] Though the exact date may be uncertain, it was written sometime between 5 February and 28 December 1918—the dates on the sketchbook with blue binding (the so-called "Sketchbook V") in which it occurs; this sketchbook also contains sketches for the *Piano-Rag-Music* of 1919, which Stravinsky had been working on when he wrote the Bell-Motive.[8] In a sketchbook with brown binding, the so-called "Sketchbook VII," which again contains sketches for the *Piano-Rag-Music*, we find an early version of the opening of the Chorale.[9] This sketch is followed by a twenty-seven-page sketch-complex, at the head of which Stravinsky later wrote "Premiers brouillons pour mes SYMPHONIES d'INSTR. à VENT"; according to Craft, as well as the editors of the facsimile, most of this material eventually found its way into the finished piece. It is known that Stravinsky used this sketchbook from June 1919 on, and because the sketch that precedes this complex bears a date, the sketch-complex very likely dates from July 1919.[10] Much of this music was scored initially for harmonium, of all instruments—a choice that Craft relates to Stravinsky's preoccupation with his main work in the spring and summer of 1919, a reinstrumentation of *Les Noces* for harmonium, two cimbaloms, a pianola and percussion.[11] After abandoning the harmonium, Stravinsky chose various combinations of strings. Indeed, the many changes of instrumentation lead Baltensperger and Meyer to characterize this sketch-complex as "experimental." The sketches also belie certain statements that Stravinsky made about his compositional technique: for example, that his pieces were composed straight through, and that his musical ideas always came to him in specific timbres, which he did not change.[12]

Now, one might argue that this compositional activity of almost two years was, in a sense, "pre-compositional": after all, no complete piece was produced, nor was one even planned, apparently. Thus Baltensperger and Meyer locate what they call the "actual beginning" of the compositional process with the request for a contribution to the Debussy-Memorial collection of short pieces planned by the periodical *Revue Musicale*. The Chorale appeared in a piano arrangement as part of the *Tombeau de Claude Debussy* included in the second issue of *Revue Musicale*, December 1920; among other composers who contributed to the collection were Ravel, Bartók, de Falla and Satie. Stravinsky later described this project as follows:

> The composition of this page [. . .] made me feel bound to give rein to the development of a new phase of musical thought conceived under the influence of the work itself and the solemnity of the circumstances that had led to it. I began at the end, and wrote a choral [*sic*] piece which later on became the final section of my *Symphonies pour Instruments à Vent*, dedicated to the memory of Claude Achille Debussy. This I gave to the *Revue Musicale* in a version arranged for the pianoforte.[13]

The "page" to which Stravinsky refers is actually two remarkably austere-looking facing pages in the issue of *Review Musicale*, containing few indications of phrasing, and utterly devoid of dynamic indications. At the top, the first page bears the inscription "Fragment des Symphonies pour instruments à vent"—strangely, *not* a direct quotation of the eventual title. But then the character of the handwriting on the title page of the autograph clearly indicates that the title was added sometime after the page was finished. The date of the chorale at the end of the short score agrees with Stravinsky's testimony—20 June 1920—and evidence seems to indicate that he submitted a copy of it to *Revue Musicale* by early August. Clearly, the chorale was the first part of the piece to be completed, but its still somewhat rudimentary form in *Revue Musicale* seems to indicate that Stravinsky may have added more than just the two "adumbrative bits of chorale" to the short score after 2 July 1920.

Apparently, Stravinsky had started work by continuing from his notes in Sketchbooks V and VII, though Baltensperger and Meyer say that he did not make direct use of other material there. This phase of the compositional process is documented by twenty-three more loose sketch pages and a sixteen-page short score. To judge by a fragment published with the facsimile, these pages might well afford a fascinating glimpse into Stravinsky's compositional method.[14] In the fragment, which comes from an ink short score of an early version of the work, a forerunner of the alto flute tune at rehearsals 9 or 17 (notated at the top in very light pencil) is apparently interpolated within an already-composed ink segment that seems like the alto clarinet "accompaniment."

Most importantly, however, this cluster of documents shows that Stravinsky developed the piece out of the chorale in a much more literal sense than had been thought heretofore. The earlier draft of the piece *starts* with the chorale, and upon closer examination, it becomes clear (even in the facsimile) that the autograph short score at one point took the same order! Even the first page with title still shows clear traces of its former number, seven. (See Fig. 2.) Upon examining all sixteen pages of the short score, Baltensperger and Meyer found that twelve of these pages were renumbered, and then proceeded to reconstruct the original sequence of pages of the short score. It began with the chorale, which was considered a self-contained section, and is dated at the end. To this Stravinsky added the winds' "pendulum motive," the "dance section," and the transition to the chorale (rehearsals 24–39 in the 1920 version)—without the two chorale fragments, of course, since no "adumbrations" of a *final* chorale were necessary. Only at this point did the present opening "bell motive" enter, with the following "litany episodes." From here on the piece continued in the same order as its final order, up to the pick-up to rehearsal 24, at which point all of the remaining music had already been used previously. Pages 7–10 of the short score (that is, rehearsals 17–24) would have been the last four pages; significantly, the numbers on these pages were never altered. Clearly, by the time Stravinsky wrote these pages, he had decided to revise the overall form of the piece, so that pages 7–10 never occupied any other location in the piece. Here it is important to emphasize that this earlier ordering of the piece never made it to the full-score stage, and thus, from what we can tell, there was never really a question of another ending to the work. However, it did survive almost to the end of the preparation of the final short score. For some time then, Stravinsky apparently found this a compelling sequence of compositional events.

The autograph full score is of particular importance as the authentic source for the first performances. (See Fig. 3, which shows the first page of this score.) This score, and one set of parts extracted from it, were rented out first by the English firm Chester, and then, after 1923, by Editions Russes de Musique. The English notation "18 parts" and the French copyright stamp (see Fig. 3) attest to the role this score played: Koussevitsky used it with its matching instrumental parts for the first performance, and in subsequent performances it was used by Ansermet, Goosens and Stravinsky himself. Though other copies must have been made (for Stokowski in America, for example), the earliest printed score—and the only published score—of the piece was the piano reduction made by Stravinsky's friend of the early twenties, Arthur Lourié, published by Editions Russes in 1926. The first printed—but never published—version of the full score is the set of proofs that Ansermet corrected on Stravinsky's behalf in 1933. This score apparently lead to another printed full score that is presently used by Boosey and Hawkes for its rental of the 1920 version, and is, presumably, the score that Kalmus copied for their rental score and pocket score (with the Editions Russes number cut off, so one cannot be absolutely sure). To make matters more complicated still, a third printed proof score exists, which conflicts with both of the previous printed full scores; however, it apparently bears a close relationship to the autograph, incorporating some of the changes indicated there in red: for example, the first page of the autograph includes the direction *aux bassoons* written over the horn parts at the opening, and the horn music appears in bassoons in this printed score. The dates for the three printed scores are unclear, but are presumably between 1933 and 1939, when Stravinsky left for America. These three printed scores were for awhile at the Sacher Foundation, where scholars were able to examine them, but unfortunately, while the second one (the Boosey and Hawkes score) has been transferred to the Library of Congress, the first and third are no longer available, having been returned to Craft's private collection.[15]

The less-than-enthusiastic reception of the first performances of *Symphonies* is well-known.[16] Klaus Schweizer has spoken of the two-pronged strategy that Stravinsky developed to deal with this setback: on the one hand, he complained of the crass expectations of the public, claiming that this was a piece for connoisseurs, not one designed "to arouse the passions" of the public, and give immediate gratification; on the other hand, he complained of the poor quality of the performance.[17] But regardless of his public posture, as we have seen, it is clear that Stravinsky had begun privately to tinker with the piece. Craft maintains that Stravinsky was from the beginning dissatisfied with the instrumentation of the work (one wonders if the public reception might have had something to do with this), and he strongly implies that the possibility of revision was on the composer's mind.[18] That Stravinsky did not actually undertake such a revision until 1947 Craft ascribes to two factors: "lack of demand for the piece, and the circumstances of World War II, during which the publisher . . . was inactive and inaccessible."[19]

It is important to point out here that the revisions marked in red on the autograph full score are not directly connected to the major revisions that Stravinsky undertook starting in 1945 and culminating with the 1947 version. Since the autograph score was still in Europe, he was forced to undertake these later American revisions with only his *Revue Musicale* copy of the Chorale, and what, in a letter to Craft, he called a "very dirty proof of the score in the last version made before the war."[20] The inspiration for the full-scale revision of the score was finally furnished by a very practical circumstance. In 1945, Stravinsky undertook a reorchestration of the Chorale for use in a broadcast concert of *Symphony of Psalms*— to fill the half hour. He wrote to his agent:

All they [CBS] need from me are an additional few minutes; that is their problem— quite easy—but mine, to fit those minutes to the Psalm Symphony (exact timing, 21 minutes, 30 seconds), is another question. Fortunately I have the solution for it. I will begin with the final chorale of my Wind Instruments Symphony. . . . In order to avoid extra expenses, I am myself rearranging this short piece (about 2 m. 15 s.) to make it fit the general sound.[21]

According to Craft, this rescored version of the Chorale (which is also at the Sacher Foundation) "eliminates the clarinets, but employs some of the extra flutes, oboes, bassoons, and trumpets required for the *Psalms*." It appears to be this reorchestration which reawakened Stravinsky's interest in the piece. He announced his intention to revise the piece as a whole in a letter to his publisher of 7 October 1947, and completed work on 25 November, remarking that although "the barring is completely different, I have not made many changes in the music itself," an assessment with which few students of the piece would agree.[22]

This lengthy chronological account, while of at least anecdotal interest to performers of *Symphonies*, is absolutely crucial to the "wrong note" issue, for it demonstrates a compositional continuum of almost thirty years that is not easily divided. Of course, if we take Stravinsky's point of view, all problems are solved: we simply write "not to be performed" on all versions of the piece earlier than the final 1947 score. Under these circumstances, our proposed "critical edition" reprints or at least collates changes from all relevant material (that is, the early sketch pages, the additional sketches and draft for the autograph piano and orchestral score, the *Revue Musicale* score, the published piano score of 1926, the three printed proofs of the 1920 version, sketches and score of the 1945 Chorale, and the sketches and score of the final 1947 version); but essentially, all of these are "items of information" for those interested in the compositional evolution of *Symphonies*. The integrity of the final text is never really in doubt (except, perhaps, for a couple of apparent misprints in the 1947 score).

The real problems begin when we take the point of view which even Craft has espoused recently, that "the 1920 version should be corrected and performances permitted, if only for the sake of the instrumental colors" (Craft also goes on to recommend the publication of the 1945 version of the Chorale).[23] But just how are these corrections to be carried out? As Craft himself shows, for almost every piece of evidence adduced in favor of a particular correction, one may also find evidence which contradicts it. And the most serious problem in this whole business is the question of whether we can read *backwards* on the compositional continuum in order to arrive at such corrections. If it were really true that Stravinsky "had not made many changes in the music itself" (with regard to the 1947 score), perhaps we could, with impunity. But Stravinsky's "not many" is highly questionable: in fact, one can make quite a good case that the two "versions" are really two different pieces. In any event, there are still too many changes to support using the 1947 score to determine "right notes" in the 1920 score in all but the most obvious cases of misprints, for the question immediately becomes, where do we stop? Obviously we must stop somewhere short of turning the 1920 score into the 1947 score; but where?

The Theoretical Literature on *Symphonies*

Let us leave these vexing problems temporarily and review the theoretical literature to see if there is anything there which might help us. With regard to formal analysis, quite a literature has grown up around this piece. Perhaps the most well-known analysis is the one by Eric Walter White, which is difficult to fault from a methodological point of view, since it is essentially a taxonomic description.[24] Edward T. Cone's excellent and most influential analysis, on the other hand, presents a real methodology;[25] Thomas Tyra passes on much of Cone's analysis in his article, and attempts to postulate tonal areas in the piece as well.[26] Cone—to oversimplify his method somewhat—tries to hold a middle course between continuity and discontinuity as primary determinants of form in *Symphonies*. While Cone's first stage, "stratification," is marked by discontinuity ("the separation in musical space of ideas—or better, of musical areas—juxtaposed in time"), continuity is restored increasingly in the latter two stages, "interlock" and "synthesis." This "dialectical" version of Stravinskian form is admittedly attractive; problems emerge, however, when on a number of occasions (as for example with Cone's analysis of the opening Bell-Motive and the subsequent sustained chord) musical materials contrast highly with regard to register, instrumentation, articulation, etc., but may be regarded as more closely related from the point of view of harmony and motive.

In a not-so-well-known analysis, but one which is still profitable reading, Laszlo Somfai takes a more traditional European "organicist" tack. To give him proper credit, Somfai refuses to see the work only from this point of view; for him, the Chorale is both simultaneously there all the time *and* the product of the "transformation—variation—simplification of different musical materials."[27] Indeed, Somfai proposes many interesting motivic relationships in the piece. It is also interesting to note in this context the extent to which Somfai's analytical approach may parallel the compositional process: Craft says that the sketchbook which contains our Ex. 2 also "contains several variations and elaborations on this motif, showing the relationship between it and such phrases as that at one measure before 2, and again at 3, 6 and in the three measures at 11."[28]

More recently, a debate over the form of *Symphonies* has reemerged among theorists who take more extreme views. Jonathan Kramer has maintained that *Symphonies* is "probably the first moment-form piece ever composed"[29] ("moment-form," the invention of Stockhausen, may be understood as assuming radical discontinuity in the present context), while Christopher Hasty has attempted to shore up the case for continuity, and in the process is of course lead to reject discontinuity.[30]

Now, it must be admitted that this theoretical debate appears to have little to do with as mundane an issue as "wrong notes" (though these would hardly appear "mundane" to the editor of our "critical edition"). But at about the same time that Cone's analysis appeared, Arthur Berger's article appeared, marking the first successful step towards the definition of Stravinsky's pre-serial pitch language.[31]

Indeed, Berger's discussion of diatonic vs. octatonic (and particularly the latter) pitch structure in Stravinsky's music has had far-reaching influence. Pieter van den Toorn's book and Richard Taruskin's article are only two of the more recent and important results of this kind of thinking.[32] And despite Alan Forte's study of *The Rite of Spring*, which attempts to subject harmonic structure of that work to his "set complex" model, refusing in the process to accept the hegemony of the octatonic scale, van den Toorn makes a more persuasive case for viewing the *Rite* also in terms of the octatonic.[33]

In the present case—*Symphonies*, that is—there can be no doubt of the importance of the octatonic. The particular octatonic in question is the one which may be thought of as the union of C-sharp and D diminished-seventh chords. Subcollections of this scale (at this transposition) include the five-note collection of the Bell-Motive, which might be thought of as a G^7 chord with B-flat; or the five-note sustained chord that follows it (this is the source of the earlier criticism of Cone); or the flute/clarinet duo motive; or the first chord of the Chorale. Similarly, larger articulations of G, B-flat, E tonal centers (obviously latent in this scale, since it contains the major and minor triad over each of these degrees) are important to the piece. This also brings up the controversy over the ending: Somfai reads the first Chorale chord as an inversion of $G7\flat9$, and thus the last chord marks the reaching of the "tonic."[34] Even van den Toorn is willing to read this chord as a "dominant" in the last bars, maintaining that it acquires the "feel" of a dominant "retroactively."[35] Hasty, on the other hand, reads the piece as ending on E (clearly the most prominent bass tone), with the C in the bass as a "Debussean added sixth, ending the work with a gesture of the opening."[36]

The octatonic has implications for our interpretation of the sketches as well. Craft notes that our Ex. 2 shows that the Bell-Motive first occured to Stravinsky a fourth lower than he actually used it;[37] could the composer not have purposely transposed it into the G tonal center (and consequently the "correct" octatonic) after having firmed up the chorale material?

Unfortunately, saying that a piece is essentially octatonic is (as yet, at least) hardly as powerfully predictive a statement as saying that a piece is a twelve-tone piece, where we might argue about details of segmentation, but at least we can account for most or even all of the pitches. That is, from the general statement that *Symphonies* is an octatonic piece, one cannot claim to be able to infer reliably the rules of syntax for local chord-to-chord motion in this piece. Nevertheless, when historical evidence fails in the assessment of possible "wrong notes," I would probably tend to favor octatonic pitch collections. But of course this general preference would be tempered by close examination of local pitch structure, to see what context might recommend. Thus, as a general working method, we shall first examine historical documentary evidence (to the extent that the documents are available), and then supplement this with analytical work when the historical evidence is either lacking or inconclusive.

The "Wrong Notes" in the 1920 Score of *Symphonies*

A number of alleged "wrong notes" have been discussed by Craft, both in "On the *Symphonies of Winds*" and *Stravinsky in Pictures and Documents*. In addition, a list of errata for the 1920 score has recently been proposed by L. Keating Johnson.[38] The order of our "wrong notes" will follow the sixteen alleged pitch errors on Johnson's list, which also incorporates the ones that Craft has discussed. Each numbered paragraph begins with an italicized paraphrase of Johnson's directions for changes; unless otherwise noted, all rehearsal numbers refer to the 1920 score.

As explained above, because the 1920 and 1947 versions are so different, any editorial alterations of the 1920 version should be supported by documents pertaining directly to that edition. If only the 1947 version supports a particular correction, it is usually preferable to let the 1920 score stand as is, though on some occasions it is possible to argue that the 1947 version corrects an obvious "error" in the 1920 version. In general I have refrained from making close calls below, preferring instead to present all evidence, and leave the final decision to the reader.

1. *Rehearsal 3, fourth bar: second beat in Clarinet II should be B-flat.* This proposed correction is treated by Craft both in "On the *Symphonies*" (p. 453) and *Pictures and Documents* (p. 228). Ansermet is the one who raised the question, and in *Pictures and Documents* Craft says that "Stravinsky verified [concert] A-flat as the correct pitch." Here we can look at the contemporaneous piano score, which indeed confirms the A-flat. When we check this spot in the facsimile of the autograph full score, we find that the B-flat is absolutely clear; thus there is now no doubt that it is correct, and that the flat was simply left out by the printer.

2. *Rehearsal 9: Alto Flute's second note should be C-natural.* The next correction is one of the most difficult to deal with. Craft treats this in "On the *Symphonies*," in which he quotes an early sketch of the flute motive, which verifies the natural in both places. But the autographs of both short score and full score require a sharp on the first (concert) G, and a natural on the second (Craft goes on to say that the three proof scores also require this).[39] Since Lourié's piano score also corresponds to the 1920 score, we can say that all contemporaneous sources are in agreement that this is not an error—i.e., that the pitch should be sharp and then natural. The problem with this conclusion is first of all that the 1947 score corrects them both to naturals, that rehearsals 9 and 17 are inconsistent in the 1920 score (the sharp is missing from rehearsal 17), and that the 1947 score renders them consistent. (Moreover, Stravinsky confirms the two naturals in the 1947 score in a letter to Ansermet.[40]) Because the change in the 1947 score is corroborated in the letter to Ansermet, one might even argue (as Johnson presumably does) that this is one of the rare instances of an "error" in the 1920 score corrected in 1947. Yet, from the structural point of view, the sharp/natural alteration seems superior, paralleling as it does the succeeding clarinet motive. And after all, the resulting 0347 (major/minor) tetrachord is one of the essential octatonic subsets of the piece (recall, for example, the Bell-Motive). Thus one might also argue for leaving the sharp at rehearsal 9 and entering one at rehearsal 17 for consistency. Unfortunately, there is no documentary evidence to support either of these alternative corrections.

3. *Rehearsal 9: Alto Clarinet's first note should be B-natural.* In fact, (written) B-flat occurs in the 1920 score, the Lourié piano score, and the autographs of the short score and full score as well, though there is an earlier sketch that contains (concert) E. Once again, Stravinsky himself confirms the concert E found in the analogous place in the 1947 score in the letter to Ansermet cited above. As with error 2, the only support for changing this is the 1947 version. But unlike error 2, there are no pressing analytical reasons here to support such a change.

4. *Rehearsal 11, third bar: Alto Clarinet's second note should be B-flat, but its fourth note should be B-natural.* Although Johnson's presumed "missing flat" might indeed be a error, it is also missing in the autographs of the short score and full score. Once again, the only evidence for this change is the reading of the 1947 score.

5. *Rehearsal 14: first note in Flute II should be B.* In this case, the 1947 version retains the flute part just as it was in the 1920 version, but the autograph of the 1920 version does in fact have the B-natural, as does Lourié's piano score. Thus, documentary evidence clearly favors this change.

6. *Rehearsal 17, second bar: second note should be C-natural.* This is likewise verified by Stravinsky with respect to the 1947 score, but here the autographs of the 1920 scores are not in agreement. The autograph of the short score has all naturals right at rehearsal 17, and merely uses a repeat sign to notate the next bar (thus it is clearly inconsistent with the parallel passage at rehearsal 9). The autograph of the full score, on the other hand, corresponds to the printed score. Due to the agreement of 1947 score and autograph (1920) short score, I would tend to favor this correction.

7. *Rehearsal 17, fourth bar: Alto Flute's second note could be E.* Again, the E in the analogous spot in the 1947 score is the only evidence in favor of this, and thus this correction is questionable. (This is one of those cases where Ansermet obviously preferred the older version; in the letter cited above, Stravinsky says that the B of the new score is correct—not the G-sharp of the old score.)

8. *Rehearsal 19, fifth bar: Alto Clarinet's last note should be G-sharp.* Here, Johnson cites the 1947 score (which indeed does have the sharp), but more importantly, the parallel spot four bars after rehearsal 14. In fact, the autographs of both short score and full score do have the sharp, so it is clear that the "missing sharp" is a printer's error.

9. *Rehearsal 22, third bar: first note in Clarinet I (in A) should be B.* The fact that the sounding G-sharp occurs in the 1947 score, and that this clarinet D overlapping of the Bell-Motive tune is also missing from the piano score, makes one think that the apparent D might well be a typical printer's ledger-line error. The autograph full score confirms that suspicion; the B is absolutely clear.

10. *Rehearsal 26: add Ds to agree with 1947 version.* Again, this one is supported only by the 1947 version; there is no other evidence to support this correction.

11. *Rehearsal 30, starting on the 2nd bar, up to rehearsal 32: change all low B-flats to E.* Stravinsky has written beyond the lower limit of the English horn, so obviously something has to be done: this solution works without doing any violence to the harmony. The parallel spot in the 1947 score is so different that it offers little assistance, and the documents are of no help in this instance.

12. *Rehearsal 32: third note in Trombone II should be G-sharp.* This again is supported only by the 1947 score, but in the letter to Ansermet, Stravinsky has an interesting explanation for preferring the G-sharp: he likes the consistent major thirds thus produced in the trombones, in opposition to the minor thirds in the trumpets. However, G-natural was not a mistake in the first version; it is quite clear in the autograph.

13. *Rehearsal 40, third bar: Trumpet III should begin with A-natural.* At this point we begin to deal with questionable pitches in the Chorale, which Craft has treated, and for which we have considerable (but as usual, conflicting) documentary evidence. The story on this particular problem starts with Ansermet writing to Stravinsky, asking if the A-natural in the twelfth bar of the Chorale should not really be an A-sharp. As Craft remarks, Ansermet obviously wants an exact sequence of the previous phrase.[41] In fact, Ansermet thought so highly of the sharp that he inserted it into the second set of proofs for the 1920 score, it was passed on to the final proofs, and hence we have it here. But although Craft finds a sketch with the A-sharp in Stravinsky's hand, there is no evidence of it in the autograph short score or full score, the *Revue Musicale* score, or in Lourié's piano score; and Stravinsky took it out of the 1947 version, probably because he was working from the *Revue Musicale* score. The right note is clearly A-natural, not A-sharp.

14. *Rehearsal 40, third bar: Tuba's last note should be E-natural.* This one likewise has a long and involved history which Craft discusses.[42] An earlier sketch of this passage, as well as the autographs of short score and full score all have E-natural. Moreover, according to Craft, the three proofs of the 1920 score also have E-natural, and Stravinsky cancelled the flat in his copy of the piano score. Yet for some curious reason he never cancelled the flat in his copy of the *Revue Musicale* score, from which he worked in orchestrating the 1947 version, and so this E-flat—which is clearly an error from any musical/structural point of view—may be found there as well.

If we move to the upper voices of this chord, we note an error which Johnson has neglected to put on his list. The F-sharp in Trumpet III is in the 1920 score, and the autographs as well. Craft is certain that the right note is F-natural, noting that Stravinsky himself corrected the F-sharp to F-natural in his copy of the Debussy Album. Consequently, the natural appears in the 1947 score. Of course, one might ask when Stravinsky made this correction, since he used the Debussy Album score in his orchestration of the 1947 version.

15 and 16. *Last note in next to the last bar should be G in English Horn, C in Trombone.* Johnson cites a letter from Ansermet, which Craft discusses; Craft claims that both English Horn and Trombone should have concert C here.[43] The autograph of the full score, on the other hand, has (written) F-sharp in English Horn, and faint notes in the autograph of the short score, may well support this, though this conjecture would require further study; Craft's opinion notwithstanding, the documents do not support this change.

This concludes our discussion of wrong notes in *Symphonies*, though needless to say, this is one small contribution to a project that remains incomplete at present, for there are surely other textual problems in the 1920 Boosey and Hawkes score—a score that was really only a proof for a published version that never appeared. In undertaking the larger project, it is important to emphasize that we must continue to approach each wrong note on a case-by-case basis. Furthermore, the only useful list of errata is a thoroughly annotated one, since, in a number of cases, there are no cut-and-dry answers regarding the integrity of the score. In such problematic cases, it is vital that the conductor have all available information on textual variants, in order to be able to make the most informed decisions possible.

Some Thoughts on Stravinsky's Compositional Method and Its Implications for Analysis

In closing I should like to summarize briefly what we have learned of Stravinsky's compositional method in our study of these scores. The composition of *Symphonies* took place in what Baltensperger and Meyer read as four stages: (1) the writing of isolated, disconnected sketches, some not associated with any work in particular, (2) the collation of these, as well as their editing and connection into a single short score, (3) the writing of the full score of 1920, and finally (4) the tentative revisions of this score, and ultimately the full-scale revision of 1947.[44] Though somewhat more complicated than is the case with other pieces by Stravinsky that do not involve two different versions, this method proves to be typical for him. In a broader context, Volker Scherliess has reported as follows on Stravinsky's compositional method in general:

> Stravinsky's compositional method consisted essentially of three stages: The first ideas were preserved on loose sketch pages, covers of envelopes, or whatever else they might have been written down on (in the case of "The Rite of Spring" for example, a telegram and a restaurant bill offer material for the piece); then he assembled the single sketches into a piano score, usually on large paper, books or notebooks, which he sometimes ruled himself with his "Stravigor" (this is not an incidental detail, since it shows us that while ruling out the page, he was already pretty clear about the instrumentation, approximate length, etc. of the passage in question). In the third stage, the various single elements are brought together and written out in more or less final form, often with many changes of order, deletions, and interpolations.[45]

More provocatively, Scherliess continues as follows:

> In general, the following picture emerges: Stravinsky writes various sketches, from short motives, to longer sections in context. Here we are speaking of single elements that he can manipulate freely: he can place them in various orders, repeat or eliminate them, join them together or break them apart, shorten them or lengthen them, etc. His work method thus deals with *ordering* and *combining* material. Therein lies the key to understanding Stravinsky's music [. . .]: Its primary characteristic is not development of a motivic seed and growth to some organic whole, as is the case in the romantic tradition (and in the New Viennese School); its analytical description should not include such words as line, development, spinning out, etc.—all words associated with Goethe's notion of organicism that was taken up by countless artists and aestheticians. The metaphor for Stravinsky's composition is not the "plant," but rather the construction kit. Bluntly expressed, the artist not as gardener, but as building engineer.[46]

Scherliess goes on to relate this compositional method to the "montage principle" that one sees so prominently in the visual arts of the first part of this century.

Indeed, we have seen this montage principle at work in Stravinsky's manipulation of small details, and even in his manipulation of the overall form of the piece.

Clearly, a "poietic analysis" of this piece, as Jean-Jacques Nattiez might call the compositional history presented earlier, is useful to have, at least as a first step in understanding the work.[47] Unfortunately, its relationship to the "immanent work"—the work viewed from a purely structural perspective—is problematic at best. Still, it seems likely that we will have to rework analytical tools that were fashioned to deal with the great tradition of Austro-Germanic organicist music (approximately from Bach to Schoenberg) in order to get to the essence of Stravinsky's work. Certainly "organic" connections are there, but they enter as part of the "editing" stage of composition, as Stravinsky superimposes them upon elements of the piece that were originally conceived in isolation, with little thought of a common "work" (cf. Craft's testimony, above). Indeed, could it even be that some of these "organic connections" discussed in the analytical literature might rather be general stylistic traits of Stravinsky's musical language, rather than piece-specific attributes of the material of *Symphonies*? Such a question can hardly be answered here, but any future work on *Symphonies* would certainly profit from considering the piece in that broader context. While it may be too much to hope that the poietic view of *Symphonies* might serve to narrow the focus and methodology of a potential analysis, or even to eliminate certain analytical strategies as inappropriately *a priori*, the complex story surrounding the composition of *Symphonies* certainly gives one pause for thought: it seems hardly coincidental that *Symphonies*, which took shape in such a protracted and complex manner, has engendered the most wide-ranging—and conflicting—analytical literature of any Stravinsky composition.

NOTES

The present article is a synthesis of two previous papers: "The 'Wrong Notes' in Stravinsky's *Symphonies of Winds*," presented at the CBDNA National Conference in Evanston, 1986, and "Compositional Method in Stravinsky's *Symphonies of Winds*: A Report from the Paul Sacher Foundation," presented at the Fortieth Anniversary of the Eastman Wind Ensemble in Rochester, 1992.

1. L. Keating Johnson, "*Symphonies of Wind Instruments*: The History, Orchestration, Formal Organization, and Suggestions toward Performing Either the 1920 Original or 1947 Revised Edition" (Washington State University: unpublished paper, 1986).

2. André Baltensperger and Felix Meyer, eds., *Igor Strawinsky:* Symphonies d'Instruments à Vent*: Faksimileausgabe des Particells und der Partitur der Erstfassung (1920)* (Winterthur: Amadeus Verlag, 1991). I wish to thank Dr. Paul Sacher, as well as the editors of the facsimile, André Baltensperger and Felix Meyer, for their generosity in providing me with these documents as soon as they were published. The reproductions in the present article were photographed from plates included in the facsimile edition, with the kind permission of the Sacher Foundation, and much of the present discussion of chronology is indebted to Baltensperger's and Meyer's research while preparing the critical introduction to the facsimile edition, as well as to discussions that I had with them in the spring of 1991 in Basel.

3. Igor Stravinsky and Robert Craft, *Themes and Episodes* (New York: Alfred A. Knopf, 1966), p. 29.

4. Baltensperger and Meyer, *Faksimileausgabe*, p. 35. Robert Craft also transcribes a sketch that contains the music of our Example 1b in Vera Stravinsky and Robert Craft, *Stravinsky in Pictures and Documents* (New York: Simon and Schuster, 1978), p. 227.

5. Eric Walter White, *Stravinsky: The Composer and His Works* (Berkeley and Los Angeles: University of California Press, 1969), p. 253.

6. For a facsimile of Stravinsky's sketch, see Robert Craft, "On the *Symphonies of Wind Instruments*," *Perspectives of New Music* 22 (1983–84): 449 (reprinted as Appendix E in Robert Craft, ed., *Stravinsky: Selected Correspondence*, vol. 2 [New York: Knopf, 1984]), or Baltensperger and Meyer, *Faksimileausgabe*, p. 39.

7. Craft, p. 449.

8. Baltensperger and Meyer, *Faksimileausgabe*, p. 28.

9. Ibid., p. 39.

10. Ibid., p. 29.

11. V. Stravinsky and Craft, *Stravinsky in Pictures and Documents*, p. 225; see pp. 222–29, in general, for important information on *Symphonies*.

12. Ibid., p. 224.

13. Igor Stravinsky, *Chronicle of My Life* (London: Victor Gollancz, 1936), p. 148.

14. Baltensperger and Meyer, *Faksimileausgabe*, p. 40; Craft published a similar sketch in *Stravinsky in Pictures and Documents*, plate 9 (opposite p. 240).

15. See Stephen Walsh, *The Music of Stravinsky* (London and New York: Routledge, 1988), p. 282, n. 21, the main source of the present account.

16. See Baltensperger and Meyer, *Faksimileausgabe*, pp. 41–43, for quotations from the musical press.

17. Klaus Schweizer, "...nicht zur Befriedigung sentimentaler Bedürfnisse: Anmerkungen zu Igor Stravinskys 'Bläsersinfonien,'" in *Analysen: Beiträge zu einer Problemgeschichte des Komponierens*, Beihefte zur Archiv für Musikwissenschaft (Stuttgart: Steiner Verlag, 1984), p. 377.

18. We may note parenthetically that it is at this point in the chronology—the early twenties—that the first "wrong-note" questions arrive from Ansermet, although he would have more queries after performing the 1947 score as well.

19. V. Stravinsky and Craft, *Stravinsky in Pictures and Documents*, p. 228.

20. Ibid.

21. Craft, *Stravinsky: Selected Correspondence*, 2: 457.

22. V. Stravinsky and Craft, *Stravinsky in Pictures and Documents*, p. 229.

23. Craft, "On the Symphonies," p. 454.

24. White, *Stravinsky*, pp. 254ff.

25. Edward T. Cone, "Stravinsky: The Progress of a Method," in *Perspectives on Schoenberg and Stravinsky*, rev. ed., ed. Benjamin Boretz and Edward T. Cone (New York: Norton, 1972), pp. 155–64.

26. Thomas Tyra, "An Analysis of Stravinsky's *Symphonies of Wind Instruments*," *Journal of Band Research* 8, no. 2 (spring 1972): 6–39.

27. Laszlo Somfai, "*Symphonies of Wind Instruments (1920)*: Observations on Stravinsky's Organic Construction," *Studia Musicologica* 14 (1972): 355–83.

28. V. Stravinsky and Craft, *Stravinsky in Pictures and Documents*, p. 226.

29. Jonathan Kramer, "Moment Form in Twentieth Century Music," *The Musical Quarterly* 64, no. 2 (1978): 177–94.

30. Christopher Hasty, "On the Problem of Succession and Continuity in Twentieth-Century Music," *Music Theory Spectrum* 8 (1986): 58–74.

31. Arthur Berger, "Problems of Pitch Organization in Stravinsky," in *Perspectives on Schoenberg and Stravinsky*, rev. ed., ed. Benjamin Boretz and Edward T. Cone (New York: Norton, 1972), pp. 123–54.

32. Pieter van den Toorn, *The Music of Igor Stravinsky* (New Haven: Yale University Press, 1983), especially pp. 337–44; Richard Taruskin, "Chernomor to Kashchei: Harmonic Sorcery; or, Stravinsky's 'Angle,'" *Journal of the Americal Musicological Society* 38, no. 1 (spring 1985): 72–142.

33. Allen Forte, *The Harmonic Organization of the "Rite of Spring"* (New Haven: Yale University Press, 1978). Forte, however, has become steadily more interested in the octatonic in his more recent work; see his article "Harmonic Syntax and Voice Leading in Stravinsky's Early Music" in *Confronting Stravinsky: Man, Musician and Modernist*, ed. Jann Pasler, pp. 95–129 (Berkeley, Los Angeles and London: University of California Press, 1986). For a particularly effective introduction to van den Toorn's ideas, see his article "Octatonic Pitch Structure in Stravinsky," also in *Confronting Stravinsky*, pp. 130–56.

34. Somfai, "*Symphonies*," p. 360.

35. Van den Toorn, *Stravinsky*, p. 343.

36. Hasty, "Succession," p. 69.

37. V. Stravinsky and Craft, *Stravinsky in Pictures and Documents*, p. 227.

38. See n. 1.

39. Craft, "On the *Symphonies*," p. 454.

40. Craft, *Stravinsky: Selected Correspondence*, 1: 230.

41. Craft, "On the *Symphonies*," p. 452.

42. Ibid., p. 451.

43. Ibid., p. 453.

44. Baltensperger and Meyer, *Faksimileausgabe*, p. 28.

45. Volker Scherliess, *Igor Strawinsky und seine Zeit* (Laaber: Laaber Verlag, 1983), pp. 157ff.

46. Ibid., p. 160.

47. Jean-Jacques Nattiez, *Music and Discourse*, trans. C. Abbate (Princeton: Princeton University Press, 1990).

Ex. 1a

Ex. 1b

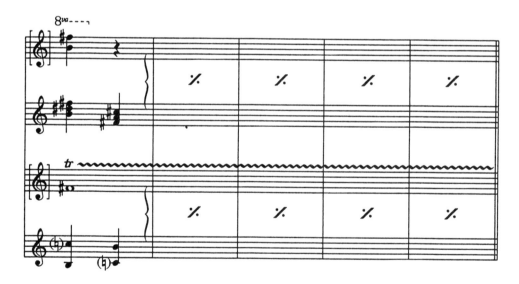

Example 1: Baltensperger and Meyer, reconstruction from Stravinsky's autograph short score.

Ex. 2

Example 2: Sketchbook V, diplomatic transcription of first sketch of "Bell Motive".

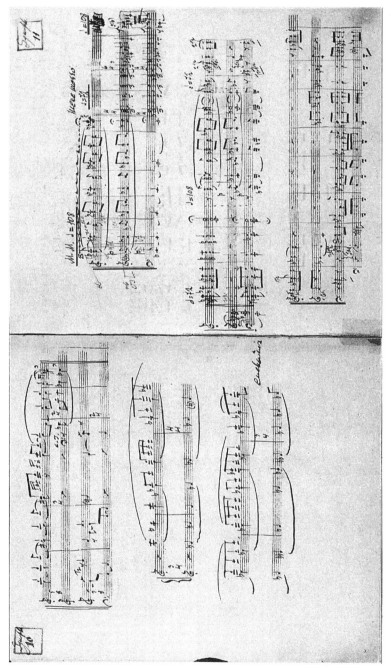

Figure 1: Autograph short score, p. 11. Reproduced by kind permission of the Sacher Foundation.

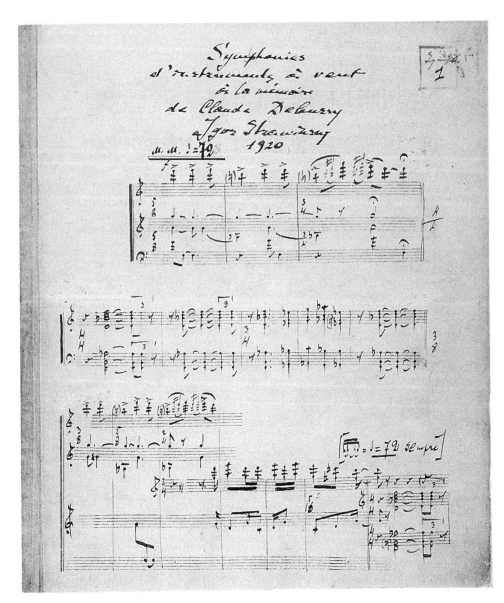

Figure 2: Autograph short score, p. 1. *Reproduced by kind permission of the Sacher Foundation.*

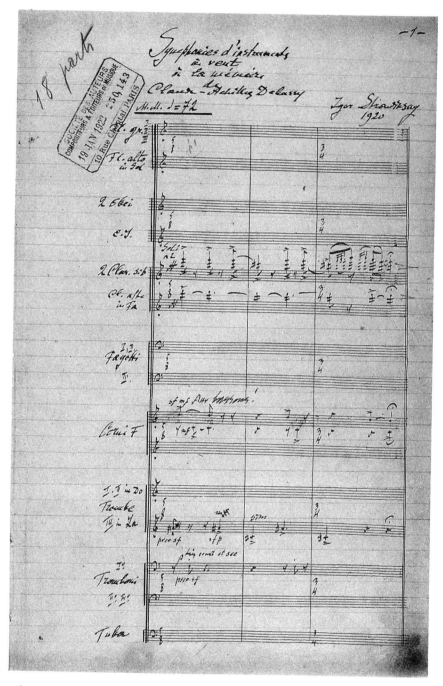

Figure 3: Autograph full score, p. 1. *Reproduced by kind permission of the Sacher Foundation.*

Sousa Marches

Principles for Historically Informed Performance

FRANK P. BYRNE, JR.

IN performing marches of John Philip Sousa, we face twin challenges of interpreting notation and recreating an unwritten performance tradition. Although marches were conceived as functional music for moving groups of people or soldiers from one place to another, Sousa elevated this form into the realm of art. The phenomenon of what Frederick Fennell calls the "sit-down concert band" provided performers capable of giving this music its due, and Sousa provided music with which to do it.[1] Functional music became concert music.[2]

To hear Sousa's marches performed by his band was memorable—not only to hear them interpreted by their composer but to observe the nature of his interpretations.[3] Perhaps the most surprising revelation is that Sousa did not perform his marches as they were published. Dr. Mark Hindsley (former Director of Bands at the University of Illinois) recounted that "Magical wand waving it was, and the result was magical music. Sounds, particularly in the first trio, that I never knew were there from the printed parts."[4] Sousa's performances were unique to his band, and these unpublished techniques have faded from the corporate memory of our American band heritage. To complicate matters, there has been a dearth of scholarly documentation on this subject.

Documenting Sousa Performance Practices

A number of Sousa Band members are sources for this information. August Helmecke (known as "Gus" to his many friends) was Sousa's bass drummer for twenty-two years.[5] His playing has been credited by Sousa Band members as a vital element of the Band's exciting performance style.[6] Of Helmecke's musicianship, Sousa testified:

> The average layman does not realize the importance of the bass drummer to a band. . . . I sometimes think that no band can be greater than its bass drummer, because it is given to him, more than to any person except the director, to reflect the rhythm and spirit of the composition.[7]

In an August 1950 article in *The Etude* entitled "How Sousa Played His Marches," August Helmecke wrote that:

141

People have no idea how Sousa wanted his marches played, because the tricks and effects that brought them to such vivid life under the Big Boss' own direction never got marked into the scores. . . . the notes alone can give you but the barest skeleton of what a Sousa March can be. . . . In some of the Marches, for instance, not a single bar of rest is written for cornets and clarinets (this was done so that the Marches could be played by small bands); but when Sousa led his own band in those works, he'd simply wave the unwanted brasses into silence at his own discretion.[8]

This practice was also noted by Dr. Raymond Dvorak, former Director of Bands at the University of Wisconsin: "To his men he would say, 'Any band can play these printed arrangements the same as we, but we shall play them differently.' And that is exactly what his band did but none of this was ever written down on paper."[9]

One of the most interesting commentaries on Sousa's performance style came from Dr. Frank Simon, Sousa's solo cornetist 1914–1921 and a well-known authority on Sousa's music:

You don't hear the dynamics as they should be, the accented notes . . . the differences in the volume of tone . . . where the brass drop out . . . and where the clarinet section will drop down an octave, then they reverse it and, oh there are so many things that he did to make it colorful. Not to make it just a march where you go through and play it . . . he made it colorful . . . he doctored them up, in other words, to make them interesting to the public . . . and that's why he became so famous. Not only for the marches but HOW he played the marches.[10]

In a rare account of a discussion with the composer on this subject, Sousa flutist Joe Lefter related the following exchange:

I asked him one time why he changed his music when he played it in the marches. When it's marked loud, why he didn't play it loud. He told me, he says [sic], "Mr. Lefter, if everybody played it the way it's written, then everybody's band would sound like Sousa's Band so we make some changes now and then just to make it a little bit different."[11]

Even musicians outside his Band noted the Sousa style. Fellow band composer Karl King wrote the following in a 1946 letter to a colleague:

Even in his marches Sousa pulled some strains down to a whisper which always made the last strain sound that much heavier by contrasts [sic]. Also Sousa had a few little tricks on *pianissimos* that I observed and wondered why other leaders who heard him didn't get "hep" to how he did it but apparently they didn't. Like the first strains of trios. Brass laid out entirely. Clarinets played but dropped it down an octave lower than written, etc.[12]

To address inevitable questions about consistency, there almost certainly must have been some refinements of Sousa's interpretations during the nearly forty-year history of his Band. However, there is a stronger case for largely standardized and consistent interpretations.

Edmund Wall (solo clarinetist of the Sousa Band for the last six years of its existence) noted that "one of the first things a new man in the Sousa Band had to learn was what march strains to play an octave lower (in the clarinets), or what strains not to play in at all (brass players)."[13] Such memorization would be impossible if the interpretive scheme changed on a random basis. In a separate interview,

Wall said, "Once he established a pattern that he liked, he let it alone."[14] Sousa percussionist John Heney also related that the march interpretations were the same all years he played with the Sousa Band, and that these interpretations were passed down from earlier bandsmen.[15]

The consistency of Sousa's interpretations may also be confirmed by the corroboration between markings in performance parts used by the Sousa Band and written accounts by former Sousa Band members, notably Dr. Frank Simon.[16] While Sousa may have, on rare occasions, adjusted the interpretation, the evidence leans toward a consistent scheme rather than an impulsive approach.

Questions Regarding the Interpretation of the Data

Having established the existence of Sousa performance practices, we face a philosophical question. How does one interpret this music when the score is only the half-way point to achieving a performance similar to what Sousa would have conducted? Leo Steinberg addresses a similar interpretive dilemma in writing about the frescoes of Michelangelo:

> There are, after all, two ways to inflict injustice on a great work of art: by overinterpreting it, or by underestimating its meaning. If unverifiable interpretations are rightly regarded as dangerous, there is as much danger of misrepresentation in restrictive assertions that feel safe only because they say little.[17]

For years wind conductors and musicians may have underestimated the meaning and the value of Sousa marches. By learning techniques Sousa employed in his own performances, we may discover that this music possesses more subtlety and sophistication than we previously gave it credit.

In *The Composer's Advocate*, Erich Leinsdorf expresses his conviction that "composers have very clear ideas about how they want their works performed, and they are more likely than anyone else to be correct."[18] Leinsdorf quotes from Johann Mattheson's 1739 publication, *Der Vollkommene Capellmeister*: "He who has never learned how the originator himself would like to have it done will hardly do well but will take away the vitality and charm, often in such manner that an author, were he to hear it, might be hard put to recognize his own work."[19]

These are essential concepts in the performance of Sousa and music of other composers. No matter how great our devotion to the score, its limitations place demands upon us, as Arthur Mendel asserts in *Modern Musical Scholarship*:

> The performer is invited—indeed compelled—by the incompleteness of even the most explicit notation, to put the stamp of his personality on a performance. . . . If today no two performances even of works notated in such minute detail as, say, those of Schoenberg are the same, how much more widely must performances have varied when [notation was less specific].[20]

Leinsdorf concurs:

> Nevertheless, however well a conductor observes a composer's stated desires and the
> traditions of his time, there are still areas in which he must fall back upon his own
> judgement. For this reason it is essential to understand where interpretation begins
> and where it ends.[21]

Here lies the dilemma of any historically informed endeavor: what is a musical
"original" and what may be considered "authentic"? Discussing the interpretation
of Beethoven symphonies, Richard Taruskin writes, "There are three schools of
thought on this matter: one holds that the musical work is the score, another that it
is whatever the first performance was, and a third holds the question absurd."[22]

In *Authenticity in Music*, Raymond Leppard addresses the tension between
historically-informed performance and interpretive freedom:

> Research has contributed wonderfully to illuminating and giving greater insight and
> freedom to the bringing of older music back to life. On the other hand, it has
> sometimes resulted in restriction and a sort of mean-spirited isolationism promoting
> the formation of musical cults. Their exclusivity has in some cases seemed willfully to
> impede access to . . . the music . . . just as religious cults exclude those outside their
> beliefs from their sort of salvation.[23]

Our knowledge of Sousa's performance practices is significant but not all-
encompassing. It is compelling, convincing, even convicting at times, yet we cannot
claim absolute knowledge. In *The Journal of Musicological Research*, Standley Howell
writes that

> Because of this inescapable element of uncertainty, some music historians have begun
> to wonder if the entire historical performance movement is misdirected. But our
> inability to achieve absolute authenticity should not prevent us from trying to under-
> stand as much as we can. Historically-oriented performances can afford real insights
> into period musical style as long as we remember that all such efforts are experimental
> and subject to criticism and eventual revision.[24]

We seek the vigor to search for every shred of data and the courage to resist the
urge to substitute our preferences for those of the composer. We must commit
ourselves, in Taruskin's words, to "a preference for the 'facts' over anyone's
designs . . . or, put another way, an ostensible preference for value-free 'what'
questions over value-laden 'why' questions."[25]

In our pursuit of the 'what' questions, we rely almost entirely on "first person"
experience in the belief that those who performed with and who heard Sousa's
Band are more likely than we to know these traditions, whether or not these
traditions agree with our preconceptions about the nature of the music. Further,
we seek a clear delineation between fact and opinion, recognizing the value of each
while requiring boundaries between them.

Documenting the Nature of the Practices

To document the nature of the Sousa performance changes, we can consult the following sources:

1. original Sousa manuscripts and published first editions;
2. performance parts with markings by Sousa musicians;
3. information from former Sousa Band members and other sources;
4. recordings of the Sousa Band.

Although Sousa's performance practices were not documented in published editions, a discussion of manuscript and published scores will point out additional problems apart from the absence of performance changes. There is evidence that Sousa created full scores for virtually all his marches; for Sousa's 136–plus marches,[26] only fifty or so full band scores have survived intact.[27] Those which have survived provide a mixed bag of information.

Sousa was reported to have carried manuscript paper at all times in the event a theme came to him.[28] In the preparation of his marches, the exact chronology is not certain, but it is believed Sousa first made sketches of the melodies, next may have prepared a short score, and then the full score.[29] Reports indicate that he could copy and orchestrate a score vertically (one measure at a time for all parts) rather than completing each part individually.[30] This is questionable based on inconsistencies found within his scores, for Sousa did not always transfer certain markings, dynamics, and articulations into every part.[31] August Helmecke explained why:

> Sousa wrote for performance, not for publication. In odd moments on trains, in hotel rooms, or shipboard, he'd simply jot down his immortal themes, hand them over to the band copyist, and then snap right into action on them. Consequently, when they came to be published, nothing but the notes got onto the printed page.[32]

Haste may have been one contributing factor to discrepancies within Sousa's manuscript scores, but other inconsistencies between instrumental parts in dynamics, articulations, and use of accents seem to contradict the idea that Sousa created the scores vertically. It is possible that the full scores in ink were completed at more than one sitting. Upon resuming work, Sousa may have neglected to transfer some details into adjacent parts.[33]

Regarding published editions, those printed within Sousa's lifetime are most reliable, but even these are problematic. Discrepancies indicate that published parts may have been engraved from manuscript instrumental parts, as opposed to having been engraved directly from the score. This procedure would also have allowed multiple engravers to work simultaneously.

First editions remain a valuable resource, if only as a starting point for preparing a modern edition. Two instrumental parts in these editions are particularly important: Solo Cornet and Solo Clarinet. Since the marches were originally published with neither full nor condensed scores, these parts were used by conductors and

Example 1: *The Fairest of the Fair*, excerpt.

usually include the most correct markings.[34] In some cases, however, variations between the parts are so great that the editor must reach a conclusion based on his or her own musical judgment. Consider the variety of phrasings published in four instrumental parts of *The Fairest of the Fair* (Ex. 1):[35]

In the absence of critically-edited full scores or other independent sources for verification, most conductors are unaware that contemporary editions (even those which claim "As played by the Sousa Band") may contain bogus instrumental parts not composed or performed by Sousa.[36] This is demonstrated in a comparison between the original 1897 John Church edition of *The Stars and Stripes Forever!* and the 1951 edition published by Theodore Presser. This comparison was motivated by the discovery that cornet parts in the 1951 edition had been distributed and marked differently than those in the 1897 edition. The 1897 solo cornet part is re-marked "1st" in the 1951 edition. Similarly, the 1897 first cornet part is re-marked "2nd" in the 1951 edition and the second and third cornet part is simply re-marked "3rd."[37]

A complete survey of the instrumentation reveals the full extent of the changes. Instrumentation was compared from four sources: the original Sousa manuscript score, the manuscript "original parts" (believed to be the first set of instrumental parts, although not done in Sousa's hand) in the University of Illinois library, the 1897 Church edition, and the 1951 Presser edition. The comparison reveals that the 1951 edition contains ten new instrumental parts which, either in whole or in part, were not written by Sousa. The most blatant of these changes is the addition of two entirely new trumpet parts. These contain the now well-known trumpet flourishes in the trio, yet those lines are found nowhere in Sousa's original score, nor in the 1897 edition, nor in the encore books of the Sousa Band.

The motivation for expanding the instrumentation of Sousa marches in the 1950s has two possible explanations: first, it would have allowed the marches in public domain to be recopyrighted in the new edition.[38] Second, it would have allowed the publication to conform to a "standardized" band instrumentation, as was popular then with several band organizations, not the least being the American Bandmasters Association.[39]

Variations in newer march editions were noticed by former Sousa Band members. William Gens, President of the Sousa Band Fraternal Society, describing the Society's ninth annual meeting, reported that:

> Dr. Franko Goldman attended as a guest of Dr. Simon and asked us all to do everything in our power to stop publishers from murdering Sousa marches. It is a crime what they are doing to make a sale. We should all refuse to buy, play, or handle anything but those from the original publishers. Be careful when you buy that you get the copies you know are genuine.[40]

Three additional points: first, the physical size of these small march editions put limitations on the amount of information which could be included on the page. As Frederick Fennell observed, "Art form nuance and stylistic expression found little space (and little place) in the early quick-step format."[41] Second, in some earlier marches, Sousa was grateful to have them published at all, having been paid $35.00 outright for *The Washington Post*,[42] and was hardly in a position to control publication details. Finally, Sousa may have been relatively unconcerned with publication because he intended to perfect the interpretation when on the podium. Sousa did not wish that other bands perform this music exactly as his band did.[43]

Performance parts with markings by Sousa musicians can be found in the Sousa Band encore books, now in the Marine Band library.[44] The encore books are bound volumes containing approximately one hundred selections which were used at every performance. Most Sousa marches performed on his concerts were encores rather than printed program selections.[45]

Although it was not common practice to mark these parts, the few markings which do exist have high correlation to other sources: accounts from Sousa Band members and recordings conducted by Sousa Band members. The players' reluctance to mark performance changes can perhaps be explained by Dr. Leonard Smith, Director of the Detroit Concert Band. Regarding the use of special interpretive devices, Dr. Smith reported that "as a matter of pride, conductors and players alike would purposely not indicate them on the parts but instead, memorize them."[46] The encore books also include manuscript parts for harp, bass drum, and mallet percussion, which give additional insight into the interpretations.

Former Sousa Band members are extremely valuable sources. The most comprehensive information has come from Dr. Frank Simon, solo cornetist and assistant conductor of the Sousa Band from 1914–1921. Simon sat directly under Sousa's right arm and was in an ideal position to observe his interpretations at close range.[47] Following his tenure with Sousa, Simon presented clinics to coach conductors and bands in the Sousa style.[48]

In 1966, Simon gave a series of interviews in which he documented performance techniques of thirty-five Sousa marches.[49] These interviews were published by the American School Band Directors Association under the title "The Sounds of John Philip Sousa."[50] The Simon narratives are especially important to this research. Other Sousa Band members have contributed valuable information in articles, lectures, and oral history interviews. When taken collectively they make a compelling case for Sousa's unique performance style.

A fourth source of information is recordings of the Sousa Band. It was one of the most recorded ensembles of its time, making nearly twelve hundred sides for the Victor Company alone. Sousa conducted his band in only six of those recordings, however;[51] the rest were done by his assistants.[52] In addition to recordings with his band, Sousa conducted two Victor recordings of his marches with the Philadelphia Rapid Transit Company Band. There also exists a 1929 radio broadcast transcription from a special Thanksgiving broadcast sponsored by the General Baking Corporation (Bond Bakers).[53]

Sousa was averse to recordings. He called them "canned music,"[54] and predicted that recordings would eventually be used in lieu of live music. He was also concerned with composers not receiving remuneration for their work.[55] Sousa wrote, ". . . the composers of the music now produced so widely by the mechanical players . . . draw no profit from it whatsoever. . . . without a penny of remuneration to himself for the use of this original product of his brain."[56]

The recordings Sousa conducted himself are a valuable resource. Whether they represent the same performance techniques Sousa employed on stage is unclear. Technical limitations may have required modification of the performance changes in order to insure a successful recording.

Other Sousa Band recordings are stylistically interesting but, without Sousa on the podium, we must question the conditions under which they were made. Clarinetist Eugene Slick related, "Jack Richardson made several recordings with Sousa's Band. He said they never used more than fourteen in the band. They couldn't see the conductor, they just started the band . . ."[57] Among the evidence that these recordings departed from Sousa's tradition is the use of a *da capo* in several instances, a practice to which Sousa objected.[58] A more complete discussion of observations about the recordings Sousa conducted will be undertaken in examination of specific performance techniques.

Recreating Sousa Performance Practices in Modern Performance

Sam Harris, Sousa Band clarinetist for ten years, wrote that "It was Sousa's belief that a march is one of the most difficult of all musical compositions to play correctly. He stressed the importance of being on the alert for all details—tempo, accents, dynamics, nuances breathing, articulations, and proper balance."[59] Sousa echoed these sentiments in his autobiography, *Marching Along*: "The chief aim of the composer is to produce color, dynamics, nuances, and to emphasize the story-telling quality. The combination and composition which gains that result is most to be desired."[60]

Col. Howard C. Bronson asked:

> How did he obtain such rich tonal coloring and why did Sousa's compositions take on a different character when played by his Band? The answer to the first question lies, I believe, in the fact that he knew exactly how he wanted his band to sound and he developed a playing character that expressed it. . . . His own compositions were played with meticulous attention to dynamics, shading and tone coloring. The printed scores did not carry the dynamic markings as actually played by the Band.[61]

Attempts to recreate the Sousa performance style must have the same "meticulous attention" to all details of the performance.

Among the first prerequisites of good Sousa march performance are properly edited performance materials. When Sousa was on the podium, many details and nuances were either worked out in rehearsal or carried on in an aural tradition by his players. Without Sousa's coaching, we must reconcile differences in articulations, accents, and dynamics between the various instrumental parts, as follows:

1. Discrepancies in written pitch and rhythmic values should be clarified from the manuscript score.
2. Lines which are rhythmically identical should be articulated alike.
3. Dynamics should be identical unless altered to achieve a performance effect.
4. Dynamic changes should occur simultaneously.
5. Other inconsistencies should be resolved to conform with the majority of the other voices.

Correcting inconsistencies will make an immediate effect upon the ensemble's performance.

Contrast is the other essential element to effective performance. Effects, dynamic changes, and accents must be executed with conviction and enough emphasis to make them stand out from the surrounding texture. While some are subtle and others dramatic, the challenge is to make as much contrast as is musically prudent.

Style and Rhythm

Beyond consistency and contrast, the playing style of Sousa and his Band is more difficult to define. Leinsdorf noted, "The performer must distinguish music written during a period of strong and generally accepted traditions from that written at times of little or no traditions."[62] Working to Sousa's benefit was a well-established performance style known by all his players. Col. Howard Bronson recounted that "The turn-over of personnel was slight. Each player knew exactly how Sousa wanted certain passages to be played—just the right shading and perfect coordination."[63] Frederick Fennell noted the same phenomenon: "We can easily forget that 100 years ago when many of the great marches were published for the first time, there was a *band style*, a way of playing which composers assumed and conductors *expected* would be fulfilled by the players—automatically and correctly!"[64]

While exact definitions are nearly impossible, two specific clues are in note length and rhythm. Arthur Pryor, Sousa trombone soloist and later conductor of his own professional band, devoted an entire article to the subject in the August 1932 issue of *The Metronome*. Pryor wrote, "Usually a march is not so difficult to play. Perhaps that is one of its disadvantages. At any rate, it is only the exceptional band that brings out the real possibilities of this movement."[65]

Pryor indicated that shorter note values should be separated from one another and particularly separated from longer notes which surround them. Regarding two-four marches, Pryor directed that "All quarter notes, dotted notes and half notes must be given full value. Each and every eighth note must be separated from the next note, unless tied over." Regarding six-eight marches, he wrote, "All quarter notes and dotted notes must have full value. Eighth notes should be played short."[66] Similar admonitions can be found in the writings of Edwin Franko Goldman.[67]

According to clarinetist Sam Harris, "[Sousa] did not use the term 'staccato.' He called it 'spacing the notes.' He stressed articulation as well, and often mentioned that many players get careless. . . ."[68] Frank Simon indicated that this was one of Sousa's pet peeves: "It used to burn the 'Governor' up when someone would fail to space their notes."[69] Paul Bierley noted that "Except for sustained passages, the Sousa Band played their notes slightly shorter or crisper so as to create an impression of cleanly separated rhythmic patterns."[70] The separation between short and long notes makes long notes seem even longer and gives additional rhythmic emphasis, taking advantage of the agogic accent.[71] "Spacing the notes" gives a lighter character to the marches and emphasizes their dance-like qualities.

The stylish rhythm of his march performances can be heard on the recordings of Sousa conducting his band. When an interviewer once asked Sousa "how he managed to achieve rhythm so successfully," Sousa replied,

> . . . that's a part of the question why one musical enterprise gets ahead and another does not . . . Why does one band give you goose-flesh, while another fails to stir you in the least. I'm sure I don't know. The thing has never been explained. Rhythm, of course, you must have in music that is alive.[72]

The evidence shows that Sousa knew *exactly* what he was doing in performances with his band. He was simply not interested in sharing it with the entire world.

Concerning rhythm, Gus Helmecke advised, "The trick here is to keep it steady. Conductor and men should be thoroughly familiar with the proper marching tempo and then stick to it. . . . You get variety by a number of means, but jiggling the rhythm isn't one of them. . . . Keep it steady."[73] It is unclear whether Helmecke was discussing rhythm only as a function of tempo. The Sousa Band recordings exhibit an abundance of rhythmic nuance which does not disturb the tempo. We find rubato within the beat where, at times, shorter note groupings are compressed toward the strong beats of the measure, or in which slight hesitations emphasize the rhythm.

Tempo

Frank Simon wrote that not all Sousa marches were played at the same tempo, that the tempo depended entirely on the character of the march.[74] Paul Bierley has noted from his interviews with former Sousa Band members that Sousa's tempos increased over the years. In the early days of the Sousa Band, the march tempo was said to have been around M.M. = 120–126.[75]

Dr. Raymond Dvorak noted, "His tempo was a lively march tempo, 120 beats a minute. In later years he stepped up the tempo to 132 beats in some of his marches."[76] Bierley also reported that Sousa took tempos up to M.M. = 140 at times, but not at every concert, and that Sousa might take faster tempos to rush to meet train schedules.[77] The "train schedule" tempos were corroborated to Bierley by Albertus Meyers, late conductor of the Allentown (Pennsylvania) Band, in a discussion at the 1963 Sousa Band Fraternal Society Dinner in New York City.[78]

Sousa discussed his march tempo in the Sydney (Australia) *Evening News* published as he left Australia during the world tour of 1911. The paper observed, "The opinion has been expressed that your march time is too quick," to which Sousa responded,

> If you play my marches for troops to march to in the streets . . . they must, of necessity, be played slower than I play them on the stage. . . . My marches, with the exception of one, are used entirely as encores. . . . I play them at a quick step rather than keep them down to a slow patter. The American regulation step is 120 to the minute . . . I have heard people say they would like me to play my marches slower. Well, if I had to play in front of a regiment, I would do so; but never on the stage.[79]

It is unclear whether the Australian audiences' opinion of Sousa's "quick" tempos was based on comparison to the British march tempo of M.M. = 110.[80] Nor is it clear exactly how Sousa's performance tempo related to the "American regulation step" of M.M. = 120, except that we must assume it was faster. An article in the July 1924 edition of *The Etude* entitled "The Fascinating March" documented the following standards for march tempos: ". . . the Quickstep, calling for about 103 steps; to the *Pas de charge* or Double-quick, demanding 120 steps."[81]

There may be a correlation between Sousa's faster tempi and the function of his marches as encores. These unprogrammed selections were sprinkled liberally throughout Sousa's concerts, executed within moments of the completion of the preceding work.[82] There is reason, however, to consider more moderate tempi based on examination of Sousa's own recordings. The nine recordings Sousa conducted (seven with his band, two with the Philadelphia Rapid Transit Band) display tempi of between M.M. = 116 and M.M. = 126. I believe that off the concert stage, when given the opportunity to interpret the marches for recordings, Sousa chose tempos which more closely reflected his intended tempos.

Frank Simon remembered, "When we were on tour, the musicians sometimes got in the habit of creeping up the tempo. When this happened, Mr. Sousa would call a meeting after a concert and tell the band to slow down and that *he* would set the tempo."[83] On another occasion, Simon commented on one of the most common Sousa march "affectations" by saying, "Sousa condoned no tempo change, once the tempo was set, including the last time of trio."[84]

Edmund Wall related the following story about Sousa's experiences conducting school bands while on tour:

> . . . almost every day, we had a high school band on stage at the intermission, which Mr. Sousa would conduct. . . . Like all high school bands, they had rehearsed this march who knows how many times and always at a pretty lively clip. And I knew what was going to happen because the Old Man conducted his marches at a marching tempo of 120 to the minute. And these kids would all watch him and the moment he gave the downbeat, their eyes would all drop to the music. From then on, they'd leave him behind. Sometimes, he would just smile and catch up and follow them through to the end.[85]

August Helmecke wrote that "Sousa never played his Marches as fast as they're generally taken today. He kept to a good, firm marching tempo. A march, remember, isn't a gallop. When people march, they don't run."[86] George Reynolds, writing in *The Instrumentalist* on the 1951 Sousa march clinic which Frank Simon conducted at the University of New Hampshire and in which August Helmecke played bass drum, reported this:

> I have had the opportunity to observe Sousa done in Sousa style. Traugott Rohner once clocked King Cotton at 118 for a cadence! Dr. Simon was on the podium and the band sound was literally alive with rhythm. Study has shown the average Sousa march tempo at 120 to 132.[87]

One theory regarding Sousa's increasing tempos over the years has been offered by Dr. Leon Bly:

> Until the early 1920s, Sousa performed his marches at tempos of 120 to 128 beats per minute, but during the last years of his life, he frequently performed his marches at tempos of 136 to 140 beats per minute. . . . when it became fashionable after World War I to play marches at a faster tempo, Sousa increased the tempo at which he performed his marches (it should be noted that the military increased the tempo of the quick march from 120 to 128 in 1922, retaining the faster tempo until 1939).[88]

The change in the military marching cadence was also documented by Dr. Raymond Dvorak, who indicated that "At the present time, the United States Army regulation tempo is 128 beats per minute which is modeled after the French Army."[89]

While this offers one possible explanation for Sousa's increasing tempos, it does not necessarily prescribe tempos for modern performance. Historically, we have Sousa's tempos reported from M.M. = 120 to M.M. = 140. Study of his recorded performances shows tempos ranging from M.M. = 116 to M.M. = 126. Furthermore, information from Helmecke and Wall leans toward slower tempos. I believe that the slower tempos are more effective and allow for more detail to be heard in the performances.

Dynamics and Balance

One challenge of proper dynamic placement is that published markings are often misplaced. In addition, dynamic indications are regularly printed in the first measure of the strain and do not cover pick-up notes leading into the strain. The conductor must ensure that dynamic changes occur on the pick-up notes rather than playing them at a different dynamic than the upcoming strain. In making other performance changes (such as when brass instruments are tacit the first time through), the dynamic contrast sought is dramatic, as going from *pianissimo* to *fortissimo*. The change should be immediate, much like turning a switch.

In terms of balance between sections, brass must not predominate throughout. A study of Sousa Band instrumentation from 1892 to 1928 shows a preference for numbers of woodwinds over brass instruments in the Sousa Band.[90] The trend toward larger woodwind sections peaked in the early 1920s, when the Sousa Band had a total of forty-three woodwinds to twenty-four brass. Joe Lefter commented:

> The sound of the band was entirely different than any of the smaller bands I had been playing in. It was really a full sound because he had lots of clarinets . . . at least twice as many as he had cornets and trumpets and the balance with the trombones and the baritones and the horns and all was very, very, very good. And, of course, he had alto and bass clarinets. That helped the fullness of the band. He had a full range of saxophones from altos, tenors, baritones, and bass. It was really a full sounding band and I thought it was very, very wonderful.[91]

Edmund Wall reported, "Sousa really held the band down in dynamics and rarely let them play full out."[92] Robin W. "Doc" Davis is quoted as saying, "In a *pianissimo,* if you couldn't hear the man next to you, you were playing too loudly."[93] In recreating Sousa dynamics, contrast should be of paramount importance, with special emphasis on the softer end of the dynamic range.

Orchestration and Instrumentation Changes

In a general discussion of these techniques, Dr. Raymond Dvorak wrote that

> Repeated strains were seldom played twice the same way; if there was a counter-melody in the first strain it was played only once usually on the repeat. The second strain was frequently played softly the first time and loudly on the repeat. Some of his trios are played three times, each time with a different instrumentation with the last strain *tutti.* There was always the element of contrast. . . . In the performance of a march the full band played sparingly.[94]

George Reynolds reported that Sousa

> would wave out sections, mainly brass, . . . and allow the woodwinds and special effects to take over. He would use the brass on alternate phrases and reverse the series on the repeat of the strain. Each of his marches achieved a variety of tonal colors by this and similar devices.[95]

In *The Band on Parade*, Dr. Raymond Dvorak offered the following summary:

> From the standpoint of arrangement Mr. Sousa usually played his marches in the following manner: Introduction and first strain as written; second strain: first time cornets, trombones, piccolos and oboes *tacet*, second time as written; trio: cornets, trombones, piccolos and oboes *tacet* with clarinets an octave lower; break or episode: as written; last strain of trio same as first strain of trio, then on the repeat of the break or episode as written to the end of the march.[96]

The most specific performance information comes from the Frank Simon narratives of thirty-five Sousa marches as part of the "Sounds of John Philip Sousa" series, and from marked parts in the Sousa encore books. Study of these two sources has revealed exactly which changes were made and also confirms differences which made each march unique. Clarinetist Edmund Wall noted, "There is no pattern for playing the Sousa Marches in the style which Mr. Sousa played them, they were all different. In his marches, he made good use of the double reeds."[97] In his interview for the Sousa Foundation Oral History Project, Wall said, "There was not a set style . . . it depended on which march it was."[98]

There are variables within the structure of Sousa's marches which make it impossible to impose one iron-clad formula on every march. Variations were linked to differences in the marches. Sousa's interpretations were consistent from performance to performance but were not necessarily consistent from march to march. Knowing of the memorized performance changes which have been previously noted, reports of "waving sections of the band out and in" were almost certainly a function of Sousa's showmanship rather than an improvisational approach to the music.[99]

Although no absolute formulas exist, we can distill frequently used patterns which are representative of those changes documented by Simon and others. Side-by-side comparison also raises questions which can best be answered by seeking trends within the various interpretations.

The Brass Instruments

It has been mentioned numerous times that "the brass" would not play the first time through repeated strains and that clarinets were "down an octave." These general statements require clarification.

In Frank Simon's narratives, his references to brass being tacet are almost categorically limited to the phrase "cornets and trombones are tacet" or "cornets and trombones are out."[100] When brass instruments were eliminated, cuts were confined to the cornets, trombones, and almost certainly the trumpet players as well. The Sousa Band carried two trumpet players during all the years of its existence, but most Sousa marches do not have separate parts for trumpet.[101] In most cases, the trumpets doubled the principal cornet parts[102] and would, therefore, be tacet as well.

In deciding which other instruments may or may not have been playing, no evidence exists that French horns, euphonium, or tubas were eliminated in these strains. The tubas would provide harmonic and rhythmic support on the down-beats, French Horns would play afterbeats in harmony (which can actually be heard in these soft strains), and euphoniums would handle the melody in a register more conducive to the mellow sound Sousa was seeking. Sousa did not use string bass at any time with his Band and it should not be used in his marches.

The Woodwind Instruments

Regarding woodwinds, the problematic phrase is "clarinets down an octave." A more accurate phrase refers to the clarinets playing "in the staff."[103] Examination of the clarinet parts in most Sousa marches will find solo and first clarinet parts written in the upper register or "above the staff." The second and third clarinet parts are most often written an octave lower or "in the staff." When we read instructions stating simply "clarinets are down an octave," it becomes clear that it is not possible to lower all clarinet parts an octave. To do so would often place the lower parts out of the range of the instrument.

In solving this dilemma, consider "in the staff" as the ultimate goal for selecting the proper clarinet register. Those parts which are above the staff and can easily be lowered an octave should be marked as such. If the other clarinet parts can be lowered as well, the conductor can instruct the section to do so. If, however, the written range will not allow it to be played an octave lower, play as written.

On occasion, Simon instructs, "clarinets play an octave lower whenever possible."[104] The most important advice is to drop clarinet parts an octave when-ever possible; but at no time should the solo and first clarinet parts (when dropped an octave) go below the second and third clarinet parts. The octaves should be adjusted to ensure separation between these parts whenever possible and unison playing at other times. When cornets and trombones return for the second time through a strain, clarinet parts are played as written, including any pick-ups into the repeat. As mentioned in the discussion of dynamic contrast, these octave changes (clarinets) or tacit sections (cornets and trombones) take effect simul-taneously and include any pick-up or lead-in notes.

Oboes, bassoons, and saxophones are very important to the texture when the "brass" are tacit and clarinets play in the lower octaves. The use of oboes in soft strains is not consistent with Dvorak's report of the Sousa style, but Edmund Wall was previously quoted as having said, ". . . he (Sousa) made good use of the double reeds."[105]

Sousa's preference for the saxophones can be found in the quote, "There is much to be done in standardizing this instrument with its strange sweetness of tone and its variety of effects."[106] From 1915 on, the number of saxophone players in the Sousa Band increased from five to a total of eight saxophones in the early 1920s.[107] The Sousa saxophone octet was a popular part of his concerts in the 1920s.[108]

The Sousa Band used alto and bass clarinet players almost continuously throughout its history,[109] but there were no published parts for these instruments in most of the earlier marches. The Sousa encore books contain mostly E-flat cornet or alto saxophone parts for alto clarinet and tenor sax, and baritone or treble clef B-flat bass parts for bass clarinet. Whether or not these parts were actually played as such is not known.

Sousa used E-flat clarinet with his band, even having two players on this instrument in some years.[110] However, his preference for E-flat clarinet players was well defined. Clarinetist Edmund Wall reported that Sousa had a "wonderful E-flat clarinet player but when he left Sousa couldn't find anyone as good." Wall noted that from this time on, Sousa had the fifth flute player transpose and play the E-flat clarinet parts.[111] Sousa demanded a player whose tone and finesse allowed him to blend with the band and not stand out from the texture.

As for flute and piccolo, we know Sousa's fondness for the piccolo if for no other reason than the famous solo in *The Stars and Stripes Forever!* It is not clear whether flute and piccolo played during the softer strains when the clarinets were dropped an octave.[112] The addition of the flutes brightens the timbre and helps prevent the texture from sounding hollow. Piccolo sounds out of place here, riding two octaves above the clarinets, when the desired sound of the band is more mellow; the same applies to the E-flat clarinet. Accordingly, I recommend eliminating both piccolo and E-flat clarinet in the strains when the clarinets are dropped an octave. Both acoustically and musically, this leads to a more homogenous sound.

The Percussion Instruments

Percussion instruments and effects are among the most essential elements in good Sousa march performance, as Sousa drummer John Heney testified:

> My friend, the late John Philip Sousa, called the drum the KING OF INSTRU-MENTS. He was more particular about his drummers and drum section, perhaps, than any other section of his band. Sousa's drum section was his pride and joy and without the marvelous cooperation of leader and drummer, his band probably would not been what it was.[113]

As mentioned earlier, Sousa had immense respect for his bass drummer, August Helmecke. Dr. Raymond Dvorak related that a bandmaster once told Sousa, "Your bass drummer can almost play a tune on a bass drum" and that Mr. Sousa had replied without the slightest hesitation, "He *can* play a tune on a bass drum."[114] During the 1920 tour of the Sousa Band, many members of the band went on strike for one performance to protest the working and travelling conditions. August Helmecke was one of only two musicians later re-hired by Sousa.[115]

Throughout its history, Sousa's percussion section was limited to three players. As Dr. Leonard Smith noted, "Professional bands prior to the 1940s rarely used more than 3 percussion players, one on bass drum & cymbals, one on snare drum and one on timpani, including the bands of Gilmore, Sousa, Pryor, Conway, Creatore and Goldman."[116] This meant that the bass drummer played with attached cymbal and handled both parts simultaneously.

Although this has almost become a lost art, some feel it is the only way to obtain proper balance between bass drum and cymbal.[117] Whether the original union of bass drum and attached cymbal was a marriage of convenience due to limited personnel or a matter of preference, is not clear. But once the tradition was established, it never wavered in Sousa's Band. With the increasing size of his band, Sousa could have hired additional percussionists if he wished to do so, but he did not. During his twenty-two years with the Sousa Band, Gus Helmecke was the undisputed king of bass drum and cymbal parts. Today, players who can effectively perform this "double duty" are rare. Most bands will want separate players for each instrument (the most common problem is that cymbals often overbalance the sound of the bass drum). In general terms, Helmecke advised, ". . . percussions [sic] should never predominate in a band. Sometimes, alas, they do!" He added, "Don't overdo loudness. Percussionists should be especially careful about dynamics. They should do only what the indications tell them. Zeal is a beautiful thing— but not when it causes someone to pound drums and cymbals out of all musical proportion."[118]

Leonard Smith has noted confusion regarding the interpretation of march percussion parts: ". . . as a rule of thumb, compositions bearing a copyright circa 1937 or earlier imply that the stem-up is for snare drum and stem-down for bass drum & cymbals," without regard for the number of available players. "If bass drum is to be played alone, it is marked 'B.D.' To return to both, it is marked 'Tog.,' implying 'together.' Cymbal alone is marked with an 'X,' or by 'Cymb.'"[119]

Regarding the choice of instruments, recordings of the Sousa Band under his direction demonstrate a snare drum sound lower in pitch than the concert snare drums most commonly in use today. The bass drum used by Gus Helmecke with the Sousa Band measured thirty-six inches across by eighteen inches deep, as documented by Dr. Leonard B. Smith.[120] Both the size and the tuning of the drum contributed to the reported effect that Sousa's bass drum was "felt" more than "heard."[121]

One of the most interesting documents of Helmecke's virtuoso style can be found in his editions of the bass drum parts to marches published by Theodore Presser. These parts demonstrate note values to indicate exactly where long and short notes are to be played, as well as precise dynamic markings. One of the most interesting is *The Stars and Stripes Forever!* Two times in the march, the bass drum part is notated as three different written pitches. Instructions on the part read: "The B.D. should be struck in the following positions for these two measures; 1st note (2nd space) just below the center of head, 2nd note (4th space) near top of head, 3rd note (3rd space) between top and center, and 4th note (2nd space) just below center."[122] The distinction between short and long notes in bass drum playing, use of accents, and subtle dynamic changes are all part of the Helmecke style.

Sousa did not use timpani in his marches.[123] No timpani parts can be found in earlier editions. These were among the parts added in the 1950s when the instrumentation was expanded.

Other Percussion Techniques

Study of recordings under Sousa's direction reveals that the snare drum is silent except during the "break-up" strains and the last time through the final strains of the marches.[124] Due to the limited frequency range of these recordings, it is nearly impossible to tell whether or not the bass drum is playing.

Paul Bierley has documented that Sousa either reduced or eliminated percussion in certain strains of his marches.[125] This is confirmed by the recordings under Sousa's direction. Conductors may consider eliminating percussion from the softer strains of the marches. The snare drumming on the Sousa Band recordings reflects a very "open" style, giving what John Heney describes as a more "drummy" sound.[126]

Perhaps the most significant innovation is the "five stroke roll with flam attack." It may have been the secret to the "lift" described by many who heard the Sousa Band.[127] This technique is covered in John Heney's book, *The Correct Way to Drum*:

> In this group you will learn a new beat heretofore unpublished . . . which will enable you to play the finish of nearly all of the Sousa marches as we played them under his direction. . . . This lesson takes up what this writer considers the most important beat used on the famous Sousa Band. It is the beat used in the finish of nearly all of his marches.[128]

The technique is as follows: whether a five- or seven- stroke roll is written in the music, a five-stroke roll is to be played in the last strain of the march. Each roll is preceded by a flam and, unlike traditional practice, each roll begins quite loud with the flam attack and makes an immediate decrescendo, thereby placing the accent on the upbeat rather than the downbeat.[129] Heney explained:

> The proper phrasing of this very fine beat is just the opposite of the ordinary five stroke roll. On the plain five stroke roll you were taught to accent the last beat very forcibly, which was correct. On the five stroke roll with a flam attack we reverse this procedure and accent the first of the roll or the flam beat itself. This note should be accented with a considerable force . . . and then the rest of the beat is decrescendoed down to the last beat which is played about one fourth as heavily as the start of the beat.[130]

Regarding the preference for the five-stroke roll, Heney wrote:

> . . . this author suggests its use in place of a seven stroke roll nearly all of the time. Incidentally very few seven stroke rolls were played on Sousa's Band. The five stroke roll with a flam attack was substituted instead. It not only sounds more 'Drummy' but does not have the crowded feeling of a seven stroke roll.[131]

The five-stroke roll gives a more open feeling, a very desirable effect. Heney added, "This beat should be played very open all the time. Under no conditions should this beat be played close [*sic*]. Do not forget to play it open."[132] The most important feature is to reverse the usual dynamics and accent the after beat firmly.[133] The player must not rush when making the after beat accent. When done effectively, the final strain of the march will come alive, producing a spectacular result.[134]

Cymbal crashes are another important effect. In the Sousa recordings, the crashes sound very much as if they were played on suspended cymbal. The technique is substantiated by John Heney as he described how to play Sousa marches: "In the ninth measure we have a very effective cymbal solo which must be played by the snare drummer hitting a cymbal with the shoulder of the drum stick; it should not be played by the bass drummer."[135] This instruction is duplicated concerning another march: "There is a cymbal solo in the second strain of the trio which, by all means, should be played by the snare drummer and the cymbal should be struck with the shoulder of the snare drum stick and not with the soft head of the bass drum stick."[136] The sharp attack on the cymbal crashes heard on the Sousa recordings seems to substantiate the use of the snare drum stick. But Dr. Raymond Dvorak has reported: "On cymbal solos in marches, he always struck the free cymbal held in the hand with a bass drum beater."[137]

Dr. Leonard Smith, who played with Gus Helmecke in the Goldman Band for many years, reported that Helmecke and fellow percussionists used all manner of cymbal crashes. For most crashes in marches, Gus would hit the cymbal held in his left hand with the bass drum beater.[138] For some, he would hit the cymbal in his hand against the cymbal attached to the drum. On occasion, when the music called for it, Gus would pick up a pair of crash cymbals for a big effect. Positioned between Helmecke and the snare drummer was a suspended crash cymbal played only by the snare drummer and only with the snare drum stick (similar to Heney's report). Dr. Smith also reported that Helmecke never hit the drum in the center but most often below center, half way between the center and the rim.[139] The varied placement when striking the drum is consistent with the information previously discussed.

Accents

Among the most famous Sousa percussion techniques were dramatic bass drum and cymbal accents. More than any other feature of Sousa march performance, former Sousa Band members consistently praised Gus Helmecke for his effective use of accents. The 1972 edition of the *Sousa Band Society News* reported, "A Sousa march played without changes of dynamics or accents would be a dull thing, but Mr. Sousa and Gus would bring it to life by . . . sudden changes to *pianissimo*, or by placing accents in unexpected spots."[140]

Sousa offered the following testimonial: ". . . no one who has watched and heard Helmecke with my band playing a march will differ with me when I declare that my bass drummer has the spirit and the soul of a great artist."[141] Concerning the accents, Helmecke wrote,

> . . . in Sousa, they're by far the most important. Sousa's Marches gained most of their stirring effectiveness from the crisp, wonderful accents he put into them. As I said,

these never got marked into the music and never were published. . . . Sousa didn't print his accents, and he never explained them—he just made them known through his conducting.[142]

Gus Helmecke continued to perform the Sousa accents with the Goldman Band until his retirement from that organization at age 82.[143] Dr. Leonard Smith, solo cornetist of the Goldman Band during these years, sat almost directly in front of Helmecke's drum and has vivid memories of these accents:

> The Sousa accents were placed logically, not whimsically. The interpretation is found in the music itself. It has nothing to do with sentiment or caprice. Sousa's accents were so effective because he conceived them. Gus *did not* do it on his own. People fantasize about this but it's not true.[144]

Without written documentation, recreating Sousa accents is difficult. Some accents reinforce the stresses in the melodic contour. Others add variety by providing rhythmic contrast to the melodic line. Frank Simon recorded another characteristic of the Sousa accents: "In some bands I have noted that these [accents] are observed by the percussion section alone. In the Sousa band we were all responsible to make the accents with the full band ensemble."[145]

Sousa apparently made no distinction between the two different written accents, the ˆ sign (known as sforzando accent, wedge, or "tent accent") and the > sign (known as the marcato accent). These seem to have been used at random throughout his manuscript scores with no apparent consistency.

Analysis of the melodic line to determine the musical climaxes will provide the best starting point. The climax of a crescendo is always an obvious place for an accent. In some cases, accents occur on the downbeat, in others on the second beat of the measure—attractive since the downbeat is already well emphasized by habit. Wherever the big accents are placed, they should be played with bass drum and cymbal *together*. Above all, accents should not be overdone and must not become predictable. During soft strains when brass are not playing, accents should be very subtle, almost inaudible (if percussion are playing at all in the soft strains). The big accents are reserved for the loud strains, a factor which also reduces their predictability.

Another Helmecke technique is the use of a slight hesitation before big accents. Mark Hindsley observed:

> One other impression remains vividly in my mind. . . . we were able to observe the famous bass drummer, Gus Helmecke. It was particularly interesting to watch him when the band played marches to see him bring up a Sousa crescendo to a climactic accent . . . to feel no amateurish rushing of the tempo, to the point that his accent seemed to come just in the nick of time, if not even a little delayed.[146]

Clarinetist Roy Miller observed the same phenomenon: "Most bands rush accents—Sousa's band played accents exactly in time which made them seem late."[147] Based on Hindsley's and Miller's comments, the big accents may have been slightly delayed, a technique which created extra tension until the accent did come.

Psychologist Caroline Palmer, formerly of Cornell University and now on the faculty of Ohio State University, conducted a long-term research project to identify through scientific examination which elements comprise what we define as a musical (versus non-musical) interpretation.[148] She found that rhythmic elements, i.e. note lengths and rhythm, were among the most measurable phenomena. One of the most basic recurring patterns in "musical" performances was that melody was often brought out (or emphasized) by playing it slightly out of synchronization with other parts. I believe the technique of playing a part "out of synch" to add emphasis is not unlike delaying the bass drum/cymbal accents.

Mallet Instruments

Mallet instruments were used in march performance with some regularity. The most common is the use of orchestra bells to double the melody in the trio.[149] The Sousa Band encore books contain a number of manuscript bell parts and also have markings in other percussion parts indicating "Bells" in the trios of the marches.

The bell parts used by Sousa simply outline the melody. John Heney wrote, "Do not roll any of the notes while playing the bells. Striking the notes with wooden hammers and letting the bar ring is sufficient and infinitely more pleasing than rolling with metal hammers."[150] This admonition is repeated later when he adds, "The bars should be struck and not rolled upon."[151] Conductors who wish to use bells in the soft trio are advised to use the first oboe part for this purpose. Any bell part which departs from the melody is not authentic.

On certain marches, Sousa had the melody played on xylophone. Heney reported in his discussion of *U.S. Field Artillery March*, "If there are more than two snare drummers and a small xylophone is present, one of the drummers should play the first strain of the trio on the xylophone."[152] Sousa's recording of *Sabre and Spurs* also includes the use of xylophone in the first time through the last strain. (Unlike the instructions for bell parts, the xylophone player on the Sousa recording rolls on longer notes, no doubt due to the fact that the xylophone, once struck, does not ring as the bells do.) The manuscript bell parts in the Sousa encore books also contain a part marked "Xylophone" for *Sabre and Spurs*.[153] The use of xylophone is far less frequent than bells.

Overview of Sousa Performance Practices

Individual elements of Sousa performance practice having been detailed, it may be helpful to the reader to provide a conservative overview of typical performance techniques:

1. The introduction and first strains were usually played as written.
2. The second strain was usually altered. The first time through, the dynamic level was adjusted to *piano*. Cornets and trombones did not play, upper clarinet parts were dropped an octave, piccolo and E-flat clarinet were eliminated. On the repeat, all instruments were back in as written.
3. At the trio, the same instruments listed above were tacit and the upper clarinets were lowered an octave. Snare drum, bass drum, and cymbals may have been

eliminated as well. Bells could double the melody at the trio. If the trio was repeated, the dynamic would be *piano* the first time, *pianissimo* the second.

4. The "dogfight" or episode was usually played as written, with all instruments back at written pitch.

5. The final strain was usually played twice, separated by the interlude or break-up strain. It was performed in the de-orchestrated fashion the first time through (piccolo and E-flat clarinet out, cornets and trombones out, upper clarinets down an octave, all with a dynamic of *piano*). On the repeat, all instruments were back in at the break-up strain and played *fortissimo* through the end of the march. Climactic accents were most common in the final repeat of the last strain and here the "five stroke roll with flam attack" may have been added to give additional lift to the performance.

Conclusion

Armed with a body of historical evidence, we are in a better position to "understand where interpretation begins and where it ends," as Leinsdorf stated, and to have a framework within which to make our own inevitable judgments. Beyond the unattainable pursuit of "absolute authenticity," we have the knowledge to present "historically informed" performances representative of those Sousa conducted with his own band. Responsible application of these performance practices will bring us closer to what Sousa conducted than will an antiseptic performance of the published notation. Such responsible application will follow a thoughtful and conservative path, consistent with the principles outlined in this paper. It must not be allowed to become capricious or arbitrary, for this is not the model which Sousa's own performances displayed.

NOTES

1. Frederick Fennell, "The Sousa March: A Personal View," in *Perspectives on John Philip Sousa*, edited by Jon Newsom (Washington: Library of Congress, 1983), p. 81.

2. Ibid., p. 83.

3. Paul E. Bierley, *The Works of John Philip Sousa* (Westerville, Ohio: Integrity Press, 1984), p. 39.

4. Mark Hindsley, Oral History Interview, n.p., 10 December 1980, *The Sousa Oral History Project*, unpublished transcript in U.S. Marine Band Library, Washington, D.C., p. 20.

5. August Helmecke, "Why the accents weren't written in . . . ," *The Instrumentalist* 5, no. 5 (March-April 1951): 15.

6. Praises for Helmecke's work are found throughout the issues of the *Sousa Band Society News* and in oral history accounts. His name is probably mentioned more frequently than any other Sousa Band member.

7. "Sousa Claims Bass Drummer in His Band Best in World, and True Artist," Tucson, Arizona *Star*, 14 January 1924 (from Sousa Band Press Books in U.S. Marine Band archives).

8. August Helmecke, "How Sousa Played His Marches," *The Etude* 68, no. 8 (August 1950): 23.

9. Raymond F. Dvorak, "Recollections of Sousa's March Performances," *The School Musician/Director and Teacher* 41, no. 4 (December 1969): 59.

10. Frank Simon, interview as part of "In Search of Sousa" radio documentary by Tony Thomas. Simon's credibility as a Sousa march authority is attested in August Helmecke's article, "Gus Helmecke Reports on the John Philip Sousa March Clinic Held at the University of New Hampshire . . . Durham, N.H., January 11–12–13th, 1951," *Sousa Band Society News* (February 1951): 14.

11. Joe Lefter, Oral History Interview, n.p., August 1980, *The Sousa Oral History Project*, unpublished transcript in U.S. Marine Band Library, Washington, D.C., pp. 65–66.

12. Karl L. King to "Barney," 29 October 1946 (from collection of Paul E. Bierley).

13. Edmund C. Wall to Keith Brion, 5 April 1978 (from the collection of Paul E. Bierley).

14. Edmund C. Wall, Oral History Interview, n.p., 24 July 1981, *The Sousa Oral History Project*, unpublished transcript in U.S. Marine Band Library, Washington, D.C., p. 143.

15. John J. Heney, interview with Paul E. Bierley, n.p., 9 February 1964 (from collection of Paul E. Bierley).

16. Dr. Simon's detailed and insightful accounts of Sousa's interpretive style are one of the most important resources to this research.

17. Leo Steinberg, *Michelangelo's Last Paintings* (London, 1975), quoted in *Modern Musical Scholarship*, edited by Edward Olleson (Boston: Oriel Press, 1978), p. 21.

18. Erich Leinsdorf, *The Composer's Advocate* (New Haven, Conn.: Yale University Press, 1981), p. 47.

19. Ibid., p. 49.

20. Arthur Mendel, "The Purposes and Desirable Characteristics of Text-Critical Editions," from *Modern Musical Scholarship*, edited by Edward Olleson (Boston: Oriel Press 1978), p. 16.

21. Leinsdorf, *Composer's Advocate*, p. 51.

22. Richard Taruskin, "Beethoven Symphonies—The New Antiquity," *Opus* (October 1987): 32.

23. Raymond Leppard, *Authenticity in Music* (Portland, Oreg.: Amadeus Press, 1988), p. 28.

24. Standley Howell, Review-Essay in *Journal of Musicological Research* 7, no. 1 (1986): 101, as quoted in Richard Taruskin, "Beethoven Symphonies—The New Antiquity," *Opus* (October 1987): 31.

25. Taruskin, "Beethoven Symphonies," p. 36.

26. Several unknown Sousa march manuscripts and sketches have recently been uncovered at the Library of Congress, making a final count of Sousa's march output impossible until all manuscripts have been sorted and catalogued.

27. This information is based on knowledge of Sousa manuscript sources documented by Paul E. Bierley.

28. Paul E. Bierley, *John Philip Sousa, American Phenomenon* (Westerville, Ohio: Integrity Press, 1973), p. 129.

29. This sequence was confirmed by Paul E. Bierley in a discussion with the author, 10 January 1992.

30. Bierley, *American Phenomenon*, p. 125.

31. In a number of original Sousa manuscripts studied by the author, Sousa appears to have been rather careless about the exact positioning of slurs, consistent placement of staccato markings, and so forth.

32. Helmecke, "How Sousa Played His Marches," p. 23.

33. This theory was supported by Paul E. Bierley in a conversation with the author, 10 January 1992.

34. This fact seems to be consistent in nearly every edition the author has studied. The principal cornet and clarinet parts must have received additional care in the engraving process.

35. John Philip Sousa, *The Fairest of the Fair* (John Church Co., 1908).

36. A series of Sousa marches published beginning in 1951 by Theodore Presser contain the designation "As played by the Sousa Band." These editions have bass drum parts edited by Sousa bass drummer Gus Helmecke and, therefore, the bass drum parts may be said to be "As played by the Sousa Band," but not the entire edition, particularly when new parts have been added to expand the instrumentation. The determination of which parts were used by Sousa and his band was made by examination of the Sousa encore books in the Marine Band Library.

37. John Philip Sousa, *The Stars and Stripes Forever!* (Theodore Presser Co.; copyright 1951 by John Church Co.).

38. This theory was corroborated by Arnold Broido, President of Theodore Presser Co., in a conversation with the author in Washington, D.C. on 13 April 1988.

39. John Philip Sousa, "We Must Have A Standard Instrumentation," *The Musical Observer* 29, no. 7 (July 1930): 28.

40. William C. Gens, "A Message from the President," *Sousa Band Society News* (January 1953): 3.

41. Frederick Fennell, "I Really Do Love Marches!," *BD Guide* 4, no. 4 (March/April 1990): 17.

42. Bierley, *Works*, p. 95.

43. Helmecke, "Why the accents weren't written in . . . ," p. 15.

44. This is one of three known sets of encore books used by the Sousa Band in its forty-year history. The Marine Band collection includes several complete books from an earlier green set, and there are empty red-covered books in the collection of the band department at the University of Illinois. This red set is empty since all music was pulled off the pages and apparently re-used in the next set of books. Parts which could not be removed remain in fragments.

45. John Philip Sousa, "Sousa Says Goodbye," Sydney (Australia) *Evening News*, 24 July 1911, from Sousa Press Book No. 34, p. 75 (in U.S. Marine Band archives).

46. Leonard B. Smith, "Concerning the Interpretation of Sousa and Other Marches," unpublished monograph, 1987 (available from author), p. 3.

47. In the seating of the Sousa Band, the solo cornet player was to the conductor's right with the section seated behind. This placed the cornet section directly opposite the clarinet section.

48. Frank Simon conducted a Sousa march clinic at the University of New Hampshire and even had brochures printed and a manager engaged to book what was billed as the "The Frank Simon Sousa March Clinic and Concert." The obvious goal was to present clinics of this nature all across the country.

49. Frank Simon, "Sounds of John Philip Sousa," vol. 1, 1966; vol. 2, 1969; booklets accompanying recordings produced by the American School Band Directors Association.

50. The Simon narratives were published in two volumes to accompany recordings of the marches. Volume 1 was released with Frank Simon conducting a student band comprised of players from Northern Virginia. Volume 2 was recorded by the U.S. Army Band under the direction of Lt. Col. Samuel Loboda. At present, vol. 1 has been newly recorded and is available from the American School Band Directors Association.

51. Keith Brion, "Sousa's Marches—As He Conducted Them," essay from booklet to accompany U.S. Marine Band recording *Semper Fidelis* (USMBCD-3), 1990.

52. James R. Smart, *The Sousa Band: A Discography* (Washington, D.C.: Library of Congress, 1970).

53. Bierley, *American Phenomenon*, p. 90 n.

54. Ibid., p. 19.

55. Ibid., pp. 70–72.

56. John Philip Sousa, "The Menace of Mechanical Music," *Appleton's Magazine* 8, no. 3 (September 1906), pp. 278–84.

57. Eugene Slick, interview with Paul E. Bierley, n.p., 11 April 1964 (from collection of Paul E. Bierley).

58. John Philip Sousa, Letter, *The Etude* 16, no. 8 (August 1878): 231.

59. Sam Harris, "Sousa As I Knew Him," *The Instrumentalist* 5, no. 5 (March-April 1951): 17.

60. John Philip Sousa, *Marching Along* (Boston: Hale, Cushman & Flint, 1928, reprinted 1941), p. 332.

61. Howard C. Bronson, "Sousa—The Man and His Music," (speech given at Eastern Division, College Band Directors National Association, at Fordham University, 14 April 1951), reprinted in *Sousa Band Society News* (May 1951): 18–24.

62. Leinsdorf, *Composer's Advocate*, p. 50.

63. Bronson, "Sousa—The Man and His Music."

64. Fennell, "I Really Do Love Marches!," p. 17.

65. Arthur Pryor, "How to Play a March," *The Metronome* (August 1932): 8.

66. Ibid.

67. Edwin Franko Goldman, *Band Betterment* (New York: Carl Fischer, 1934), pp. 88–89.

68. Harris, "Sousa As I Knew Him," p.17.

69. Simon, "Sounds of John Philip Sousa," vol. 1, p. 9.

70. Bierley, *Works*, p. 39.

71. Leinsdorf, *Composer's Advocate*, p. 91.

72. "Why Sousa's Band Succeeds," *The Musical Messenger* 18, no. 10 (October 1922): 9.

73. Helmecke, "How Sousa Played His Marches," p. 23.

74. Simon, "Sounds of John Philip Sousa," vol. 1, p. 4.

75. In discussion with the author during research at his home, Westerville, Ohio, February 1989.

76. Dvorak, "Sousa's March Performances," p. 65.

77. Paul E. Bierley to Leon J. Bly, 26 February 1977.

78. Albertus Meyers, interview with Paul E. Bierley, Sousa Band Fraternal Society Dinner, Gilhuly Brothers Cafe, New York, New York, 3 November 1963.

79. Sousa, "Sousa Says Goodbye."

80. Smith, "Concerning the Interpretation of Sousa and Other Marches," p. 4.

81. C. A. Browne, "The Fascinating March," *The Etude* 42, no. 7 (July 1924): 458, reprinted in *Band Fan*, newsletter of the Detroit Concert Band, vol. 13, no. 2 (fall 1989): 7.

82. Bierley, *American Phenomenon*, p. 140.

83. Frank Simon, interview with Paul E. Bierley, Manchester Motor Court, Middletown, Ohio, 29 June 1963 (from collection of Paul E. Bierley).

84. Helmecke, "Why the accents weren't written in . . .," p. 15.

85. Wall, Oral History Interview, 24 July 1981, pp. 144–145.

86. Helmecke, "How Sousa Played His Marches," p. 23.

87. George E. Reynolds, "Sousa," *The Instrumentalist* 5, no. 5 (March-April 1951): 12.

88. Leon J. Bly, *The March in American Society* (Ph.D. diss., University of Miami, Coral Gables, Fla., 1977), p. 194.

89. Raymond F. Dvorak, *The Band on Parade* (New York: Carl Fischer, 1937), p. 2.

90. Bierley, *American Phenomenon*, p. 148.

91. Lefter, Oral History Interview, August 1980, pp. 63–64.

92. Edmund C. Wall, interview with Keith Brion, n.p., 25 March 1983 (from collection of Paul E. Bierley).

93. Dvorak, "Sousa's March Performances," p. 59.

94. Ibid., p. 65.

95. Reynolds, "Sousa," p. 13.

96. Dvorak, *The Band on Parade*, p. 3.

97. Dvorak, "Sousa's March Performances," p. 59.

98. Wall, Oral History Interview, 24 July 1981, p. 143.

99. Showmanship was an integral part of Sousa's performance style. He and his managers created an image which was evident in all phases of his public life, most notably on stage. This led to observations such as the one offered by Otis Skinner: "Sousa is the best actor America has produced."

100. These phrases appear throughout the booklets for both volumes of the "Sounds of John Philip Sousa."

101. Bierley, *American Phenomenon*, p. 148.

102. Based on parts found in the Sousa encore books.

103. Simon, "Sounds of John Philip Sousa," vol. 2, p. 12.

104. Simon, "Sounds of John Philip Sousa," vol. 1, p. 8.

105. Having experimented with the instrumentation in soft strains, I believe using oboes here is a wonderful effect. The other instruments Dvorak recommends dropping (cornets, trombones, and piccolo) all have greater carrying power than the oboes. Their absence in soft strains would seem to make more sense.

106. John Philip Sousa, "Sousa's Message to Young America," *Musical Truth* 17, no. 44 (fall 1927): 3.

107. Bierley, *American Phenomenon*, p. 148.

108. Ibid., p. 178.

109. Ibid., p. 148.

110. Ibid.

111. Wall, interview with Brion, 25 March 1983.

112. Dvorak's recollection is that piccolo was not used in the soft strains.

113. John J. Heney, *The Correct Way to Drum* (St. Augustine, Fla.: Heney School of Percussion, 1934), p. 12.

114. Dvorak, "Sousa's March Performances," p. 59.

115. Frank Simon had claimed that Helmecke was the only striking member who was re-hired. Paul Bierley believes that there were actually two members hired back: Helmecke was one and the other was said to also be a percussionist. It could be that Helmecke insisted that his fellow percussionist also be rehired as a condition of his own return (information from conversation with Paul Bierley, 12 January 1992).

116. Smith, "Concerning the Interpretation of Sousa and other Marches," p. 2.

117. Ibid., p. 2.

118. Helmecke, "How Sousa Played His Marches," p. 23.

119. Smith, "Concerning the Interpretation of Sousa and other Marches," p. 2.

120. Dr. Smith measured Gus Helmecke's bass drum during his time with the Goldman Band. The author saw the replica during a visit with Dr. Smith in Phoenix, Arizona on 7 March 1989.

121. Bierley, *Works*, p. 39.

122. Sousa, *The Stars and Stripes Forever!* (published Presser, copyright 1951 John Church Co.).

123. Leonard B. Smith, telephone conversation with the author, 5 January 1992.

124. This is especially audible on *Dauntless Battalion, Solid Men to the Front,* and *Liberty Loan.*

125. Conversation with the author, Westerville, Ohio, February 1989.

126. Heney, *The Correct Way to Drum*, p. 51.

127. Bierley, *Works*, p. 39.

128. Heney, *The Correct Way to Drum*, pp. 51–52.

129. Professional percussionists with whom the author has discussed this beat have speculated that it was an outgrowth of the drumming style popularized in ragtime music.

130. Heney, *The Correct Way to Drum*, p. 53.

131. Ibid.

132. Ibid.

133. In 1969 John Heney recorded an instructional cassette tape in which he discussed and demonstrated the "five stroke roll with a flam attack." He made the point very distinctly that the use of the five-stroke roll was not important but that the interpretation of the roll was important.

134. This five-stroke roll with flam attack is also documented in an essay as part of vol. 2 of the "Sounds of John Philip Sousa" series produced by the American School Band Directors Association.

135. Heney, *The Correct Way to Drum*, p. 62.

136. Ibid., p. 57.

137. Dvorak, "Sousa's March Performances," p. 59.

138. This can be seen in a Fox Movietone newsreel of the Goldman Band playing in Central Park (from the author's collection).

139. Smith, telephone conversation with the author, 5 January 1992.

140. Jake Freeman, "Reminiscences of a Tuba Player," *Music World* (Chicago Musical Instrument Co.), reprinted in *Sousa Band Society News* (November 1972): 8–9.

141. "Sousa Claims Bass Drummer . . . Best in World, and True Artist."

142. Helmecke, "How Sousa Played His Marches," p. 23.

143. Robert A. Poteete, "Goldman Band Bass Drummer, 82, Retires With a Flourish," n.p., n.d., reprinted in *Sousa Band Society News* (July 1952): 7.

144. Leonard B. Smith to Frank Byrne, 7 March 1989.

145. Simon, "Sounds of John Philip Sousa," vol. 2, p. 4.

146. Hindsley, Oral History Interview, 10 December 1980, p. 21.

147. Dvorak, "Sousa's March Performances," p. 59.

148. "What is Music?," part of the PBS "Nova" series, WGBH, Boston 1989.

149. The Sousa-conducted recording of *Dauntless Battalion* is an excellent example.

150. Heney, *The Correct Way to Drum*, p. 57.

151. Ibid., p. 62.

152. Ibid., p. 59.

153. In the collection of the U.S. Marine Band Library.

Figure 1: Solo Cornet part to *Washington Post March.*

This Solo Cornet part to Sousa's *Washington Post March* is taken from the Sousa Band Encore books, now in the archives of the U.S. Marine Band Library in Washington, D.C. It is one of the best examples of Sousa's style as documented by a player in a performance part. The original pencil markings have been darkened to make them readable in this reproduction. The angled and haphazard penmanship suggests that these markings were added hurriedly with the music on the stand, possibly by a new Solo Cornetist who had not yet memorized the performance changes. The performance practices we can see clearly indicated are as follows: (1) tacet second strain first time, with a *crescendo* on each of the dotted half notes in mm. 3, 5, 7, and 11 of this strain leading to a *sforzando* on the downbeat of each successive measure, (2) tacet both times through the trio and in the episode (or "break-up strain"), entering at *piano* after the first quarter note three measures before the last strain which, although not indicated with a double bar, starts sixteen measures from the end, and (3) tacet the first time through the last strain. These changes match exactly the narrative information on Sousa performance practice documented by Dr. Frank Simon, Sousa's Solo Cornetist 1914–1921.

Richard Wagner's *Trauermusik*, WWV 73

[*Trauersinfonie*]

MICHAEL VOTTA

O NE of the landmark works of the nineteenth-century wind repertoire is Richard Wagner's so-called *Trauersinfonie*. This work, actually referred to as *Trauermusik* by Wagner,[1] now exists in at least three separate versions: the original manuscript score (1844—hereafter identified as W);[2] the first published full score, edited by Michael Balling (1926—hereafter B);[3] and Erik Leidzen's "revision" for symphonic band (1948—hereafter L).[4] Leidzen's version is most commonly performed because it includes parts for full symphonic band instrumentation, and because no performing edition of the original had been made. Consequently, I have worked to create a practical performing edition that is faithful to Wagner's original.[5]

In the 1980s, two articles by Keating Johnson[6] and a catalog of Wagner's works[7] opened the discussion of the genesis and history of this important work. Johnson and the compilers of the *Wagner Werk-Verzeichnis* (WWV), however, disagree on the compositional history of the work. Johnson mentions an "edition by Breitkopf und Härtel from the late 1800s" that was "*re*-published . . . in 1926 as part of the Complete Works of Richard Wagner" (emphasis added),[8] while other sources maintain 1926 as the first publication date of the full score.[9] Johnson's "edition from the late 1800s," if it exists, would be an important source in preparing a new edition. It is not listed, however, in catalogs of Wagner's works,[10] in Breitkopf & Härtel catalogs of the period,[11] in the holdings of the British Museum, the Library of Congress, the New York Public Library, or in the OCLC (Online Computer Library Center) or RLIN (Research Libraries Information Network) systems.[12] Unfortunately, the original performance parts, potentially one of the best sources for determining a definitive version, have not been mentioned by anyone. I have sought these parts in all known repositories of Wagner's manuscripts, but have yet to locate them.[13]

Johnson's articles also contain some curious statements. He states that no account of the premiere performance survives,[14] even though there is a detailed account by Wagner himself.[15] Johnson also expresses surprise that the work lay dormant after its premiere until a 1927 performance by the New York Philharmonic conducted by Willem Mengelberg.[16] Part of Johnson's surprise may be due to his belief that the nineteenth-century Breitkopf edition was widely circulated. The 1927 performance date is, of course, only one year after the first known full score was published. Most importantly, the work was composed for enlarged orchestral wind section—there was no version for band until 1948.

Johnson's main contribution, therefore, has been a tabulation of differences in articulation between the three versions.[17] No one has produced an edition of the original instrumentation for modern wind ensembles, nor has anyone attempted to resolve some of the ambiguities in the Wagner manuscript.[18] It is surely time to take these final steps to establish a modern performing edition.

History of the Work

On 14 December 1844 the remains of Carl Maria von Weber were moved from English to German soil. Wagner composed *Trauermusik* for the torch-light procession to Weber's final resting-place, the Catholic Cemetery in Friedrichstadt.[19] The subtitle to the work, "Funeral Music on Themes of Carl Maria von Weber," and the preface to the Leidzen transcription are misleading. Both imply that Wagner borrowed and arranged only Weber's melodies. Actually, Wagner took both melody and harmony from Weber. *Trauermusik* is Wagner's "band transcription" of Weber's music.

The first part of *Trauermusik* is an arrangement of music from the overture to *Euryanthe* (mm. 129–143) which represents the vision of Emma's spirit in the opera (Ex. 1). Wagner transposed the music down one-half step to B-flat minor and added a dominant-seventh chord to connect the passage to the next section. Wagner also altered Weber's tempo indication, "Largo," to "Adagio." However, Wagner retained Weber's meter signature of 4/4.

The main section of the work (mm. 17–71) is taken from the cavatina "Hier dicht am Quell" ("Near to this spring") from Act III, scene 2, in which Euryanthe grieves over the loss of her beloved, Count Adolar.[20] Wagner's choice of this passage may have been influenced by the numerous textual references to death (Ex. 2). Wagner transposed this music from G major to B-flat major; he also added a repeat marking at the end of this section (returning to the beginning) to allow the work to be used throughout the two-and-one-half mile procession. Most importantly, Wagner doubled Weber's note values, which calls into question the tempo relationship between this section and the opening.

The coda of *Trauermusik* is taken from Act III, scene 7 (just before the final chorus) where Count Adolar "falls on his knees before Euryanthe, then rises in prophetic ecstasy at their reunion (Ex. 3)."[21] Wagner probably chose this passage because it is an altered version of the "vision music" which opens *Trauermusik*. Wagner transposed this passage from C major to B-flat major, adjusted the part-writing, and once again doubled the note values. In addition, he eliminated repeated notes and changed the rhythm of Adolar's melody in *Trauermusik's* final trumpet passage.

From 1844 until 1926, the only generally known copies of the full score were W and a score in the hand of Felix Mottl.[22] The lack of an available full score and parts undoubtedly made performances of the work difficult. Only one performance of the work between its premiere and 1926 is known: a concert performance conducted by Johann Siebenkäs in October 1864. The origin and current location of these performance parts are unknown.

A piano arrangement published in 1860 by C. F. Meser gave the work its long-standing title, *Trauersinfonie*.[23] This title, however, was added by Meser; Wagner repeatedly referred to the work as *Trauermusik*.[24] Ironically, this arrangement, the only version of the work published during Wagner's lifetime, was done without his knowledge. Wagner, believing the work to be unpublished, wrote to the publisher Fritzsch in 1871: "You could issue my *Trauermusik* in full score and in piano arrangement. . . ."[25] Wagner later wrote to Fritzsch that Meser's edition was done "against my [Wagner's] wishes."[26] It was not until 1926 that the first generally known published full score, edited by Balling (B), was issued by Breitkopf & Härtel in volume 20 of Wagner's collected works.[27]

Balling made a fundamental and significant change, altering W's tempo and meter signature "Adagio, C" to "Andante maestoso, alla breve" (Ex. 4). Balling possibly took tempo and meter markings, as he did the title, from Meser's piano version or from Mottl's handwritten copy of the score. Wagner clearly intended to preserve the slow tempo of Weber's music. The fact that he doubled the note values in the cavatina and coda may have led to Balling's *alla breve* indication.

Because the work was to be performed in a procession, Wagner may have avoided tempo changes—this score is entirely free of the numerous tempo modifications found in his other works. In a concert performance, however, one can judge relative tempos from Weber's metronome markings for the original material. Weber indicates quarter note = M.M. 52 for the opening material and eighth note = M.M. 66 for the cavatina (see Exx. 1 and 2), hence my suggested addition of "poco più mosso" at m. 17.

There are also two minor notational differences between these scores. First of all, there is one flute part. W specifies three first flutes and two second flutes, playing in unison throughout. B indicates one part played by five flutes.[28] Secondly, there are four separate clarinet parts. W requests two clarinet parts with ten players each. Both parts use *divisi*. B specifies four clarinet parts with five players each—W's first part becomes B's "clarinet 1 & 2," and W's second part becomes B's "clarinet 3 & 4."[29] Other discrepancies between W and B include numerous differences in articulation, and some small variances in instrumentation.

Erik Leidzen's "revision" of *Trauermusik* (L), done in 1948 for the Goldman Band, made the work available to wind bands in a performing edition. This edition remains the most widely performed version of the work, even though it is now permanently out of print. Richard Franko Goldman, in the preface to L, stated that it was "in faithful accordance with the original except for very minor revisions . . . necessitated by the changes in wind instruments and usages since Wagner's early years." Leidzen himself, in his preface to the first printing of his arrangement, used words like "serviceable and effective" to describe his numerous additions to Wagner's original. Leidzen never claimed that his version had any scholarly relation to original sources. His aim clearly was to produce a useful version of the piece for American symphonic bands rather than a definitive edition of the original.

Although many of Leidzen's emendations are logical, his version continues

Balling's misrepresentation of title, tempo marking, meter, signature and articulations, probably because he worked from B, not from the manuscript.[30] Leidzen also misquotes the original in m. 6. W's bass line (first and second bassoons and second horn) has a B-double-flat on the fourth beat (Ex. 5); L alters this to B-flat in his bass clarinet, bassoon, tenor saxophone, second horn, and euphonium parts. Most importantly, however, "wind instruments and usages" as well as wind bands have undergone a major evolution since 1948. Consequently, Leidzen's revisions in instrumentation are anything but "minor" by today's standards.

Leidzen's "Modernized" Instrumentation

Military bands were common in mid-nineteenth-century Germany, and Wagner was surely aware of their instrumentation.[31] Although these military bands existed in several different instrumentations, none used orchestral winds exclusively.[32] Since W is scored for augmented orchestral wind section, it seems that Wagner chose to write only for orchestral winds. Leidzen, on the other hand, wrote for the instrumentation of the twentieth-century American symphonic band.

W and B both specify the number of players for each part. L was prepared for "the Goldman Band," a symphonic band of sixty players whose exact instrumentation is amply documented.[33] We can therefore compare the specific instrumentations of Wagner's original score, Balling, and Leidzen (Table 1).

Wagner asked for substantial doublings of each part. The Goldman Band's instrumentation, which is common in modern symphonic bands, approximates Wagner's in the flute, clarinet, trumpet, trombone and tuba sections, but falls considerably short of Wagner's oboe, bassoon, and horn sections. Modern "wind ensembles" that follow the one-player-per-part concept have substantially smaller clarinet sections (and therefore proportionally larger flute, saxophone, and trumpet sections) than either of the earlier ensembles. Consequently, the overall sound and balance can be quite different from Wagner's intention when the work is performed by either modern symphonic bands or wind ensembles.

Leidzen was, of course, forced to add numerous parts to complete the standard symphonic band instrumentation. Some of these, such as alto and bass clarinet, alto, tenor and baritone saxophone, and euphonium parts are used to strengthen clarinet, bassoon, and horn parts to help compensate for the differences in instrumentation described above. Others, like E-flat clarinet, bass saxophone, and percussion are obvious "instrumentation fillers" which were peculiar to the performance practice of large bands of the early and mid-twentieth-century. Table 2 lists the doublings of these added parts.

In all versions, the principal melodic line is played in unison by flute, first oboe, and first clarinet throughout the work. Wagner probably intended an equal blend of flute, oboe, and clarinet on this line (he apparently realized that the more penetrating quality of the oboe allows four of that instrument to balance equally with five flutes and five clarinets). In performance with modern bands, therefore, the flute and first clarinet parts should be assigned with the view of providing an equal balance on this crucial line. Since most modern bands have less than four first oboes, dynamics must be adjusted to ensure that the oboe timbre remains fully one-third of the overall woodwind sound.

Wagner also specifies fourteen horns and six trumpets, while most modern bands use more trumpets than horns. The original F horn parts (L's first and second parts) carry the principal melodic lines, while the B-flat horns (L's third and fourth) provide harmonic support. L frequently strengthens the two melodic parts with saxophones, altering the timbre Wagner intended. To preserve the timbral clarity of the original, balance between the trumpet and horn parts should be corrected only by adjusting dynamics or by reducing the number of trumpets. On the other hand, the supporting (B-flat) horn parts are doubled frequently with trumpets and trombones in all versions.

Leidzen's Rewritten Parts

Besides changing the instrumentation of the ensemble, Leidzen altered timbres within the woodwind, brass, and percussion sections by rewriting passages according to traditional band scoring practices.

In W and B, the first and second clarinet parts are independent while the third and fourth parts play mostly in unison, producing a section of 5 first, 5 second, and 10 third/fourth. L, however, shifts the original third/fourth part between his second and third parts (Ex. 6). Unless L's second and third parts are played by sections of equal strength, the balance of the original clarinet lines will be distorted. L condensed these four parts into a standard three-part clarinet section by replacing the fourth part with alto saxophone, making this instrument essential to achieving correct woodwind balance. L also occasionally uses the alto saxophones to double the original first and second parts, giving undue prominence to these lines.

If the work is to be performed using Leidzen's version, equal numbers of players should be assigned to the second and third parts (remembering that the first clarinet parts should be assigned to balance with the flutes and oboes). A better solution would be to dispose of Leidzen's clarinet parts and substitute the original four clarinet parts, allowing the saxophone doublings to be eliminated in sensitive passages such as the delicate opening measures of the work.

In mm. 6–11, m. 14, and mm. 31–32, L scores W's second trumpet part for trombone. The passage in mm. 6–11 could be played by either instrument. L, however, scores the G-flat (concert pitch) whole note in m. 9 for the entire trumpet section—in W it is for first trumpets only (three players total)—making the fifth of the C-flat "German" sixth chord unnecessarily strong (Ex. 7). In m. 14, L re-orchestrates the final eighth note, but omits the B-flat from the chord entirely (Ex. 8). B omits W's trombone chord in m. 16; L created trombone parts that double the third trumpet and second and fourth horns. The parts should be rewritten to restore W's trombone notes. Measures 31–32 in L defy the logic of W's trombone parts (Ex. 9).

W merely specifies "muffled drums" (*trommeln gedämpft*). B amplifies this to tenor drums (*Rührtrommeln*), but L calls for snare drum. Karl Peinkofer clarifies the type of drums intended by Wagner. Peinkofer (a native German) maintains that *Rührtrommel* should actually be translated as "long drum"—a drum often used with fifes in early military bands. Peinkofer further suggests that this is the drum intended by Wagner in *Lohengrin, Meistersinger,* and *Parsifal.* "Long drums" are 20–30 inches (50–75 cm.) deep and 16–20 inches (40–50 cm.) in diameter. Modern long drums have four to six gut snares. The strong resonance of the large shell, combined with the distance of the snares from the batter head results in very little snare noise in the overall sound. Peinkofer describes the drum as having a "low, dark and muffled" timbre.[34] In any case, modern concert snare drums do not belong in *Trauermusik.*

The number of drums Wagner intended is also open to question. W and B specify six muffled drums, yet Wagner, in his commentary on the first performance, wrote: "I set the ghostly viola tremolo [in Weber's original] for *twenty* muffled drums in the softest *piano. . .*" (emphasis added).[35]

The concept of flexible instrumentation, the artistic idea that led to the creation of the Eastman Wind Ensemble in 1952, allows modern wind ensembles to represent faithfully the composer's ideal instrumentation. A fundamental concern, therefore, is the selection of an appropriate medium for performances of *Trauermusik.* Wagner wrote for orchestral winds, not for military band. There is a clear timbral difference between these media, produced by the presence of auxiliary clarinets, saxhorns, and saxophones in the band instrumentation. We cannot, therefore, accept Leidzen's arrangement as "faithful to the original" simply because both versions are for wind instruments.

There is a clear need for a modern performing edition of the original version. Johnson suggests using the 1926 edition with corrected articulation. This approach, however, leaves the questions of ensemble size and balance unanswered. Wagner's original calls for seventy-five winds, of which seven are oboes, ten are bassoons, and fourteen are horns. Beyond the severely practical reason that very few modern ensembles could amass such a large number of these instruments, we should also consider whether an indoor concert performance requires so many players. Wagner's decision to use such large forces was undoubtedly influenced by the fact that the work was to be performed in an outdoor procession. We must, however, also consider the texture that results from such massive doublings, a property of which Wagner was surely aware.

Reducing Wagner's original instrumentation while keeping the same proportions within the ensemble seems to be a logical and practical solution. In reducing Wagner's instrumentation we must try to balance two conflicting principles. On one hand, a too-small ensemble (such as one player per part) has a significantly "leaner" sound than Wagner's ensemble. Further, Wagner's long phrases cannot be projected at slow tempi with such an ensemble—there are too few places in the music for solo winds to breathe. On the other hand, Wagner's ensemble calls for a bassoon section that is fully one-half the size of the clarinet section; a large ensemble therefore quickly requires an impractical number of bassoons. The best compromise, I believe, is detailed in Table 1 under the heading "proposed concert version."

This instrumentation requires dynamic adjustment of some parts to maintain the balance of the original.[36] It would, however, allow the original balance and timbre to be projected with an ensemble of relatively modest dimensions (twenty-nine winds). This instrumentation with dynamic adjustments as needed, combined with the restoration clarification of W's articulations is a first step to producing a modern, practical edition of *Trauermusik*.

Articulations and Dynamics

Articulations in both B and L differ substantially from W. Wagner seems to have used slur marks primarily to show phrases, not to indicate breathing points.[37] B shortened these phrase markings, and L further modified B's articulations. Restoring Wagner's original markings visually reinforces the long, sweeping melodic lines that are the essence of *Trauermusik*. However, the long slurs raise some issues for the editor.

The manuscript has numerous examples of repeated notes under slurs, some with dots, some with accents, and some with no markings. The flute, oboe and clarinet passage in mm. 41–42 has repeated notes in both measures, yet dots only in m. 42. Both B and L added dots in m. 41. W's markings, however, are consistent in all voices: all slurred in m. 41 and "dotted" in m. 42 (Ex. 10). This passage is scored for strings in Weber's original, and Wagner copies Weber's markings exactly.

W combines three different articulations at the end of m. 66: notes at the end of a slur with a ^ mark (flute, oboe, clarinet); accented notes slurred into the following measure (bassoons, B-flat horns, trumpets, and first trombone); and accented notes with no slur (F horns, lower trombones, and tuba). Clearly the F horns' upbeat should be slurred and the low trombones and tuba should have a tenuto mark to ensure that the brass sustain uniformly as the woodwinds release their note (Ex. 11).

W's use of slurs is inconsistent at several points in the manuscript. For example, most of the upbeats in the main tune of the cavatina are slurred while those in mm. 21–22 are articulated (Ex. 12). There are also inconsistent articulations between parts, such as the different markings for second oboe and third and fourth clarinet in mm. 6–11 (Ex. 13). Considering the speed with which Wagner prepared this score (the manuscript represents the "first and only" draft), I believe that articulations should be made consistent but that Wagner's long phrase markings should be retained.

Although published versions of *Trauermusik* have been available for sixty-five years, only one set of parts (L) was ever readily available, and no editions are currently in print. The work has yet to be published in the new edition of Wagner's complete works and is not likely to be for some time, according to the publisher.[38]

With the advent of the wind ensemble and the concept of adapting the ensemble to the needs of the music (rather than vice versa), wind conductors gained an invaluable resource for expressive, faithful interpretation. My edition of *Trauermusik* will make the original instrumentation of one of our masterworks available in a practical performing edition.

NOTES

1. The term "Trauermusik" was applied generically to funeral music.

2. Berlin, Deutsche Staatsbibliothek, Mus. ms. autogr. R. Wagner 3. Other copies in Wagner's hand have reportedly been seen in the Richard Wagner-Gesamtausgabe (Schott) offices in Mainz. I have been unable to trace these.

3. Michael Balling, ed., *Richard Wagners Werke*, vol. 20 (Leipzig: Breitkopf & Härtel, 1926); reissued New York: Da Capo Press, 1971.

4. Richard Wagner, *Trauersinfonie*, arr. Erik Leidzen (New York: Associated Music Publishers, Inc., 1949).

5. Cleveland: Ludwig, Inc., forthcoming.

6. L. Keating Johnson, "The Wind Band Compositions of Richard Wagner, 1813–1883," *Journal of Band Research*, vol. 15, no. 2 (spring 1980): 10–14, and "Richard Wagner's *Trauersinfonie*," *Journal of Band Research*, vol. 16, no. 2 (spring 1981): 38–42.

7. John Deathridge, Martin Geck, and Egon Voss, *Wagner Werk-Verzeichnis* (Mainz: B. Schotts Söhne, 1986).

8. Johnson, "Richard Wagner's *Trauersinfonie*," p. 38.

9. These sources include the *Wagner Werk-Verzeichnis*, *The New Grove Dictionary of Music and Musicians*, ed. Stanley Sadie (London: Macmillan, 1980), and *Die Musik in Geschichte und Gegenwart*, ed. Friedrich Blume, (Kassel: Bärenreiter, 1949).

10. Including Horst Klein's *Erstdrücke der Musikalische Werke von Richard Wagner* (First Publications of Wagner's Musical Works) (Tutzing: Hans Schneider, 1983).

11. Summarized in Oskar von Hase, *Breitkopf und Härtel Gedankenschrift und Arbeitsbericht*, 5th edition (Wiesbaden: Breitkopf & Härtel, 1968).

12. In a telephone conversation, Johnson confirmed that he had found a copy of this edition in the library of the U.S. Marine Band in Washington, D.C. It was published with score and parts, and is identical to the 1926 edition. It is not mentioned by any other source. Since it is identical to the 1926 Breitkopf edition, it does not represent a new version of the work.

13. They were probably destroyed during World War II.

14. Johnson, "Richard Wagner's *Trauersinfonie*," p. 12.

15. Richard Wagner, "Bericht über die Heimbringung der sterblichen Überreste Karl Maria von Webers aus London nach Dresden—aus meinen Lebenserinnerungen ausgezogen" (Report on the return of the remains of Karl Maria von Weber from London to Dresden—from my memoirs), *Gesammelte Schriftungen und Dichtungen* (Leipzig, 1887), 2:41–48.

16. Johnson, "Richard Wagner's *Trauersinfonie*." Johnson mentions only "an orchestra." Details are contained in the preface to the first printing of L. The New York Philharmonic program does not state whether the original, winds-only version or an orchestral arrangement was performed.

17. Johnson compared a microfilm of W with B and L.

18. These ambiguities include inconsistent articulations and Wagner's use of slurs.

19. Like most wind works of its time, *Trauermusik* was composed as ceremonial music. Wagner also composed a work for men's chorus, *An Webers Grabe* (At Weber's Grave), WWV 72, for the same occasion.

20. See Michael Tursa, *Carl Maria von Weber's Euryanthe* (Ph.D diss., Princeton University, 1983).

21. I am indebted to Robert Garofolo of Catholic University for identifying and describing this passage from *Euryanthe*.

22. Mottl's score, which is currently in the Richard Wagner Gedenkstätte der Stadt Bayreuth, may have been the source for the 1926 edition.

23. The arrangement, made by A. D. Blassman, was reprinted in 1885.

24. The original manuscript is untitled.

25. ". . . meiner Partitur der Trauermusik . . . könnten Sie in Partitur und Klavierauszugher-ausgeben. . . ," quoted in Georg Kinsky, *Musik-Autographen*, vol. 4 of *Musikhistorisches Museum von Wilhelm Heyer in Köln—Katalog* (Cologne, 1916), p. 705 f.

26. Ibid.

27. Although the Breitkopf & Härtel edition was originally conceived as a complete collection of Wagner's works, the full project was never completed.

28. Wagner originally may have intended to write two separate flute parts.

29. Wagner probably used *divisi* to save paper.

30. Johnson, in a telephone conversation, reported his belief that Leidzen worked from an orchestral arrangement of Balling's edition, and recreated a wind setting of the piece. Considering the numerous similarities between B and L, however, I believe that Leidzen worked from the 1926 edition.

31. Eugen Brixel, "Richard Wagners Beziehung zur Militärmusik," in *Bläserklang und Blasinstrumente im Schaffen Richard Wagners*, report from the 1983 Congress of the International Society for the Promotion and Investigation of Wind Music, ed. Wolfgang Suppan (Tutzing: Hans Schneider, 1985), pp. 177–87.

32. Common additional instruments included piccolo clarinets in A-flat and E-flat, alto clarinets in F and E-flat, basset horns, saxophones, cornets, tenorhorns, and other saxhorns.

33. Kirby R. Jolly, *E. F. Goldman and the Goldman Band* (Ph.D. diss., New York University, 1971).

34. Karl Peinkofer, *Handbook of Percussion Instruments*, trans. Kurt and Else Stone (Mainz: B. Schotts Söhne, 1969).

35. ". . . das schaurige Tremolo der Bratsche . . . ließ ich durch zwanzig gedämpfte Trommeln im leisesten Piano erseßen. . . ." Richard Wagner, *Gesammelte Schriftungen und Dichtungen*, pp. 43–44.

36. The oboe dynamics must be raised and the horn dynamics lowered.

37. This use of slurs is analogous to that in Wagner's string writing, in which slurs often show phrasing, not bowing.

38. Telephone conversation. The new edition is *Richard Wagner: Sämtliche Werke*, Carl Dahlhaus and Egon Voss, eds. (Mainz: B. Schotts Söhne, 1970–). *Trauermusik* is to appear in vol. 18, part 2.

Numbers in parentheses are number of players per part. Parts in brackets were included in Leidzen's published set of parts but were not used by the Goldman Band.

Original Instrumentation	Goldman Band, 1946*	Proposed Concert Version
flute (5)	flute (4)	flute (2)
1st oboe (4)	1st oboe (1)	1st oboe (1: raise dynamics)
2nd oboe (3)	2nd oboe (1)	2nd oboe (1: raise dynamics selectively)
——	E♭ clarinet (1)	——
1st clarinet (5)	1st clarinet	1st clarinet (2)
2nd clarinet (5)	2nd clarinet†	2nd clarinet (2)
3rd clarinet (5)	3rd clarinet† (19 total)	3rd clarinet (2)
4th clarinet (5)	——	4th clarinet (2)
——	[alto clarinet]	——
——	bass clarinet (1)	——
1st bassoon (5)	1st bassoon (1)	1st bassoon (2)
2nd bassoon (5)	2nd bassoon (1)	2nd bassoon (2)
——	1st alto saxophone (1)	——
——	[2nd alto saxophone]	——
——	tenor saxophone (1)	——
——	baritone saxophone (1)	——
——	[bass saxophone]	——
1st F horn (4)	1st horn (1)	1st F horn (2)
2nd F horn (4)	2nd horn (1)	2nd F horn (2) (reduce dynamics)
1st B♭ (basso) horn (3)	3rd horn (1)	3rd horn (1)
2nd B♭ (basso) horn (3)	4th horn (1)	4th horn (1)
1st F trumpet (3)	1st cornet/trumpet	1st trumpet (1)
2nd F trumpet (3)	2nd cornet/trumpet†	2nd trumpet (1)
——	3rd cornet/trumpet (7 total)	——
alto trombone (3)	1st trombone† (2)	1st trombone (1)
tenor trombone (3)	2nd trombone† (2)	2nd trombone (1)
bass trombone (3)	3rd trombone (2)	bass trombone (1)
——	euphonium (2)	——
tuba (4)	tuba (4)	tuba (2)
——	string bass	——
——	tympani	——
tenor drum—muffled	snare drum	tenor/long drum (2)
[long drum?]	——	
——	cymbals	——
——	tam-tam	——

*Kirby R. Jolly, *E. F. Goldman and the Goldman Band* (Ph.D. diss., New York University, 1971).
†Differs substantially from the original version.

Table 1: Instrumentations of original (Wagner and Balling), Goldman Band (Leidzen), and proposed concert versions.

E♭ clarinet: doubles the first clarinet part throughout. *Omit this part and have the player join the clarinet section.*

Alto clarinet: not used by the Goldman Band, and probably included at the request of Leidzen's publisher. Primarily doubles first bassoon; also reinforces second clarinet (m. 12), third clarinet (mm. 14 and 41), and second horn (mm. 13–14). *Alto clarinet is a good reinforcement for the first bassoon part, since its timbre is compatible with Wagner's instrumentation, and especially considering Wagner's large bassoon section. Change articulations to match original bassoon or trombone lines as needed.*

First alto saxophone: problematic. Leidzen's version will not work without it because it replaces the fourth clarinet part (except in m. 12 and mm. 72–76 where it doubles second oboe, and mm. 62–65 where it doubles first horn). If Wagner's clarinet parts are used, this part becomes optional.

Second alto saxophone: not originally used by the Goldman Band. Reinforces second clarinet (mm. 1–3, 12–15, 17–18, 21–22, and 78–85), third clarinet (mm. 4, 25–31, and 37–42), first horn (mm. 6–11, 19–20, 34–36, 43–44, 49–50, 57–63, and 72–77), third horn (mm. 32–33 and 64–65), and second cornet (mm. 47–48 and 55–56). The clarinet doublings are illogical: Leidzen attempts to achieve the original weight within the clarinet section by replacing fourth clarinet with first alto, then again distorts the clarinet balance with this part. *Omit.*

Tenor saxophone: primarily doubles first bassoon; adds a spurious bottom octave to the melody in mm. 17–18 and 21–22; also reinforces bottom *divisi* of third clarinet [original fourth clarinet part] (mm. 37–41), first horn (mm. 32–33), third horn (mm. 34–36), and second trombone (mm. 86–87). *If this part is used, be sure to match articulations with the original and eliminate the "new" bottom woodwind octave described above.*

Baritone saxophone: primarily doubles second bassoon, as well as second/third trombone in mm. 25–28, 54–80. *The least distortion of the original is accomplished with first alto, tenor (with editing), and baritone.*

Bass saxophone: a case in point of "changes in wind instruments and usages." Doubles tuba throughout. *Omit.*

Euphonium: primarily doubles fourth horn; also doubles second bassoon (mm. 81–88), second horn (m. 42), first trombone (mm. 70–71), and third trombone (mm. 17–41, 49–50, and 56–61). *Adds weight and smoothness to low brass parts and can be especially useful in filling out the lower horn parts. The part is also extensively cued with important bass lines. Match articulations with trombones or horns as needed, editing out the woodwind doublings.*

String bass: doubles bass line throughout. *Note that the slurs in the part in mm. 32–36 are not good bowings.*

Percussion: Leidzen added parts for tympani, cymbals (!), and tam-tam (!!). *They should be omitted. If the tympani part is used, a third drum, tuned to E♭, should be added in mm. 17, 21, and 49 so that the tympani follows the bass line accurately, thus eliminating the 6/4 chords produced with the written B♭.*

Table 2: Leidzen's added parts with doublings. Specific recommendations for their use are in italics.

Example 1: "Vision music" from overture to *Euryanthe*.

Example 2: Excerpt from Act III, scene 2 (Cavatina: "Hier dicht am Quell").

Example 3: Excerpt from Act III, scene 7 (altered "vision music").

Example 4: Opening. a. Wagner's autograph. b. Balling.

Example 5: Wagner's autograph, m. 6.

a.

b.

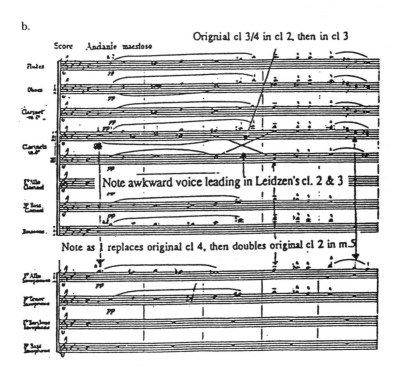

Example 6: Woodwinds, mm. 1–5.
    a. Wagner (Balling).
    b. Leidzen.

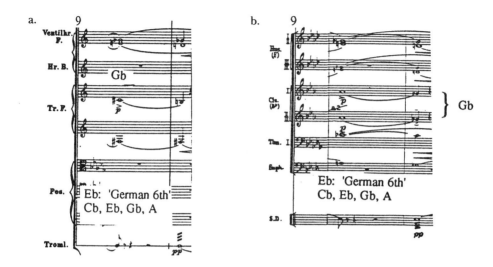

Example 7: Doublings in brass chord, m. 9.
   a. Wagner (Balling).
   b. Leidzen.

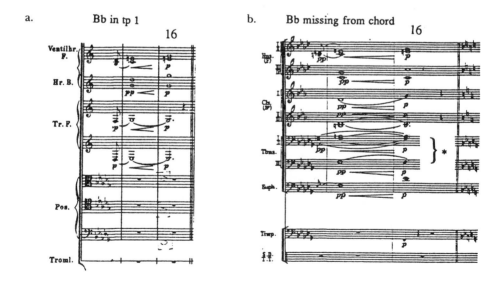

Example 8: Brass chords, mm. 14–16.
   a. Wagner (Balling). B♭ in Trumpet 1; no trombone parts in m. 16 of Balling.
   b. Leidzen. B♭ missing from chord; trombones double horns.

All trombones play complete phrase

Example 9: Trombone parts, mm. 31–34.
    a. Wagner (Balling). All trombones play complete phrase.
    b. Leidzen. Trombone 2 begins melody in mid-phrase.

Example 10: Wagner's autograph, mm. 41–42.

Example 11: Wagner's autograph, m. 66.

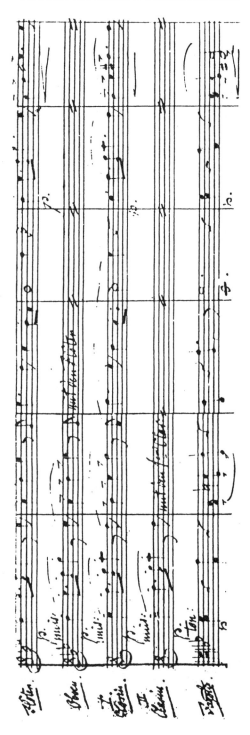

Example 12: Wagner's autograph, mm. 17–22.

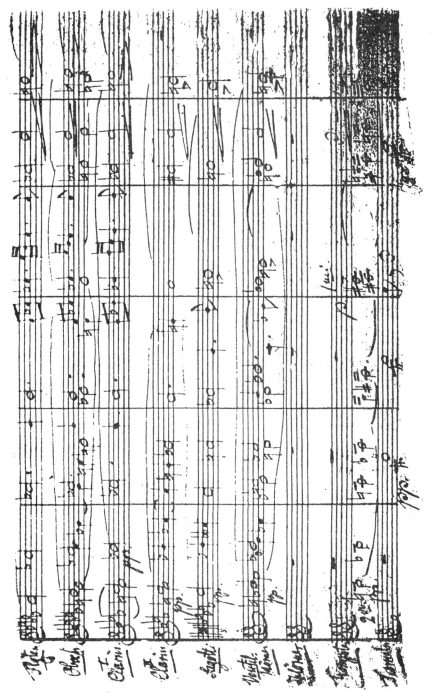

Example 13: Wagner's autograph, mm. 6–11.

Contemporary British Music
for Band and Wind Ensemble

TIMOTHY REYNISH

IN his book, *Basic Band Repertory*, Frederick Fennell states that "At least 90% of the band music now published and played in the United States is patterned after the British Army band repertory of the early 1900s."[1] Such is the influence of a handful of works, all of which were published by the Boosey Company, and are well known to all band conductors: Gustav Holst's Suite for Military Band in E-flat (1909) and Suite No. 2 in F (1911), Ralph Vaughan Williams' *Toccata Marziale* and *English Folk Song Suite* (both 1924), and Gordon Jacob's *William Byrd Suite* (1924). The next six decades saw a virtual neglect of the wonderful possibilities opened by Holst and Vaughan Williams. After early flirtation with two of Britain's leading young composers, military musicians returned to their appointed business of providing music for ceremony or entertainment while the classical musical establishment continued to develop in other ways. The symphonies of Elgar, the concerti of Walton, the operas of Britten and Tippett, plus a host of works by the young lions of today, have placed Britain firmly back on the world musical map; however, in the field of the wind band and wind ensemble, only sporadic attempts were made during the fifty years following the 1920s.

Of the few outstanding works in this period, the most significant was, of course, *Hammersmith* by Holst in 1930. Composed for the Wireless Military Band, it remains to this day a challenge to interpreters and audience alike with its "chamberish" qualities and careful construction. Gordon Jacob, student, friend, and amanuensis of Vaughan Williams, also continued to write during this period, and his status was finally recognised during the 1951 Festival of Britain, through the commissioning of a large scale work for the Royal Festival Hall—*Music For A Festival*. The first performance was greeted in the *London Times* as one Festival commission that had immediately justified itself; however, other works and composers received a warning in the newspaper concerning the possibility of banality in a medium capable of broad effects and massive designs. Jacob's own repertoire listing contained fourteen works for wind band; additional works such as the Concerto for Timpani and Band (R. Smith) have been published posthumously.

During the 1960s and 70s, several composers contributed major additions to the wind repertoire. The first was Alun Hoddinott, whose Piano Concerto No. 1, Op. 19 (Oxford University Press, hereafter OUP, 1960) is a fine work scored for orchestral winds, brass, and percussion. Hoddinott followed the Concerto with an

187

equally splendid work, *Ritornelli* (OUP, 1974) for trombone and chamber ensemble and the charming *Welsh Airs and Dances* (OUP, 1975) for symphonic band instrumentation.

Many wind works from this period were composed as *pieces d'occasion*, a major reason for their lack of notice in succeeding years. One such work is Elizabeth Maconchy's *Music for Wind and Brass* (Chester/Music Sales, 1966), a superbly crafted piece scored for 2–2–2–2:4–3–3–1:T, that was written for the Thaxed Festival founded by Gustav Holst. (Maconchy herself forgot about the work until it was restored to the repertoire in the 1980s.) A composition by another distinguished female composer, Priaulx Rainier of South Africa, is *Ploermel* (1972). This work, like Alan Bush's *Scherzo for Wind Orchestra* (Novello, 1969), was a commission for the BBC Proms concerts. Rainier's compositional idiom is excitingly abrasive, owing something to the sound-world of Stravinsky's *Le Sacre du Printemps*, combined with her own primitivism.

Hoddinott's *Welsh Dances* (OUP, 1975) and *The English Dance Suite* (OUP, 1977), written by John Gardner for Queen Elizabeth's Silver Jubilee, continued the folk-song-based tradition of Holst and Vaughan Williams. The first truly modern work from this British "dark age" of composition for winds to remain in the repertoire today is *Metamorphoses* by Edward Gregson (Novello, 1977). Composed for orchestral winds, brass, and percussion ensemble along with piano and string basses, it explores simple aleatoric and electronic techniques. The composition remains an excellent introduction to contemporary music and finds positive audience reaction. Of Gregson's more recent works, the Tuba Concerto (Novello, 1984) is now firmly in the international repertoire for tuba players; *Festivo* (Novello, 1985) is a highly successful light overture combining traditional band formulae with Stravinsky-like energy; and his *Missa Brevis* (Novello, 1988), for treble and baritone vocal soloists, SSA choir, and band, is a simple yet deeply felt setting of the Ordinary of the Mass. All these latter works are in a populist vein, but none the less very effective.

In 1981, the First International Conference for Conductors, Publishers and Composers, organized by New England Conservatory Wind Ensemble conductor Frank Battisti, under the auspices of the College Band Directors National Association (CBDNA), happily chose the Royal Northern College of Music in Manchester for its venue. The level of music making, the range of compositions performed, and the potential of the medium were more than amply demonstrated. The main commission for the Conference was awarded to Derek Bourgeois for his *Symphony of Winds* (R. Smith, 1981), which was performed at the final concert. Bourgeois' scoring here, as in his *Sinfonietta* (R. Smith, 1983), is brilliantly effective, although it has been suggested that the technical demands for the performers are not equaled by the intellectual demands of the score. Bourgeois' musical language is deliberately traditional, using the wind band almost as an extension of the brass band, with massive doublings and a luxuriant palette. Perhaps his most effective works thus far are his little Serenade, set in 11/8 and 13/8, and his Trombone Concerto (R. Smith, 1989), although the latter is little more than a vehicle for solo trombone virtuosity.

The effects and influence of the 1981 Conference were immediately felt. The same year both the World Association for Symphonic Bands and Ensembles

(WASBE) and the British Association of Symphonic Bands and Wind Ensembles (BASBWE) were founded. The years since then have become an ongoing voyage of musical discovery as new works are commissioned and older works emerge from libraries or composer's archives.

BABSWE has undertaken the initiative of creating a new repertoire through a commissioning program. What has emerged is a series of works based upon musical merit, not merely a set of dances or folk songs. Most of the works commissioned are now well established in the international wind band repertoire, and all have been published (publishers are given in parentheses):

1983   Guy Woolfenden, *Gallimaufry* (Ariel)
       Philip Wilby, *Firestar* (Chester)
1984   Arthur Butterworth, *Tundra* (Vanderbeek)
       Joseph Horovitz, *Bacchus on Blue Ridge* (Molenaar)
1985   David Bedford, *Sea and Sky and Golden Hill* (Novello)
1986   Guy Woolfenden, *Illyrian Dances* (Ariel)
1987   Richard Rodney Bennett, *Morning Music* (Novello)
       Michael Ball, *Omaggio* (Novello)
1988   George Lloyd, *Forest of Arden* (R. Smith)
1990   James MacMillan, *Sowetan Spring* (Universal)
1991   Paul Patterson, *The Mighty Voice* (Weinberger)
       Richard Rodney Bennett, *The Four Seasons* (Novello)
       John McCabe, *Canyons* (Novello)
       Nicholas Maw, *American Games* (Faber)
       Robin Holloway, *Entrance; Carousing; Embarkation* (Boosey)

Additional composers who have recently been commissioned include Michael Tippett (1992), Colin Matthews, Michael Ball, Martin Butler, and David Bedford (1993), and Thea Musgrave (1994). It is interesting to note that, for the first time since the 1920s, British publishers are once again printing important repertoire for winds. The commissions listed above are from composers not necessarily familiar with the traditional use of the medium nor the repertoire, and thus, we have arrived at new perspectives of the problems posed in writing for the wind band. In general, the more easily accessible works have been written for a full band instrumentation, usually playable by a wind ensemble, while more challenging works have been scored with specified instrumentation.

Of the composers listed above, a slight word concerning other works in their catalogs and the style of composition might be of assistance at this point. Guy Woolfenden, director of music at the Royal Shakespeare Theatre, Stratford-on-Avon, brings his experience of theater writing. Both *Gallimaufry* and *Illyrian Dances* draw upon the Shakespeare canon for their program, with the musical language being pastiche English Renaissance, recalling both the 16th century and the early 20th century. High points include the metrical structure and a harmonic piquancy which avoids the obvious.

Philip Wilby's practical background resembles that of Woolfenden, but he brings a more advanced harmonic language and occasional use of aleatoric techniques. Three works mark his most recent contribution: *Firestar*, virtually a scherzo for wind orchestra with very carefully controlled elements; the more ambitious

Sinfonia Sacre, commissioned by Larry Sutherland of California State University, Fresno, ranges from Messiaen-like chords to a lone offstage trumpet which is finally silenced by the swish of six suspended cymbals; and the imaginative *Catcher of Shadows*, on a more simple plane and designed primarily for school band.

The 1984 BASBWE Conference brought forth Joseph Horovitz's first work, *Bacchus on Blue Ridge*, a divertimento in which jazz elements and the American Wild West rub shoulders. His second work, *Wind Harp*, is a rare, evocative, slow, single movement requiring great sensitivity in its performance; the splendid Euphonium Concerto still awaits a setting for wind band. His catalog also includes *Ad Astra*, written for the Central Band of the Royal Air Force, *Fête Galante*, a tribute to the Rococo period, and the recent *Dance Suite*, which was premiered by the Japanese Kosei Wind Orchestra and its regular conductor, Frederick Fennell.

In 1981 the Huddersfield Festival of Contemporary Music commissioned a work from David Bedford, a British composer who had studied with Luigi Nono in Italy, and who has been caught up in teaching and writing for children. His first wind band work, *Sun Paints Rainbows Over the Vast Waves*, derives from his experiences with the rock music of Kevin Ayres and Mike Oldfield in the 1970s; pop harmonies are treated in a pointilistic minimalist manner. His present wind catalog is completed by the 1985 BASBWE commission, *Sea and Sky and the Golden Hill*, with its gentle use of wine goblets to produce some beautiful effects, the Symphony No. 2, the variant *Ronde for Isolde*, and the *Praeludium* for antiphonal groups placed around the auditorium.

In 1987, WASBE held its International Conference in Boston. While there were no British ensembles performing, BASBWE was well represented through two major commissions: *Omaggio* by Michael Ball, a virtuosic homage to Italy, and *Morning Music* by Richard Rodney Bennett. *Morning Music*, like Bennett's *The Four Seasons*, which was commissioned for the 1991 WASBE Conference, is essentially a work for orchestral winds with harp and piano. Both works are examples of post-Schoenbergian technique with wonderfully etched orchestration that is very much a part of the compositional experience.

In 1990 the BASBWE Conference was held in Glasgow, where the world premiere of an outstanding wind ensemble work, James MacMillan's *Sowetan Spring*, was given by the Scottish National Orchestra, conducted by John Paynter. The following year WASBE and BASBWE held a joint meeting at the Royal College of Music in Manchester, and five commissioned works received first performances: *Canyons* by John McCabe, commissioned by the Guildhall School as part of a consortium; *The Mighty Voice* by Paul Patterson; Nicholas Maw's *American Games*; *Entrance-Carousing-Embarkation* by Robin Holloway; and the aforementioned *Four Seasons* of Richard Rodney Bennett. Each composition strikes an evocative voice for the new wind band era, and is a striking addition to the now-emerging literature for serious wind conductors.

A number of other commissions offered in the 1970s and 80s include works by the late Adrian Cruft, assiduous in his support of the symphonic wind band, and Stephen Dodgson, whose *The Eagle* and *Capriccio Concertante* are perhaps the most substantial. Several pieces for wind ensemble and solo strings, often for the London Sinfonietta, deserve a wide audience. Gordon Crosse's *Ariadne* (OUP, 1972), for solo oboe and ensemble, is a wonderful work, as is Dominic Muldowney's Saxophone Concerto (Universal). Another particularly fine work is Anthony Gilbert's *Dream Carousels* (Schott, 1989), a three-movement programmatic piece premiered at the Royal Northern College.

Two strands of thought may be perceived in the wind music of the past decade. On the one hand there is a repertoire cast in a more populist mold, usually well-suited for the large symphonic band. Written in a pastiche style, more European than American, are such works as Martin Dalby's *A Plain Man's Hammer*, Joseph Horovitz's *Fête Galante*, Buxton Orr's *John Gay Suite*, and Guy Woolfenden's *Gallimaufry* and *Ilyrian Dances*. On the opposite side, there are the composers who rely on traditional forms and languages: David Bedford's *Ronde for Isolde*, Edward Gregson's Tuba Concerto and *Festivo*, Stephen Dodgson's *Concerto Capriccioso*, Adrian Cruft's *Overture Tamburlaine*, Iain Hamilton's *Overture 1912*, and Paul Patterson's *The Mighty Voice*. It might chauvinistically be claimed that many of these works possess a refreshing vigour and spontaneity which one does not always find in the "formula" music of their American contemporaries.

Robin Holloway, one of the more serious composers to have responded to recent commissions, sums up the current state of a great deal of British music of today in his statement:

> I am trying to write music which, though conversant with most of the revolutionary technical innovations of the past 80 years or so, and by no means turning its back on them, nonetheless keeps a continuity of language and expressive intention with the classics and romantics of the past.

The commissioning program of BASBWE has deliberately encouraged leading composers who might subscribe to this creed, and Bennett, Gilbert, Holloway, Maw, McCabe, and Wilby have already done so. Their contributions to the wind literature follow in the highest traditions set forth by the Eastman Wind Ensemble concept.

Contemporary Composers, a new book which lists five hundred international composers active today or recently deceased, is intended as a listener's guide to the broadest spectrum of contemporary music.[2] While including composers such as Andriessen, Corigliano, Erb, Finney, Gould, Husa, Keuris, Krenek and Schuller as representatives outside the U.K., the list of British composers contains most of the names discussed above as part of the new contemporary wind movement. While this might be considered bias on the part of the dictionary's British compilers, the most surprising omission is of the wind works of Holst, Vaughan Williams, Hindemith, and Schoenberg.

Major composers give primary thought to the compositional process while minor composers offer useful teaching tools. We must, therefore, continue to build upon the repertoire of the past decade and expect within the next two decades to see a tremendous upsurge of wind orchestra and wind ensemble music of the highest caliber.

The composers and the players are there; the audience can also be there but only if conductors, publishers, broadcasters, and record companies have faith in our composers and performers. Light band music will always be with us in the form of ceremonial and entertainment music, but given the wind ensemble principles now firmly in place, I look forward to a new and different repertoire that will challenge the players, stimulate the audience, and extend the canon of significant works for winds by such illustrious predecessors as Mozart, Dvořák, and Strauss.

NOTES

1. Fennell, Frederick, *Basic Band Repertory* (Chicago: The Instrumentalist Co., 1980).
2. Brian Morton and Pamela Collins, eds., *Contemporary Composers* (Chicago: St. James Press, 1992).

Wind Bands
in Continental Europe

LEON JOSEPH BLY

TO understand the influence of the symphonic wind ensemble movement on continental European bands, it is necessary to comprehend the diversity and extent of the band movement in Europe. European bands are as varied as the countries and cultures in which they flourish or wane. Bands are presently flourishing throughout Western Europe, but economic conditions and political upheaval have forced many Eastern European bands into inactivity. The extent of this inactivity can not be ascertained exactly, since in most Eastern European countries the publication of statistics was forbidden by the former communist governments.

Unlike the United States, where bands are found primarily in schools and are student oriented, most continental European bands are community bands with mainly adult members. Although there are a number of municipal and military bands which are supported with tax money, and a few works bands supported by industries, most bands are amateur ensembles which raise their own funding. Thus, these organizations are dependent upon their respective communities for support. Attracting large audiences to their concerts and participating in a multitude of service-related performances are necessary to raise monies for continued existence.

In the Netherlands, Belgium, and Switzerland there is a great deal of band activity. The Netherlands alone has around 3,000 amateur bands. However, in all three countries there are not only wind bands, but also brass bands and fanfare bands.[1] In Switzerland, for example, there are about 2,200 amateur bands, of which about 60% are wind bands, 28% brass bands, and 2% fanfare bands; and in Belgium, with around 2,000 amateur bands, approximately 200 are fanfare bands, and 30 are brass bands, with the remainder being wind bands. Other continental European countries with more than one type of band are France, which has fanfare as well as wind bands; Luxembourg, with about 50 amateur wind bands and 80 fanfare bands; Norway, where of the approximately 2,200 bands that belong to the Norwegian Band Federation there are brass bands and wind bands; Sweden with around 1,000 wind bands and about 500 brass bands; and Denmark, where of the nearly 150 member bands of the National Band Association there are both brass and wind bands.

Not only do three different types of bands exist, but the traditional instrumentation of the wind bands varies from country to country. For example in Spain, where large symphonic bands tend to be the rule, three to six cellos are regularly used, while in the rest of Europe cellos are rarely employed. In Scandinavia and the Benelux countries the use of trumpets and cornets follows the British and North American practice, whereas in Germany (with approximately 7,200 amateur bands), Austria (with roughly 2,200), South Tirol (with 200), Slovakia (with 500), the Czech Republic (with 1,000), and Slovenia (with close to 110 amateur bands), trumpets and flugelhorns are traditionally employed. In Italy (with some 3,000 amateur bands), Austria, and parts of Eastern Europe, the use of the small A-flat clarinet is still quite common. In Central and Eastern Europe three B-flat tenor horns as well as a B-flat euphonium are part of the standard band instrumentation, as is the use of both E-flat and BB-flat tubas. In Eastern Europe, and to some extent in France, a complete family of saxhorns (i.e., flugelhorns, E-flat alto horns, B-flat tenor horns, baritones, E-flat tubas, and BB-flat tubas) are prevalent.

Although these differences in instrumentation may seem incidental, they reveal a very important historical development. Whereas composers have always determined the size and instrumentation of the orchestra they wished to use, bandmasters or military commissions have normally been the determining force for the instrumentation of the wind band from the time of the French Revolution to the middle of the twentieth century. With the exception of march music, most of the band music composed during this period was conceived in terms of the sound of the symphony orchestra, rather than the acoustical properties of wind and percussion instruments. Thus various attempts were made to find a family of instruments (clarinets, saxophones, saxhorns, etc.) that could take the place in the wind band of the strings in the symphony orchestra. Each country attempted to solve this problem in its own way, the success of which is an open question. However, these attempts resulted in the bands in each country developing their own national sound based upon their unique instrumentation and performance practices. This further resulted in most major composers writing only occasional works for wind band to be performed at a specific time and place, and minor composers writing pieces for bands within their national or cultural borders. Thus composers like Stephan Jaeggi and Paul Huber in Switzerland, Sepp Tanzer and Sepp Thaler in Tirol, Gerard Boedijn in the Netherlands, Gabriel Parès in France, Willy Schneider and Hellmut Haase-Altendorf in Germany, Jos Moerenhout and Philippe-Jules Godard in Belgium, Giovanni Orsomando in Italy, and Herbert König and Franz Königshofer in Austria, did much to enrich the band music of their native countries, but their compositions are rarely applicable to other cultures.

This is not to imply that the occasional works written by major composers have not helped to enrich the repertoire. One need only consider the *Trauersinfonie* by Richard Wagner or the *Symphonie funèbre et triomphale* by Hector Berlioz from the nineteenth century. In the twentieth century numerous works by major composers have had this type of origin. In 1936, for example, the French Minister of Education Jean Zay commissioned seven leading French composers: Jacques Ibert, Georges Auric, Darius Milhaud, Albert Roussel, Charles Koechlin, Arthur Honegger, and Daniel Lazarus to write music for a production of Romain Rolland's *Quatorze Juillet*, and in 1937 the twentieth anniversary of the October Revolution in Russia gave rise to an overture by Reinhold Glière and a cantata for choir and band by Serge Prokofiev.

One should also not get the impression that continental European wind bands have not generated any significant compositions. Where fine bands with distinguished conductors with vision have existed, noted composers have long been encouraged to write works for them. Thus the Garde Républicaine in France was the impetus for Florent Schmitt's *Dionysiaques*, op. 62 and Gabriel Faure's *Chant Funéraire*, op. 117, as well as Paul Fauchet's Symphony in B-flat and Lucien Haudebert's *Rapsodie Celtique*. The many distinguished conductors of the Belgian Guides encouraged such prominent composers as Jean Absil, Paul Gilson, Marcel Poot, Maurice Schoemaker, René Bernier, Gaston Brenta, Jules Strens, and Théo Dejoncker to write works for that band, and during the 1930s and 1940s the German Luftwaffenorchester in Berlin under the direction of Hans Felix Husadel stimulated such composers as Harald Genzmer, Paul Höffer, Erwin Dressel, Bruno Stürmer, Hermann Grabner, and Eberhard L. Wittmer to produce works for the wind band. The excellent band of the Soviet Ministry of Defense helped to stimulate compositions by such leading composers as Nicholas Miaskovsky, Dmitri Kabalevsky, Reinhold Glière, Alexander Glazunov, and Dmitri Shostakovich, and in Bulgaria the Sofia Wind Orchestra under the direction of Sasho Mihailov provided the stimulus for Dimiter Hristov's Concerto No. 2 for Piano and Large Wind Band, Liltscho Borrisov's *Concertino Capriccio* for Alto Saxophone and Large Wind Band, Jul Levi's Symphony No. 4 for Large Wind Band, Dimitar Sagaev's Symphony No. 2 for Speaker, Large Wind Band, Baritone, Male Choir, and Children Choir, and Todor Assenov Stojkov's Concerto for Two Pianos and Symphonic Wind Band. Other fine wind bands such as the Stockholm Symphonic Wind Orchestra and the Central Wind Orchestra of the Hungarian Army have also had a lasting impact on the band's repertoire.

Paul Hindemith's initiative in 1926 at the Donaueschingen Kammermusiktage, which produced Hindemith's own *Konzertmusik*, op. 41, Ernst Krenek's *Drei Märsche*, op. 44, Ernst Pepping's *Kleine Serenade*, Ernst Toch's *Spiel*, and Hal Gál's *Promenadenmusik* is well known. What is less well known are the other farsighted undertakings which have had an impact on the band's repertoire. Under the guidance of Albert Häberling, 116 compositions for wind band and eight for choir and wind band were premiered at the Festliche Musiktage in Uster, Switzerland between 1956 and 1989. Although most of these works can not be compared with the compositions mentioned above, works like *Salute to the Lone Wolves*, op. 89 by Peter Jona Korn, *Epiphany* by Henk Badings, *Der kleine Schelm* by André Besancon, *Incantation et sacrifice* by Jean Balissant, *Elegie für Chor, 10 Bläser und Stabspiele* by Peter Wettstein, and the *Sinfonie für Bläser* by Werner Wolf Glaser are important additions to the repertoire.

In the Netherlands the "Stichting Overkoepeling Nederlandse Muziek Organisaties" (SONMO) has through the "Fonds voors de Scheppende Toonkunst" commissioned many works for wind band, including *Conflicts and Confluences* by Henk Badings, *Overture for an Imaginary Play* by Jurriaan Andriessen, and *Drieluik* by Oscar van Hemel. Since its founding in 1988, the Swiss Blas-Orchester-Forum (BFO) has annually commissioned a work for wind band from a Swiss composer, resulting in such works as Peter Wettstein's *Rhapsodie für Blasorchester*, Martin Wendel's *Ostinato*, and Peter Benary's *Konzertstück Nr. 2 für Blasorchester*. In Sweden the Rikskonserter has taken innumerable initiatives resulting in over thirty wind band compositions by such composers as Csaba Deák and Bengt Hambraeus, and the Organisationskommittén för Regionsmusiken has commissioned compositions by various composers including Eberhard Eyser and Lars Edlund.

Wind band contests have also had an impact on the repertoire, as various contest committees have commissioned test pieces. A large number of compositions, for example, have been commissioned for the annual Certamen in Valencia, Spain; and the Bavarian Radio's Band Competition of 1986, commissioned the *Ouvertüre für Blasorchester* by Harald Genzmer. The World Music Contest Kerkrade Foundation has commissioned such works as Jurriaan Andriessen's *Sinfonia "Il Fiume"* and Ida Gotkovsky's *Brillante Symphonie*.

With the establishment of the Eastman Wind Ensemble in 1952, a new phase in the development of the wind band began, which is still foreign to practically all of the literature mentioned above. According to the symphonic wind ensemble concept, the instruments to be used and the number of players to a part should be determined by the creator of the music, rather than being left solely in the hands of the recreators. Hence the composers become the originators of the colors, weights, and balances, rather than the commissioners, conductors, or number of available players for a particular band. Unfortunately, this concept is still largely misunderstood among European bandsmen, who continue in the belief that a symphonic wind ensemble is a band with too few clarinets, or tubas, or other instruments. What is misunderstood is that the goal of the symphonic wind ensemble is to follow the desires of the composer, with flexibility being the key element. A performance of the *Symphonie funèbre et triomphale* by Hector Berlioz with four horns and eight clarinets is thus no more in keeping with the rationale than is a performance of the *Petite Symphonie* by Charles Gounod with a band of eighty players.

Unlike in the United States, where the development of the wind ensemble took place in an academic setting, to date there has been no catalyst for such a merger in continental Europe. Most European conservatories and music academies do not have wind bands, even where band conducting training is offered, such as at the Basel and Lucerne Conservatories. In music academies where bands do exist, such as in Graz, Brussels, Luxembourg, Rotterdam, and Maastricht, the rationale for their existence is the training of conductors for amateur and military bands.

Throughout continental Europe, however, there are excellent chamber wind ensembles such as the New Winds Ensemble of Rome, the Netherlands Wind Ensemble, the Omnibus Wind Players of Sweden, Belgium's Octophorus, and the Mainz Wind Ensemble, but they perform only chamber music. Beginning with the creation of the large alfresco wind band during the last part of the eighteenth century, the chamber winds and the wind band began a long period of independent development. These two traditions continue to develop independently of one another, but the founding of the symphonic wind ensemble has brought about the beginnings of a merger, at least in North America and the British Isles.

Although in continental Europe most performers of wind chamber music seldom play in wind bands, and wind band players rarely play chamber music, a few ensembles have been organized in accordance with the symphonic wind ensemble concept. Among these are the Stockholm Symphonic Wind Orchestra, the Larvik Wind Ensemble of Norway, the Swiss National Youth Wind Orchestra, the German Wind Philharmonic, and the Amsterdam Wind Orchestra. A look at the sample programs provided below reveals the flexibility of these ensembles in programming works for both large and small combinations of instruments.

Concert by the Swiss National Youth Wind Ensemble
Felix Hauswirth conducting, April 28, 1992

Serenade, op. 7	Richard Strauss
Aubade für Klavier und Kammerensemble	Francis Poulenc
Rheinische Kirmestänze	Bernd Alois Zimmermann
Concertino für Violoncello, Bläserensemble, Klavier, und Schlagzeug	Bohuslav Martinu
Der brave Soldat Schweik, op. 22	Robert Kurka

Concert by the Swiss National Youth Wind Ensemble
Felix Hauswirth conducting, July 24, 1987

A Festival Anthem	Franco Cesarini
Der kleine Schelm	André Besancon
Hochzart	Mani Planzer
Suite francais	Darius Milhaud
Al Fresco	Karel Husa
Suite of Old American Dances	Robert Russell Bennett

Concert by the Stockholm Symphonic Wind Orchestra
Osmo Vänskä conducting, February 3, 1992

Fanfares pour Britannius	André Jolivet
Ebony Concerto	Igor Stravinsky
Kjell Fagéus, Clarinet	
Hammersmith, op. 52	Gustav Holst
Arktis	Torbjörn Iwan Lundquist
Concerto for Clarinet	Nicolai Rimsky-Korsakoff
Kjell Fagéus, Clarinet	
Konzertmusik, op. 41	Paul Hindemith

The influence, however, of the symphonic wind ensemble movement on the European band scene has been far greater than the mention of these five ensembles reveals. In the areas of performance standards and repertoire, beginning with the recordings made during the 1950s and 1960s by Frederick Fennell and the Eastman Wind Ensemble, the symphonic wind ensemble has been a key factor in raising performance standards and in disseminating an international repertoire of the highest order. Thus the suites by Gustav Holst and Ralph Vaughan Williams may be heard today from the Atlantic to the Urals and from the North Cape to the Mediterranean, and leading bands throughout Europe play *Music for Prague 1968* and *Lincolnshire Posy*.

In the area of performance practices the influence has also been much greater than a casual overview may disclose. For better or for worse, during the past decades the sound of symphony orchestras throughout the world has tended to homogenize. The same can be said for the wind band. Although the national differences described above continue to exist, leading European wind bands are beginning to adjust their instrumentation and style of playing in order to perform the repertoire espoused by the symphonic wind ensemble. While this can be understood in positive terms regarding an international repertoire, it has often had amusing and/or negative effects on the performance of traditional literature. For example, in performances of traditional marches in central Europe, the flugelhorns and B-flat tenor horns are often eliminated and saxophones employed. Even in performances of compositions like Ernst Toch's *Spiel*, op. 39, and Boris Blacher's *Divertimento,* op. 7, "orchestral instruments" or saxophones are often used in lieu of flugelhorns and B-flat tenor horns.

Finally, current developments and trends may eventually lead to a flourishing of symphonic wind ensembles in continental Europe in the twenty-first century. Since World War II, wind bands have become an increasingly important part of the music education of adolescents and young adults. For example, of the 500 bands in Hungary about 70% are youth bands, and most of the 7,200 amateur adult bands in Germany support a youth band as a training ensemble. Furthermore, around 1,000 communities in Germany support a music school for the instrumental music instruction of children and amateur musicians.[2] During the past decade a large number of these music schools have organized symphonic wind bands, which perform serious wind band literature. In fact, these youth bands have already been the leaven for a few significant new compositions, including Axel D. Ruoff's *Konzert für Klavier und sinfonisches Blasorchester* (1989), Hanno Haag's *Cantica Sacra,* op. 36, and Matthias Pintscher's *Invocazioni per orchestra sinfonica da strumenti a fiato* (1991).

Although wind bands are still a rarity at most music academies and conservatories, there seems to be a growing interest in making them a part of the curriculum. A wind band was formed at the Peter Cornelius Conservatory in Mainz in 1991, and a wind band became a part of the curriculum at the Vienna Academy in the fall of 1992. All that seems now to be missing for a forward surge in symphonic wind ensemble activity in continental Europe is a greater interest in joining the wind band and chamber wind ensemble traditions.

NOTES

1. Originally, fanfare bands consisted of complete families of saxophones and saxhorns, with other instruments such as trumpets and/or trombones occasionally being employed for additional color. Eventually the E-flat alto horns were replaced with F horns, and the E-flat sopranino saxophone and the E-flat flugelhorn were eliminated. Although the number of players varies from band to band, the basic instrumentation of the fanfare band today is as follows: soprano saxophone(s), alto saxophone(s), tenor saxophone(s), baritone saxophone(s), B-flat flugelhorns in three parts, B-flat cornets in three parts, B-flat trumpets in two parts, F horns in four parts, trombones in three parts, small bore B-flat baritones in two parts, B-flat euphoniums in two parts, E-flat tuba(s), BB-flat tuba(s), and percussion. A small number of significant original compositions have been written for this type of band, including works by Paul Gilson (1865–1942), Marcel Poot (1901–1988), and Henk Badings (1907–1987).

2. In Germany, as in most other continental European countries, professional musicians are trained in music academies or conservatories, rather than at universities or colleges. Applied music instruction for children and amateur musicians takes place in municipal or private music schools, not in academic institutions.

BIBLIOGRAPHY

Biber, Walter. "Aus der Geschichte der Blasmusik in der Schweiz." In *Bericht über die erste Internationale Fachtagung zur Erforschung der Blasmusik, Graz 1974*, edited by Wolfgang Suppan and Eugen Brixel. Alta Musica 1. Tutzing, Germany: Hans Schneider, 1976.

———. *Die Geschichte der Blasmusik im Kanton Uri.* N.p., 1981.

Birsak, Kurt and Manfred König. *Das Große Salzburger Blasmusikbuch.* Vienna: Christian Brandstätter, 1983.

Blank, Ludwig. "Die Entwicklung des zivilen Blasmusikwesens in Nordwürttemberg." In *Bericht über die erste Internationale Fachtagung zur Erforschung der Blasmusik, Graz 1974*, edited by Wolfgang Suppan and Eugen Brixel. Alta Musica 1. Tutzing, Germany: Hans Schneider, 1976.

Bly, Leon. "Der Status der Musik für Blasorchester im 20. Jahrhundert im Spiegel der 'Festlichen Musiktage Uster.'" In *Johann Joseph Fux und die barocke Blasertradition: Kongreßbericht Graz 1985*, edited by Bernhard Habla. Alta Musica 9. Tutzing, Germany: Hans Schneider, 1987.

Brera, Gianni and Franco Calvetti. *La Banda nella Provincia di Como.* Como: Amministrazione Provinciale di Como, 1981.

Brixel, Eugen. *Das Große Oberösterreichische Blasmusikbuch.* Vienna: Christian Brandstätter, 1984.

Brixel, Eugen, and Wolfgang Suppan. *Das Große Steirische Blasmusikbuch.* Vienna: Christian Brandstätter, 1981.

Brixel, Eugen, Martin Gunther and Gottfried Pils. *Das ist Österreichs Militärmusik.* Graz: Verlag Styria, 1982.

———. "Instrumentierung und Instrumentation aus der Sicht der österreichischen Blasmusikpraxis unserer Zeit." In *Johann Joseph Fux und die barocke Blasertradition: Kongreßbericht Graz 1985*, edited by Bernhard Habla. Alta Musica 9. Tutzing, Germany: Hans Schneider, 1987.

Courroyez, G. *Etude sur les Musiques d'Harmonie.* Paris: Andrieu Freres, 1931.

Degele, Ludwig. *Die Militärmusik.* Wolfenbüttel, Germany: Verlag für musikalische Kultur und Wissenschaft, 1937.

Deutsch, Walter. *Das Große Niederösterreichische Blasmusikbuch.* Vienna: Christian Brandstätter, 1982.

Egg, Erich and Wolfgang Pfaundler. *Das Große Tiroler Blasmusikbuch.* Vienna: Christian Brandstätter, 1979.

Ferrero, Bernardo Adam. *Las Bandas de Musica en el Mundo.* Madrid: Sol Editorial S.B., 1986.

Gmasz, Sepp and Hans Hahnenkamp. *Das Große Burgländische Blasmusikbuch.* Vienna: Christian Brandstätter, 1987.

Gundersen, Egil A. *Alltid Foran! Telemark Krets av NMF 1938–1988*. Stathelle, Norway: Trio Forlag, 1988.

Habla, Bernhard. *Besetzung und Instrumentation des Blasorchesters seit der Erfindung der Ventile für Blechblasinstrumente bis zum Zweiten Weltkrieg in Österreich und Deutschland*. Alta Musica 12. Tutzing, Germany: Hans Schneider, 1990.

Kalkbrenner, A. *Die Organisation der Militärmusikchöre aller Länder*. Hannover: Louis Oertel, 1884.

——. *Wilhelm Wieprecht*. Berlin: Emil Prager, 1882.

Kastner, Georges. *Manuel général de musique militaire a l'usage des armées françaises*. Paris: Didot Frères, 1848. Reprinted Geneva: Minkoff, 1973.

Ligasacchi, Giovanni. "Amilcare Ponchielli und die Blasmusik." In *Kongreßbericht Oberschutzen/Burgenland 1988, Toblach/Südtirol 1990*, edited by Wolfgang Suppan and Eugen Brixel. Alta Musica 14. Tutzing, Germany: Hans Schneider, 1992.

Mahling, Christoph-Hellmut. "Die Rolle der Blasmusik im Saarländischen Industriegebiet im 19. und frühen 20. Jahrhundert." In *Bericht über die erste Internationale Fachtagung zur Erforschung der Blasmusik, Graz 1974*, edited by Wolfgang Suppan and Eugen Brixel. Alta Musica 1. Tutzing, Germany: Hans Schneider, 1976.

Maréchal, Henri and Gabriel Parès. *Monographie Universelle de L'Orphéon*. Paris: Librarie Ch. Delagrave.

Masel, Andreas. *Das Große Ober- und Niederbayerische Blasmusikbuch*. Munich: Schwingenstein-Verlag, 1989.

Milani, Giuseppe. *Le bande musicali della svizzera italiana*. Vol. 1. Agni, Switzerland: Edizione Arti Grafische Bernasconi, 1981.

Neukomm, Edward. *Histoire de la musique militaire*. Paris: L. Baudouin & Co., 1889.

Oggier, Alex, Josef Meier and Herbert Frei. *125 Jahre Eidgenössicher Musikverband*. Luzern: Selbstverlag des Eidgenössicher Musikverband, 1987.

Panoff, Peter. *Militärmusik in Geschichte und Gegenwart*. Berlin: K. Siegismund, 1938.

Pieters, Francis. *Blaasmuziektusen gisteren en morgen*. Wormerveer, Holland: Molenaar Edition, 1992.

——. *Van Trompetsignaal tot Muziekkapel*. Kortrijk, Belgium: VZW Muziekcentrum, 1981.

Rameis, Emil. *Die österreichische Militärmusik, von ihren Anfängen bis zum Jahre 1918*. Supplemented and edited by Eugen Brixel. Alta Musica 2. Tutzing, Germany: Hans Schneider, 1976.

Roth, J. Chretien. *Les Musiques Militaires en France*. Strasbourg: the author, 1852.

Ruhr, Peter and Wolfgang Blass. "Eine Strukturanalyse des Badischen Blasmusiklebens." In *Bericht über die Vierte Internationale Fachtagung zur Erforschung der Blasmusik, Uster/Schweiz 1981*, edited by Eugen Brixel. Alta Musica 7. Tutzing, Germany: Hans Schneider, 1976.

Schneider, Erich. *Blasmusik in Vorarlberg*. Lustenau: Selbstverlag des Vorarlberg Blasmusikverband, 1986.

——. "Die Entwicklung des Blasmusikwesens in Vorarlberg." In *Bericht über die erste Internationale Fachtagung zur Erforschung der Blasmusik, Graz 1974*, edited by Wolfgang Suppan and Eugen Brixel. Alta Musica 1. Tutzing, Germany: Hans Schneider, 1976.

Steinmetz, Horst and Armin Griebel. *Das Große Nordbayerische Blasmusikbuch*. 4 vols. Munich: Schwingenstein-Verlag, 1990.

Suppan, Wolfgang. *Blasmusik in Baden*. Freiburg-Tiengen, Germany: Blasmusikverlag Schulz, 1983.

——. *Komponieren für Amateure: Ernest Majo und die Entwicklung der Blasorchesterkomposition*. Alta Musica 10. Tutzing, Germany: Hans Schneider, 1988.

Veit, Gottfried. *Die Blasmusik*. Innsbruck: Helbling, 1972.

Vessella, Alessandro. *La Banda dalle Origini Fino ai Nostri Giorni*. Milano: Istituto Editoriale Nazionale, 1935.

Whitwell, David. *Band Music of the French Revolution*. Alta Musica 5. Tutzing, Germany: Hans Schneider, 1979.

——. *The History and Literature of the Wind Band and Wind Ensemble*. 11 vols. Northridge, California: WINDS, 1982–90.

Yperen, R. van. *De Nederlandse Militaire Muziek*. Bussum, Holland: van Dishoeck, van Holkema & Warendorf N.V., 1966.

Historical Development of Wind Bands
in Japan

TOSHIO AKIYAMA

WIND band development in Japan can be traced to the arrival of the American Admiral Matthew Perry in 1853. Initially ordered to leave, Admiral Perry insisted on being received by the Japanese Government in order to present documents which led to the first treaty between the United States and Japan being concluded in 1854. This signaled the end to the Japanese national policy against foreign contact. However, it took another fifteen years (the beginning of the Meiji Period) for Western culture and educational principles to begin the process of gaining eventual acceptance. Among the earliest of foreign bands in Japan were an English Marine band and a French Army band. Both were stationed in Yokohama, one of Japan's principal seaports. Their influence brought about the formation of the first Japanese military band in 1869, organized under the tutelage of an English bandmaster, John William Fenton (1829–?). Two years later this thirty-six-piece band was formally designated the Japanese Navy Band with an instrumentation consisting of:

Piccolo	E-flat alto horn (4)
E-flat clarinet	B-flat tenor horn (2)
B-flat clarinet (9)	Tenor trombone (2)
Bass clarinet (2)	Bass trombone
Cornet (3)	Euphonium (2)
Flugelhorn (2)	B-flat Bass (4)
E-flat trumpet (2)	Percussion (2)

The instrumentation was rather well balanced for its day, even though it reflected the makeup of the English brass band with the addition of piccolo, B-flat clarinets, and two bass clarinets.

In 1872, the Japanese Army Band was established with a French bandmaster as teacher and leader. Their use of the French transposition system, with its treble clef notation for all brasses, caused a problem within the military, since the Navy Band, under its English leader, utilized treble and bass clefs. The result was that individual music libraries had to be maintained. For example, the official Japanese national anthem, composed in 1880 by Hiromori Hayashi (1830–1896), Court Musician to the Emperor, and Franz Eckert (1852–1916), a German bandmaster who worked with both the Army and Navy bands, required Eckert to make two separate versions in order for it to be performed by each group.

The first Japanese bandmaster to study abroad was sent to France in 1882 to learn French band repertoire and procedures. In 1900, a Navy bandmaster was sent, but this time to Germany for training in band practices and techniques of that country. Other band activities included the founding of the first commercial, or "business" band, in Tokyo in 1886. This organization was influenced by American professional bands such as the Patrick Gilmore Band.

Band activity in the public and private schools did not begin until much later. The first high school band was established in Kyoto in 1912; however, the school band program did not become popular until two pioneers in the movement, Yoshio Hirooka and Terumi Jinno, initiated band programs in their junior high schools in 1929 and 1931, respectively. It may appear incongruous to American band directors, but the junior high school level band has been one of the primary influences in the growth of the entire country's wind program. The importance and level of development of junior high school ensembles remains to this day and frequently eclipses senior high school wind programs in level of repertoire and performance standards.

School bands multiplied rapidly following Hirooka and Jinno's lead; prior to the beginning of World War II, there were approximately thirteen hundred bands in Japan. Many of these groups were small "pep bands" with poor instrumentation— no French horns, tenor or baritone saxophones, or bass clarinets. Also during this time, numerous small industrial bands developed, following the English industrial bands as a model.

With the conclusion of World War II, band groups reflected the state of the country, with its shortages of housing and clothing, plus a lack of musical instruments and supply of adequate teachers. Then in 1947 the Ministry of Education adopted the American school grade system of 6–3–3 (the previous Japanese system utilized five years for the junior high school), and instrumental music programs were introduced to complement vocal programs that had been in place since before the war. Major contributors to the development of Japanese bands during this post-war period were the American military bands stationed in Japan and their numerous musicians, who offered new instrumentation ideas, musical repertoire, and provided assistance to the instrumental programs. Local town bands began to revive around 1947, and exchange concerts between communities led once again to an interest in bands.

In 1949 several colleges and universities began schools of music with instrumental music courses, but without actual band programs. In 1951 the Fine Arts Music Department of the University of Tokyo organized a symphonic band as a club activity that later became part of the official school curriculum. Their first concert, conducted by Professor Masato Yamamoto on 17 October 1951, included:

Light Cavalry Overture	Franz von Suppe
Gold and Silver Waltz	Franz Lehar
Star Dust	Hoagy Carmichael, arr. Paul Yoder
"Dance of the Hours" from *La Gioconda*	Amilcare Ponchielli
The Nutcracker Suite	Peter Tchaikovsky
"Unfinished" Symphony	Franz Schubert

Athletic Festival March	Sergei Prokofiev
Hungarian Dances, Nos. 5 and 6	Johannes Brahms
The Glass Slipper	Paul Yoder

The first professional band to resume activities following World War II was the Osaka City Concert Band, directed by Ichitaro Tsujii. This fine ensemble is still a major presence among the professional bands in Japan. It enjoys full-time sponsorship by the City of Osaka and continues to provide adult leadership in a field predominantly located in the various levels of the school system—junior high, senior high and university. Their first concert, performed 18 April 1960, included the following repertoire:

*Canzona	Peter Mennin
Dedication, A Symphonic Poem	Carl Frangkiser
*Symphony in B-flat	Paul Hindemith
*Fest-Konzert für Klavier und Blasorchester	Russell Schmidt
*Lieutenant Kije Suite	Sergei Prokofiev (arr. Ichitaro Tsujii)

*First performance in Japan

The attitude toward repertoire in these two bands reflects totally opposing directions, a condition that is still prevalent today. The Tokyo University program contained six transcriptions from the orchestral repertoire, one wind re-orchestration (*Athletic Festival March*), an arrangement (*Star Dust*), and one original work (*The Glass Slipper*). In contrast, the Osaka City Band program featured four original works for band (including the Japanese premiere of the Hindemith symphony) and one transcription (by the conductor of the band for his ensemble). Unfortunately, audiences then and now often prefer transcribed classical repertoire to the newer original works for band.

In 1960 the Musashino School of Music in Tokyo (the largest private school of music in Japan) introduced chamber wind music. In the same year the second-largest conservatory, the Kunitachi School of Music, presented the premiere concert of their new Blasorchester.

Presently, there are a large number of bands and a great amount of band activity throughout Japan. This is directly due to a number of factors, among which are: the formation of the All Japan Band Association and its revival and implementation of regional and national band contests; publication of band journals and band repertoire; visits and influence of leading band conductors, composers, and publishers from other countries; the formation of the Japan Bandmasters Association; and the establishment of bands and wind curriculum on the university level. Each of these developments will be examined separately.

The All Japan Band Association and the All Japan Band Contests

The All Japan Band Association was founded in 1939 with sponsorship by the Asahi Newspaper Company. Shortly thereafter it inaugurated the first All Japan Band Contest, which was discontinued in 1943 because of World War II. With the revival of local band associations and activities after the war (exchange concerts by community and school bands, etc.), there was renewed interest in reestablishing the contests. In 1951 the Osaka region presented its area contest, and a year later the Tokyo Band Association began its regional contest. The Tokyo registration included bands from seven junior high schools, nine senior high schools, and fifteen industrial bands. Contest programs included works by American band composers Paul Yoder, Carl Frangkiser, and Joseph Olivadoti.

The year 1953 marked the beginning of the reorganization of the All Japan Band Association, with the boards of directors from several band associations meeting in Tokyo to discuss a national program. The newly-structured All Japan Band Association agreed to reactivate the National Band Contests in 1956, the first being held in Osaka with five junior high, five senior high, three industrial, and two community bands competing. The prize-winning junior high school band performed *In a Persian Market* by Albert Ketelbey as its free-choice composition, while the first prize senior high school band performed Bela Bartok's *Rumanian Folk Dances*.

Through the next few years, the National Contest gained widespread attention, and the number of participating bands greatly increased. In 1961 the Contest was held in Tokyo with ten junior high, ten senior high, four college, seven industrial, and seven community bands. The first prize senior high school band performed the *Symphonic Suite* by Clifton Williams (seven years after its introduction to Japan by the U.S. Air Force Band). A major change in repertoire occurred in 1964, when the All Japan Band Association began requiring contest compositions to be overtures or comparable types of pieces, rather than marches. They also inaugurated a requirement that each competing group perform a work commissioned for the contest from a Japanese composer.

The increase in repertoire awareness and performance techniques was demonstrated when, in 1968, the Izumo Junior High School Band performed a near-perfect rendition of the Toccata and Fugue in D minor by J.S. Bach, thus establishing goals for the future rapid growth in the junior high school band movement. Four years later an additional formative step was taken by the All Japan Band Association when it established new instrumentation and personnel numbers for contest participation (since 1952 all bands had been performing with a required forty members):

Junior High School band	45 members
Senior High School band	45 members
College/University band	55 members
Industrial band	55 members
Community band	60 members

The use of more complete, modern instrumentation and full percussion was also encouraged.

The year 1976 marked another high point for the junior high school level when the Izumo Daiichi Junior High School Band won first prize with a performance of the *Daphnis and Chloe Suite* No. 2 by Ravel. In all, twenty junior high school bands participated, with three receiving the Gold Prize (First Division), five receiving the Silver Prize, and twelve receiving the third level Copper Prize. The success of the

Izumo School and its repertoire, which relies heavily on transcriptions for concert and contest use, reflects a long-persistent pattern. In 1991, however, that transcription mold was broken when one of the eight Gold Prize (First Division) winners performed "... *and the mountains rising nowhere*" by Joseph Schwantner. The performance of Schwanter's piece at the contest also demonstrated the major influence of the Eastman Wind Ensemble, which had just performed this work on its 1990 concert tour of Japan under the sponsorship of Sony Corporation, and had recorded it in Osaka for Sony Classical Records. The All Japan Band Contest has been a most positive force in the development of the Japanese band program on all levels.

Authors, Publishers, and Instrument Manufacturers

Following World War II, quality instruments, instruction books, and music were almost impossible to find, even if one had the necessary money. Therefore, it became essential that Japanese publishers undertake the task of rebuilding their country's educational system with indigenous materials. In 1954, the year of the official reorganization of the All Japan Band Association, the Kyodo Music Publishing Company began publishing *Band News*, a magazine to publicize band activities, new music, instructional materials, and instrumental techniques. Two years after this innovation, Professor Irving Cheyette of Syracuse University visited Japan as a Fulbright Lecturer at Tokyo University School of Fine Arts. He reported on Japanese music education in the January 1956 issue of the *Music Educators Journal*. In addition, Cheyette left a copy of the *Boosey Band Method* in the library of Tokyo University where it was noticed by this author; the text was introduced throughout Japan through the *Japanese Music Educators Journal* in 1956. About this same time, the American military occupation bands sold their instruments to the Japanese market, thus making high-quality instruments available for the first time. The first recordings of the Eastman Wind Ensemble under Frederick Fennell on Mercury Records also became available.

In 1958 Ongakuno Tomosha (currently the country's largest music publisher) began its activities and the following year introduced the *Band Journal*. This author's book, *How To Organize and Teach School Bands*, was also published by Ongakuno Tomosha and became a primary source for school band directors.

The Yamaha Corporation, which had merged with the Nippon Kangakki Company, a pre-World War II wind instrument manufacturer, began making wind instruments in 1965 and quickly established a leadership role in the promotion of bands and band programs. Much of this development was in conjunction with the Japan Band Directors Clinic presented annually at Nemo Nu Sato, and through the numerous foreign visitors brought to Japan by Yamaha. Over the past thirty years, Yamaha has continued to be a leading support organization and has broadened its instrument, keyboard, and educational facilities throughout the country and abroad to include practically every type of performance medium.

Visiting Foreign Musicians and Wind Bands

The influence of visiting musicians from abroad must be measured as one of the most influential aspects affecting Japanese band growth. Although the effect of Japanese musicians traveling to the United States or Europe has been beneficial, the overall impact on large numbers of people has been more directly due to the visitors from abroad.

Following World War II, the first ensemble to make a tour of Japan (1956) was the United States Air Force Band under the direction of Col. George S. Howard. Although the program was primarily of an entertainment style created for general audiences, this was the first experience for Japanese musicians to hear high-level professional performers with modern American band sounds, a quality less brilliant than used in Japan at the time. The program performed by Col. Howard and the Air Force Band was:

Triumphal March	Miklos Rosza
Overture to *If I Were King*	Adolphus Adam
Vocal solo from *Il Pagliacci*	Leoncavallo
Caribbean Fantasy	John Morrisey
Accordian solo: *Carnival of Venice*	arr. Richard Cray
Selections from *The King and I*	Richard Rodgers
American Folk Songs	The Singing Sergeants
Symphonic Suite	Clifton Williams
Vocal solo: "Fedora"	Giordano
Gold and Silver Waltz	Franz Lehar
Trumpet Trio: *Bugler's Holiday*	Leroy Anderson
A Bit of American Jazz	Hill
The Stars and Stripes Forever	J. P. Sousa

The Air Force Band returned the following year for a second tour; a highlight of that tour's programs was William Schuman's *Newsreel Suite*.

Another major influence for Japanese band people was the 1961 tour by the Musique de la Garde Republicaine of Paris. Its performances demonstrated what many considered to be a truly legato concept in wind playing. The band, with its very large and complete woodwind section, performed an entire program of transcribed orchestral music, reflecting a philosophy that remains evident to this day in the group's annual visits to Japan. The profound impression made by the French band's sound and programming was quickly manifest in the performances of many of the bands hoping to make a favorable impression at the annual contests. This influence is still very apparent in today's National Contests.

In 1969 the American High School Band, a mixed tour group conducted by William Revelli, presented a concert and clinic at the Yamaha Music Camp at Nemuno-Sato. The following year the Osaka World Expo was held with bands invited from many countries; among those present were the Purdue University Marching Band and the University of California-Berkeley Marching Band. In

1972 the Fifth U.S. Air Force Band, conducted by Captain Benny Knudsen, was invited to perform at that year's Japan Band Clinic.

In 1978 the Eastman Wind Ensemble, under the sponsorship of the Kambara Music Office, Tokyo, was invited to perform a three-week tour, including a concert and workshop at the Yamaha Music Clinic at Nemuno-Sato. The program, which consisted primarily of original music for wind band, presented yet another approach for Japanese band directors; this model became very popular in Japan. The selection of pieces included *The Leaves Are Falling* by Warren Benson, Persichetti's Symphony No. 6, Bach's Passacaglia and Fugue in C minor as transcribed by Donald Hunsberger, and Ingolf Dahl's *Sinfonietta*. Following the Japan tour, the Ensemble performed in Hong Kong, Manila, Singapore, Kuala Lumpur, Jakarta, and Taegu and Seoul, Korea, sponsored by the United States Department of State.

In 1981 Larry Curtis conducted the Concert Band of California State University, Long Beach, in a performance of "*. . . and the mountains rising nowhere*" by Joseph Schwantner at the Japan Band Clinic. Six years later, in 1987, Craig Kirchhoff and the Ohio State University Band were invited to the Japan Band Clinic, where they offered the first performance in Japan of Michael Colgrass's *Winds of Nagual*.

A most important development for Japanese bands took place in 1984, when Frederick Fennell was appointed regular conductor of the Tokyo Kosei Wind Orchestra, establishing a continuous leadership that exists to this day. Previously, American wind conductors and teachers had visited Japan for several weeks or months, but Fennell's participation with Kosei has been an ongoing and highly contributory relationship through the many concerts, guest appearances, television appearances, and in particular, recordings he has made with the Tokyo Kosei Wind Orchestra.

Among the Americans who have been invited to Japan for rehearsal/concert and clinic/workshop presentations are: Irving Cheyette (1954–55), Clarence Sawhill (1964), Paul Yoder (1965), Harold Walters (1966), Fred Weber (1967), James Berdahl and Paul Whear (1971), George Cavendar (1972), Francis McBeth and William Gower (1974), Robert Jager and Mark McDunn (1975), John Paynter (1977), and Donald Hunsberger (1976, 1989, and 1991). In addition, Alfred Reed has been most active in Japan during the past few years, presenting concerts and clinics.

Individual Study and Travel Abroad

The importation of foreign, particularly American, personalities and ensembles led to new standards and methodology in rehearsal techniques, performance traditions, and repertoire. An equally important step lay in the formation of Japanese band associations which were directly or indirectly influenced by outside models. Also, the gradual interest of Japanese band and wind musicians to travel abroad for study has led to a broader awareness for potential future development.

In 1963, this author studied at the Eastman School of Music for one year, and during this period, Shoji Katoh, Professor at the Musashino School of Music, also spent a month studying at Eastman. Mr. Katoh introduced the wind ensemble concept to Japan in 1965 and continued to develop this approach until he retired in 1971. Yuichi Omuro (1940–1989), a saxophone graduate of Tokyo University School of Fine Arts, studied at Eastman and became the first Japanese performer to play as a regular member of the Eastman Wind Ensemble. Omuro returned to Japan where he was very active in teaching and became the principal saxophonist of the Tokyo Kosei Wind Orchestra.

An important step forward for many Japanese band directors began in 1968 when numerous directors attended the annual meeting of the Midwest Band Clinic, held each December in Chicago. This tradition has continued and many musicians from Japan have been introduced not only to new music and performance techniques, but also have had the opportunity to hear many of America's finest educational and military service organizations.

One of the special invited guests to the Fortieth Anniversary Weekend Celebration of the Eastman Wind Ensemble was Toru Miura. He attended the Eastman School in 1973, during which time he performed as the principal euphonium player of the Eastman Wind Ensemble. Upon his return to Japan, Mr. Miura became the principal euphonium player of the Tokyo Kosei Wind Orchestra and faculty member at the Kunitachi Music College, Tamagawa University, and the Soai College of Music.

Another positive influence in the development of young Japanese wind performers has been William Gower, who visited Japan in 1974. Many young performers travelled to study at Mr. Gower's school, Mississippi Southern University, and through his influence these students received their introduction to American education, life and music.

Eastman Wind Ensemble Recordings and Appearances

A high percentage of the positive influences upon the growth and development of Japanese bands and band directors during the past forty years may be traced directly to the many recordings and in-person appearances of the Eastman Wind Ensemble. In addition, the presence of Frederick Fennell in Japan as conductor of the Tokyo Kosei Wind Orchestra and the several visits of Donald Hunsberger have contributed immensely to an expansion of thought and methodology in wind band activities. It is interesting to compare the situation in the 1950s, as described above, with the movement evident in Japan today. The increase in the number of bands and people involved in them is most impressive, as the following census of bands in Japan as of October, 1991, shows:

Professional		5
Military:	Army	21
	Navy	6
	Air Force	5
Police		48
Schools of Music		10
Elementary		910
Junior High School		6,046
Senior High School		3,469
College		221
Industrial		103
Community		1,061
Total:		11,905

It is with a sense of gratitude that we acknowledge the contributions of the Eastman Wind Ensemble and its conductors, for without them our progress would not have been so well directed.

Complete Repertoire of the Eastman School Symphony Band
1935–1952

[Titles and composers appear as they did in the original programs. Corrections have been made only in the cases of missing or misleading information.]

PROGRAMS

January 18, 1935, Strong Auditorium

Sousa	*Semper Fidelis*
Wagner (Grabel)	Overture to *Rienzi*
Meyer-Helmund	*Serenade Rococo*
Ketelby	
The Clock and the Dresden Figures for Piano and Band	

PHILLIP MANGOLD, SOLOIST

INTERMISSION

Goldman	*University Grand March*
Goldmark (Armbruster)	
Scherzo from "The Rustic Wedding" Symphony	
Ketelby (Amers)	*Cockney Suite*
Fennell	*The Spirit of Youth*

FREDERICK FENNELL, CONDUCTOR

March 18, 1935, Kilbourn Hall

Sousa	*Semper Fidelis*
Wagner (Grabel)	Overture to *Rienzi*
Goldman	*University Grand March*
Ketelby	*The Clock and the Dresden Figures*
	For Piano and Band

PHILLIP MANGOLD, SOLOIST

INTERMISSION

Ketelby (Amers)	*Cockney Suite*
Bach (Godfrey)	
Chorale Prelude—"We All Believe in One God"	
Fennell	*The Spirit of Youth*
Fennell	*Hail Sinfonia*

FREDERICK FENNELL, CONDUCTOR

Second Annual Concert
March 23, 1936, Kilbourn Hall

Weber (Godfrey)	Overture to *Euryanthe*
Fauchet (Gillette)	Symphony in B-Flat, mvt. 1
Hanson (Maddy)	*Nordic Symphony*, mvt. 2
Bach (Holst)	*Fugue à la Gigue*
Wagner (Winterbottom)	
	Wotan's Farewell and Magic Fire Music
White	*Five Miniatures*
Glière (Leidzen)	*Russian Sailor's Dance*

FREDERICK FENNELL, CONDUCTOR

Radio Performances, NBC, April 2, 4, 12, 1936

Bach (Holst)	*Fugue à la Gigue*
Glière (Leidzen)	*Russian Sailor's Dance*
Hanson (Maddy)	*Nordic Symphony*, mvt. 2
Wagner (Winterbottom)	
	Wotan's Farewell and Magic Fire Music
Weber (Godfrey)	Overture to *Euryanthe*
White	*Five Miniatures*

Radio Performance, NBC, March 11, 1937

Cline	*Valor and Victory March*
Beethoven (Winterbottom)	*Egmont* Overture
Bach (Quarles)	Fugue in G Minor ("Lesser")
Bach (Quarles)	Fantasia in G Major
Bach (Lyon)	Fugue in G Minor ("Lesser")
Bach (Gillette)	Chorale Prelude in G Minor
McKay	"Burlesque March"
Keller	Suite
Stravinsky	Berceuse and Finale from *The Firebird*

FREDERICK FENNELL, CONDUCTOR

Third Annual Concert

March 20, 1937, Eastman Theatre

Beethoven (Winterbottom)	*Egmont* Overture
Bach (Gillette)	Chorale Prelude in G Minor
Bach (Lyon)	Fugue in G Minor ("Lesser")
Bach (Quarles)	Fantasia in G Major

INTERMISSION

Holst (Smith)	"Mars" from *The Planets*
Cline	*Valor and Victory March*
McKay	
	"Burlesque March" from *Caricature Dance Suite*
Keller	Suite for Symphony Band
Turina (Boyd)	*Danzas Fantasticas* No. 1, "Exaltación"
Stravinsky (Quarles)	
	Berceuse and Finale from *The Firebird*
Wilkins (Woolston)	*The Genesee*

FREDERICK FENNELL, CONDUCTOR

April 26, 1937, Eastman Theatre

Seventh Annual Festival of American Music

Mason (Simmons)	*Divertimento* for Symphony Band
Gillette	*Vistas Sinfonietta in Olden Style*

INTERMISSION

Alessandro	*Sinfonietta* for Wind Instruments
Cline	*Valor and Victory*
Keller	Suite for Symphony Band
McKay	
Symphonic Prelude in American Idiom (for brass alone)	
McKay	
	"Burlesque March" from *Caricature Dance Suite*
Read	"Prayers of Steel" from *Sketches of a City*

FREDERICK FENNELL, CONDUCTOR

[EASTMAN SCHOOL SYMPHONY BAND]

4th SEASON: 1937–38

January 8, 1938, Eastman Theatre

Bach (Lyon)	Fugue in C Minor
Franck (Godfrey)	"Redemption"
	from *Morceau Symphonique*
Berlioz (Safranek)	*Roman Carnival Overture*

INTERMISSION

Three Characteristic Pieces:

Rossini (Respighi)	*Danse Cosaque*
Debussy (Weiss)	*The Girl with the Flaxen Hair*
Debussy (Weiss)	*Golliwog's Cake Walk*
Elgar (Godfrey)	
	Suite, "From the Bavarian Highlands"
Prokofieff (Duthoit)	
	Scherzo and March from *The Love of Three Oranges*
Glière (Dvorak)	*Russian Sailor's Dance*

FREDERICK FENNELL, CONDUCTOR

February 26, 1938, Eastman Theatre

Vaughan Williams	*Toccata Marziale*
DeNardis (Caravaglios)	
	Nocturne and Procession from *Scenes Abruzzesi*
Alford	*The Purple Carnival*
Fennell	*Palestra*
Franchetti	Symphony in E Minor

INTERMISSION

Weber (Lake)	Concerto for Clarinet
DOUGLAS DANFELT, SOLOIST	
Jacob	*An Original Suite*
Bendel (Watson)	
	"Sunday Morning at Glion" from *By The Lake at Geneva*
Weinberger (Bainum)	
	Polka and Fugue from *Schwanda, the Bagpiper*
GERALD VOGT, ORGAN	
Trad. (Woolston)	*The Genesee*

FREDERICK FENNELL, CONDUCTOR

Radio Performance, NBC, March 17, 1938

Vaughan Williams	*Toccata Marziale*
De Nardis (Caravaglios)	
	Nocturne and Procession from *Scenes Abruzzesi*
Franchetti	Symphony in E Minor
Alford	*The Purple Carnival*
Fennell	*Palestra*
Weber (Lake)	Concerto for Clarinet
DOUGLAS DANFELT, SOLOIST	
Jacob	*An Original Suite*
Weinberger (Bainum)	
	Polka and Fugue from *Schwanda, the Bagpiper*

FREDERICK FENNELL, CONDUCTOR

April 25, 1938, Eastman Theatre
Eighth Annual Festival of American Music

Alford	*Glory of the Gridiron*
Morgenstern	Quartet for Horns
McKay	Sonata for Clarinet
Tuthill	Overture for Symphonic Band
Lyon	Chorale for Two Brass Choirs
Alford	*The Skyliner*
Grofé (Leidzen)	
	"On the Trail" from *Grand Canyon Suite*
Cline	*Cowboy Lament*
Read	*Prayers of Steel*

FREDERICK FENNELL, CONDUCTOR

5th SEASON: 1938–39

January 13, 1939, Eastman Theatre

Bach (Godfrey)	
	Prelude, Chorale and Fugue in G minor
(Clark)	*Suite of Classic Dances*
Couperin	Sarabande (*La Lugubre*)
Krebs	Bourrée
Gluck	*Dance of the Sylphs*
Gretry	Gavotte
Mattheson	Slow Minuet
Rameau	Rigaudon
Mozart (Duthoit)	Overture to the *Marriage of Figaro*
Humperdinck (Winterbottom)	
	Suite from "The Miracle"
Smetana (Winterbottom)	Symphonic Poem—*Vltava*
Dukas (Winterbottom)	*The Sorcerer's Apprentice*

FREDERICK FENNELL, CONDUCTOR

Radio Performance, NBC, January 17, 1939

Bach (Godfrey)	Prelude and Chorale in G Minor
Mozart (Duthoit)	Overture to *Marriage of Figaro*
Dukas (Winterbottom)	*The Sorcerer's Apprentice*

FREDERICK FENNELL, CONDUCTOR

February 28, 1939, Eastman Theatre

Handel (Lyon)	Suite from the *Water Music*
Bach (Cailliet)	Fugue in G minor
Bach (Holst)	*Fugue à la Gigue* in B flat
Weber (Gready)	Overture to *Oberon*

INTERMISSION

Stravinsky (Quarles)	
	Berceuse and Finale from *The Firebird*
Vaughan Williams	*English Folk Song Suite*
Tschaikowsky (Westphal)	*Romeo and Juliet Fantasie*

FREDERICK FENNELL, CONDUCTOR

6th SEASON: 1939–40

Concert for the Seventh Annual Clinic of the New York State School Music Association

December 1, 1939, Eastman Theatre

Glinka (Winterbottom)	
	Overture to *Russlan and Ludmilla*
Humperdinck (Maddy)	
	Prayer and Dream Pantomime from *Hansel and Gretel*
Clarke	Euphonium Solo: *Debutante*

ROBERT MARSTELLER, EUPHONIUM

Enesco	*Rumanian Rhapsody*

FREDERICK FENNELL, CONDUCTOR

January 23, 1940, Eastman Theatre

Cimarosa (Winter)	Overture to *The Secret Marriage*
Tchaikowsky (Winterbottom)	
	Theme and Variations from Suite No. 3, op. 55
Purcell (Garland)	Trumpet Voluntary

SIDNEY MEAR, TRUMPET

Brahms (Duthoit)	
	Variations on a Theme by Haydn, op. 56a

INTERMISSION

Wagner (Cailliet)	
	Siegfried's Rhine Journey from *Götterdämmerung*
Wagner (Cailliet)	
	Elsa's Procession to the Cathedral from *Lohengrin*
Wagner (Winterbottom)	Prelude to *Die Meistersinger*

FREDERICK FENNELL, CONDUCTOR

May 10, 1940, Eastman Theatre

Weber (Godfrey)	Overture to *Euryanthe*
Mozart (Garland)	Minuet from Symphony No. 39
Barat (Mear)	Andante and Scherzo

SIDNEY MEAR, TRUMPET

Tschaikowsky (Godfrey)   Suite from *Swan Lake*

INTERMISSION

Texidor (Winter)   *Amparita Roca*
Smetana (Lotter)   Suite from *The Bartered Bride*
Jeanjean (End)   *Au Clair de la Lune*
       CLEMENT HUTCHINSON, CLARINET
White (Lyon)   *Overture To Youth*
       FREDERICK FENNELL, CONDUCTOR

Radio Performance [n.d.]
Enesco   *Roumanian Rhapsody* No. 1
Glinka (Winterbottom)
              Overture to *Russlan and Ludmilla*
Humperdinck (Maddy)
      Prayer and Dream Pantomine from *Hansel and Gretel*
       FREDERICK FENNELL, CONDUCTOR

7th SEASON: 1940–41

November 29, 1940, Eastman Theatre
*Concert for the Eighth Annual Clinic of the New
York State School Music Association*
Bach (Leidzen)   Chorale—"Come Sweet Death"
Debussy (Winterbottom)   *Petite Suite*
Wagner (Godfrey)
       Prelude and Love Death from *Tristan and Isolde*
       FREDERICK FENNELL, CONDUCTOR

December 3, 1940, Eastman Theatre
Bach (Leidzen)   Chorale—"Come Sweet Death"
Debussy (Winterbottom)   *Petite Suite*
Shostakovitch (Dike)   Prelude in E-flat Minor
Hanson (Goldberg)
              Symphony No. 2 ("Romantic"), mvt. 1
Wagner (Godfrey)
       Prelude and Love Death from *Tristan and Isolde*
       FREDERICK FENNELL, CONDUCTOR

January 17, 1941, Eastman Theatre
Rossini (Rollinson)   Overture to *Semiramide*
(Clark)   *Suite of Classic Dances*
Schubert (Safranek)   Ballet music from *Rosamunde*
Bizet (Laurendeau)   *L'Arlesienne Suite* No. 1

Weinberger (Bainum)
      Polka and Fugue from *Schwanda, the Bagpiper*
       FREDERICK FENNELL, CONDUCTOR

March 24, 1941, Eastman Theatre
Bach (Abert)
              Prelude, Chorale, and Fugue in G Minor
Bach (Holst)   *Fugue à la Gigue*
Prokofieff (Duthoit)
      Scherzo and March from *The Love of Three Oranges*
Wagner (Winterbottom)
              Prelude to Act III from *Die Meistersinger*
Cailliet
      Variations on the theme "Pop Goes the Weasel"
Strauss (Godfrey)   Overture to *Die Fledermaus*
       FREDERICK FENNELL, CONDUCTOR

8th SEASON: 1941–42

November 3, 1941, Eastman Theatre
Bach (Whybrew)
      Chorale—"Christ Lay in the Bonds of Death"
Bach (Wright)
      Chorale Prelude—"Fervent is My Longing"
Franck (Gillette)   Symphony in D Minor, Finale
Wagner (Cailliet)
      Elsa's Procession to the Cathedral from *Lohengrin*
Hanson (Garland)   Suite from *Merry Mount*
Strauss (Cailliet)   Waltzes from *Der Rosenkavalier*
Rossini (Duthoit)   Overture to *The Barber of Seville*

Radio Performance, NBC, December 9, 1941
Tuthill   Overture for Symphonic Band
McKay   "Burlesque March"
Mason (Simmons)   March from *Divertimento*
Sousa   *The Liberty Bell*
       FREDERICK FENNELL, CONDUCTOR

December 11, 1941, Eastman Theatre
Tuthill   Overture for Symphonic Band
Bach (Falcone)   Passacaglia and Fugue in C Minor
Paganini (Falcone)   *Perpetual Motion*
       26 CLARINETISTS FROM THE CLASS OF
              RUFUS AREY, SOLOISTS

December 11, 1941 (cont.)

Jacob	*William Byrd Suite*
Mason (Simmons)	*Divertimento* for Symphonic Band
Gershwin (End)	Three Songs from *Porgy and Bess*
Glière (Leidzen)	*Russian Sailor's Dance*

FREDERICK FENNELL, CONDUCTOR

February 16, 1942, Eastman Theatre

Tschaikowsky (Westphal)
Overture Fantasy from *Romeo and Juliet*
Shostakovich (Woolston)
Symphony No. 5, mvts. 2 (Allegretto) and 4 (Allegro
non troppo)

INTERMISSION

Moussorgsky (Leidzen/Fennell)
Pictures at an Exhibition
FREDERICK FENNELL, CONDUCTOR

Radio Performance, NBC, March 15, 1942

Gershwin (End)	Three Songs from *Porgy and Bess*
Harris	*Cimarron Overture*
Gould	*Cowboy Rhapsody*

FREDERICK FENNELL, CONDUCTOR

March 16, 1942, Eastman Theatre

Gould	*Cowboy Rhapsody*
Harris	*Cimarron Overture*
Rachmaninoff (Leidzen)	*Italian Polka*
Grieg (Falcone)	Piano Concerto in A Minor, mvt. 1

ROBERT BAUSTIAN, SOLOIST

INTERMISSION

Strauss (Godfrey)	Waltzes from *Die Fledermaus*
Sarasate (Cailliet)	*Zigeunerweisen*

ROBERT BOYD, SOLOIST

Hanson (Leidzen)	*March Carillon*
De Falla (Goldberg)	

Spanish Dance from *La Vida Breve*
Group of Marches:

Alford	*Purple Carnival*
Sousa	*Black Horse Troop*
Bagley	*National Emblem*
Sousa	*Semper Fidelis*

FREDERICK FENNELL, CONDUCTOR

9th SEASON: 1942–43

November 23, 1942, Eastman Theatre

Bach (Gillette)
Chorale Prelude—"We All Believe in One God"

Beethoven (Godfrey)	*Leonore* Overture No. 3
Brahms (Duthoit)	*Variations on a Theme by Haydn*
Grainger	*The Immovable Do*

Rimsky-Korsakof (Leidzen)
"Procession of the Nobles" from *Mlada*
Borodin (Glazounoff/Duthoit) Overture to *Prince Igor*
FREDERICK FENNELL, CONDUCTOR

February 9, 1943, Eastman Theatre

Bach (Wright)	Toccata and Fugue in D Minor
Mozart (Garland)	Minuet in E-flat
Liszt (Falcone)	*Hungarian Fantasie*

NORMA BESS HOLMES, PIANO

Copland (Haldane)	*El Salon Mexico*
White (Fennell)	*College Caprice*
Strauss (Brown)	*Emperor Waltz*

FREDERICK FENNELL, CONDUCTOR

May 11, 1943, Eastman Theatre

Handel (Sartorius) *The Royal Fireworks Music*
Schubert (Cailliet)
Symphony No. 8 ("Unfinished"), Andante con moto
Mendelssohn (Meyer)
Overture to *A Midsummer Night's Dream*
Beethoven (Winterbottom) *Egmont* Overture

INTERMISSION

Schuman	*Newsreel (In Five Shots)*
McKay	*Bravura Prelude*
End	*Floor Show*

FREDERICK FENNELL, CONDUCTOR

10th SEASON: 1943–44

February 4, 1944, Eastman Theatre

Rossini (Duthoit)   Overture to *The Barber of Seville*
Bach (Wright)
Chorale Prelude—"Herzlich thut mich verlangen"
Handel (Beecham / Duthoit)
Suite—"The Gods Go A-Begging"

Franck (Gillette)   Symphony in D Minor

INTERMISSION

Rimsky-Korsakow (Luckhardt)
Wedding March and Death of King Dodon from *Le Coq d'Or*
Palestrina (Harvey)   *Adoramus Te* and *Sanctus*
Moussorgsky (Leidzen)
            Coronation Scene from *Boris Godounow*
      PATTEE EVENSON, CONDUCTOR

11th SEASON: 1944–45

December 5, 1944, Eastman Theatre

Wagner (Grabel)   Overture to *Rienzi*
Schuman   *Newsreel in 5 Shots*
Dukas (Winterbottom)   *The Sorcerer's Apprentice*
Turlet   *Le Regiment de Sambre-et-Meuse*

INTERMISSION

Bach (Leidzen)   Toccata and Fugue in D Minor
Gould (Yoder)   Pavanne
Rachmaninoff (Leidzen)   *Italian Polka*
Cailliet
      Variations on the theme "Pop Goes the Weasel"
Shostakovitch (Woolston)
                  Symphony No. 5, op. 47, Finale
      PATTEE EVENSON, CONDUCTOR

May 1, 1945, Eastman Theatre

Rimsky-Korsakoff (Leidzen)
            Procession of the Nobles from *Mlada*
Handel (Lyon)   Suite from *The Water Music*
Barat (Mear)
      Andante and Scherzo for Solo Trumpet and Band
            EDWIN BETTS, SOLOIST
Berlioz (Foulds/Brown)
      Symphonie Fantastique, op. 14, mvts. 2 (A Ball) and 4
                        (March to the Scaffold)
Alford   *Colonel Bogey*

INTERMISSION

Gould   *Jericho Rhapsody*
Bach (Leidzen)   Chorale—"Komm, süsser Tod"
Bach (Gillette)
      Chorale Prelude—"Wir glauben all' an einen Gott"

Weinberger (Bainum)
      Polka and Fugue from *Schwanda, the Bagpiper*
            PATTEE EVENSON, CONDUCTOR

12th SEASON: 1945–46

November 26, 1945, Eastman Theatre

Weber (Godfrey)   Overture to *Euryanthe*
(Clark)   *Suite of Classic Dances*
Schubert (Cailliet)   Symphony No. 8 ("Unfinished")
Handel (Sartorius)   *The Royal Fireworks Music*

INTERMISSION

Debussy (Winterbottom)   *Petite Suite*
Humperdinck (Winterbottom)
  Prayer and Dream Pantomime from *Hansel and Gretel*
Hadley   *Youth Triumphant Overture*
      FREDERICK FENNELL, CONDUCTOR

February 9, 1946, Eastman Theatre

Rossini (Rollinson)   Overture to *Semiramide*
Wagner (Cailliet)
  Elsa's Procession to the Cathedral from *Lohengrin*
Wagner (arr. unknown)
        Closing Scene from Act III of *The Valkyrie*
            ARTHUR SCHOEP, SOLOIST

INTERMISSION

Moussorgsky (Leidzen/Fennell)
                  Pictures at an Exhibition
      FREDERICK FENNELL, CONDUCTOR

April 11, 1946, Eastman Theatre
Sixteenth Annual Festival of American Music
Hanson   *Festival Fanfare*
Key   *The Star Spangled Banner*
Tuthill   Overture for Symphonic Band
Kohs   *Life with Uncle Sam*
Sanders   Symphony in B-flat for Band

INTERMISSION

Gould   *Cowboy Rhapsody*
McKay   *Bravura Prelude*
End   *Floor Show*
      FREDERICK FENNELL, CONDUCTOR

13th SEASON: 1946–47

November 19, 1946, Eastman Theatre
Bach (Wright)
        Chorale Prelude—"Fervent is my Longing"
Bach (Holst)   *Fugue à la Gigue*
Smetana (Winterbottom)
        Symphonic poem *The Moldau*
Wagner (Godfrey)
        Prelude and Love Death from *Tristan und Isolde*
Rimsky-Korsakoff (Leidzen)
        "Procession of the Nobles" from *Mlada*

INTERMISSION

Holst (Smith)   "Mars" from *The Planets*
Bizet (Laurendeau)   *L'Arlesienne Suite* No. 1
Dukas (Winterbottom)   *The Sorcerer's Apprentice*
Texidor (Winter)   *Amparita Roca*
    FREDERICK FENNELL, CONDUCTOR

January 20, 1947, Eastman Theatre
Borodin (Duthoit)   Overture to *Prince Igor*
Handel (Beecham/Duthoit)
        Suite—"The Gods Go A-Begging"
Bach (Abert)
        Prelude, Chorale, and Fugue in G Minor
Holst   First Suite in E-flat

INTERMISSION

Strauss (Godfrey)   Overture to *Die Fledermaus*
Strauss (Brown)   *Emperor Waltz*
Grieg (Holvik)   *The Last Spring*
Wagner (Winterbottom)
        Prelude to Act III of *Die Meistersinger*
Wagner (Cailliet)
        Siegfried's Journey to the Rhine from
                Götterdämmerung
    FREDERICK FENNELL, CONDUCTOR

March 6, 1947, Eastman Theatre
Jacob   *William Byrd Suite*
Bach (Whybrew)
        Chorale—"Christ Lay in the Bonds of Death"
Bach (D. Wright)   Toccata and Fugue in D Minor

INTERMISSION

Tchaikowsky (J. Woldt)
    Concerto No. 1 in B-flat Minor, op. 23, for Piano and
                  Orchestra
    MARYA SIELSKA, SOLOIST
Wagner (Godfrey)   *A Faust Overture*
Tchaikowsky (T. C. Brown)   *1812 Overture*, op. 49
    FREDERICK FENNELL, CONDUCTOR

May 3, 1947, Eastman Theatre
Seventeenth Annual Festival of American Music
Riegger   Passacaglia and Fugue
Barber   *Commando March*
Tuthill   Suite for Band, op. 26
Cazden   *Elegy Before Dawn*
Cowell   *Shoonthree*
San Juan   *Yoruba Song*
Read   *Prayers of Steel*
Sousa   *Manhattan Beach*
Sousa   *Liberty Bell*
Sousa   *High School Cadets*
    FREDERICK FENNELL, CONDUCTOR

14th SEASON: 1947–48

November 4, 1947, Eastman Theatre
Rossini (Duthoit)   Overture to *The Barber of Seville*
Vaughan Williams   *Folk Song Suite*
Prokofieff (Duthoit)
    Scherzo and March from *The Love of Three Oranges*
Weinberger (Bainum)
    Polka and Fugue from *Schwanda the Bagpiper*

INTERMISSION

Shostakovitch (Woolston)   Symphony No. 5,
        Allegretto and *Allegro non troppo*
Bach (Falcone)   Passacaglia and Fugue in C Minor
    FREDERICK FENNELL, CONDUCTOR

January 14, 1948, Eastman Theatre
Wagner (Godfrey)
    Entry of the Gods into Valhalla from *Das Rheingold*
Wagner (Winterbottom)
    Siegfried's Funeral March from *Twilight of the Gods*
Wagner (Winterbottom)
    Symphonic Synthesis of the Music from *Parsifal*

Berlioz (Godfrey)   *Roman Carnival Overture*
Berlioz (Goldman)   *Grand Symphony for Band*, op. 15
FREDERICK FENNELL, CONDUCTOR

15th SEASON: 1948–49

November 3, 1948, Eastman Theatre
Bach (Whybrew)
            Chorale—"Christ Lay in the Bonds of Death"
Wagner (Grabel)   Overture to *Rienzi*
Smetana (Winterbottom)
                    Symphonic Poem *The Moldau*
Hanson (Garland)   Suite from *Merry Mount*

INTERMISSION

Moussorgsky (Leidzen/Fennell)
                        Pictures at an Exhibition
FREDERICK FENNELL, CONDUCTOR

January 17, 1949, Eastman Theatre
Beethoven (Winterbottom)   *Egmont* Overture
Holst   Suite No. 2 in F Major
Weber (Lake)   Concertino for Clarinet, op. 26
GEORGE SELTZER, SOLOIST

INTERMISSION

Respighi   Ballad for Band *Huntingtower*
Roussel   *A Glorious Day*
E. Hansen   *Little Norwegian Suite*
Ganne   *Marche Lorraine*
Rimsky-Korsakoff (Leidzen)
            "Procession of the Nobles" from *Mlada*
Sousa   *Manhattan Beach*
FREDERICK FENNELL, CONDUCTOR

March 15, 1949, Eastman Theatre
Vaughan Williams   *Toccata Marziale*
Schoenberg
            Theme and Variations in G Minor, op. 43a
Holst   Suite No. 1 in E-flat

INTERMISSION

Strauss   *Solemn Entry of the Knights of St. John*

Milhaud   *Suite Française*
Stravinsky
        Circus Polka ("Composed for a Young Elephant")
Sousa   *Sabre and Spurs*
Sousa   *Northern Pines*
Sousa   *Black Horse Troop*
FREDERICK FENNELL, CONDUCTOR

16th SEASON: 1949–50

November 8, 1949, Eastman Theatre
Festival of Marches
Bagley   *National Emblem*
Handel (Goldman)   March from *Judas Maccabeus*
Holst   March from Suite No. 1
Gounod (Lake)   *Funeral March of a Marionette*
Texidor (Winter)   *Amparita Roca*
Chabrier (Miller)   *March Joyeuse*
Barber   *Commando March*
Turlet   *French National Défile*
Goldman   *On the Mall*

INTERMISSION

Elgar (Evans)   *Pomp and Circumstance* March No. 2
Debussy (Weiss)   *Cortège* from *Petite Suite*
Wagner (Winterbottom)
        Siegfried's Funeral March from *Götterdämmerung*
Pierne (Beeler)   *March of the Little Lead Soldiers*
Prokofieff (Duthoit)
            March from *The Love of Three Oranges*
Schubert (Laurendeau)
                Marche Militaire Française No. 1
Bigelow   *Our Director*
Petersen   *Our Commander*
Sousa   *Stars and Stripes Forever*
FREDERICK FENNELL, CONDUCTOR

December 8, 1949, Eastman Theatre
Bach (Wright)   Chorale Prelude—"Fervent is My
                            Longing"
Bruckner (Falcone)
            Symphony No. 7 in E-flat Major, Adagio
R. Strauss (Cailliet)   Waltzes from *Der Rosenkavalier*

December 8, 1949 (cont.)

INTERMISSION

Brahms (Winter)	*Variations on a Theme by Haydn*
Britten (Brown)	
	Soirées Musicales on Themes of Giaccomo Rossini
Sousa	*Hands Across the Sea*
Sousa	*Corcoran Cadets*
Sousa	*Washington Post*

FREDERICK FENNELL, CONDUCTOR

March 1, 1950, Eastman Theatre

Rossini (Rollinson)	Overture to *Semiramide*
Jacob	*William Byrd Suite*
Tchaikowsky (Godfrey)	Suite from *Swan Lake*

INTERMISSION

Hadley	*Youth Triumphant Overture*
Tuthill	Suite for Band, op. 26
Cowell	*Shoonthree*
Grainger	*Lads of Wamphray*
Lithgow	*Invercargil*
Belsterling	*March of the Steel Man*
Alford	*Glory of the Gridiron*

FREDERICK FENNELL, CONDUCTOR

April 25, 1950, Eastman Theatre

Bach (Wright)	Toccata and Fugue in D Minor
(Clark)	*Suite of Classic Dances*
Barrow	*A Suite of Variations*
Wagner (Winterbottom)	
	Siegfried's Journey to the Rhine from *Die Götterdämmerung*

INTERMISSION

Pryor

Fantasie on the Air "The Blue Bells of Scotland" with Theme and Variations

RICHARD MYERS, SOLOIST

Rossini (Respighi/Godfrey/Leidzen)

	La Boutique Fantasque
Sibelius (Cailliet)	*Finlandia*
Goldman	*Interlochen Bowl*
Seitz	*Grandioso*
Alford	*The Purple Carnival*

FREDERICK FENNELL, CONDUCTOR

October 30, 1950, Eastman Theatre

Second Annual Festival of Marches

Key	*Star Spangled Banner*
Sousa	*High School Cadets*
Handel (Sartorius)	
	March from *The Royal Fireworks Music*
Rimsky-Korsakoff (Luckhardt)	
	Wedding March from *Le Coq d'Or*
Byrd (Jacob)	*Earl of Oxford's March*
Hanson (Leidzen)	*March Carillon*
Berlioz (Brown)	
	"March to the Scaffold" from *Symphonie fantastique*
Goldman	*Interlochen Bowl*
Fennell	*Palestra*

INTERMISSION

Meacham	*American Patrol*
Rimsky-Korsakoff (Leidzen)	
	"Procession of the Nobles" from *Mlada*
Holst (Smith)	"Mars" from *The Planets*
Belsterling	*March of the Steelmen*
Vaughan Williams	*Folk Songs*
Grainger	*Lads of Wamphray*
Prokofieff (Goldman)	
	Triumphal March from *Peter and the Wolf*
Alford	*Glory of the Gridiron*
Respighi (Leidzen)	
	"Pines of the Appian Way" from *Pines of Rome*

FREDERICK FENNELL, CONDUCTOR

December 4, 1950, Eastman Theatre

Glinka (Winterbottom)	
	Overture to *Russlan and Ludmilla*
Bach (Leidzen)	Chorale—"Come Sweet Death"
Handel (Beecham) Suite—"The Gods Go A-Begging"	
Wagner (Seidel)	Overture to the *The Flying Dutchman*
Hanson (Garland)	Suite from *Merry Mount*

INTERMISSION

Bizet (Falcone)	Selections from *Carmen*
Kern (Jones)	Selections from *Showboat*
Weinberger (Bainum)	
	Polka and Fugue from *Schwanda, the Bagpiper*
Lithgow	*Invercargil*
Jenkins/Neff	*Pieces of Eight*

FREDERICK FENNELL, CONDUCTOR

February 5, 1951, Kilbourn Hall
Concert Music for Wind Instruments (Orchestral Department)

Willaert   *Ricercare for Wind Instruments*
Scheidt
            Canzon XXVI (Bergamasca) for Five Instruments
Di Lasso
            Motet—*Tui sunt coeli* for Eight-voice Double Brass
                                    Choir
Gabrieli   *Sonata pian'e forte*
Gabrieli   *Canzon noni toni a 12* from *Sacre Symphonie*
Pezel   Suite No. 2 for Brass Instruments (*Turmmusik*)
Beethoven   Three Equali for Four Trombones

INTERMISSION

Mozart
            Serenade No. 10 in B-flat Major for Wind
                                    Instruments

INTERMISSION

Strauss
            Serenade in E-flat Major, op. 7, for Thirteen Wind
                                    Instruments
Ruggles
            "Angels" from *Men and Angels* for Multiple Brass
                                    Choir
Stravinsky
            Symphonies of Wind Instruments (in Memory of Claude
                                    Debussy)
FREDERICK FENNELL, CONDUCTOR

February 14, 1951, Kilbourn Hall
Mozart (Duthoit)   Overture to *The Marriage of Figaro*
Tchaikowsky (Westphal)
            Overture and Fantasie from *Romeo and Juliet*
Gershwin (Bennett)   Selections from *Porgy and Bess*

INTERMISSION

Wagner (Fennell)
Nachtgesang, Prelude to Act III and Shepherd's Song
                        from *Tristan und Isolde*
FREDERICK FENNELL, CONDUCTOR

March 14, 1951, Eastman Theatre
Rossini (Duthoit)   Overture to *The Barber of Seville*

Bach (Mairs)
            Chorale—"Christ Lay in the Bonds of Death"
Pierne (Beeler)   March of the Little Lead Soldiers
Dvořák (Ertl)   *Slavonic Dance* No. 2
Tchaikowsky (Winterbottom)
            Theme and Variations from Suite No. 3

INTERMISSION

De Sarasate (Cailliet)   *Zigeunerweisen*
            RICHARD BARNETT, SOLOIST
MacDowell (Winterbottom)   *Woodland Sketches*
Stravinsky   *Circus Polka*
Gould   *Cowboy Rhapsody*
Jenkins/Neff   *Pieces of Eight*
Sousa   *Manhattan Beach*
FREDERICK FENNELL, CONDUCTOR

April 30, 1951, Eastman Theatre
Twenty-first Annual Festival of American Music

Bagley   *National Emblem*
Effinger   Prelude and Fugue
Barrow   *A Suite of Variations*
Harris   Symphonic Fantasy *The Fruit of Gold*
Persichetti   *Divertimento* for Band, op. 42

INTERMISSION

Riegger   Music for Brass Choir, op. 45
Bennett   *Suite of Old American Dances*
Thomson   *A Solemn Music*
Tuthill   *Rowdy Dance*
Sousa   *The Invincible Eagle*
Goldman   *Cheerio*
FREDERICK FENNELL, CONDUCTOR

18th SEASON: 1951–52

October 30, 1951, Eastman Theatre
Third Annual Festival of Marches

Key   *Star-Spangled Banner*
Alford   *Colonel Bogey*
Verdi (Seredy)   Grand March from *Aida*
Beethoven   Turkish March from *The Ruins of Athens*
Milhaud   March from *Suite Française*
Bizet   March of the Smugglers from *Carmen*
Handel (Leidzen)   Slow March from *Scipio*
Persichetti   *Divertimento* for Band, March

October 30, 1951 (cont.)

Wagner (Leidzen)
  Trauersinfonie, Funeral Music on Themes from
                        Weber's *Euryanthe*
Fennell   *Tally-Ho!*

INTERMISSION

Mendelssohn (Laurendeau)
  Wedding March from *A Midsummer Night's Dream*
Gould   *American Salute*
Riegger   *Processional*
Saint-Saens (Lake)   *French Military March*
Tchaikowsky (Laurendeau)   *March Slav*
Jenkins/Neff   *Pieces of Eight*
Sousa   *Corcoran Cadets*
Alford   *The Vanished Army*
Goldman   *Cheerio*

FREDERICK FENNELL, CONDUCTOR

November 29, 1951, Eastman Theatre

*In a Concert for the Sixteenth Annual Conference of the
New York State School Music Association*
Weber (Godfrey)   Overture to *Euryanthe*
Bach (Wright)
  Chorale and Chorale Prelude—"Fervent Is My
                              Longing"
Schoenberg   Theme and Variations, op. 43a
Handel (Goldman)
        March and Chorus from *Judas Maccabaeus*
Walton (Duthoit)   *Crown Imperial March*
Sousa   *Corcoran Cadets*

FREDERICK FENNELL, CONDUCTOR

December 3, 1951, Eastman Theatre

Weber (Godfrey)   Overture to *Euryanthe*
Bach (Wright)
  Chorale and Chorale Prelude—"Fervent Is My
                              Longing"
Schoenberg   Theme and Variations, op. 43a
King   *Pride of the Illini*

INTERMISSION

Handel (Goldman)
        March and Chorus from *Judas Maccabaeus*
Miaskovsky
  Symphony No. 19 in E-flat Major for Band, Andante
                   serioso and Moderato

Walton   *Crown Imperial March*
Davies   *Royal Air Force March*

FREDERICK FENNELL, CONDUCTOR

January 16, 1952, Eastman Theatre

Jacob   *Music for a Festival*

INTERMISSION

Goldmark (Faulwetter)   *Sakuntala Overture*
Dvořák (arr. unknown)
            Slavonic Dance No. 4 in F, op. 46
Wagner (Godfrey)
  Entry of the Gods into Valhalla from *Das Rheingold*
Morris   *The Kilties March*
Alford   *Voice of the Guns March*

FREDERICK FENNELL, CONDUCTOR

February 12, 1952, Eastman Theatre

Beethoven (Winterbottom)   *Egmont* Overture
Britten (Brown)
  Soirées Musicales—Suite of Movements from Rossini
Schubert (Laurendeau)   *Marche Militaire Française*
Dvořák (arr. unknown)
          Slavonic Dance No. 3 in A-flat Major, op. 46
Bottesini (Zimmerman)
   Grand Duo Concertante for Violin and Double Bass

INTERMISSION

Persichetti   *Divertimento*
Wagner (Winterbottom)
            Symphonic Synthesis from *Parsifal*
Fillmore   *The Klaxon March*
Alford   *Dunedin March*

FREDERICK FENNELL, CONDUCTOR

March 18, 1952, Eastman Theatre

Wagner (Seidel)   Overture to *The Flying Dutchman*
Hindemith   Symphony in B-flat for Concert Band

INTERMISSION

Wagner (Leidzen)
  Trauersinfonie, Funeral Music on Themes from
                        Weber's *Euryanthe*
Wagner (Winterbottom)
         Prelude to Act III of *Die Meistersinger*

Wagner (Grabel)   Overture to *Rienzi*
FREDERICK FENNELL, CONDUCTOR

The Eastman School Symphony Band performances continued after the debut of the Eastman Wind Ensemble until 1975. The Eastman Wind Orchestra, which parallels the Eastman Wind Ensemble in programing style, debuted on 6 October 1975. The repertoire for the 1952–53 season of the Eastman School Symphony Band is included in order to contrast the programming content of the two ensembles.

19th SEASON: 1952–53

October 29, 1952, Eastman Theatre
Fourth Annual Festival of Marches

Key	*The Star-Spangled Banner*
Hall	*The New Colonial March*
Grundman	*March Processional*
Sibelius (Goldman)	*Alla marcia* from *Karelia Suite*
Milhaud	
	Two Marches (*In Memoriam* and *Gloria Victoribus*)
Coates	Northwards from *Suite, Four Ways*
Gounod (Lake)	Processional from *The Queen of Sheba*
Elgar (Evans)	*Pomp and Circumstance* March No. 1

INTERMISSION

Jayaloyes (Hume)	Spanish March *El Abanico*
Saint-Saens (Winterbottom)	*Marche Heroique*
Pierne (Cydalise)	*Entry of the Little Fauns*
Walton	*Crown Imperial March*
Sousa	*National Fencibles March*
Scott	*March of the Slide Trombones*
Goldman	*Onward—Upward*
J. F. Wagner	*Under the Double Eagle*

FREDERICK FENNELL, CONDUCTOR

November 18, 1952, Eastman Theatre

Sousa	*Corcoran Cadets*
Handel (Cailliet)	Overture to *The Messiah*
Holst	Suite No. 2 in F Major
Mendelssohn (Meyer)	
	Nocturne from *A Midsummer Night's Dream*

Schuman   *George Washington Bridge*

INTERMISSION

Moussorgsky (Leidzen/Fennell)
                    Pictures at an Exhibition
FREDERICK FENNELL, CONDUCTOR

December 17, 1952, Eastman Theatre

Goldman	*Bugles and Drums*
Vaughan Williams	*English Folk Song Suite*
Cazden	*Elegy Before Dawn*
Cowell	*A Celtic Set*
Bliss	Suite from the film *Things to Come*
Smetana (Winterbottom)	*The Moldau*
Sousa	*The Rifle Regiment*
Tieke	*Old Comrades March*

FREDERICK FENNELL, CONDUCTOR

February 10, 1953, Eastman Theatre

Alford	*The Vanished Army*
Ireland	*A Maritime Overture*
Kechley	Suite for Concert Band
McBride	*Lonely Landscape*
Villa-Lobos (Krance)	
	Aria and Toccata from *Bachianas Brazilieras* No. 5
Eager	*Dominion*
Goldman	*Cheerio*

FREDERICK FENNELL, CONDUCTOR

May 7, 1953, Eastman Theatre
Twenty-second Annual Festival of American Music

Sousa	*The Rifle Regiment*
Gould	*Fourth of July*
Piston	*Tunbridge Fair*
Riegger	Passacaglia and Fugue
Schuman	*George Washington Bridge*
Kay	*Solemn Prelude*
Mennin	*Canzona*
Reed	*Russian Christmas Music*
Teike	*Old Comrades*
Goldman	*Bugles and Drums*

FREDERICK FENNELL, CONDUCTOR

APPENDIX A1B

Complete Repertoire of the Eastman School Symphony Band
1935–1952

CATALOGUE OF PERFORMANCES BY COMPOSER AND TITLE

Season(s) of performance indicated after each entry

A

Alessandro, Victor: *Sinfonietta* for Wind Instruments 36–37

Alford, Harry: *Glory of the Gridiron* 37–38; 50–51

Alford, Harry: *Purple Carnival March* 37–38; 49–50

Alford, Harry: *Skyliner* 37–38

Alford, Kenneth: *Colonel Bogey* 44–45; 51–52

Alford, Kenneth: *Dunedin March* 51–52

Alford, Kenneth: *The Vanished Army* 51–52; 52–53

Alford, Kenneth: *Voice of the Guns March* 51–52

B

Bach, J. S. (Whybrew): Chorale—"Christ Lay in Bonds of Death" 41–42; 46–47; 48–49

Bach, J. S. (Leidzen): Chorale—"Come Sweet Death" 40–41(2); 44–45; 50–51

Bach, J. S. (Wright): Chorale Prelude—"Fervent Is My Longing" 41–42; 43–44; 46–47; 51–52

Bach, J. S. (Gillette): Chorale Prelude in G Minor 36–37

Bach, J. S. (Gillette): Chorale Prelude—"We All Believe in One God" 35–36; 44–45

Bach, J. S. (Quarles): Fantasia in G Major 36–37

Bach, J. S. (Holst): *Fugue à la Gigue* 35–36; 38–39; 40–41; 46–47; 50–51

Bach, J. S. (Lyon): Fugue in C Minor from the *Musical Offering* 37–38

Bach, J. S. (Cailliet): Fugue in G Minor 38–39

Bach, J. S. (Lyon): Fugue in G Minor ("Lesser") 36–37

Bach, J. S. (Quarles): Fugue in G Minor ("Lesser") 36–37; 38–39

Bach, J. S. (Falcone): Passacaglia and Fugue in C Minor 41–42; 47–48

Bach, J. S. (Abert): Prelude, Chorale, and Fugue in G Minor 40–41; 46–47

Bach, J. S. (D. Godfrey): Prelude, Chorale and Fugue in G Minor 38–39

Bach, J. S. (Wright): Toccata and Fugue in D Minor 44–45; 46–47; 49–50

Bagley, E. E.: *National Emblem* 49–50; 50–51

Barat, Edward (Mear): Andante and Scherzo 39–40; 44–45

Barber, Samuel: *Commando March* 46–47; 49–50

Barrow, Edward: *Suite of Variations* 49–50; 50–51

Beethoven, Ludwig van (F. Winterbottom): *Egmont* Overture 36–37; 42–43; 47–48; 51–52

Beethoven, Ludwig van (D. Godfrey): *Leonore* Overture No. 3 42–43

Beethoven, Ludwig van: Three Equali for Trombones 50–51

Beethoven, Ludwig van (Lake): Turkish March from *The Ruins of Athens* 51–52

Belsterling, Charles: *March of the Steelmen* 49–50; 50–51

Bendel, Franz (Watson): *Sunday Morning at Glion* 37–38

Bennett, Robert Russell: *Suite of Old American Dances* 50–51

Berlioz, Hector: *Grand Requiem Mass* (with Chorus and Orchestra) 37–38

Berlioz, Hector (Goldman): *Grand Symphony (Funeral and Triumphal)* for Band, Chorus and Orchestra 47–48

Kern, Jerome (Jones): Selections from *Show Boat* 49–50

Ketelbey, Albert: *The Clock and the Dresden Figures* 34–35

Ketelbey, Albert (Amers): *The Cockney Suite* 34–35

Key, Francis Scott: *The Star Spangled Banner* 46–47; 50–51; 51–52; 52–53

King, Karl: *The Goldman Band March* 42–43

King, Karl: *Pride of the Illini* 51–52

Kohs, Ellis B.: *Life with Uncle Sam* 45–46

L

Lasso, Orlando di: Motet *Tui sunt coeli* for Eight-Voice Double Brass Choir 50–51

Liszt, Franz (Falcone): *Hungarian Fantasie* 42–43

Lithgow, Charles: *Invercargil* 49–50

Lyon, Ernst: Chorale for Two Brass Choirs 37–38

M

MacDowell, Edward (Winterbottom): *Woodland Sketches* 50–51

Mason, Daniel G. (Simmons): *Divertimento* 36–37

Mason, Daniel G. (Simmons): March from *Divertimento* 41–42

McBride, Robert: *Lonely Landscape* 52–53

McKay, George F.: *Bravura Prelude* 42–43; 45–46

McKay, George F.: "Burlesque March" from the *Caricature Dance Suite* 36–37; 41–42

McKay, George F.: Sonata for Clarinet and Band 37–38

McKay, George F.: *Symphonic Prelude in an American Idiom for Brass Alone* 36–37

Meacham, F. W.: *American Patrol* 50–51

Mendelssohn, Felix (Meyer): Nocturne from *A Midsummer Night's Dream* 52–53

Mendelssohn, Felix (Meyer): Overture to *A Midsummer Night's Dream* 42–43

Mendelssohn, Felix (Laurendeau): Wedding March from *A Midsummer Night's Dream* 42–43; 51–52

Mennin, Peter: *Canzona* 51–52

Meyer-Helmund, Erik *Serenade Rococo* 34–35

Miaskovsky, Nicholas: Symphony No. 19 in E-Flat Major for Band 51–52

Milhaud, Darius: March from *Suite Française* 51–52

Milhaud, Darius: *Suite Française* 48–49

Milhaud, Darius: Two Marches (*In Memoriam* and *Gloria Victoribus*) 52–53

Morgenstern, Elliot: Quartet for Horns 37–38

Morris, S. E.: *The Kilties March* 51–52

Moussorgsky, Modeste (Leidzen): Coronation Scene from *Boris Godounov* 43–44

Moussorgsky, Modeste (Leidzen/Fennell): *Pictures at an Exhibition* 41–42; 45–46; 48–49; 52–53

Mozart, W. A. (Duthoit): Overture to *The Marriage of Figaro* 38–39; 50–51

Mozart, W. A. (Garland): Minuet in E-Flat from Symphony No. 39 39–40; 42–43

Mozart, W. A.: Serenade No. 10 in B-Flat Major, K. 361 (new K. 370a) 50–51

P

Paganini, Nicolo (Falcone): *Perpetual Motion* 41–42

Palestrina (Harvey): *Adoramus te* 43–44

Palestrina (Harvey): *Sanctus* 43–44

Persichetti, Vincent: *Divertimento* for Band 50–51; 51–52

Peterson, Theodore: *Our Commander* 49–50

Pezel, Johann: Suite No. 2 for Brass Instruments 50–51

Pierne, Gabriel (Cydalise): *Entrance of the Little Fauns* 52–53

Pierne, Gabriel (Beeler): *March of the Little Lead Soldiers* 49–50; 50–51

Piston, Walter: *Tunbridge Fair* 51–52

Prokofieff, Sergei (Duthoit): March and Scherzo from *The Love of Three Oranges* 37–38; 40–41; 47–48

Prokofieff, Sergei (Goldman): Triumphal March from *Peter and the Wolf* 49–50

Pryor, Arthur: Fantasie on the Air "Blue Bells of Scotland" 49–50

Purcell, Henry (Garland): Trumpet Voluntary 39–40; 40–41

R

Rachmaninoff, Sergei (Leidzen): *Italian Polka* 41–42; 44–45

Read, Gardner: "Prayers of Steel" from *Sketches of the City* 36–37; 37–38; 46–47

Read, Alfred: *Russian Christmas Music* 51–52

Respighi, Ottorino: *Huntingtower Ballad* 48–49

Respighi, Ottorino (Leidzen): "Pines of the Appian Way" from *The Pines of Rome* 50–51

Riegger, Wallingford: *Music for Brass Choir* 50–51

Riegger, Wallingford: Passacaglia and Fugue 46–47

Riegger, Wallingford: Processional 51–52

APPENDIX A2A

Complete Repertoire of the Eastman Wind Ensemble 1952–1992

[Titles and composers appear as they did in the original programs. Corrections have been made only in the cases of missing or misleading information.]

PROGRAMS

PREMIÉRE SEASON: 1952–53

January 5, 1953
NYSSMA Concerts—Rural Radio Network
Handel, G. F. (Goldman)
  March and Chorus from *Judas Maccabaeus*
Bach, J. S. (Lake)
  Chorale—"Jesu, Who in Sorrow Dying"
Grundman, Clare *American Folk Rhapsody*
Weinberger, Jaromir (Bainum)
  Polka and Fugue from *Schwanda, the Bagpiper*

January 12, 1953
NYSSMA Concerts—Rural Radio Network
Bach, J. S. (Leidzen) Chorale—"Come Sweet Death"
Hanson, E. (Brown) *Little Norwegian Suite*
Humperdinck, E. (Maddy)
  Prayer from *Hansel and Gretel*
Gould, Morton *Ballad* for Band

January 26, 1953
NYSSMA Concerts—Rural Radio Network
Grundman, Clare *Two Moods Overture*
Fiorillo, Dante *South American Holiday*
Yoder, Paul *Sleepytime*
Weber, Carl Maria (Godfrey) *Euryanthe* Overture

February 2, 1953
NYSSMA Concerts—Rural Radio Network
Bach, J. S. (Moehlmann)
  Chorale—"If Thou Be Near"

Gluck, Christoph Willibald von (DeLamarter)
  Dance of the Blessed Spirits from *Orpheus*
Grieg, Edvard (Holmes)
  Ase's Death from *Peer Gynt Suite* No. 1
Holst, Gustav Suite No. 1 in E-flat

February 8, 1953, Kilbourn Hall
Première Concert
Mozart, W. A. Serenade No. 10 in B-Flat Major,
      K. 361

INTERMISSION

Riegger, Wallingford Nonet for Brass
Hindemith, Paul Symphony in B-Flat
 FREDERICK FENNELL, CONDUCTOR

February 9, 1953
NYSSMA Concerts—Rural Radio Network
Palestrina, Giovanni (Harvey) *Adoramus te* and *Sanctus*
McKay, George Frederick *Three Street Corner Sketches*
Reed, H. Owen *Spiritual*
Chabrier, Emmanuel (Safranek) *España*

February 16, 1953
NYSSMA Concerts—Rural Radio Network
Bach, J. S. (Cailliet) Prelude and Fugue in G Minor
McBride, Robert *Lonely Landscape*
Cowell, Henry *Shoontree*
Hanson, Howard (Maddy)
  Andante from Symphony No. 1 ("Nordic")
Milhaud, Darius "Provençe" from *Suite Française*

February 23, 1953
NBC Coast-to-Coast Broadcast

Vaughan Williams, Ralph	*Toccata Marziale*
Gould, Morton	*Ballad* for Band
Persichetti, Vincent	*Divertimento* for Band
Schuman, William	*George Washington Bridge*
Sousa, John Philip	*Corcoran Cadets*

March 23, 1953
NBC Coast-to-Coast Broadcast

Hadley, Henry	*Youth Triumphant Overture*
Thomson, Virgil	*A Solemn Music*
Bennett, Robert Russell	*Suite of Old American Dances*
Harris, Roy	Finale from Symphony for Band

May 7, 1953, Eastman Theatre
23rd Annual Festival of American Music

Schuman, William	*George Washington Bridge*
Gould, Morton	*Ballad* for Band
Gould, Morton	Symphony for Band (*West Point*)

INTERMISSION

Piston, Walter	*Tunbridge Fair*
Persichetti, Vincent	*Divertimento* for Band
Bennett, Robert Russell	*Suite of Old American Dances*
Barber, Samuel	*Commando March*

FREDERICK FENNELL, CONDUCTOR

2nd SEASON: 1953–54

November 1, 1953, Kilbourn Hall
(Chorales preceding concert by the Trombone Choir)
Lasso, Orlando di (Hanson)
  Motet: *Tui sunt coeli* for Eight-Voice Double Brass
Choir

Pezel, Johann	Suite No. 2 for Brass Instruments
Locke, Matthew	*Music for King Charles II*
Gabrieli, Giovanni (King)	*Sonata pian e forte*
Gabrieli, Giovanni (Fennell)	*Canzon noni toni a 12*

INTERMISSION

Strauss, Richard
  Symphony for Wind Instruments, op. posth.
  (first performance in America)
FREDERICK FENNELL, CONDUCTOR

November 19, 1953, Kilbourn Hall
Fifth Annual Festival of Marches

Goldman, Edwin Franko	*Cheerio*
Bigelow, F. E.	*Our Director*
Fillmore, Henry	*His Honor*
Hanson, Howard	*March Carillon*
Alford, Harry L.	*Glory of the Gridiron*
Jenkins, Joseph Wilcox (Neff)	*Pieces of Eight*
King, Karl	*Pride of Illini*
Bagley, Edwin E.	*National Emblem*

INTERMISSION

Sousa, John Philip	*Rifle Regiment*
	Corcoran Cadets
	Daughters of Texas
	Fairest of the Fair
	The Black Horse Troop
	Hands Across the Sea
	Manhattan Beach
	Semper Fidelis

FREDERICK FENNELL, CONDUCTOR

December 19, 1953, Kilbourn Hall
Symposium of Manuscript Works for Wind Band held in association with the Eastern Division Meeting of the College Band Directors National Association

Bassett, Leslie	*Symphonic Sketch*
Bottje, Will Gay	*Symphonic Allegro*
Breydert, Frederick M.	Suite in E-flat
Frankenpohl, Arthur	Variations
Fuerstner, Carl	Overture
Hart, Weldon	*Song and Celebration*
Headley, H. Klyne	Chorale and Passacaglia
Pyle, Francis Johnson	*Edged Night*
Rusch, Harold W.	*Menominee Sketches*
Resseger, Robert	*Metamorphosis on a March*
Shanley, Frank	*Concertino*

FREDERICK FENNELL, CONDUCTOR

January 4, 1954
NYSSMA Concerts—Rural Radio Network

Hadley, Henry	*Youth Triumphant Overture*
Bach, J. S. (Lake)	
Chorale—"Thou Prince of Life, O Christ, O Lord"	
Humperdinck, E. (Maddy)	
Prayer and Dream Pantomime from *Hansel and Gretel*	
Grundman, Clare	*Blue Tail Fly*

January 11, 1954

NYSSMA Concerts—Rural Radio Network

Bach, J. S. (Richardson)
　　　　Chorale—"Sheep May Safely Graze"
Rimsky-Korsakoff, Nicolai (Leidzen)
　　　　Procession of the Nobles from *Mlada*
Whitney, Maurice　　　　*Thendara Overture*
Strauss, Richard (Harding)
　　　　Excerpt from *Death and Transfiguration*

January 25, 1954

NYSSMA Concerts—Rural Radio Network

Beethoven, L. van (Winterbottom)
　　　　　　　　Overture to *Egmont*
Bizet, Georges　　　　　　*Agnus Dei*
Wagner, Richard (Leidzen)　　*Trauersinfonie*
Barber, Samuel　　　　*Commando March*

February 1, 1954

NYSSMA Concerts—Rural Radio Network

Bach, J. S. (Abert/Weiss)
　　　　Chorale and Fugue in G Minor
Grainger, Percy　*Irish Tune from County Derry*
Rota, Nino (Dawson)　*Legend of the Glass Mountain*
LaGassey, Homer　　　　　*Sequoia*

February 8, 1954

NYSSMA Concerts—Rural Radio Network

Still, William Grant　　　*From the Delta*
Handel, G. F. (Beecham)
　　　　Suite from *The Gods Go A-Begging*
Vaughan Williams, Ralph　*English Folk Song Suite*

February 15, 1954

NYSSMA Concerts—Rural Radio Network

Bach, J. S. (arr. unknown)　　Fugue in F Major
Hanson, Howard (Leidzen)　　*March Carillon*
Wagner, Richard (Godfrey)
　　Entry of the Gods into Valhalla from *Das Rheingold*
Alford, Harry L.　　*Glory of the Gridiron*
Jenkins, Joseph Wilcox (Neff)　　*Pieces of Eight*

May 10, 1954, Kilbourn Hall

24th Annual Festival of American Music

Mennin, Peter　　　　　　*Canzona*
Bottje, Will Gay　　　　　*Contrasts*
Reed, H. Owen　　　*La Fiesta Mexicana*

INTERMISSION

Word, William R.　*Variations on a Western Tune*
Persichetti, Vincent　　*Psalm for Band*
Thomson, Virgil　　　*A Solemn Music*
Hanson, Howard　*Chorale and Alleluia*

FREDERICK FENNELL, CONDUCTOR

3rd SEASON: 1954–55

December 13, 1954, Kilbourn Hall

Vaughan Williams, Ralph　　*Toccata Marziale*
Holst, Gustav　　　First Suite in E-Flat
Persichetti, Vincent　*Divertimento for Band*
Reed, H. Owen　　　*La Fiesta Mexicana*

INTERMISSION

Bennett, Robert Russell　*Suite of Old American Dances*
Gould, Morton　　　　*Ballad* for Band
Hanson, Howard　　*Chorale and Alleluia*
Goldman, Edwin Franko　　*Cheerio March*
Sousa, John Philip　　*Corcoran Cadets*
Jenkins, Joseph Wilcox (Neff)　*Pieces of Eight*

FREDERICK FENNELL, CONDUCTOR

December 15, 1954, Ashtabula High School,
Ashtabula, Ohio

Vaughan Williams, Ralph　　*Toccata Marziale*
Holst, Gustav　　　First Suite in E-Flat
Persichetti, Vincent　*Divertimento for Band*
Reed, H. Owen　　　*La Fiesta Mexicana*
Bennett, Robert Russell　*Suite of Old American Dances*
Gould, Morton　　　　*Ballad* for Band
Hanson, Howard　　*Chorale and Alleluia*
Goldman, Edwin Franko　　*Cheerio March*
Sousa, John Philip　　*Corcoran Cadets*
Jenkins, Joseph Wilcox (Neff)　*Pieces of Eight*

FREDERICK FENNELL, CONDUCTOR

December 17, 1954
Orchestra Hall, Chicago, Illinois

A concert for the Biennial Conference of the College Band
Directors National Association

Vaughan Williams, Ralph	*Toccata Marziale*
Holst, Gustav	First Suite in E-Flat
Persichetti, Vincent	*Divertimento for Band*
Reed, H. Owen	*La Fiesta Mexicana*
Bennett, Robert Russell	*Suite of Old American Dances*
Gould, Morton	*Ballad for Band*
Hanson, Howard	*Chorale and Alleluia*
Goldman, Edwin Franko	*Cheerio*
Sousa, John Philip	*Corcoran Cadets*
Jenkins, Joseph Wilcox (Neff)	*Pieces of Eight*

FREDERICK FENNELL, CONDUCTOR

May 7, 1955, Rehearsal Room, 50 Swan Street

Vaughan Williams, Ralph	*Toccata Marziale*
Holst, Gustav	First Suite in E-Flat
Vaughan Williams, Ralph	*English Folk Song Suite*
Holst, Gustav	Second Suite in F

INTERMISSION

Grainger, Percy	*Hill Song* No. 2
Anderson, Leroy	Two excerpts from the *Irish Suite*:
"The Girl I Left Behind Me"	
"The Rakes of Mallow"	
Perkins, Frank	*Fandango*
Key, Francis Scott	*The Star Spangled Banner*

FREDERICK FENNELL, CONDUCTOR

4th SEASON: 1955–56

October 30, 1955, Eastman Theatre

Mozart, W. A.	Serenade No. 12 in C Minor, K. 388
Grainger, Percy	*Hill Song* No. 2
Frankenpohl, Arthur	*Overture Giocoso*
Hindemith, Paul	Symphony in B-Flat

FREDERICK FENNELL, CONDUCTOR

December 12, 1955, Eastman Theatre

Mozart, W. A.
        Serenade No. 11 in E-Flat Major, K. 375
Shahan, Paul Willard
        Leipzig Towers for Brass and Percussion

McCarthy, Patrick	*Ballade* for Band
Stravinsky, Igor	*Symphonies of Wind Instruments*
Creston, Paul	*Celebration Overture*

FREDERICK FENNELL, CONDUCTOR

January 18, 1956, Eastman Theatre
Sixth Annual Festival of Marches

Goldman, Edwin Franko	*On the Mall*
Meacham. F. W.	*American Patrol*
Klohr, John	*The Billboard*
McCoy, Earl E.	*Lights Out*
Alford, Kenneth J.	*Colonel Bogey*
King, Karl	*Barnum and Bailey's Favorite*

INTERMISSION

Sousa, John Philip	*The U.S. Field Artillery*
	King Cotton
	The Thunderer
	El Capitan
	Stars and Stripes Forever

FREDERICK FENNELL, CONDUCTOR

March 25, 1956, Kilbourn Hall

Mozart, W. A.   Serenade in B-flat No. 10, K.361

INTERMISSION

Stravinsky, Igor   Octet for Wind Instruments

INTERMISSION

Stravinsky, Igor
    Concerto for Piano and Wind Instruments
      RICHARD WOITACH, PIANO
Rogers, Bernard   *Three Japanese Dances*
    CHARLENE CHADWICK, MEZZO-SOPRANO
    FREDERICK FENNELL, CONDUCTOR

May 4, 1956, Kilbourn Hall

"Ruffles and Flourishes"—A program of music for fifes and drums and for bugles, cymbals, and drum, based upon the Field Music of the United States Army from the Revolutionary War to the present day.

Fifes and Drums:
The camp duty of the U.S. Army
    The Three Camps, The Slow Scotch, The Austrian,

May 4, 1956 (cont.)

Dawning of the Day, The Hessian, Dusky Night, The Prussian, The Dutch, The Quick Scotch, The Three Camps

Traditional rudimental music for fifes and drums

The Breakfast Call, The Dinner Call, Wrecker's Daughter, Hell on the Wabash, Downfall of Paris

Traditional marching tunes for fifes and drums

Yankee Doodle, Sergeant O'Leary, The Belle of the Mohawk Vale, Gary Owen, Dixie, Sentry Box, Rally 'round the Flag, Bonnie Blue Flag, White Cockade

Bugles, Drums, and Cymbals—excerpts from the official U.S. Army manual:

Bugle calls of the Army—Played in unison

Ruffles and Flourishes, Assemble, Adjutant's Call, Church Call, Drill Call, General Call, Mail Call, Mess Call, Retreat, Call to Quarters, Reveille, Tattoo, Taps

Music for rendering honors

Ruffles and Flourishes, General's March, To the Colors, Funeral March

Traditional marches and inspection pieces

Rip Van Winkle, Holy Joe, Soapsuds Row, The Colonel's Daughter, The Prisoner, The Garrison Belle, General Burt, General Dooley, The Old Guard, The American Flag, The Cavaliers, Old Six-eight, I've Got Three Years To Do This In, Hens and Chickens, So Slum Today, You're in the Army Now, Spanish Guard Mount, The Red Hussars, A-Hunting We Will Go, Pay Day, Double Time, The President's March

May 7, 1956, Eastman Theatre

26th Annual Festival of American Music

Frankenpohl, Arthur	*Overture Giocoso*
Williams, Clifton	*Fanfare and Allegro*
McCarthy, Patrick	*Ballata*
Bottje, Will Gay	Symphony No. 4

INTERMISSION

Lo Presti, Ronald	*Pageant*
Shanan, Paul	*Spring Festival in Five Scenes*
Kraehenbuehl, David	*Ritual*
Rogers, Bernard	*Three Japanese Dances*

CHARLENE CHADWICK, MEZZO-SOPRANO

FREDERICK FENNELL, CONDUCTOR

5th SEASON: 1956–57

November 16, 1956, Eastman Theatre

Grainger, Percy	*Lincolnshire Posy*
Fauchet, Paul (Campbell-Watson)	
	Nocturne from Symphony in B-flat
Beversdorf, Thomas	
	Symphony for Band and Percussion

INTERMISSION

Strauss, Richard	Serenade in E-Flat Major, op. 7
Gauldin, Robert	
	Variations on a Theme by Bartók for Wind Ensemble
Persichetti, Vincent	*Psalm for Band*

FREDERICK FENNELL, CONDUCTOR

December 12, 1956, Eastman Theatre

Casella, Alfredo	*Introduction, Chorale, and March*
Schmitt, Florent	
Lied and Scherzo for Double Wind Quintet and Solo Horn, op. 54	

BARRY BENJAMIN, HORN

Holst, Gustav	*Hammersmith*, op. 52
Scianni, Joseph	*Court Square: An Impression*
Milhaud, Darius	*Suite Française*

FREDERICK FENNELL, CONDUCTOR

March 21, 1957, Eastman Theatre

Schoenberg, Arnold	Theme and Variations, op. 43a
Stravinsky, Igor	*Symphonies of Wind Instruments*
Hindemith, Paul	Symphony in B-Flat

FREDERICK FENNELL, CONDUCTOR

6th SEASON: 1957–58

October 16, 1957, Eastman Theatre

Seventh Festival of Marches

Honoring Edwin Franko Goldman, 1878–1956

Goldman, Edwin Franko	*Illinois March*
	Boy Scouts of America
	Onward-Upward
	Children's March
	Interlochen Bowl
	Bugles and Drums

INTERMISSION

Seitz, Roland F.	*Grandioso*
Rodgers, Richard	*Guadalcanal March*
Reeves, Daniel W.	
	Second Regiment Connecticut National Guard
Alford, Kenneth J.	*Mad Major*
Hall, Ronald B.	*Officer of the Day*
Fillmore, Henry	*Americans We*

FREDERICK FENNELL, CONDUCTOR

December 4, 1957, Eastman Theatre

Jacob, Gordon	*William Byrd Suite*
Strauss, Richard	Serenade in E-Flat Major, op. 7
Grainger, Percy	*Lincolnshire Posy*

INTERMISSION

Beversdorf, Thomas	*Serenade*
Milhaud, Darius	*Suite Française*
Bennett, Robert Russell	*Symphonic Songs*

FREDERICK FENNELL, CONDUCTOR

February 27, 1958, Orchestra Annex

Mozart, W. A.

Serenade No. 10 in B-Flat Major, K.361

FREDERICK FENNELL, CONDUCTOR

February 28, 1958, Orchestra Annex

Grainger, Percy	*Lincolnshire Posy*
Milhaud, Darius	*Suite Française*
Strauss, Richard	Serenade in E-Flat Major, op. 7
Rogers, Bernard	*Three Japanese Dances*

CAROL DAWN MOYER, SOPRANO

FREDERICK FENNELL, CONDUCTOR

May 3, 1958, Eastman Theatre

28th Annual Festival of American Music

Williams, Clifton	*Symphonic Suite*
Bottje, Will Gay	*Theme and Variations*
Mailman, Martin	*Partita*
End, Jack	*Portrait by a Wind Ensemble*

INTERMISSION

Gauldin, Robert	*Three Symphonic Sketches*

Hartley, Walter

Concerto for Twenty-three Wind Instruments

Rogers, Bernard	*Three Japanese Dances*

CAROL DAWN MOYER, SOPRANO

FREDERICK FENNELL, CONDUCTOR

7th SEASON: 1958–59

October 16, 1958, Eastman Theatre

Jacob, Gordon	*William Byrd Suite*
Bennett, Robert Russell	*Symphonic Songs*

INTERMISSION

Holst, Gustav	*Hammersmith*
Walton, William (Duthoit)	*Crown Imperial*

November 14, 1958, Eastman Theatre

8th Annual Festival of Marches—Program of International Marches

Sousa, John Philip	*Hands Across the Sea*
Ganne, Gustave Luis (Roberts)	*Father of Victory*
San Miguel, Mariano	*The Golden Ear*
Teike, Carl	*Old Comrades*
Hanssen, Johannes (Bainum)	*Valdres*
Prokofieff, Serge	March, op. 99
Delle Cese, Davide	*Inglesina*
Coates, Eric	*Knightsbridge March*

November 19, 1958, Orchestra Annex

Jacob, Gordon	*William Byrd Suite*

INTERMISSION

Holst, Gustav	*Hammersmith*
Walton, William (Duthoit)	*March Crown Imperial*

FREDERICK FENNELL, CONDUCTOR

November 20, 1958, Orchestra Annex

Eighth Annual Festival of Marches
Program of International Marches

Sousa, John Philip	*Hands Across the Sea*
Ganne, Gustave Luis	*Father of Victory*
San Miguel, Mariano	*The Golden Ear*
Teike, Carl	*Old Comrades*
Hanssen, Johannes (Bainum)	*Valdres*

November 20, 1958 (cont.)

Prokofieff, Serge	March, op. 99
Delle Cese, Davide	*Inglesina*
Coates, Eric	*Knightsbridge March*

FREDERICK FENNELL, CONDUCTOR

January 21, 1959, Eastman Theatre

Tomasi, Henry	*Fanfares Liturgiques*
Anderson, Leroy	*Suite of Carols*
Persichetti, Vincent	Symphony No. 6

INTERMISSION

Kurka, Robert	Suite from *The Good Soldier Schweik*
Vaughan Williams, Ralph	*English Folk Song Suite*

FREDERICK FENNELL, CONDUCTOR

March 13, 1959, Eastman Theatre

Gabrieli, Andrea (Ghedini)	*Aria della battaglia*
Strauss, Richard	Suite in B-Flat, op. 4
Work, Julian	*Autumn Walk*
Grainger, Percy	*Hill Song* No. 2
Gould, Morton	*Ballad for Band*
Williams, Clifton	Fanfare and Allegro

FREDERICK FENNELL, CONDUCTOR

April 29, 1959, Eastman Theatre

Grainger, Percy	*Hill Song* No. 2
Hartley, Walter	Concerto for Twenty-three Winds
Work, Julian	*Autumn Walk*
Khachaturian, Aram	*Armenian Dances*

April 30, 1959, Eastman Theatre

29th Annual Festival of American Music

Williams, Clifton	Fanfare and Allegro
Hartley, Walter	Concerto for Twenty-three Winds
Gould, Morton	*West Point Symphony*

INTERMISSION

Hodkinson, Sydney	*Litigo*
Persichetti, Vincent	Symphony No. 6
Bennett, Robert Russell	*Symphonic Songs*

FREDERICK FENNELL, CONDUCTOR

8th SEASON: 1959–60

November 22, 1959, Strong Auditorium, River Campus

Schuman, William	*Chester*
Gauldin, Robert	Variations on a Theme by Bartók
Holst, Gustav	First Suite in E-Flat

INTERMISSION

Berger, Theodor	*Rondo Ostinato*
Schmitt, Florent	*Dionysiaques*
Jenkins, Joseph Wilcox	*An American Overture*
Delle Cese, Davide	*Inglesina March*

FREDERICK FENNELL, CONDUCTOR

January 15, 1960, Eastman Theatre

Creston, Paul	*Celebration Overture*
Vaughan Williams, Ralph	*Scherzo alla Marcia*
Strauss, Richard	Suite in B-Flat, op. 4
Latham, William	*Three Choral Preludes*

INTERMISSION

Schoenberg, Arnold	Variations, op. 43a
Stevens, Bernard	Adagio and Fugue, op. 31
Miaskovsky, Nicholas	
Symphony No. 19 for Wind Orchestra, op. 46	
Sousa, John Philip	*Black Horse Troop*
Heed, J. C.	*In Storm and Sunshine*
Strauss, Johann, Sr.	*Radetzky March*, op. 228

FREDERICK FENNELL, CONDUCTOR

March 11, 1960, Eastman Theatre

Hindemith, Paul	Symphony in B-Flat
Mozart, W. A.	Serenade No. 10 in B-Flat, K. 361
Grainger, Percy	*Lincolnshire Posy*

INTERMISSION

Holst, Gustav	First Suite in E-Flat
Stravinsky, Igor	*Symphonies of Wind Instruments*
Hanson, Howard	*Chorale and Alleluia*
Prokofieff, Serge	March, op. 99
Delle Cese, Davide	*Inglesina*
Bagley, Edwin E.	*National Emblem*

FREDERICK FENNELL, CONDUCTOR

March 20, 1960, Atlantic City, New Jersey

Music Educators National Conference,
Seventeenth Biennial Convention

Grainger, Percy	*Lincolnshire Posy*
Mozart, W. A.	Serenade No. 10 in B-Flat, K. 361
Holst, Gustav	First Suite in E-Flat
Stravinsky, Igor	*Symphonies of Wind Instruments*
Hanson, Howard	*Chorale and Alleluia*
Prokofieff, Serge	March, op. 99
Delle Cese, Davide	*Inglesina*
Bagley, Edwin E.	*National Emblem*

FREDERICK FENNELL, CONDUCTOR

April 28, 1960, Eastman Theatre

30th Annual Festival of American Music
A Program of Marches by John Philip Sousa

Sousa, John Philip	*High School Cadets*
	The Picadore
	The Belle of Chicago
	Bullets and Bayonets
	Nobles of the Mystic Shrine
	The Gallant Seventh
	The Invincible Eagle
	Sound Off
	Riders for the Flag
	Sabre and Spurs
	Solid Men to the Front
	The Liberty Bell

FREDERICK FENNELL, CONDUCTOR

9th SEASON: 1960–61

October 28, 1960, Eastman Theatre

Schuman, William	*George Washington Bridge*
Persichetti, Vincent	*Divertimento for Band*
Riegger, Wallingford	
Introduction and Fugue for Cello and Symphonic Winds	

RONALD LEONARD, CELLO

Milhaud, Darius	*Suite Française*

INTERMISSION

Mellers, Wilfred	*Samson Agonistes*
Gould, Morton	*Ballad for Band*
Seitz, Roland	*University of Pennsylvania Band March*

Fillmore, Henry	*Men of Ohio*
Chambers, W. Paris	*The Chicago Tribune*

FREDERICK FENNELL, CONDUCTOR

October 30, 1960, Cutler Union

Concerts at Cutler Series—First Concert

Mozart, W. A.	Serenade No. 12 in C Minor, K.388
Strauss, Richard	Serenade, op. 7
Riegger, Wallingford	
Introduction and Fugue for Cello and Symphonic Winds	

RONALD LEONARD, CELLO

INTERMISSION

Reynolds, Verne	Serenade for Thirteen Winds
Blackwood, Easley	
Chamber Symphony for Fourteen Winds, op. 2	

FREDERICK FENNELL, CONDUCTOR

The Civil War Albums were recorded 13 and 15 December 1960. A four-hour concert was presented in the Eastman Theater prior to the recording sessions:

Hail to the Chief
Cape May Polka
Tenting Tonight
Easter Galop
Tramp, Tramp, Tramp
Come where my Love Lies Dreaming
When Johnny Comes Marching Home
Listen to the Mocking Bird
Old Hundredth
Dixie and Bonnie Blue Flag
Come Dearest the Daylight is Gone
Marching Thru Georgia
Lulu's Quickstep
Palmyra Schottische
Goober Peas
Carry Me Back
Old Kentucky, Kentucky
Garry Owen
St. Patrick's Day in the Morning
Port Royal Galop
We Are Coming Father Abra'am
Hail Columbia
Freischutz Quickstep
Cheer Boys Cheer

December 13 and 15, 1960 (cont.)

Nightingale Waltz

The Star Spangled Banner

Field Music of Union and Confederate Troops:

Cavalry Bugle Signals

Camp and Field Calls for Fifes and Drums

Cavalry Quickstep

Lulu's Gone

Tramp, Tramp, Tramp

Waltz

Storm Galop

Maryland, My Maryland

The Battle Hymn of The Republic

January 8, 1961, Cutler Union

Concerts at Cutler Series—Second Concert

Mozart, W. A.   Serenade No. 11 in E-Flat, K.375

Barlow, Wayne   *Intrada, Fugue, and Postlude for Brass*

Strauss, Richard   Suite in B-Flat, op. 4

FREDERICK FENNELL, CONDUCTOR

January 20, 1961, Eastman Theatre

Copland, Aaron   *Fanfare for the Common Man*

Crane, Robert   *Five Baroque Choral Preludes*

Persichetti, Vincent   *Psalm for Band*

Vaughan Williams, Ralph   *English Folk Song Suite*

INTERMISSION

Humel, Gerald   *Five Quotations from a Czech Fairy Tale*

Bennett, Robert Russell   *Suite of Old American Dances*

Alford, Harry L.   *Law and Order*

Sousa, John Philip   *The Legionnaires*

King, Karl   *Barnum and Bailey's Favorite*

FREDERICK FENNELL, CONDUCTOR

February 19, 1961, Cutler Union

Concerts at Cutler Series—Third Concert

Russell, Armand   *Suite Concertante* for Tuba

ROGER BOBO, TUBA

Dvorak, Antonin   Serenade in D Minor, op. 44

FREDERICK FENNELL, CONDUCTOR

March 3, 1961, Eastman Theatre

Schuman, William   *When Jesus Wept*

Krenek, Ernst

Symphony for Wind Instruments and Percussion

Mennin, Peter   *Canzona*

INTERMISSION

Toch, Ernst   *Spiel für Blasorchester*

Holst, Gustav   Second Suite in F

Stravinsky, Igor   *Circus Polka*

Sousa, John Philip   *Rifle Regiment*

Black Horse Troop

Manhattan Beach

FREDERICK FENNELL, CONDUCTOR

March 5, 1961, Cutler Union

Concerts at Cutler Series—Fourth Concert

Varèse, Edgard   *Intégrales*

Rogers, Bernard   *The Musicians of Bremen*

CALVIN CULLEN, NARRATOR

Ibert, Jacques

Concerto for Violoncello and Wind Instruments

RONALD LEONARD, VIOLONCELLO

FREDERICK FENNELL, CONDUCTOR

April 16, 1961, Vassar College Chapel

Vassar College Centennial Concert

Vassar College Choir, Harvard Glee Club

Gabrieli, Giovanni   Two Motets

Bruckner, Anton   Mass in E Minor

DONALD PEARSON, CONDUCTOR

April 21, 1961, Eastman Theatre

13th Annual Festival of Marches

Sousa, John Philip

Ancient and Honorable Artillery Company

Sesqui-Centennial Exposition March

Golden Jubilee March

The National Game

The Kansas Wildcats

The Rifle Regiment

The Pride of the Wolverines

The Black Horse Troop

The Glory of the Yankee Navy

The Gridiron Club

New Mexico March

Manhattan Beach

FREDERICK FENNELL, CONDUCTOR

April 28, 1961, Eastman Theatre

Sousa, John Philip	*High School Cadets*
	The Picador
	The Belle of Chicago
	Bullets and Bayonets
	Nobles of the Mystic Shrine
	The Gallant Seventh

INTERMISSION

	The Invincible Eagle
	Sound Off
	Riders for the Flag
	Sabre and Spurs
	Solid Men to the Front
	Liberty Bell

May 1, 1961, Eastman Theatre

31st Annual Festival of American Music

Hartley, Walter	Rondo for Winds and Percussion
Erickson, Frank	*Time and the Winds*
DeLone, Peter	Symphony No. 1
Bottje, Will Gay	
Concerto for Trumpet, Trombone, and Winds	
BOYDE HOOD, TRUMPET	
ROBERT GILLESPIE, TROMBONE	
Wilder, Alec	*An Entertainment*

FREDERICK FENNELL, CONDUCTOR

May 10, 1961, Eastman Theatre

Jacob, Gordon	*William Byrd Suite*
Strauss, Richard	Serenade in E-Flat, op. 7
Bennett, Robert Russell	*Suite of Old American Dances*

INTERMISSION

Hanson, Howard	*Chorale and Alleluia*
Sousa, John Philip	*The Black Horse Troop*
Goldman, Edwin Franko	*March Illinois*
Heed, J. C.	*In Storm and Sunshine*

FREDERICK FENNELL, CONDUCTOR

10th SEASON: 1961–62

November 10, 1961, Eastman Theatre

Vaughan Williams, Ralph	*Toccata Marziale*
Jacob, Gordon	*William Byrd Suite*

Grainger, Percy	*Lincolnshire Posy*
Sullivan, Arthur (Mackerras/Duthoit)	*Pineapple Poll*

INTERMISSION

Stravinsky, Igor	*Symphonies of Wind Instruments*
Schoenberg, Arnold	Theme and Variations, op. 43a
Persichetti, Vincent	Symphony No. 6
Bagley, Edwin E.	*The National Emblem*
Hanssen, Johannes (Bainum)	*Valdres*
Sousa, John Philip	*The Black Horse Troop*

FREDERICK FENNELL, CONDUCTOR

November 16, 1961, State University of New York at Albany, Page Hall

Jacob, Gordon	*William Byrd Suite*
Persichetti, Vincent	Symphony No. 6
Grainger, Percy	*Lincolnshire Posy*

INTERMISSION

Vaughan Williams, Ralph	*Toccata Marziale*
Schoenberg, Arnold	Theme and Variations, op. 43a
Sullivan, Arthur (Mackerras/Duthoit)	*Pineapple Poll*
Bagley, Edwin E.	*The National Emblem*
Hanssen, Johannes (Bainum)	*Valdres*
Sousa, John Philip	*The Black Horse Troop*

FREDERICK FENNELL, CONDUCTOR

November 17, 1961, Carnegie Hall, New York City

Vaughan Williams, Ralph	*Toccata Marziale*
Jacob, Gordon	*William Byrd Suite*
Grainger, Percy	*Lincolnshire Posy*
Sullivan, Arthur (Mackerras/Duthoit)	*Pineapple Poll*

INTERMISSION

Stravinsky, Igor	*Symphonies of Wind Instruments*
Schoenberg, Arnold	Theme and Variations, op. 43a
Persichetti, Vincent	Symphony No. 6
Bagley, Edwin E.	*The National Emblem*
Hanssen, Johannes (Bainum)	*Valdres*
Sousa, John Philip	*The Black Horse Troop*

FREDERICK FENNELL, CONDUCTOR

December 3, 1961, Cutler Union
Concerts at Cutler Series—Fifth Concert
Buxtehude, Dietrich (D. Ross [Hunsberger])
Benedicam Dominum
Blomdahl, Karl-Birger
Kammerkonzert for Piano, Woodwinds, and
Percussion
JUDITH BORLING, PIANO
DONALD HUNSBERGER, CONDUCTOR

December 13, 1961, Cutler Union
Dukas, Paul	Fanfare from *La Peri*
Jenkins, Joseph Wilcox	*Cumberland Gap*
Holst, Gustav	First Suite in E-flat
Scianni, Joseph	*Court Square: An Impression*
Respighi, Ottorino	*Huntingtower Ballad*
Giannini, Vittorio	Praeludium and Allegro
Tieke, Carl	*Old Comrades*
Grafulla, Claudio	*Washington Greys*

DONALD HUNSBERGER, CONDUCTOR

February 16, 1962, Eastman Theatre
Milhaud, Darius	*Suite Française*
Angelini, Louis	*Evocation*
Hindemith, Paul	Symphony in B-flat

INTERMISSION

Rorem, Ned
Sinfonia for Fifteen Winds and Percussion
Persichetti, Vincent	*Serenade* for Band
Williams, Clifton	*Symphonic Suite*
Fucik, Julius	*The Florentiner March*

DONALD HUNSBERGER, CONDUCTOR

March 7, 1962, Eastman Theatre
Creston, Paul	*Celebration Overture*
Vaughan Williams, Ralph	*English Folk Song Suite*
Gould, Morton	*Ballad* for Band
Tuthill, Burnet	*Rowdy Dance*

INTERMISSION

Bernstein, Leonard (Beeler)	Overture to *Candide*
Jacob, Gordon	*An Original Suite*
Mennin, Peter	*Canzona*
Blankenburg, H. L.	*Action Front*
Alexander, Russell	*Rival Rovers*
Seltzer, M.	*Trombone Solidity*

DONALD HUNSBERGER, CONDUCTOR

May 4, 1962, Eastman Theatre
32nd Annual Festival of American Music
"The Jazz Idiom" with the Modern Jazz Quartet—
John Lewis, Director
Illustrated History of Jazz
MODERN JAZZ QUARTET
JOHN LEWIS, CONDUCTOR
Lewis, John	Excerpt from *The Comedy*
End, Jack	*Variations in the Style of Sauter*
	Blues for a Killed Cat
Wilder, Alec	Excerpts from *An Entertainment*

FREDERICK FENNELL, CONDUCTOR

11th SEASON: 1962–63

October 19, 1962, Eastman Theatre
Rimsky-Korsakov, Nicolai (Leidzen)
Procession of the Nobles from *Mlada*
Bach, J. S. (Leidzen)
Chorale—"Jesu, Joy of Man's Desiring"
Milhaud, Darius	*West Point Suite*

Berlioz, Hector (Boyd)
Royal Hunt and Storm Scene from *The Trojans*

INTERMISSION

Dukas, Paul (Cailliet)
Scherzo from *The Sorcerer's Apprentice*
Creston, Paul	*Prelude and Dance*

Weinberger, Jaromir (Bainum)
Polka and Fugue from *Schwanda, the Bagpiper*
A. CLYDE ROLLER, CONDUCTOR

November 30, 1962, Eastman Theatre
Bach, J. S. (Leidzen)	Toccata and Fugue in D Minor
Hartley, Walter	*Sinfonia* No. 4
	Rondo for Winds and Percussion
Rachmanninoff, Sergei (Leidzen)	*Italian Polka*
Tohno, Shigeo	*Dance of the Japanese Youth*

INTERMISSION

Bright, Houston	Prelude and Fugue in F Minor
Reed, H. Owen	*Spiritual* for Band
Verdi, Giuseppe (Mollenhauer)	*Manzoni Requiem*

A. CLYDE ROLLER, CONDUCTOR

February 8, 1963, Eastman Theatre

Bach, J. S. (Hunsberger)

             Passacaglia and Fugue in C Minor

Piston, Walter   *Tunbridge Fair*

Persichetti, Vincent   *Psalm* for Band

Reed, H. Owen   *La Fiesta Mexicana*

Menotti, Gian Carlo (P. Lang)

         Excerpts from the ballet *Sebastian*

Schreiner, Adolph (Osterling) *The Worried Drummers*

JUSTIN DI CIOCCIO AND JOHN WYRE, SOLOISTS

A. CLYDE ROLLER, CONDUCTOR

March 15, 1963, Eastman Theatre

Gabrieli, Andrea (Ghedini)   *Aria della battaglia*

Vaughan Williams, Ralph

 Scherzo alla marcia from Symphony No. 8 in D Minor

Gould, Morton

            West Point Symphony I. Epitaphs

INTERMISSION

McCarthy, Patrick   *Ballata*

Giannini, Vittorio   Symphony No. 3 for Band

DONALD HUNSBERGER, CONDUCTOR

April 7, 1963, Eastman Theatre

Lyndol Mitchell Memorial Concert

Mitchell, Lyndol   *River Suite*

                    Red River

              Red River Valley

               Golden Sands

A. CLYDE ROLLER, CONDUCTOR

April 29, 1963, Eastman Theatre

33rd Annual Festival of American Music

Washburn, Robert   *Partita* for Band

Hovhaness, Alan   Symphony No. 4, op. 165

Velke, Fritz   *Concertino for Band*

INTERMISSION

White, Donald   *Miniature Set for Band*

Presser, William   *The Devil's Footprints*

Rogers, Bernard

    Tribal Drums for Wind Band from the Symphony

                          Africa

A. CLYDE ROLLER, CONDUCTOR

May 2, 1963, Eastman Theatre

Hovhaness, Alan   Symphony No. 4, op. 165

Giannini, Vittorio   Symphony No. 3 for Band

A. CLYDE ROLLER, CONDUCTOR

12th SEASON: 1963–64

October 11, 1963, Eastman Theatre

Bach, J. S. (Leidzen) Chorale—"Komm, süsser Tod"

Hindemith, Paul   Symphony in B-flat

Latham, William   Passacaglia and Fugue for Band

INTERMISSION

Dukas, Paul   Fanfare from *La Peri*

Bennett, Robert Russell *Suite of Old American Dances*

Stravinsky, Igor

    Berceuse and Finale from *The Firebird*

A. CLYDE ROLLER, CONDUCTOR

November 8, 1963, Eastman Theatre

Bach, J. S. (Richardson)

         Chorale—"Sheep May Safely Graze"

Persichetti, Vincent   Symphony No. 6 for Band

Silliman, Cutler   Variations for Band

INTERMISSION

Debussy, Claude (Schaefer)

          "Fêtes" from *Three Nocturnes*

Turina, Josquin (Reed)   *La Procession du Rocio*

Jacob, Gordon   Overture to *Flag of Stars*

A. CLYDE ROLLER, CONDUCTOR

December 5, 1963, Eastman Theatre

Concert Presented for the NYSSMA Twenty-eighth Annual Directors' Conference

Mailman, Martin   *Geometrics* No. 1

Villa-Lobos, Heitor *Fantasy in the Form of a Chorus*

Giannini, Vittorio   Preludium and Allegro

DONALD HUNSBERGER, CONDUCTOR

February 14, 1964, Eastman Theatre

Shostakovich, Dmitri (Hunsberger)

Festive Overture, op. 96

Ward, Robert   *Night Fantasy*

Stevens, Noel Scott   *Cameos*

GERALD WELKER, ALTO SAX
JASON WEINTRAUB, ENGLISH HORN
RICHARD RAUM, TROMBONE
GLEN BELL, TRUMPET

INTERMISSION

De Lone, Peter

Introduction and Allegro from Symphony No. 1

Kennan, Kent   *Night Soliloquy*

NANCY HOWE, FLUTE

Holst, Gustav

Prelude and Scherzo from *Hammersmith*

DONALD HUNSBERGER, CONDUCTOR

March 6, 1964, Eastman Theatre

Mendelssohn, Felix (Boyd)

Overture for Band, op. 24

Ward, David   Symphony for Wind Ensemble

INTERMISSION

Pace, Pat   *Music for Winds*

Russell, Armand   Theme and Fantasia

Orff, Carl (Moerenhout)   *Carmina Burana*

A. CLYDE ROLLER, CONDUCTOR

**April 15, 1964, Kulp Auditorium,
Ithaca High School, Ithaca, New York**

*The Ithaca High School Band and the Bach, J. S. Honor
Society present a Contemporary Music Festival*

Bach, J. S. (Hunsberger)

Passacaglia and Fugue in C Minor

Bennett, Robert Russell

Concerto for Woodwind Quintet and Wind
Symphony

NANCY HOWE, FLUTE
DON JONES, OBOE
ROBERT UMIKER, CLARINET
PAUL MINERT, BASSOON
DAVID PINKOW, HORN

Benson, Warren   *The Leaves Are Falling*

Russell, Armand   *Theme and Fantasia*

Dello Joio, Norman   *Variants on a Medieval Tune*

A. CLYDE ROLLER, CONDUCTOR

April 30, 1964, Eastman Theatre

34th Annual Festival of American Music

Asenjo, Gunzalez   Concerto for Wind Instruments

Starer, Robert   Dirge for Band

Washburn, Robert   Symphony for Band

INTERMISSION

Benson, Warren   *The Leaves Are Falling*

Bennett, Robert Russell

Concerto for Woodwind Quintet and Wind
Symphony

THE INTERLOCHEN ARTS QUINTET:
RAMONA DAHLBORG, FLUTE;
DONALD JAEGER, OBOE;
FRANK ELL, CLARINET;
MELINDA DALLY, BASSOON;
DONALD HADDAD, HORN

Dello Joio, Norman   *Variants on a Medieval Tune*

A. CLYDE ROLLER, CONDUCTOR

13th SEASON: 1964–65

November 13, 1964, Eastman Theatre

Gabrieli, Giovanni (King)   *Sonata octavi toni*

Gabrieli, Giovanni (Hunsberger)

Canzona quarti toni a 15

Strauss, Richard   Serenade, op. 7

Milhaud, Darius   *Suite Française*

INTERMISSION

Roussel, Albert   *A Glorious Day*

Grainger, Percy   *Lincolnshire Posy*

Hindemith, Paul   Symphony in B-Flat

DONALD HUNSBERGER, CONDUCTOR

January 8, 1965, Eastman Theatre

Catel, Charles Simon   Overture in C

Vivaldi, Antonio (Rogers)

Concerto for Two Trumpets in C

JAMES ODE AND GLENN KOPONEN, SOLOISTS

Britten, Benjamin (Brown)   *Soirées Musicales*

INTERMISSION

Prokofieff, Serge   *Athletic Festival March*

Grainger, Percy   *Hill Song No. 2*

Surinach, Carlos   *Paeans and Dances of Heathen Iberia*

DONALD HUNSBERGER, CONDUCTOR

February 26, 1965, Eastman Theatre

Bach, J. S. (Hunsberger)
Prelude in E-Flat ("St. Anne")
Sibelius, Jean (Goldman)
Three Movements from the *Karelia Suite*
White, Donald   *Miniature Suite*

INTERMISSION

Rorem, Ned   *Sinfonia* for 15 Winds and Percussion
Benson, Warren
Symphony for Drums and Wind Orchestra
DONALD HUNSBERGER, CONDUCTOR

April 2, 1965, Eastman Theatre

Jacob, Gordon   *The Battell*
Dvorak, Antonin   Serenade in D Minor, op. 44
Riegger, Wallingford
Introduction and Fugue for Violoncello and
Symphonic Winds
RONALD LEONARD, CELLO

INTERMISSION

Debussy, Claude (Schaefer)   *March Ecossaise*
Ibert, Jacques
Concerto for Violoncello and Wind Orchestra, op. 74
RONALD LEONARD, CELLO
Rossini-Respighi (Godfrey)   *La Boutique Fantasque*
DONALD HUNSBERGER, CONDUCTOR

April 29, 1965, Eastman Theatre

35th Annual Festival of American Music
Benson, Warren
Symphony for Drums and Wind Orchestra
Dello Joio, Norman   *From Every Horizon*
George, Thom Ritter
Symphonic Variations for Wind and Percussion
Instruments

INTERMISSION

Dahl, Ingolf   *Sinfonietta* for Concert Band
Copland, Aaron   *Emblems*
DONALD HUNSBERGER, CONDUCTOR

14th SEASON: 1965–66

October 27, 1965, Eastman Theatre

Concert for the Rochester Association for the United Nations
Shostakovich, Dmitri (Hunsberger)
Festive Overture, op. 96
Jacob, Gordon   *William Byrd Suite*
Nixon, Roger   *In Memoriam—Adlai Stevenson*
Persichetti, Vincent   Symphony No. 6

INTERMISSION

Van Baaron, Kees   *Partita*
Ganne, Louis   *Marche Lorraine*
Van Blon, Franz   *Under the Banner of Victory*
Codina, Genaro   *Marcha Zacatecas*
Costa, P. M. (Seredy)   *A Frangesa*
DONALD HUNSBERGER, CONDUCTOR

November 19, 1965, Eastman Theatre

Peeters, Flor   *Modale Suite*
White, Donald   *Aeterna Christi Munera*
Hindemith, Paul *Konzertmusik für Blasorchester*, op. 41

INTERMISSION

Briccetti, Thomas   *Turkey Creek March*
Schuman, William   *When Jesus Wept*
Schuman, William   *Chester*
DONALD HUNSBERGER, CONDUCTOR

December 14, 1965, Kilbourn Hall

Strauss, Richard   Suite in B-flat, op. 4
Otterloo, Willem van   *Sinfonietta*
Haufrecht, Herbert
Symphony for Brass and Timpani

INTERMISSION

Rogers, Bernard   *Pictures from "The Tale of Aladdin"*
GEORGE WARREN, NARRATOR
Toch, Ernst   *Spiel für Blasorchester*
DONALD HUNSBERGER, CONDUCTOR

February 11, 1966, Eastman Theatre

Transcriptions for the Wind Band:

Arnold, Malcom (Johnstone)	*English Dances*
Martinu, Bohuslav (Jarman)	
Little Suite from *Comedy on the Bridge*	
Tveitt, Geirr (Haugland)	Folk Tunes
	from *Hardanger*
Hanson, Howard (Garland)	*Merry Mount Suite*

INTERMISSION

Original Compositions for the Wind Band:

Schuman, William	*George Washington Bridge*
Bennett, Robert Russell	*Suite of Old American Dances*
Alford, Kenneth	*The Mad Major*
	Old Panama

DONALD HUNSBERGER, CONDUCTOR

March 18, 1966, Eastman Theatre

Pottenger, Harold	Suite for Wind Band
Stravinsky, Igor	*Symphonies of Wind Instruments*
Effinger, Cecil	*Silver Plume*
Kabalevsky, Dmitri (Hunsberger)	
	Overture to *Colas Breugnon*

INTERMISSION

Holst, Gustav	First Suite in E-flat
Ginastera, Alberto (John)	
"Danza Final" from the ballet *Estancia*	

DONALD HUNSBERGER, CONDUCTOR

May 6, 1966, Kilbourn Hall

36th Annual Festival of American Music

Sacco, Peter	*Four Sketches on Emerson Essays*
Serly, Tibor	Symphony for Wind Instruments
Kremenliev, Boris	
Crucifixion for Winds, Organ, Piano, and Percussion	

INTERMISSION

White, Donald	Recitative, Air and Dance
Johnston, Donald	Symphony No. 4

DONALD HUNSBERGER, CONDUCTOR

15th SEASON: 1966–67

October 21, 1966, Kilbourn Hall

Gabrieli, Giovanni	*Sonata octavi toni*
	Canzon primi toni
Mozart, W. A.	Serenade No. 12 in C Minor, K. 388

Starer, Robert	Serenade for Brass

INTERMISSION

Rogers, Bernard	*Three Japanese Dances*
ANN YERVANIAN, SOPRANO	
Hindemith, Paul	Symphony in B-flat

DONALD HUNSBERGER, CONDUCTOR

November 22, 1966, Eastman Theatre

Bach, J. S. (Hunsberger)	
Passacaglia and Fugue in C Minor	
Palestrina, Giovanni (Harvey)	Missa Brevis

INTERMISSION

Gabrieli, Giovanni	*In Ecclesiis*
De Lone, Peter	Symphony No. 1
La Montaine, John	*Te Deum*, op. 35

EASTMAN SCHOOL CHORUS

GEORGE CORWIN, CONDUCTOR

DONALD HUNSBERGER, CONDUCTOR

November 30, 1966, Eastman Theatre

Howard Hanson Week

Hanson, Howard	*Chorale and Alleluia*
Hanson, Howard (Ford)	Symphony No. 5
	(*Sinfonia Sacra*)

DONALD HUNSBERGER, CONDUCTOR

December 2, 1966, Eastman Theatre

Music of Howard Hanson

Hanson, Howard (Ford)	Symphony No. 5
	(*Sinfonia Sacra*)

DONALD HUNSBERGER, CONDUCTOR

February 17, 1967, Eastman Theatre

A Program of Original Music for the Wind Band

The English Tradition:

Vaughan Williams, Ralph	*Toccata Marziale*
Holst, Gustav	First Suite in E-Flat
Holst, Gustav	Second Suite in F

INTERMISSION

Americana:

Adler, Samuel	*Southwestern Sketches*

COMPOSER CONDUCTING

Piston, Walter   *Tunbridge Fair*
International Marches:
  Alford, Kenneth   *Dunedin*
  Teike, Carl   *The Conqueror*
  Lithgow, Alexander   *Invercargill*
  Sousa, John Philip   *Corcoran Cadets*
    DONALD HUNSBERGER, CONDUCTOR

May 5, 1967, Eastman Theatre
37th Annual Festival of American Music
Hartley, Walter   *Sinfonia* No. 4
Gilmore, Bernard Five Songs for Soprano and Winds
    CANDACE WILSON, MEZZO-SOPRANO
Persichetti, Vincent   *Masquerade*

INTERMISSION

Rogers, Bernard
  Apparitions: Scenes from *The Temptation of St.*
Anthony
Nixon, Roger   *Fiesta del Pacifico*
    DONALD HUNSBERGER, CONDUCTOR

16th SEASON: 1967–68

October 24, 1967, Eastman Theatre
*A Concert for the Rochester Association
for the United Nations*
Jacob, Gordon   *An Original Suite*
Villa-Lobos, Heitor   *Fantasy in the Form of a Chôros*
Surinach, Carlos *Paeans and Dances of Heathen Iberia*

INTERMISSION

Kabalevsky, Dmitri (Hunsberger)
             Overture to *Colas Breugnon*
Washburn, Robert   Symphony for Band
Wagner, Josef Franz   *Under the Double Eagle*
Suma, Yosaku   March—*Blue Skies*
Sousa, John Philip   *The Stars and Stripes Forever*

November 19, 1967, Page Hall,
State University of New York at Albany
Bach, J. S. (Leidzen)   Chorale—"Komm süsser Tod"
Gossec, Francois Joseph   Symphony in F Major
Jacob, Gordon   *An Original Suite*
Washburn, Robert   Symphony for Band

INTERMISSION

Kabalevsky, Dmitri (Hunsberger)
             Overture to *Colas Breugnon*
Dello Joio, Norman   *Variants on a Mediaeval Tune*
Nixon, Roger   *Fiesta del Pacifico*
Wagner, Josef Franz   *Under the Double Eagle*
Delle Cese, Davide   *Inglesina*
Grafulla, Claudio   *Washington Greys*
    DONALD HUNSBERGER, CONDUCTOR

December 12, 1967, Kilbourn Hall
Gabrieli, Giovanni (Hunsberger)
            Canzona duodecimi toni
Scheidt, Samuel (Reynolds)   *Centone* No. 5
Mozart, W.A.   Divertimento No. 3 in E-flat
Milhaud, Darius
  "Dixtour d'instruments à vent" from *Cinq symphonies*
pour petit orchestre
Reynolds, Verne   Woodwind Quintet
Krenek, Ernst   *Drei lustige Märsche*
    DONALD HUNSBERGER, CONDUCTOR

February 23, 1968, Eastman Theatre
Shostakovich, Dmitri (Hunsberger)
            Festive Overture, op. 96
Hartley, Walter   *Sinfonia* No. 4
Persichetti, Vincent   *Masquerade*
Dello Joio, Norman   *Variants on a Medieval Tune*

INTERMISSION

Dahl, Ingolf   *Sinfonietta*
Nixon, Roger   *Fiesta del Pacifico*
    DONALD HUNSBERGER, CONDUCTOR

March 3, 1968, Cambridge Springs High School
Auditorium, Alliance, Ohio
Alliance College Lecture and Artists Series
Shostakovich, Dmitri (Hunsberger)
            Festive Overture, op. 96
Vaughan Williams, Ralph   *English Folk Song Suite*
Hartley, Walter   *Sinfonia* No. 4
Williams, Clifton   Fanfare and Allegro

INTERMISSION

March 3, 1968 (cont.)

Dahl, Ingolf	*Sinfonietta*
Dinerstein, Norman	*The Answered Question*
Nixon, Roger	*Fiesta del Pacifico*

DONALD HUNSBERGER, CONDUCTOR

March 11–17, 1968

Repertoire for the tour to the Music Educator's National Conference Chicago, Denver, Los Angeles (UCLA), Redlands, Palo Alto, Bellevue (Washington); March 17—Seattle Opera House, a concert for the Music Educators National Conference General Assembly

Copland, Aaron	*Emblems*
Dahl, Ingolf	*Sinfonietta*
Dello Joio, Norman	*Variants on a Mediaeval Tune*
Dinerstein, Norman	*The Answered Question*
Hartley, Walter	*Sinfonia* No. 4
Mozart, W. A.	Serenade No. 12 in C Minor, K. 388
Nixon, Roger	*Fiesta del Pacifico*
Persichetti, Vincent	*Masquerade*
Russell, Armand	*Theme and Fantasia*
Shostakovich, Dmitri (Hunsberger)	
	Festive Overture, op. 96
Vaughan Williams, Ralph	*English Folk Song Suite*
Williams, Clifton	Fanfare and Allegro

DONALD HUNSBERGER, CONDUCTOR

April 3, 1968, Eastman Theatre

University of Rochester Alumni Theatre Party

Shostakovich, Dmitri (Hunsberger)	
	Festive Overture, op. 96
Persichetti, Vincent	*Masquerade*
Vaughan Williams, Ralph	*English Folk Song Suite*
Dinerstein, Norman	*The Answered Question*
Nixon, Roger	*Fiesta del Pacifico*

DONALD HUNSBERGER, CONDUCTOR

May 3, 1968, Eastman Theatre

38th Annual Festival of American Music

Surinach, Carlos	*Paeans and Dances of Heathen Iberia*
Reed, H. Owen	*La Fiesta Mexicana*

DONALD HUNSBERGER, CONDUCTOR

May 12, 1968, Eastman Theatre

Nixon, Roger	*Fiesta del Pacifico*

Hartley, Walter	*Sinfonia* No. 4
Dahl, Ingolf	*Sinfonietta*
Surinach, Carlos	*Paeans and Dances of Heathen Iberia*
Persichetti, Vincent	*Masquerade*
Reed, H. Owen	*La Fiesta Mexicana*

DONALD HUNSBERGER, CONDUCTOR

17th SEASON: 1968–69

November 1, 1968, Eastman Theatre

Prokofieff, Serge	March, op. 99
Bach, J. S. (Moehlmann)	
	Chorale—"If Thou Be Near"

Music for *Le Quatorze Juillet* ("The 14th of July"):

Honegger, Arthur	*La Marche sur la Bastille*
Roussel, Albert	Prelude to Act II
Auric, Georges	*Le Palais Royal*
Russell, Armand	*Symphony in Three Images*

DONALD HUNSBERGER, CONDUCTOR

December 13, 1968, Eastman Theatre

A Program of Contemporary Compositions for the Wind Band

Ketting, Otto	*Intrada Festiva*
Dello Joio, Norman	Scenes from *The Louvre*
Hovhaness, Alan	Symphony No. 4

INTERMISSION

Benson, Warren	*Remembrance*
Bielawa, Herbert	*Spectrums*
Davison, John	
Symphony for Wind Instruments and Percussion	

DONALD HUNSBERGER, CONDUCTOR

January 17, 1969, Kilbourn Hall

Music for the Classical Wind Band:

Handel, G. F.	*Music for the Royal Fireworks*
Mozart, W. A.	Serenade No. 11 in E-Flat, K. 375

Occasional Music for Military Wind Band:

Beethoven, L. van	March in F (1809)
	Polonaise
	March in F
	Ecossaise
	March in C
Haydn, F. J.	*March for the Prince of Wales*

INTERMISSION

The American Wind Orchestra:
Hovhaness, Alan
> *Return and Rebuild the Desolate Places*
PHILIP COLLINS, TRUMPET
Amram, David   *King Lear Variations*
DONALD HUNSBERGER, CONDUCTOR

**February 9, 1969, Burton Hall, York University,
Toronto, Canada (afternoon concert)**
Alexander, Russell   *From Tropic to Tropic*
Bach, J. S. (Moehlmann)
> Chorale—"If Thou Be Near"
Dello Joio, Norman   Scenes from *The Louvre*
Mozart, W. A.   Serenade No. 11 in E-flat, K. 375
McCauley, William   *Metropolis*
Bielawa, Herbert   *Spectrums*
Davison, John
> Symphony for Wind and Percussion Instruments
Alford, Kenneth   *The Vanished Army*
DONALD HUNSBERGER, CONDUCTOR

**February 9, 1969, Burton Hall, York University,
Toronto, Canada (evening concert)**
Prokofiev, Sergei   March, op. 99
Bach, J. S. (Moehlmann)
> Chorale—"If Thou Be Near"
Amram, David   *King Lear Variations*
Hovhaness, Alan *Return and Rebuild the Desolate Places*
PHILIP COLLINS, TRUMPET
Dello Joio, Norman   Scenes from *The Louvre*

INTERMISSION

Bielawa, Herbert   *Spectrums*
Davison, John
> Symphony for Wind and Percussion Instruments
DONALD HUNSBERGER, CONDUCTOR

March 19, 1969, Eastman Theatre
Grainger, Percy   *The Duke of Marlborough Fanfare*
                        Irish Tune from County Derry
                                    The Immovable Do
Milhaud, Darius   *Suite Française*

Benson, Warren
> Symphony for Drums and Wind Orchestra
COMPOSER CONDUCTING

INTERMISSION

Penderecki, Krzysztof   *Pittsburgh Overture*
Williams, John T.   *Sinfonietta*
DONALD HUNSBERGER, CONDUCTOR

April 30, 1969, Eastman Theatre
Mennin, Peter   *Canzona*
Mayuzumi, Toshiro   *Music with Sculpture*
Arnold, Malcolm (Johnstone)   *English Dances*
Williams, John T.   *Sinfonietta*

INTERMISSION

Penderecki, Krzysztof   *Pittsburgh Overture*
Ward, Robert   *Night Fantasy*
Walton, William (Duthoit)   March—*Crown Imperial*
DONALD HUNSBERGER, CONDUCTOR

May 13, 1969, Eastman Theatre
Penderecki, Krzysztof   *Pittsburgh Overture*
Mayuzumi, Toshiro   *Music with Sculpture*
Williams, John T.   *Sinfonietta*
DONALD HUNSBERGER, CONDUCTOR

18th SEASON: 1969–70

October 22, 1969, Eastman Theatre
Concert for the Rochester Association of the United Nations
Key, Francis Scott   National Anthem
Khatchaturian, Aram (Hunsberger)
> Three Dance Episodes from the ballet *Spartacus*
Auric, Georges   *Divertimento*
Husa, Karel   *Music for Prague 1968*

INTERMISSION

International Marches:
Dan, Ikuma   *Grand March "Prospera Aeterna"*
Leemans, P.   *Colonel Paddy*
Costa, P. M.   *A Frangesa*
Davies, Walford   *R.A.F. March*
Blankenburg, H. L.   *Action Front*
Chambers, Paris   *Alhambra*
Sousa, John Philip   *Stars and Stripes Forever*
DONALD HUNSBERGER, CONDUCTOR

November 21, 1969, Kilbourn Hall
A Concert of Serenades and Such

Gabrieli, Giovanni   *Canzon primi toni a 10*
Mozart, W. A.   Serenade in C Minor, K. 388
Strauss, Richard   Serenade in E-Flat, op. 7
ROBERT BLOOM, CONDUCTOR

INTERMISSION

Weinzweig, John
    Divertimento No. 5 for Trumpet, Trombone and
                                    Wind Ensemble
        PHILIP COLLINS, TRUMPET
        FREDRICK BOYD, TROMBONE
Starer, Robert   Serenade for Brass
DONALD HUNSBERGER, CONDUCTOR

December 16, 1969, Eastman Theatre

Beglarian, Grant
    Sinfonia for Band, adapted from *Sinfonia* for
                                    Orchestra
Kennan, Kent   *Night Soliloquy*
    BONITA BOYD, flute
Adler, Samuel
    Concerto for Brass, Winds and Percussion

INTERMISSION

Benson, Warren   *The Solitary Dancer*
Dello Joio, Norman   *Fantasia on a Theme of Haydn*
DONALD HUNSBERGER, CONDUCTOR

February 17, 1970, Kilbourn Hall

Zador, Eugene   Suite for Brass Instruments
Lantier, Pierre
    Andante and Scherzetto for Saxophone Quartet
Hindemith, Paul   Septet for Wind Instruments
Morawetz, Oskar   *Sinfonietta*
DONALD HUNSBERGER, CONDUCTOR

March 18, 1970, Eastman Theatre

Schuman, William   *Dedication Fanfare*
Nielson, Carl (Boyd)   Overture to *Maskarade*

Hovhaness, Alan   Suite for Band
Hindemith, Paul   Symphony in B-Flat

INTERMISSION

Holst, Gustav   Second Suite in F
Wilder, Alec   *Entertainment III*
DONALD HUNSBERGER, CONDUCTOR

April 14, 1970, Eastman Theatre
Symposium of Student Works for Wind Ensemble

Downs, Lamont   *Sinfonia* No. 1
Harris, Larry   *Dedication Te Deum*
    NORBERT BUSKEY, ALTO SAXOPHONE
Garriguenc, Pierre   *Synthesis*
DONALD HUNSBERGER, CONDUCTOR

May 12, 1970, Kilbourn Hall
40th Annual Festival of American Music

Johnston, Donald   *Montage*
Fox, Fred   *BEC-I*
Stevens, Noel Scott   *Etching*
Downs, Lamont   *Sinfonia* No. 1

INTERMISSION

Sousa, John Philip   *The Gladiator*
                                 Semper Fidelis
                                  Guide Right
                                The Bride-Elect
                                The Directorate
DONALD HUNSBERGER, CONDUCTOR

19th SEASON: 1970–71

October 16, 1970, Eastman Theatre

Vaughan Williams, Ralph   *Toccata Marziale*
Jacob, Gordon   *William Byrd Suite*
Lopatnikoff, Nikolai   Concerto for Wind Orchestra

INTERMISSION

McKay, Neil   *Evocations*
Rodrigo, Joaquin   Adagio for Wind Orchestra
White, Donald   *Miniature Set*
DONALD HUNSBERGER, CONDUCTOR

November 6, 1970, Eastman Theatre
Bach, J. S. (Hunsberger)
        Passacaglia and Fugue in C Minor
Cowell, Henry   *Celtic Set*
Mayuzumi, Toshiro
    Concerto for Percussion and Wind Orchestra
Respighi, Ottorino (Bates)   Aria *Campanae Parisienses*
Hartley, Walter   Sonata for Wind Band
Bergsma, William   March with Trumpets
DONALD HUNSBERGER, CONDUCTOR

December 11, 1970, Kilbourn Hall
Barlow, Wayne
   Intrada, Fugue and Postlude for Brass Ensemble
Padovano, Annible (Schmitt)   *Aria della battaglia*
Willey, James   *Commentary II*
Donizetti, Gaetano (Townsend)
             Sinfonia for Wind Band
Epstein, David
   Vent-Ures, Three Pieces for Symphonic Wind
                        Ensemble

INTERMISSION

Kurka, Robert
     Suite from *The Good Soldier Schweik* Suite
DONALD HUNSBERGER, CONDUCTOR

February 19, 1971, Eastman Theatre
Bach, J. S. (Boyd)   Fantasia and Fugue in G Minor
Mailman, Martin   *Geometrics in Sound*
Koch, Frederick (Nelson)   *Composites*
Badings, Henk
  Concerto for Flute and Wind Symphony Orchestra
       BONNIE BOYD, FLUTE

INTERMISSION

Downs, Lamont   *March RS-2*
Copland, Aaron   *An Outdoor Overture*
Ginastera, Alberto (John)
     "Danza Final" from the ballet *Estancia*
DONALD HUNSBERGER, CONDUCTOR

March 10, 1971, Men's Gymnasium, Alfred University
Copland, Aaron   *An Outdoor Overture*

Bach, J. S. (Boyd)   Fantasia and Fugue in G Minor
Mailman, Martin   *Geometrics in Sound*
Badings, Henk
  Concerto for Flute and Wind Symphony Orchestra
       BONNIE BOYD, FLUTE

INTERMISSION

Downs, Lamont   *March RS-2*
Cowell, Henry   *Celtic Set*
Shostakovich Festival I:
   Shostakovich, Dmitri (Hunsberger)
          Galop (*Moscow Cheremoushky*)
          Contradance (*The Gadfly*)
               Polka (*The Bolt*)
           Nocturne (*The Gadfly*)
         Folk Festival (*The Gadfly*)
DONALD HUNSBERGER, CONDUCTOR

March 12, 1971, Kilbourn Hall
Haydn, Joseph   Divertimento in D
Chou, Wen-Chung   *Soliloquy of a Bhiksuni*
   GEOFFREY RICHTER, TRUMPET
Bozza, Eugène
    Andante et Scherzo pour Quatuor des Saxophones
Stravinsky, Igor
   Concerto for Piano and Wind Instruments
     PAUL VAN NESS, PIANO
Berger, Theodor   *Rondo ostinato on a Spanish motive*
DONALD HUNSBERGER, CONDUCTOR

April 26, 1971, Monroe Community College, Rochester
Adler, Samuel   *Festive Prelude*
Baaren, Kees van   *Partita*
Lieb, Richard
  Concertino Basso for Bass Trombone and Wind Band
   ELWOOD WILLIAMS, BASS TROMBONE
Xenakis, Iannis   *Akrata*

INTERMISSION

Fillmore, Henry   *The Klaxon March*
Persichetti, Vincent
       Chorale Prelude—"So Pure The Star"
Walton, William (O'Brien)   Movements from *Façade*
DONALD HUNSBERGER, CONDUCTOR

May 4, 1971, Orchestra Annex

Symposium of Compositions for Symphonic Wind Ensemble

Downs, Lamont   *Recessional* for Chorus and Band
Forson, Thomas   *Toccata* for Winds
Ward, Wayne   *Xenophanes*
Wasson, Steven   *William Billings* Suite No. 1
Williams, Neal   *Separate*

DONALD HUNSBERGER, CONDUCTOR

20th SEASON: 1971–72

**October 29, 1971, Arts Center Auditorium,
Nazareth College, Rochester**

Concert for the Rochester Association for the United Nations

Oettinger, Alan   Fanfare for Brass and Percussion
McKay, Neil   *Dance Overture*
Vaughan Williams, Ralph   *English Folk Song Suite*
Chow, Wen-Chung   *Metaphors*

INTERMISSION

Prokofieff, Serge   March, op. 99
Dato, Julio   *Martin Fierro*
Hanssen, Johannes (Bainum)   *Valdres*
Marquina, Pasqual
      Procesión de Semana Santa en Sevilla
Delle Cese, Davide   *Inglesina*
Sousa, John Philip   *The Stars and Stripes Forever*

DONALD HUNSBERGER, CONDUCTOR

**November 29, 1971, Imperial Room,
Concord Hotel, Kiamesha Lake, New York**

*Eastman School of Music 50th Anniversary Festival: A
Concert for the New York State School Music Association*

Oettinger, Alan   Fanfare for Brass and Percussion
McKay, Neil   *Dance Overture*
Benson, Warren   *Shadow Wood*
      SHERRY ZANNOTH, SOPRANO
Chou, Wen-Chung   *Metaphors*
Shostakovich, Dmitri (Hunsberger)
      Galop (*Moscow Cheremoushky*)

DONALD HUNSBERGER, CONDUCTOR

December 10, 1971, Kilbourn Hall

*A Concert Commemorating the Fiftieth Anniversary of the
Eastman School of Music, presented as the concluding
portion of the National Music Critics Panel*

Amram, David   *King Lear Variations*
Davies, Peter Maxwell
      Saint Michael, Sonata for 17 Wind Instruments
Benson, Warren   *Shadow Wood*
      SHERRY ZANNOTH, SOPRANO
Reynolds, Verne   *Scenes*
      DONALD HUNSBERGER, CONDUCTOR
(This program was cancelled the evening of performance due to the death of Emory B. Remington, famed Professor of Trombone, at 6:30 p.m., December 10, 1971.)

January 18, 1972, Kilbourn Hall

Zielenski (Reynolds)   *Magnificat*
Boismortier, Joseph   Concerto No. 3
Mozart, W. A.   Divertimento in E-flat
Bottje, Will Gay   *Modalities*
Prokofieff, Serge   *Ouverture*, op. 42

DONALD HUNSBERGER, CONDUCTOR

February 18, 1972, Eastman Theatre

*Combined concert with Greater Rochester Youth Wind
Ensemble and Eastman Symphony Band*

Farber, Mitchell   *Concert Music* for Band
Holst, Gustav   *Hammersmith*
Reynolds, Verne   *Scenes*

DONALD HUNSBERGER, CONDUCTOR

April 6, 1972, Eastman Theatre

*A Gala Concert Celebrating the Fiftieth Anniversary of the
Eastman School of Music presented as part of a combined
meeting of the Eastern Division of the College Band Directors
National Association and the Third National Wind
Ensemble Conference.*

Hanson, Howard   *Dies Natalis*
Wagner, Richard (Leidzen)   *Trauersinfonie*
      DAVID WHITWELL, GUEST CONDUCTOR
Husa, Karel   *Apotheosis of this Earth*
      FREDERICK FENNELL, GUEST CONDUCTOR

INTERMISSION

Kane, Irving *Fourth Stream*
HENRY ROMERSA, GUEST CONDUCTOR
Schuller, Gunther *Study in Texture*
FRANK BATTISTI, GUEST CONDUCTOR
Williams, John T. *A Nostalgic Jazz Odyssey*
DONALD HUNSBERGER, CONDUCTOR

April 7, 1972, Kilbourn Hall
Music for the Orchestra Wind Section and the
Chamber Wind Ensemble
Epstein, David
Vent-Ures, Three Pieces for Symphonic Wind
Ensemble
Kurka, Robert Suite from *The Good Soldier Schweik*
Mozart, W. A. Divertimento No. 3 in E-Flat, K. 166
Schwartz, Elliott *Voyage*
Benson, Warren *Shadow Wood*
SHERRY ZANNOTH, SOPRANO
Poulenc, Francis *Suite Française*
Reynolds, Verne *Scenes*
DONALD HUNSBERGER, CONDUCTOR

April 7, 1972, Eastman Theatre
The Piano Concerto with Wind Accompaniment
Kennan, Kent
Concertino for Piano and Wind Ensemble
EDWARD EICKNER, PIANO
Stravinsky, Igor
Concerto for Piano and Wind Instruments
KIMBERLY SCHMIDT, PIANO
Starer, Robert Concerto for Piano and Winds, No. 2
REBECCA OEKERMAN, PIANO
DONALD HUNSBERGER, CONDUCTOR

21st SEASON: 1972–73

October 20, 1972, Eastman Theatre
Ives, Charles (Rhoads) Variations on "America"
Jacob, Gordon *William Byrd Suite*
Benson, Warren *The Mask of Night*
Husa, Karel
Concerto for Percussion and Wind Ensemble
(COMPOSER CONDUCTING)
DONALD HUNSBERGER, CONDUCTOR

November 10, 1972, Eastman Theatre
Joseph C. Wilson Day
Kineda, Bin *Symphonic Movement*
Bernstein, Leonard (Hunsberger)
Symphonic Dances from *West Side Story*

November 17, 1972, Eastman Theatre
Russell, Armand *Theme and Fantasia*
Persichetti, Vincent Symphony No. 6
DeLone, Peter Introduction and Allegro
Hanson, Howard
Young Person's Guide to the Six-Tone Scale
BARRY SNYDER, PIANO
DONALD HUNSBERGER, CONDUCTOR

December 13, 1972, Kilbourn Hall
Gabrieli, Giovanni (Reynolds)
Quis est iste qui venit (from *Sacrae Symphoniae*)
Sweelinck, Jan P. (Ricker)
Mein junges Leben hat ein End
Gates, Everett *Declamation and Dance*
Russell, Armand *Quest*
Debussy, Claude (Erickson)
Sarabande from *Pour le Piano* for Woodwind Choir
Binkerd, Gordon
The Battle (based on Frescobaldi's *Capriccio sopra la battaglia*)
DONALD HUNSBERGER, CONDUCTOR

February 9, 1973, Eastman Theatre
Welcher, Dan
Walls and Fences, Five Tactile Experiences for Winds
and Percussion
Castérède, Jacque *Divertissement d'Eté*
Benson, Warren *The Solitary Dancer*
DONALD HUNSBERGER, CONDUCTOR

March 15, 1973, Eastman Theatre
Eastman Wind Ensemble and Chorale
Gabrieli, Giovanni (Reynolds) *Benedicam Dominum*
Gabrieli, Giovanni (Reynolds)
Canzon per sonar duodecimi toni
Attaingant, Pierre (Randolph) *Renaissance Dance Set*
Gabrieli, Giovanni *Jubilate Deo*

March 15, 1973 (cont.)

Bernstein, Leonard   Latin Choruses from *The Lark*
    JOHN ZEIGLER, COUNTER-TENOR
    DONALD HUNSBERGER, CONDUCTOR

Mozart, W. A.   Serenade No. 11 in E-Flat, K. 375
    MICHAEL PRATT, GUEST CONDUCTOR

INTERMISSION

Persichetti, Vincent

    Celebrations for Chorus and Wind Ensemble
        EASTMAN CHORALE
        ROBERT DECORMIER, CONDUCTOR
        MILFORD FARGO, GUEST CONDUCTOR
        DONALD HUNSBERGER, CONDUCTOR

April 19, 1973, Kilbourn Hall

Holst, Gustav   Second Suite in F

Stravinsky, Igor   *Symphonies of Wind Instruments*

End, Jack

    The Rocks and the Sea (set to photographs by Louis
                                        Ouzer)

INTERMISSION

Andrews, Ray   *March MKT*

Baban, Gracian (Reynolds)   *Voce mea ad Dominum*

Reynolds, Verne   *Cantos III*
    EASTMAN HORN CHOIR
    VERNE REYNOLDS, CONDUCTOR

Surinach, Carlos   *Sinfonietta Flamenca*
    DONALD HUNSBERGER, CONDUCTOR

22nd SEASON: 1973–74

September 19, 1973, Eastman Theatre

*A Concert Celebrating the Inauguration of Robert Freeman
    as Director of the Eastman School of Music*

Dukas, Paul   Fanfare from *La Peri*

Hanson, Howard   *Dies Natalis*

October 12, 1973, Eastman Theatre

Bottje, Will Gay   *Contrasts*

Rogers, Bernard   *Three Japanese Dances*

Bassett, Leslie   *Designs, Images and Textures*
    DONALD HUNSBERGER, CONDUCTOR

November 2, 1973, Eastman Theatre

Toch, Ernst   *Spiel für Blasorchester*

Hovhaness, Alan *Return and Rebuild the Desolate Places*
    ALLEN VIZZUTTI, TRUMPET

Persichetti, Vincent   Symphony No. 6, op. 69
    DAVID HARMAN, CONDUCTOR

INTERMISSION

Poulenc, Francis   *Suite Française*

Klein, Lothar   *Symphonic Etudes*

Shostakovich, Dmitri (Hunsberger)

    A Shostakovich Festival
        DONALD HUNSBERGER, CONDUCTOR

**November 7, 1973, Central Collegiate Auditorium,
    Barrie, Ontario**
**November 8, 1973, Edward Johnson Theatre,
    University of Toronto, Toronto, Ontario**

Hanson, Howard   *Dies Natalis*

Hovhaness, Alan *Return and Rebuild The Desolate Places*
    ALLEN VIZZUTTI, TRUMPET

Persichetti, Vincent

    Symphony for Wind Band, op. 69

INTERMISSION

Rogers, Bernard   *Three Japanese Dances*

Poulenc, Francis   *Suite Française*

Shostakovich, Dmitri (Hunsberger)

    Folk Festival from *The Gadfly*
    Polka from *The Bolt*
    Galop from *Moscow Cheremoushky*
        DONALD HUNSBERGER, CONDUCTOR

December 12, 1973, Kilbourn Hall

Gabrieli, Giovanni (King)   *Canzon quarti toni a 15*

Lasso, Orlando di (Hanson)   *Tui sunt coeli*

Gabrieli, Giovanni (Fennell)   *Canzon noni toni a 12*

Perilhou, Andre   *Divertissement*

Willis, Richard   *Sonants*

Albeniz, Isaac (Mule)

    Three Pieces for Saxophone Quartet

Kelterborn, Rudolf   *Miroirs*
        DONALD HUNSBERGER, CONDUCTOR

February 1, 1974, Eastman Theatre

Schuman, William (Owen)   *Circus Overture*
Persichetti, Vincent
    Chorale Prelude—"O Cool Is The Valley"
Beall, John   Concerto for Piano and Wind Orchestra
    CAROL JEAN BEALL, PIANO
Copland, Aaron
    The Red Pony—A Film Suite for Wind Band
White, Donald
    Concertino for Timpani, Winds, and Percussion
    JOHN BECK, TIMPANI
Ginastera, Alberto (Johns)
    "Danza Final" from *Estancia*
DONALD HUNSBERGER, CONDUCTOR

March 1, 1974, Eastman Theatre

Dello Joio, Norman   *Songs of Abelard*
    WILLIAM SHARP, BARITONE
Dahl, Ingolf
    Concerto for Alto Saxophone and Wind Orchestra
    DOUGLAS WALTER, ALTO SAXOPHONE
Schoenberg, Arnold   Theme and Variations, op. 43a
Penn, William
    Designs (for Orchestral Winds, Jazz Quartet, and
            Percussion)
Makris, Andreas (Bader)   *Aegean Festival Overture*
DONALD HUNSBERGER, CONDUCTOR

April 8, 1974, Eastman Theatre

Bach, J. S. (Hunsberger)
    Passacaglia and Fugue in C Minor
Fišer, Lobos   *Report*
Stout, Gordon
    Concerto for Marimba and Wind Ensemble
    GORDON STOUT, MARIMBA

INTERMISSION

Massenet, Jules (Reynolds)   Ballet Music from *Le Cid*
    VERNE REYNOLDS, CONDUCTOR
Creston, Paul   Concerto for Alto Saxophone, op. 26
    JONATHAN RADWAY, ALTO SAXOPHONE
    DONALD HUNSBERGER, CONDUCTOR

23rd SEASON: 1974–75

September 27, 1974, Eastman Theatre

Johnston, Donald   *Montage*
Amram, David   *King Lear Variations*
Benson, Warren
    Symphony for Drums and Wind Orchestra

INTERMISSION

Vaughan Williams, Ralph   *English Folk Song Suite*
Tull, Fisher   *Sketches on a Tudor Psalm*
    DONALD HUNSBERGER, CONDUCTOR

October 11, 1974, Eastman Theatre

An Evening with Vincent Persichetti
Persichetti, Vincent   *Parable* for Band, op. 121
    Chorale Prelude—"Turn Not Thy Face," op. 105
    A Lincoln Address, op. 124a
    ROBERT DE CORMIER, NARRATOR
    DONALD HUNSBERGER, CONDUCTOR

November 8, 1974, Kilbourn Hall

Strauss, Richard   Suite in B-flat, op. 4
Schubert, Franz (Reynolds)   *Cantos V*
    EASTMAN HORN CHOIR
    VERNE REYNOLDS, CONDUCTOR
Kupferman, Meyer
    Concertino for Eleven Brass Instruments
Tuthill, Burnet
    Concerto for String Bass and Wind Orchestra
    PATRICIA HUTTER, STRING BASS
Rodrigo, Joaquin   Adagio for Wind Orchestra
    DONALD HUNSBERGER, CONDUCTOR

December 16, 1974, Eastman Theatre

Honoring Her Excellency Golda Meir upon the awarding of
an Honorary Doctorate by the University of Rochester
Jenkins, Joseph Wilcox   *An American Overture*
Persichetti, Vincent
    Chorale Prelude—"Turn Not Thy Face"
Jacob, Gordon   *William Byrd Suite*
Williams, Clifton   Fanfare and Allegro
    DONALD HUNSBERGER, CONDUCTOR

January 31, 1975, Eastman Theatre

Ives, Charles   *Omega Lambda Chi March*
Ives, Charles (Brion)
        Variations on "Jerusalem The Golden"
Penn, William   *Niagara*
Copland, Aaron   *Emblems*
        LAMONT DOWNS, CONDUCTOR

INTERMISSION

Turina, Josquin (Krance)   *Five Miniatures*
Lendvay, Kamilló
Concertino for Piano, Winds, Percussion and Harp
        DAVID LIPTAK, PIANO
        BRADLEY NELSON, CONDUCTOR
Finney, Ross Lee   *Summer in the Valley*
        DONALD HUNSBERGER, CONDUCTOR

February 21, 1975, Eastman Theatre

Reynolds, Verne   *Scenes*
Satie, Erik (Ricker)
        Fourth Nocturne (trans. for woodwind choir)
Stravinsky, Igor
        Concerto for Piano and Wind Instruments
        ROBERT SPILLMAN, PIANO
Sousa, John Philip   *George Washington Bicentennial*
Hanssen, Johannes (Bainum)   *Valdres*
Prokofieff, Serge   March, op. 99
Stokes, Eric   *Hennepin Avenue Marches and Struts!*
        LAMONT DOWNS, ASSISTING CONDUCTOR
        SYDNEY HODKINSON, GUEST CONDUCTOR
        DONALD HUNSBERGER, CONDUCTOR

April 28, 1975, Eastman Theatre

*1975 Alumni Theatre Party Honoring Dr. Howard
Hanson on the 50th Anniversary of His Appointment as
Director of the Eastman School of Music*
Hanson, Howard
        Laude, Chorale, Variations and Metamorphosis
        DONALD HUNSBERGER, CONDUCTOR

24th SEASON: 1975–76

October 3, 1975, Eastman Theatre

A Program of European Compositions for Wind Ensemble
Holst, Gustav   *Hammersmith*
Beethoven, Ludwig   March in F, WoO 18

Hindemith, Paul
        Geschwindmarsch (on Beethoven) from *Symphonia
                                              Serena*
Rodrigo, Joaquin   Adagio for Wind Orchestra
Otterloo, Willem van
                Sinfonietta for Wind Instruments
        ROBERT GRAY, CONDUCTOR

INTERMISSION

Messiaen, Olivier   *Et expecto resurrectionem mortuorum*
        DONALD HUNSBERGER, CONDUCTOR

October 6, 1975, Eastman Theatre

DEBUT CONCERT OF THE
EASTMAN WIND ORCHESTRA

Massaino, Tiburito   *Canzona trigesimaquinta*
Gabrieli, Giovanni (Hunsberger)   *Canzon quarti toni*
Reicha, Anton   *Commemoration Symphony*
Bernard, Emile   *Divertissement pour instruments à vent*

INTERMISSION

Husa, Karel   *Al Fresco*
Badings, Henk   Symphony for Wind Orchestra
        DONALD HUNSBERGER, CONDUCTOR

Tonight's concert marks the debut performance of
the Eastman Wind Orchestra. This ensemble, a
companion performance medium of the Eastman
Wind Ensemble, will present programs of original
and transcribed music for varying instrumentations
ranging in size from large wind ensemble to chamber
music combinations. [Much of the repertoire performed by the EWE from 1952 to 1975 would now
be programmed for the Eastman Wind Orchestra.]

October 10, 1975, Eastman Theatre

Weill, Kurt   *Little Threepenny Music*
        SYDNEY HODKINSON, GUEST CONDUCTOR

November 7, 1975, Eastman Theatre

*PRISM, a Concert for the New York State School Music
Association 1975 Convention featuring various ensembles
and soloists from throughout the Eastman School*
Fiser, Lubos   *Report*
        GARY BORDNER AND RICHARD BRAUN, TRUMPETS
        DONALD HUNSBERGER, CONDUCTOR

November 14, 1975, Eastman Theatre

The Wind Band and Its Repertoire

Our American Heritage:

	Yankee Doodle
	The Hessian
	Colonel Arne's March
	Garryowen
	The Austrian
	General Washington's March

The Manchester Brass Band and the
Social Orchestra:

The Band:

Anonymous	*Congo's Quickstep*
Dignam, Walter	
	Air Varie: Hope Told a Flattering Tale

ALLEN VIZZUTTI, E-FLAT TRUMPET

The Orchestra:

Foster, Stephen (arr.)	*Old Folks Quadrille*
Moore, John	*Quaker Medley Set Quadrille*
Dodworth, Allen	*Gift Polka*

The Band:

Sousa, John Philip	*Guide Right*
Ives, Charles (Sinclair)	Overture and March: 1776
Schuman, William	*When Jesus Wept*
Schuman, William	*Chester*

INTERMISSION

Two Contemporary European Views:

Loudova, Ivana

Chorale for Wind Orchestra, Percussion and Organ

Messiaen, Olivier   *Et expecto resurrectionem
                                         mortuorum*

DONALD HUNSBERGER, CONDUCTOR

February 6, 1976, Eastman Theatre

Sweelinck, Jan Pieterszoon (Walters)

                                  Ballo del Granduca

Baker, Claude   *Capriccio* for Concert Wind Band

Tull, Fisher

Variations on an Advent Tune for Brass Ensemble

Gould, Morton   Symphony for Band

INTERMISSION

Jankowsky, Loretta   *Todesband*

NEIL DePONTE, ASSISTING CONDUCTOR

Schoenberg, Arnold   Theme and Variations, op. 43a

DONALD HUNSBERGER, CONDUCTOR

February 28, 1976, Niagara-on-the-Lake, Ontario

Winter at Shaw Festival

Makris, Andreas (Bader)	*Aegean Festival Overture*
Chance, John Barnes	*Elegy*
Kay, Ulysses	*Forever Free, A Lincoln Chronicle*
Schoenberg, Arnold	Theme and Variations, op. 43a
Ives, Charles (Sinclair)	Overture and March: 1776
Benson, Warren	

Concerto for Alto Saxophone and Wind Band

RAMON RICKER, SOLOIST

Gould, Morton   Symphony for Band

March 19, 1976, Eastman Theatre

Makris, Andreas (Bader)   *Aegean Festival Overture*

Benson, Warren

Concerto for Alto Saxophone and Wind Band

RAMON RICKER, SOLOIST

Bach, J. S. (Hunsberger)

                Passacaglia and Fugue in C Minor

INTERMISSION

Ives, Charles (Sinclair)	Overture and March: 1776
Chance, John Barnes	*Elegy*
Hindemith, Paul	Symphony in B-flat

DONALD HUNSBERGER, CONDUCTOR

April 21, 1976, Kilbourn Hall

Convocation Concert in honor of Aaron Copland

Copland, Aaron   *Fanfare for the Common Man*

DONALD HUNSBERGER, CONDUCTOR

25th SEASON: 1976–77

November 5, 1976, Eastman Theatre

PRISM U.S.A.

Williams, John T.   *Sinfonietta*, mvts. 2 and 3

DONALD HUNSBERGER, CONDUCTOR

November 8, 1976, Eastman Theatre

*Concert with the Eastman Chorus, John Poellein,
guest conductor*

Binkerd, Gordon	*Noble Numbers*
Stravinsky, Igor	*Symphonies of Wind Instruments*
Williams, John T.	*Sinfonietta*

DONALD HUNSBERGER, CONDUCTOR

December 3, 1976, Kilbourn Hall

Michalsky, Donal
    Fanfare after Seventeenth Century Dances
Penderecki, Krzysztof
    Prelude für Bläser, Schlagzeug und Kontrabässe
Jolas, Betsy   *Lassus Ricercare*

INTERMISSION

Mozart, W. A.   Serenade in B-Flat, K. 361
DONALD HUNSBERGER, CONDUCTOR

February 4, 1977, Eastman Theatre

Ives, Charles   *Country Band March*
Barber, Samuel   *Commando March*
Bilik, Jerry   *Block M*
Sousa, John Philip   *Hands Across the Sea*
Benson, Warren   *Shadow Wood*
HELEN BOATWRIGHT, SOPRANO

INTERMISSION

Hodkinson, Sydney   *Cortege: Dirge-Canons*
Grainger, Percy   *Lincolnshire Posy*
Teike, Carl   *Old Comrades*
Delle Cese, Davide   *Inglesina*
Ganne, Gustav Luis (Roberts)   *Father of Victory*
Texidor, J. (Winter)   *Amparito Roca*
SYDNEY HODKINSON, CONDUCTOR

February 28, 1977, Eastman Theatre

Grainger, Percy   *Hill Song* No. 2
Mayuzumi, Toshiro   *Music with Sculpture*
Foley, Keith   *Evosträta*
BILL DOBBINS, PIANO

INTERMISSION

Schwantner, Joseph
    ". . . and the mountains rising nowhere"
BILL DOBBINS, PIANO
Reed, H. Owen   *La Fiesta Mexicana*
DONALD HUNSBERGER, CONDUCTOR

March 9–11, 1977, University of Maryland
College Band Directors National Association
Nineteenth National Conference
Krenek, Ernst   *Drei lustige Märsche*, op. 44

Grainger, Percy   *Hill Song* No. 2
FREDERICK FENNELL, GUEST CONDUCTOR
Mayuzumi, Toshiro   *Music with Sculpture*
Foley, Keith   *Evosträta*
BILL DOBBINS, PIANO
Schwantner, Joseph
    ". . . and the mountains rising nowhere"
BILL DOBBINS, PIANO
Reed, H. Owen   *La Fiesta Mexicana*
DONALD HUNSBERGER, CONDUCTOR

April 22, 1977, Eastman Theatre
PRISM III—Festa Italiana
Respighi, Ottorino (D'Elia)   *Feste Romane*
DONALD HUNSBERGER, CONDUCTOR

26th SEASON: 1977–78

September 26, 1977, Eastman Theatre
PRISM IV—Fanfare, a special prism concert
Bach, J. S. (Hunsberger)   Prelude in E-Flat
DONALD HUNSBERGER, CONDUCTOR

October 7, 1977, Kilbourn Hall
25th Anniversary Celebration Weekend Honoring
the Members of the Eastman Wind Ensemble and the
Ensemble's Founder, Dr. Frederick Fennell
Milhaud, Darius   *Suite Française*
DONALD HUNSBERGER, CONDUCTOR
Stravinsky, Igor   Octet for Wind Instruments
FRANK BATTISTI, CONDUCTOR
Reynolds, Verne   *Scenes Revisited*
H. ROBERT REYNOLDS, CONDUCTOR
Hindemith, Paul   Symphony in B-Flat
FREDERICK FENNELL, CONDUCTOR

October 8, 1977, Kilbourn Hall
25th Anniversary Celebration Weekend Honoring the
Members of the Eastman Wind Ensemble and the Ensemble's
Founder, Dr. Frederick Fennell
Schuman, William   *George Washington Bridge*
Persichetti, Vincent   *Divertimento*
Holst, Gustav   Second Suite in F
Grainger, Percy   *Lincolnshire Posy*

Bennett, Robert Russell   *Suite of Old American Dances*
Sousa, John Philip   *The Corcoran Cadets*
Jenkins, J. W. (Neff)   *Pieces of Eight*
Sousa, John Philip   *The Stars and Stripes Forever*
FREDERICK FENNELL, CONDUCTOR

November 4, 1977, Eastman Theatre
Kabalevsky, Dmitri (Hunsberger)
Overture to *Colas Breugnon*
Dahl, Ingolf   *Sinfonietta*
Benson, Warren   *The Passing Bell*
Corigliano, John   *Gazebo Dances*
DONALD HUNSBERGER, CONDUCTOR

December 2, 1977, Eastman Theatre
Nelson, Ron   *Savannah River Holiday*
Kessner, Daniel   *Wind Sculptures*
Hanson, Howard   *Variations on an Ancient Hymn*
Adler, Samuel   *A Little Night and Day Music*
Chance, John Barnes   Symphony No. 2
Sousa, John Philip   *On Parade*
Goldman, Edwin Franko   *Onward-Upward March*
Fucik, Julius   *Florentiner*, op. 214
DONALD HUNSBERGER, CONDUCTOR

February 3, 1978, Eastman Theatre
Ives, Charles (Sinclair)   *Overture and March: 1776*
Dello Joio, Norman   *Songs of Abelard*
Stravinsky, Igor   *Symphonies of Wind Instruments*
Mozart, W. A.   Divertimento No. 3 in B-Flat, K. 166
Benson, Warren   *The Leaves Are Falling*
Surinach, Carlos   *Sinfonietta Flamenca*
DONALD HUNSBERGER, CONDUCTOR

March 1, 1978, Eastman Theatre
Makris, Andreas (Bader)   *Aegean Festival Overture*
Persichetti, Vincent   Symphony No. 6
Hanson, Howard
Laude, Chorale, Variations and Metamorphoses
Sacco, Peter   *Four Sketches on Emerson Essays*
Nixon, Roger   *Fiesta del Pacifico*
DONALD HUNSBERGER, CONDUCTOR

May 10, 1978, Eastman Theatre
Holst, Gustav   First Suite in E-Flat
Benson, Warren   *The Leaves Are Falling*
Reynolds, Verne   *Scenes*
Prokofiev, Serge   March, op. 99
Wright, Rayburn   *Japanese Folk Song Fantasy*
RAYBURN WRIGHT, CONDUCTOR
Kamioka, Yoichi   *In Autumn Skies*
DONALD HUNSBERGER, CONDUCTOR

May 11, 1978, Eastman Theatre
Copland, Aaron   *Outdoor Overture*
Grainger, Percy   *Lincolnshire Posy*
Kineda, Bin   *Symphonic Movement*
Persichetti, Vincent   Symphony No. 6
Mayuzumi, Toshiro   *Music with Sculpture*
Wright, Rayburn   *Verberations*
MARK LOPEMAN, SOPRANO SAX
RAYBURN WRIGHT, CONDUCTOR
DONALD HUNSBERGER, CONDUCTOR

May 13–June 24, 1978
Six-week tour of Japan (Kambara Arts Agency) and
Southeast Asia (U.S. State Department)
25 concert appearances in Japan, Hong Kong, Philippines,
Indonesia, Malaysia, and South Korea
Bach, J. S. (Hunsberger)   Passacaglia and Fugue
in C minor
Holst, Gustav   First Suite in E-Flat
Benson, Warren   *The Leaves Are Falling*
Reynolds, Verne   *Scenes*
Prokofieff, Serge   March, op. 99
Wright, Rayburn   *Japanese Folk Song Fantasy*
(COMPOSER CONDUCTING)
Kamioka, Yoichi   *In Autumn Skies*
Copland, Aaron   *Outdoor Overture*
Grainger, Percy   *Lincolnshire Posy*
Kineda, Bin   *Symphonic Movement*
Persichetti, Vincent   Symphony No. 6
Mayuzumi, Toshiro   *Music with Sculpture*
Wright, Rayburn   *Verberations*
MARK LOPEMAN, SOPRANO SAX
(COMPOSER CONDUCTING)
DONALD HUNSBERGER, CONDUCTOR
RAYBURN WRIGHT, ASSOCIATE CONDUCTOR

27th SEASON: 1978–79

October 6, 1978, Eastman Theatre
Changes in the Winds
The Manchester Brass Band Concert of July 1, 1858:
Eaton's Grand March
"Giorno d'Orrore" (Semiramide)
Quickstep—*Free and Easy*
Serenade—*Departed Days*
Congo's Quickstep
Brant, Henry   *Angels and Devils*
BONITA BOYD, FLUTE
Schober, Brian   *Sunflower Splendour*
KATE NESBIT, MEZZO SOPRANO

INTERMISSION

Schwantner, Joseph
". . . and the mountains rising nowhere"
Hanson, Howard
Young Person's Guide to the Six-Tone Scale
BARRY SNYDER, PIANO
Copland, Aaron   *Emblems*
DONALD HUNSBERGER, CONDUCTOR

**October 19, 1978, Alice Tully Hall, Lincoln Center
for the Performing Arts**
The Manchester Brass Band Concert of July 1, 1858:
Eaton's Grand March
"Giorno d'Orrore" (Semiramide)
Quickstep—*Free and Easy*
Serenade—*Departed Days*
Congo's Quickstep
Brant, Henry   *Angels and Devils*
BONITA BOYD, FLUTE
Schwantner, Joseph
". . . and the mountains rising nowhere"

INTERMISSION

Hanson, Howard
Young Person's Guide to the Six-Tone Scale
BARRY SNYDER, PIANO
Copland, Aaron   *Emblems*

December 1, 1978, Eastman Theatre
Surinach, Carlos   *Paeans and Dances of Heathen Iberia*
Krommer, Franz   *Partita*, op. 69

Gould, Morton   Symphony for Band (*West Point*)

INTERMISSION

Kurka, Robert   Suite from *The Good Soldier Schweik*
Copland, Aaron   *The Red Pony*
DONALD HUNSBERGER, CONDUCTOR

February 7, 1979, Eastman Theatre
Hartley, Walter   *Sinfonia* No. 4
Hindemith, Paul
Concert Music for Wind Orchestra, op. 41

INTERMISSION

Maslanka, David
Concerto for Piano, Winds and Percussion
BILL DOBBINS, PIANO
Strauss, Richard   Suite in B-Flat, op. 4
Grainger, Percy   *Lincolnshire Posy*
FREDERICK FENNELL, CONDUCTOR

February 23, 1979, Eastman Theatre
PRISM VI: El Espiritu de España
Traditional (Koff)   *La Virgen de la Macarena*
GEORGE VOSBOUGH, TRUMPET
CARL ATKINS, CONDUCTOR

March 30, 1979, Kilbourn Hall
Bach, J. S. (Whitwell)
Capriccio "On the Departure of a Friend"
Kessner, Daniel   *Variations*
DANIEL KESSNER, CONDUCTOR
Beethoven, L. van   *Siegessinfonie*
Schmitt, Florent (Duker)   *Dionysiaques*
DAVID WHITWELL, CONDUCTOR

April 30, 1979, Eastman Theatre
Gabrieli, Giovanni   *Jubilate Deo*
Mozart, W. A.   Serenade in B-Flat Major, K. 361

INTERMISSION

Husa, Karel   *An American Te Deum*
MARK EDWIN JOHNSON, BARITONE
CORNELL UNIVERSITY CHORUS
KAREL HUSA, CONDUCTOR

28th SEASON: 1979–80

October 5, 1979, Kilbourn Hall

An Evening of French Music for Winds

Bozza, Eugene   *Children's Overture*
Gounod, Charles   *Petite Symphonie*
Music for Le Quatorze Juillet:
  Honegger, Arthur   *Marche on the Bastille*
  Roussel, Albert   Prelude to Act II
  Auric, George   *La Palais Royale*
Gotkovsky, Ida   *Poéme du Feu*
          DONALD HUNSBERGER, CONDUCTOR

October 20, 1979, Eastman Theatre

PRISM VII: Eastman Milestones

Hindemith, Paul   Symphony in B-Flat, mvt. 1
          DONALD HUNSBERGER, CONDUCTOR

November 9, 1979, Eastman Theatre

Nelson, Ron   *Rocky Point Holiday*
Schuman, William   *New England Triptych*
Balassa, Sándor   *Lupercalia*

              INTERMISSION

Hindemith, Paul   Symphony in B-Flat
Adler, Samuel   *Southwestern Sketches*
          DONALD HUNSBERGER, CONDUCTOR

November 30, 1979, Eastman Theatre

*Program with the Eastman Women's Chorus and
the Eastman Chorale*

Lindroth, Scott   *Medieval Transformations*
Holland, A. G.   *Ultimus*
Persichetti, Vincent   *Celebrations*
          (WITH THE EASTMAN CHORALE)
          DONALD HUNSBERGER, CONDUCTOR

February 8, 1980, Eastman Theatre

*A Program of Music for Wind Band
by American Composers*

Hanson, Howard   *Dies Natalis*
Benson, Warren   *The Leaves Are Falling*
Persichetti, Vincent   *Masquerade*

              INTERMISSION

Benson, Warren
          Symphony for Drums and Wind Orchestra
Dobbins, Bill *Celebration* for Jazz Ensemble and Winds
          EASTMAN JAZZ ENSEMBLE
          DONALD HUNSBERGER, CONDUCTOR

March 24, 1980, Kilbourn Hall

*An Adventure in 20th-century Compositions
for Large Wind Ensemble*

McCulloh, Byron   *Monographs*
Rorem, Ned   *Sinfonia*
Lewis, Robert Hall
          Osservazioni II for Winds, Keyboard, Harp and
                              Percussion
          CARL ATKINS, ASSISTING CONDUCTOR

              INTERMISSION

Reynolds, Verne   *Last Scenes*
          VERNE REYNOLDS, HORN
Finney, Ross Lee   *Skating on the Sheyenne*
          DONALD HUNSBERGER, CONDUCTOR

April 30, 1980, Kilbourn Hall

Bach, C. P. E.
          Six Sonatas for Two Horns, Two Flutes, Two
Clarinets and Bassoon, W. 184 (Sonatas I, II, IV, V)
Bottesini, Giovanni (Zimmerman)
              Grand Duo for Violin and Contrabass
          JOHN CELENTANO, VIOLIN
          J. B. VANDERMARK, BASS
Poulenc, Francis   *Suite Française*
Wilder, Alec   Serenade for Wind Ensemble
          DONALD HUNSBERGER, CONDUCTOR

29th SEASON: 1980–81

September 26, 1980, Eastman Theatre

Fall Festival of Winds

Bach, J. S. (Paynter)
          Toccata, Adagio and Fugue in C Major
Schoenberg, Arnold   Theme and Variations, op. 43a
Badings, Henk   *Greensleeves*
Grainger, Percy   *Hill Song* No. 2
Russell, Armand   *Symphony in Three Images*
          DONALD HUNSBERGER, CONDUCTOR

October 27, 1980, Eastman Theatre

Copland, Aaron   *An Outdoor Overture*
Hummel, Johann Nepomuk (Corley)
                              Concerto for Trumpet
        BARBARA BUTLER, TRUMPET
Davison, John
        Symphony for Wind Instruments and Percussion

INTERMISSION

Vaughan Williams, Ralph   *Toccata Marziale*
Grøndahl, Launy (Hunsberger)
                              Concerto for Trombone
        JOHN MARCELLUS, TROMBONE
Reed, H. Owen   *La Fiesta Mexicana*
Grafulla, Claudio   *Washington Greys*
Sousa, John Philip   *The Liberty Bell*
        DONALD HUNSBERGER, CONDUCTOR

November 19, 1980, Eastman Theatre

An Evening of Exotic Wind Textures
Williams, John T.   *Sinfonietta*
Mayuzumi, Toshiro   *Music with Sculpture*

INTERMISSION

Husa, Karel
        Concerto for Percussion and Wind Ensemble
        DONALD HUNSBERGER, CONDUCTOR

INTERMISSION

Messiaen, Olivier   *Et expecto resurrectionem mortuorum*
        RODNEY WINTHER, CONDUCTOR

January 30, 1981, Eastman Theatre

Gallus, Jacobus (Kandel)   *In Resurrectione tuae Christe*
Gabrieli, Giovanni (Smith)   Sonata XIX
Mozart, W. A.   Serenade No. 10 in B-flat, K. 361

INTERMISSION

Stravinsky, Igor
        Concerto for Piano and Wind Instruments
        DAVID BURGE, PIANO
Adler, Samuel   Symphony No. 3, "Diptych"
        DONALD HUNSBERGER, CONDUCTOR

February 23, 1981, Kilbourn Hall

Kabalevsky, Dmitri (Hunsberger)
                      Overture to *Colas Breugnon*
Albert, Thomas
                B-flat Piece for Winds and Percussion
Bassett, Leslie
        Sounds, Shapes, Symbols in Four Movements
        DONALD HUNSBERGER, CONDUCTOR
Arnold, Malcolm (Johnstone)   *Four English Dances*
Jacob, Gordon   *Music for a Festival*
        RODNEY WINTHER, CONDUCTOR

March 4, 1981, Eastman Theatre

Mendelssohn, Felix   Overture in C for *Harmoniemusik*
Holst, Gustav   Second Suite in F
        DONALD HUNSBERGER, CONDUCTOR
Giannini, Vittorio   Symphony No. 3
        MONRO SHERRILL, CONDUCTOR

INTERMISSION

Thomas, David   *Dance Men*
Stravinsky, Igor   *Symphonies of Wind Instruments*
        CARL ATKINS, CONDUCTOR

April 6, 1981, Eastman Theatre

Jolas, Betsy   *Lassus Ricercare*
Larsson, Lars-Eric (Walker)
        Concertino for Trombone, op. 45, no. 7
        STEVE WITSER, TROMBONE
Hodkinson, Sydney   *Bach Variations*

INTERMISSION

Schütz, Heinrich   *Absalom, fili mi*
        THOMAS PAUL, BASS
Benson, Warren   *The Beaded Leaf*
        THOMAS PAUL, BASS
Benson, Warren   *The Solitary Dancer*
        DONALD HUNSBERGER, CONDUCTOR

April 29, 1981, Kilbourn Hall

Music for the Young at Heart
Susato, Tilman (Iveson)   Suite from *The Danserye*
Stamitz, Karl (Reynolds)
                      Concerto for Horn and Winds
        EDWARD DESKUR, SOLOIST

Ravel, Maurice (Hunsberger)
"La Vallée des cloches" from *Miroirs*
Persichetti, Vincent   *Divertimento,* op.42

INTERMISSION

Mozart, W. A.   Serenade No. 14 in E-flat, K. 375
DONALD HUNSBERGER, CONDUCTOR

INTERMISSION

Makris, Andreas (Bader)   *Aegean Festival Overture*
Sullivan, Arthur (Duthoit)   *Pineapple Poll*
FREDERICK FENNELL, CONDUCTOR

30th SEASON: 1981–82

October 7, 1981, Kilbourn Hall
Clarke, Jeremiah (Iveson)   *Trumpet Voluntary*
FRANK TAMBURRO AND CHRISTOPHER
TRANCHITELLA, TRUMPETS
Gabrieli, Giovanni (Fennell)   *Canzon noni toni a 12*
Jacob, Gordon   *William Byrd Suite*
Bach, J. S. (Hunsberger)
Passacaglia and Fugue in C Minor
Strauss, Richard   Serenade for Winds, op. 7
Downs, Lamont   *Sinfonia II* for Wind Ensemble
Bennett, Robert Russell
Symphonic Songs for Wind Band
DONALD HUNSBERGER, CONDUCTOR

October 28, 1981, Eastman Theatre
*Tribute to Howard Hanson: An Eighty-fifth Birthday
Celebration*
Hanson, Howard   *Chorale and Alleluia*

November 6, 1981, Eastman Theatre
36th Anniversary of the United Nations
Altenburg, Johann Concerto for Clarini and Timpani
Hindemith, Paul *Konzertmusik für Blasorchester,* op. 41
Dahl, Ingolf   *Sinfonietta*
DONALD HUNSBERGER, CONDUCTOR

INTERMISSION

Hartley, Walter   Concerto for Twenty-three Winds
Holloway, John   *Wood-up Quickstep*
Sousa, John Philip   *Semper Fidelis*

Prokofieff, Serge   March, op. 99
RODNEY WINTHER, CONDUCTOR

December 10, 1981, Kilbourn Hall
Sweelinck, Jan Pieterszoon (Walters)
Ballo del Granduca
Kelterborn, Rudolph   *Miroirs*
Lendvay, Kamilló
Concertino for Piano, Winds, Percussion and Harp
YOSHIKO IMAI, PIANO

INTERMISSION

Schuller, Gunther
Symphony for Brass and Percussion
Berio, Luciano (Marciniak)   *Petite Suite*
DONALD HUNSBERGER, CONDUCTOR

January 15, 1982, Eastman Theatre
PRISM VIII: Dreams and Fantasies
Mayuzumi, Toshiro   *Music with Sculpture*
DONALD HUNSBERGER, CONDUCTOR

January 29, 1982, Eastman Theatre
Corigliano, John   *Gazebo Dances*
Hartley, Walter   *In Memoriam*
Reynolds, Verne   *Scenes*
Gould, Morton   Symphony for Band (*West Point*)
Goldman, Edwin Franko   *Onward-Upward*
Sousa, John Philip   *Belle of Chicago*
DONALD HUNSBERGER, CONDUCTOR

February 26, 1982, Eastman Theatre
Saint-Saëns, Camille (Whitwell)
Occident and Orient, op. 25
Liadov, Anatol (Goldman)   *Eight Russian Folk Songs*
Sparke, Philip
Gaudium, A Concert Piece for Wind Symphony
Orchestra
Rouse, Christopher   *Thor*

INTERMISSION

Kraft, William   *Dialogues and Entertainments*
CLARON McFADDEN, SOPRANO
Sousa, John Philip   *Jack Tar March*
Sousa, John Philip   *New York Hippodrome*
DONALD HUNSBERGER, CONDUCTOR

April 5, 1982, Eastman Theatre

Schwantner, Joseph	*From A Dark Millennium*
Ravel, Maurice (Hunsberger)	La Vallée des Cloches
Arutiunian, Alexandre (Duker)	
	Concerto for Trumpet

JONATHAN KRUGER, TRUMPET

INTERMISSION

Adler, Samuel	*Snow Tracks*

TERESA RINGHOLZ, SOPRANO
DONALD HUNSBERGER, CONDUCTOR

April 7, 1982, Eastman Theatre
A Concert of Marches by John Philip Sousa

Sousa, John Philip	*Anchor and Star*
	Comrades of the Legion
	El Capitan
	Hail to the Spirit of Liberty
	Jack Tar
	The Liberty Bell
	The Loyal Legion
	King Cotton
	The Man Behind the Gun
	Semper Fidelis
	The Stars and Stripes Forever
	The Thunderer
	Washington Post
	Who's Who in Navy Blue
	The High School Cadets
	The Corcoran Cadets

April 30, 1982, Eastman Theatre

Williams, Clifton	*Fanfare and Allegro*
Jacob, Gordon	*An Original Suite*
Grainger, Percy	*Lincolnshire Posy*
Hindemith, Paul	
Konzertmusik for Piano, Two Harps and Brass	

RUTH MARROW, PIANO
RODNEY WINTHER, CONDUCTOR

Shostakovich, Dmitri (Hunsberger)	
	Festive Overture, op. 96
Bennett, Robert Russell	*Suite of Old American Dances*
Walton, William (Duthoit)	*Crown Imperial March*

DONALD HUNSBERGER, CONDUCTOR

31st SEASON: 1982–83

September 28, 1982, Eastman Theatre

Bernstein, Leonard (Beeler)	Overture to *Candide*
Jacob, Gordon	*William Byrd Suite*
Gregson, Edward	*Metamorphoses*
Hanson, Howard	*Dies Natalis*
Ginastera, Albert (John)	
	"Danza Final" from the ballet *Estancia*

DONALD HUNSBERGER, CONDUCTOR

October 16, 1982, Eastman Theatre
PRISM IX: A Little Night Music

Holst, Gustav (Smith)	"Jupiter" from *The Planets*

DONALD HUNSBERGER, CONDUCTOR

November 3, 1982, Eastman Theatre

Grainger, Percy	*Lincolnshire Posy*
Stravinsky, Igor	*Symphonies of Wind Instruments*
Gilmore, Bernard	
	Five Folk Songs for Soprano and Wind Band

ROBYNNE REDMON, MEZZO SOPRANO

Rogers, Bernard	*Three Japanese Dances*

ROBYNNE REDMON, MEZZO SOPRANO
DONALD HUNSBERGER, CONDUCTOR

December 13, 1982, Eastman Theatre

Gotkovsky, Ida	*Poéme du Feu*
Hindemith, Paul	*Symphony for Band*
Dello Joio, Norman	Scenes from *The Louvre*
Copland, Aaron	*Emblems*

DONALD HUNSBERGER, CONDUCTOR

January 23, 1983, Eastman Theatre
Sousa Spectacular I

Makris, Andreas (Bader)	*Aegean Festival*
Liszt, Franz	Second Hungarian Rhapsody

JOHN BECK, MARIMBA

Chance, John Barnes	*Elegy*

Pryor, Arthur   *Thoughts of Love*
JOHN MARCELLUS, TROMBONE
Sullivan, Arthur (Sousa)   *The Pirates of Penzance*
Reed, H. Owen
              La Fiesta Mexicana—Prelude and Aztec Dance
Arban, J. B. (Goldman)   *Carnival of Venice*
BARBARA BUTLER, CHARLES GEYER, TRUMPETS
Sousa, John Philip   *Hands Across The Sea*
Alford, Kenneth   *The Mad Major*
Fucik, Julius   *The Florentiner*
DONALD HUNSBERGER, CONDUCTOR

March 2, 1983, Kilbourn Hall
Gabrieli, Andrea (Ghedini)   *Aria della battaglia*
Mozart, W. A.   Serenade No.10 in B-Flat, K. 361
Berg, Alban
Kammerkonzert for Piano and Violin with Thirteen
                                              Winds
VIVIAN WEILERSTEIN, PIANO
DONALD WEILERSTEIN, VIOLIN
DONALD HUNSBERGER, CONDUCTOR

April 8, 1983, Eastman Theatre
Adler, Samuel   *Snow Tracks*
TERSEA RINGHOLTZ, SOPRANO
Bach, J. S. (Hunsberger)
                    Passacaglia and Fugue in C Major
White, Donald H. (Olson)   *Tetra Ergon*
MARK LUSK, TROMBONE
Stravinsky, Igor   *Symphony of Psalms*
EASTMAN CHORALE
DONALD NEUEN, CONDUCTOR
DONALD HUNSBERGER, CONDUCTOR

32nd SEASON: 1983–84

September 30, 1983, Eastman Theatre
Dukas, Paul   Fanfare from *La Peri*
Goldstaub, Paul   *Festival Prelude*
Holst, Gustav   Second Suite in F
Benson, Warren   *The Leaves Are Falling*
Nelson, Ron   *Savannah River Holiday*
Dorff, Daniel   *Symphony of Delusions*
DONALD HUNSBERGER, CONDUCTOR

November 9, 1983, Eastman Theatre
Hindemith, Paul *Konzertmusik für Blasorchester*, op. 41
Hovhaness, Alan *Return and Rebuild the Desolate Places*
WILLIAM CAMPBELL, TRUMPET
Kelterborn, Rudolph   *Miroirs*
Dahl, Ingolf   *Sinfonietta*
DONALD HUNSBERGER, CONDUCTOR

December 7, 1983, Kilbourn Hall
Krommer, Franz   *Partita*, op. 69
Erickson, Frank   *Wind Chimes*
Bottje, Will Gay   *Symphonic Allegro*
Rachmaninoff, Sergei (Andrews)
                              Symphonic Dance No. 1
Tull, Fisher   *Toccata*
DONALD HUNSBERGER, CONDUCTOR

January 20, 1984, Eastman Theatre
Michalsky, Donal
              Fanfare after Seventeenth Century Dances
Noon, David   *Sweelinck Variations*, Set III
Strauss, Richard   Serenade in E-Flat Major, op. 7
Poulenc, Francis   *Suite Française*

INTERMISSION

Morawetz, Oscar
Memorial to Martin Luther King for Solo Violoncello
              and Winds, Percussion and Piano
PAUL KATZ, VIOLONCELLO
DONALD HUNSBERGER, CONDUCTOR

February 19, 1984, Eastman Theatre
Sousa Spectacular II
Suppé, Franz von (Tobani)
          Overture to *Morning, Noon and Night in Vienna*
Clarke, Herbert L. (Hunsberger)   *The Three Aces*
WILLIAM CAMPBELL, PETER MARGULIES, AND
PHILIP SNEDECOR, TRUMPET
Fauchet, Paul (Gillette)
              Nocturne from Symphony in B-Flat
Weber, Carl Maria von (Lake)   Concertino, op. 26
THOMAS MARTIN, CLARINET
Ponchielli, Amilcare
              Dance of the Hours from *La Gioconda*
Sousa, John Philip   *The Invincible Eagle*

February 19, 1984 (cont.)

Herbert, Victor (Hunsberger) *Ah, Sweet Mystery of Life*

Herbert, Victor (Hunsberger)

    The Italian Street Song from *Naughty Marietta*

    TERESA RINGHOLZ, SOPRANO

Tschaikovsky, Piotr Ilych (Winterbottom)

                    Capriccio Italien

    DONALD HUNSBERGER, CONDUCTOR

March 28, 1984, Eastman Theatre

Jenkins, Joseph Wilcox   *American Overture* for Band

Ives, Charles (Sinclair)   *Overture and March: 1776*

Ives, Charles (Rhoads)   Variations on "America"

Nelson, Ron   *Medieval Suite*

Buhr, Glenn   *Epigrams*

Hindemith, Paul   Symphony in B-Flat

    DONALD HUNSBERGER, CONDUCTOR

March 30, 1984, Eastman Theatre

PRISM X: "A Sesquicentennial Scrapbook"

Jenkins, Joseph Wilcox   *American Overture* for Band

    DONALD HUNSBERGER, CONDUCTOR

April 20, 1984, Eastman Theatre

Jenkins, Joseph Wilcox   *American Overture* for Band

Ives, Charles (Rhoads)   Variations on "America"

Basta, James   Concerto for Marimba and Orchestra

    MICHAEL BURRITT, MARIMBA

Wagner, Richard (Cailliett)

    Elsa's Procession to the Cathedral from *Lohengrin*

Husa, Karel   Concerto for Percussion

    KEITH ALEO, MICHAEL BURRITT,

    WADE CULBREATH, ROGER BOYCE,

    NATHAN NORMAN, PERCUSSION

    DONALD HUNSBERGER, CONDUCTOR

33rd SEASON: 1984–85

September 30, 1984, Eastman Theatre

Concert honoring the Inauguration of Dennis O'Brien as President of the University of Rochester (with Eastman Chorale and Philharmonia)

Hanson, Howard   *Chorale and Alleluia*

Benson, Warren   *Wings*

Holst, Gustav   *Hammersmith*

Prokofieff, Serge   March, op. 99

    DONALD HUNSBERGER, CONDUCTOR

October 19, 1984, Eastman Theatre

Reed, H. Owen   *La Fiesta Mexicana*

Benson, Warren

    Symphony for Drums and Wind Orchestra

Benson, Warren   *Wings*

Hanson, Howard   *Laude*

Adler, Samuel   *Southwestern Sketches*

    DONALD HUNSBERGER, CONDUCTOR

December 5, 1984, Eastman Theatre

Mennin, Peter   *Canzona*

Rogers, Rodney   *Prevailing Winds*

Rodrigo, Joaquin   *Adagio*

Hartley, Walter

    Symphony No. 2 for Large Wind Ensemble

    MALLORY THOMPSON, CONDUCTOR

White, John   Concerto for Flute and Wind Ensemble

    BONITA BOYD, FLUTE

Taub, Bruce   *Band Piece (Chromatic Essay)*

    DONALD HUNSBERGER, CONDUCTOR

February 6, 1985, Kilbourn Hall

Gabrieli, Giovanni   *Canzone*

              Sonate pian' e forte

            Canzon in double echo

           Canzon noni toni a 12

DONALD HUNSBERGER AND MICHAEL VOTTA,

    CONDUCTORS

Johnston, Donald   *Montage*

Dvorak, Antonin   Serenade in D Minor, op.44

    MALLORY THOMPSON, CONDUCTOR

Lewis, James

    You Must Remember This for Jazz Quartet and Wind Ensemble

    DONALD HUNSBERGER, CONDUCTOR

February 24, 1985, Eastman Theatre

Sousa Spectacular III

Gomez, Antonio Carlos (Clarke)   *Il Guarany* Overture

Herbert, Victor (Langey)   *Badinage*

Bach, Vincent   *Hungarian Melodies*
   BARBARA BUTLER, CORNET
Weinberger, Jaromir (Bainum)
     Polka and Fugue from *Schwanda, the Bagpiper*
Sousa, John Philip   *The Gallant Seventh*
Thiere, Charles Le   *L'Oiseau du Bois*
   DIANE SCHUMANN, PICCOLO
Gershwin, George (Bennett)
     Selections from *Porgy and Bess*
   DONALD HUNSBERGER, CONDUCTOR

May 3, 1985, Eastman Theatre

Krommer, Franz   Concerto for Two Clarinets, op. 35
   NATHAN WILLIAMS, MARY BETH SKAGGS,
     CLARINETS
   DONALD HUNSBERGER, CONDUCTOR
Wagner, Richard (Thompson)
     Prelude to Act III, Dance and Finale from *Die
          Meistersinger*
Husa, Karel   Concerto for Wind Ensemble
   MALLORY THOMPSON, CONDUCTOR

34th SEASON: 1985–86

October 10, 1985, St. Agnes High School, Rochester, New York

*Concert Honoring the Inauguration of Robert J. Joynt as
Dean of the University of Rochester Medical School*
Mendelssohn, Felix   Overture for Wind Band, op. 24
Chance, John Barnes   *Elegy*
Vaughan Williams, Ralph   *English Folk Song Suite*
Processional:
  Wagner, Richard
     Homage March for King Ludwig of Bavaria
  Elgar, Edward   *Pomp and Circumstance* No. 1, op. 39
  Walton, William   *Crown Imperial*
Concert Piece:
  Grainger, Percy   *Irish Tune from County Derry*
Recessional:
  Shostakovich, Dmitri (Hunsberger)
             Festive Overture, op. 96
   DONALD HUNSBERGER, CONDUCTOR

October 19, 1985, Eastman Theatre

PRISM XII: Tour de Force
Bernstein, Leonard (Hunsberger)
     Symphonic Dances from *West Side Story*
   DONALD HUNSBERGER, CONDUCTOR

November 1–2, 1985, Eastman Theatre

*The First Eastman Wind Ensemble Symposium,
Sponsored by the Eastman School of Music and
The Institute of American Music*
Friday, Nov. 1, 1985, 2:00 p.m.

Bulow, Harry   *Textures*
Rudin, Andrew   *Stentoriae*
   NORA CHIANG, PIANO
Stock, David
   Evensong for English Horn and Wind Orchestra
   NANCY AMBROSE, ENGLISH HORN
Speck, Frederick   Concerto for Wind Orchestra
Macchia, Salvatore   *Granite*
   PETER BLACKBURN, PIANO
   STEVEN SEARFOSS, MARIMBA
   THOMAS WOLFE, ELECTRIC GUITAR
Toensin, Richard
     Concerto for Flutes and Wind Orchestra
   BONITA BOYD, FLUTE, ALTO FLUTE AND PICCOLO
Thorne, Nicholas   *Adagio Music*
Snow, David
   Sinfonia Concertante for Piano, Horn, Percussion and
              Wind Ensemble
   SYLVIA WANG, PIANO
   CAROLYN COMFORT, HORN
   ROGER BOYCE, TIMPANI
   WAYNE KILLIUS, PERCUSSION
   STEVEN SEARFOSS, PERCUSSION
   DONALD HUNSBERGER, CONDUCTOR

Friday Nov. 1, 1985, 8:15 p.m.—Reduced Instrumentations

Myers, Robert
   Enigma Virginia for Percussion and Wind Ensemble
   EASTMAN JAZZ ENSEMBLE
   RAYBURN WRIGHT, DIRECTOR
   RUSSELL BURGE, PERCUSSION
   WAYNE KILLIUS, PERCUSSION
   CHRIS PERSAD, CORNET
Adolphe, Bruce *Chiaroscuro* for Double Wind Quintet

November 1–2, 1985 (cont.)

Miller, Eric	*Serenade for Eleven Instruments*
Meacham, Margaret	*Moonshadows* for Flute Octet
Miller, Dennis	*Piece in Three Parts*

DONALD HUNSBERGER, CONDUCTOR

Saturday Nov. 2, 1985, 10:00—Large Instrumentations

Hollomon, Samuel	Symphony No. 2
Mygatt, Louise	*Windchanges*
Rosenbaum, Joel	

Fantasia Allucinante for Flute and Wind Orchestra

BONITA BOYD, FLUTE

Rodriquez, Robert

The Seven Deadly Sins (A Ballet for Wind Ensemble)

DONALD HUNSBERGER, CONDUCTOR

December 11, 1985, Eastman Theatre

Bach, J. S. (Boyd)	Fantasia and Fugue in G Minor

DONALD HUNSBERGER, CONDUCTOR

Otterloo, Willem van	*Sinfonietta*

MICHAEL VOTTA, CONDUCTOR

Bulow, Harry	*Textures*

MICHAEL VOTTA, CONDUCTOR

Ticheli, Frank	*Concertino* for Trombone

JOHN MARCELLUS, TROMBONE

Hidas, Frigyes	*Circus Suite*

DONALD HUNSBERGER, CONDUCTOR

February 5, 1986, Kilbourn Hall

Mozart, W. A.	Serenade No. 10 in B-Flat, K. 370a

MICHAEL VOTTA, CONDUCTOR

INTERMISSION

McCulloh, Byron

Concertino No. 2, "Il Pomo della Discordia," for Large Trombone and Small Wind Ensemble"

BYRON McCULLOH, TROMBONE

DONALD HUNSBERGER, CONDUCTOR

Stravinsky, Igor	*Symphonies of Wind Instruments*

MICHAEL VOTTA, CONDUCTOR

INTERMISSION

Israel, Brian

Concerto for Clarinet and Wind Ensemble

CHARLES NEIDICH, CLARINET

DONALD HUNSBERGER, CONDUCTOR

February 23, 1986, Eastman Theatre

Sousa Spectacular IV

Walton, William (Richardson)	*Orb and Sceptre*
Thomas, Ambrose (Safranek)	
	Overture to *Raymond* (*The Queen's Secret*)
Buck, Larry	*Freckles Rag*

JOHN BECK, SOLOIST

Sullivan, Arthur (Mackerras)	*Pineapple Poll*
Fucik, Julius	*The Florentiner*

INTERMISSION

Sousa, John Philip	*The Stars and Stripes Forever*
Weber, Carl Maria von (Brown)	
	Polacca from Second Concerto for Clarinet

PERFORMED BY THE CLARINET SECTION

Tchaikovsky, Piotr Ilyich (Laurendeau)	*Marche Slav*

DONALD HUNSBERGER, CONDUCTOR

April 4, 1986, Eastman Theatre

Holst, Gustav	First Suite in E-Flat
Welcher, Dan	*Arches, An Impression* for Concert Band
Morris, Robert	*Cuts* for Large Wind Ensemble
Rossini, Giacomo (Hermann)	
	Introduction, Theme, and Variations

AYAKO OSHIMA, CLARINET

DONALD HUNSBERGER, CONDUCTOR

April 30, 1986, Eastman Theatre

Berg, Alban

Kammerkonzert for Violin and Piano with Thirteen Winds

ABRAM LOFT, VIOLIN

ROBERT SPILLMAN, PIANO

MICHAEL VOTTA, CONDUCTOR

Giannini, Vittorio	Praeludium and Allegro
Tomasi, Henri	Concerto for Trombone

MARK KELLOGG, TROMBONE

Grainger, Percy	*Lincolnshire Posy*

DONALD HUNSBERGER, CONDUCTOR

35th SEASON: 1986–87

October 1, 1986, Eastman Theatre

Copland, Aaron	*An Outdoor Overture*
Grainger, Percy	*Hill Song* No. 2

Stravinsky, Igor   *Symphonies of Wind Instruments*
Iannaccone, Anthony   *Of Fire and Ice*
Mahr, Timothy   Fantasia in G
DONALD HUNSBERGER, CONDUCTOR

October 26, 1986, Eastman Theatre
Celebration of 90th Birthday of Howard Hanson
Hanson, Howard   *Dies Natalis*
DONALD HUNSBERGER, CONDUCTOR

November 7, 1986, Eastman Theatre
Williams, Clifton   Fanfare and Allegro
Hartley, Walter   Concerto for Twenty-three Winds
DONALD HUNSBERGER, CONDUCTOR
Nelson, Ron   *Medieval Suite*
DAVID WALLACE, CONDUCTOR

INTERMISSION

Messiaen, Olivier   *Et expecto resurrectionen mortuorum*
DONALD HUNSBERGER, CONDUCTOR

December 10, 1986, Kilbourn Hall
Mendelssohn, Felix
          Overture for *Harmoniemusik*, op. 24
Strauss, Richard   Serenade, op. 7
Krenek, Ernst   *Three Merry Marches*
Rodrigo, Joaquin   *Adagio* for Wind Orchestra
Weill, Kurt   *Little Threepenny Music*
DONALD HUNSBERGER, CONDUCTOR

February 4, 1987, Eastman Theatre
Holst, Gustav   Second Suite in F
Hindemith, Paul
      Konzertmusik für Blasorchester, op. 41 (1927)
Vaughan Williams, Ralph   *English Folk Song Suite*
Kelterborn, Rudolph   *Miroirs*
Grainger, Percy   *Lads of Wamphray*
DONALD HUNSBERGER, CONDUCTOR

February 22, 1987, Eastman Theatre
Sousa Spectacular V
Walton, William (Duthoit)   *Orb and Sceptre*
Von Suppe, Franz (Meyerelles)
                          Poet and Peasant Overture
Clarke, Herbert L. (Hunsberger)   *The Three Aces*
      PHILIP GIBB, YVONNE TOLL, AND
      DAVID BAMONTE, TRUMPETS
Grainger, Percy   *Irish Tune from Country Derry*
Weinberger, Jaromir (Bainum)
      Polka and Fugue from *Schwanda, the Bagpiper*
Goldman, Edwin Franko   *On the Mall*

INTERMISSION

Texidor, J. (Winter)   *Amparito Roca*
Bernstein, Leonard (Bernstein)
            "Glitter and Be Gay" from *Candide*
      SUSAN BARKER, SOPRANO
Holst, Gustav   First Suite in E-flat
DONALD HUNSBERGER, CONDUCTOR

March 23, 1987, Eastman Theatre
Concluding concert of the East Coast and Canada tour with
Wynton Marsalis, cornet soloist
Concert appearances: Burlington (Vermont), Montreal,
Toronto, London (Ontario), Lewisburg (Pennsylvania),
Boston, Philadelphia, Washington D.C., Elmira (New
York), New York City, Rochester (New York).
Walton, William (Richardson)   *Orb and Sceptre*
Holst, Gustav   Second Suite in F
Schwantner, Joseph
            ". . . and the mountains rising nowhere"
Arban, J. B. (Hunsberger)
            Variations on *Le Carnaval de Venise*
      WYNTON MARSALIS, CORNET
Levy, Jules (Hunsberger)   *Grand Russian Fantasie*
      WYNTON MARSALIS, CORNET
Traditional (Hunsberger)
            Sometimes I Feel Like a Motherless Child
      WYNTON MARSALIS, CORNET
Grainger, Percy   *Lads of Wamphray*
Arban, J. B. (Hunsberger)   *Fantasie Brillante*
      WYNTON MARSALIS, CORNET
DONALD HUNSBERGER, CONDUCTOR

May 6, 1987, Eastman Theatre
Combined Concert with the Eastman Wind Orchestra
Strauss, Richard   *Fanfare Stadt Wien*
          COMBINED BRASS ENSEMBLE
          WAYNE JEFFREY, CONDUCTOR
Castérède, Jacques   *Divertissement d'Eté*
          EASTMAN WIND ORCHESTRA
          WAYNE JEFFREY, CONDUCTOR
DePonte, Neil   Concerto for Marimba
          LUANNE WARNER, MARIMBA
          EASTMAN WIND ENSEMBLE
       DONALD HUNSBERGER, CONDUCTOR
Liptak, David   *Soundings*
          EASTMAN WIND ENSEMBLE
       DONALD HUNSBERGER, CONDUCTOR

          INTERMISSION

Handel, G. F.   *Music for the Royal Fireworks*
          COMBINED ENSEMBLES
          WAYNE JEFFREY, CONDUCTOR
Hindemith, Paul   Symphony in B-Flat
          COMBINED ENSEMBLES
       DAVID WALLACE, CONDUCTOR

          36th SEASON: 1987–88

October 24, 1987, Eastman Theatre
Rochester Association for the United Nations Concert
Coates, Eric (Williams)   *London Every Day Suite*
Berlioz, Hector (Goldman)
  Recitative and Prayer from *Grand Symphony Funébre et*
                                    Triomphal
          MARK KELLOGG, TROMBONE
Adler, Samuel   *Double Visions* for Large Wind
                                    Ensemble
Shostakovich, Dmitri (Hunsberger)   Folk Festival
                                    Polka
                                    Galop

          INTERMISSION

Sousa, John Philip   *The Diplomat*
Beethoven, L. van   March No. 1 in F Major
Hindemith, Paul   *Geschwindmarsch*
Boccalari, E.   *Il Bersaglieri*
Leemans, P.   *Colonel Paddy*
Codina, Genaro   *Marcha Zacatecas*
Chambers, W. Paris   *Chicago Tribune*
       DONALD HUNSBERGER, CONDUCTOR

December 7, 1987, Eastman Theatre
Barlow, Wayne   *Frontiers*
Keyes, Christopher   *East-Wind Music*
          WAYNE JEFFREY, CONDUCTOR
Bennett, Richard Rodney   *Morning Music*

          INTERMISSION

Ball, Michael   *Omaggio*
Williams, John T.   *A Nostalgic Jazz Odyssey*
       DONALD HUNSBERGER, CONDUCTOR

February 5, 1988, Kilbourn Hall
Boismortier, Joseph Bodin de (Paubon)
                              Concerto à Cinque
Poulenc, Francis   *Suite Française*
Rogers, Bernard   *The Musicians of Bremen*
          ROBERT GRENIER, NARRATOR
          WAYNE JEFFERY, CONDUCTOR

          INTERMISSION

Hoffmeister, F. A.   Serenade
Hodkinson, Sydney   *Echo Preludes*
          STEVE DOANE, CELLO
       DONALD HUNSBERGER, CONDUCTOR

February 21, 1988, Eastman Theatre
Sousa Spectacular VI
Tchaikovsky, Piotr Ilyich (Boyd)   *Coronation March*
Strauss, Johann (Godfrey) Overture to *Die Fledermaus*
Gregson, Edward   Tuba Concerto
          GARY PRESS, TUBA
Copland, Aaron   *Lincoln Portrait*
          TOM RYAN, NARRATOR

          INTERMISSION

A John Philip Sousa Retrospective:
  Sousa, John Philip   *Guide Right*
                              Presidential Polonaise
Three selections from the Sousa Band appearance at
the Eastman Theatre, July 21–27, 1928:
  Sousa, John Philip   *Washington Post*
  Sullivan, Arthur   *The Lost Chord*
          JOHN HAGSTROM, CORNET
  Sullivan, Arthur
    "I, too, was born in Arcadia" from *Three Quotations*

Sousa, John Philip
      Easter Morning on the White House Lawn
Sousa, John Philip   *Comrades of the Legion*
    DONALD HUNSBERGER, CONDUCTOR

May 4, 1988, Eastman Theatre
Stravinsky, Igor
    Concerto for Piano and Wind Instruments
    JEFFREY WATSON, PIANO
    WAYNE JEFFREY, CONDUCTOR
Stravinsky, Igor   Octet for Wind Instruments
    TIMOTHY MUFFITT, CONDUCTOR
Stravinsky, Igor   *Symphony of Psalms*, mvt. 3
    EASTMAN CHORALE
    WAYNE JEFFREY, CONDUCTOR

May 21, 1988, Indianapolis, Indiana
National MENC Convention, Indianapolis Convention
Center and Tour
Vaughan-Williams, Ralph (Hunsberger)
    Variations for Wind Band
Bennett, Richard Rodney   *Morning Music*
Hindemith, Paul
    Konzertmusik für Blasorchester, op. 41
Husa, Karel   *Music for Prague 1968*
    DONALD HUNSBERGER, CONDUCTOR

37th SEASON: 1988–89

October 7, 1988, Kilbourn Hall
Holst, Gustav   First Suite in E-flat
Stravinsky, Igor   *Symphonies of Wind Instruments*
Schoenberg, Arnold   Theme and Variations, op. 43a
Grainger, Percy   *Lincolnshire Posy*
    DONALD HUNSBERGER, CONDUCTOR

October 15, 1988, Eastman Theatre
PRISM XIV: Micro/Macro
Holst, Gustav   First Suite in E-Flat
    FREDERICK FENNELL, CONDUCTOR

October 28, 1988, Eastman Theatre
Bach, J. S. (Hunsberger)
    Passacaglia and Fugue in C Minor
Iannaccone, Anthony   *Apparitions*
Persichetti, Vincent   *Masquerade*
Dalby, Martin   *A Plain Man's Hammer*
Grainger, Percy   *Lincolnshire Posy*
    DONALD HUNSBERGER, CONDUCTOR

December 13, 1988, Eastman Theatre
Mozart, W. A.   Serenade No. 10 in B-Flat, K. 370a

INTERMISSION

Messiaen, Olivier   *Et expecto resurrectionem mortuorum*
    DONALD HUNSBERGER, CONDUCTOR

January 22, 1989, Eastman Theatre
Rochester Conference (A University of Rochester Week of
Seminars, Lectures and Concerts)
Mozart, W. A.   Serenade No. 10 in B-Flat, K. 370a

INTERMISSION

Messiaen, Olivier   *Et expecto resurrectionem mortuorum*
    DONALD HUNSBERGER, CONDUCTOR

February 8, 1989, Kilbourn Hall
Stravinsky, Igor   Suite from *L'Histoire du Soldat*
    DONALD HUNSBERGER, CONDUCTOR
Hindemith, Paul
    Konzertmusik for Piano, Brass and Harps, op. 49
    ELIZABETH AZCONA, PIANO
    JEFFREY RENSHAW, CONDUCTOR
Weill, Kurt   *Kleine Dreigroschenmusik*
    MARK SCATTERDAY, CONDUCTOR

March 9, 1989, Eastman Theatre
Sousa Spectacular VII
Sousa, John Philip   *Hail to the Spirit of Liberty*
Verdi, Giuseppe (Rogers)
    Overture to *La Forza del Destino*
Dahl, Ingolf
    Concerto for Alto Saxophone and Wind Orchestra
    KENNETH FOERCH, ALTO SAXOPHONE
Grieg, Edvard (Godfrey)   *Three Symphonic Dances*

March 9, 1989 (cont.)

Sousa, John Philip (Bourgeois)
Marching Along—A Pass in Review of Sousa
marches as compiled by Col. John Bourgeois,
Director of the U.S. Marine Band

Three Fireside Favorites:

Balfe (Hunsberger) *The Last Rose of Summer*
Sullivan, Arthur *The Lost Chord*
Traditional (Hunsberger)
Believe Me, If All Those Endearing Young Charms
KATE HEARDON, LYRIC SOPRANO

Chabrier, Emmanuel (Safranek) *España*
DONALD HUNSBERGER, CONDUCTOR

April 14, 1989, Eastman Theatre

Husa, Karel Fanfare for Brass Ensemble
Husa, Karel *Music for Prague 1968*
MARK SCATTERDAY, CONDUCTOR

INTERMISSION

Husa, Karel *Apotheosis of the Earth*
COMPOSER CONDUCTING

May 10, 1989, Eastman Theatre

Schwantner, Joseph
"*. . . and the mountains rising nowhere*"
HOLLY ROADFELDT, PIANO
JEFFREY RENSHAW, CONDUCTOR
Thorne, Nicholas *Adagio, op. 12*
MARK SCATTERDAY, CONDUCTOR
Benson, Warren *Symphony II—Lost Songs*
DONALD HUNSBERGER, CONDUCTOR

38th Season: 1989–90

September 29, 1989, Eastman Theatre

Giannini, Vittorio Symphony No. 3 for Wind Band
Gregson, Edward *Festivo*
Sacco, P. Peter *Four Sketches on Emerson Essays*
Kraft, William *Dialogues and Entertainments*
MARGARET BISHOP, SOPRANO
DONALD HUNSBERGER, CONDUCTOR

October 27, 1989, Eastman Theatre

Concert for the Rochester Association for the United Nations

Sousa, John Philip *Hands Across the Sea*
Schuman, William *New England Triptych*
Ohguri, Hiroshi *Fantasy on Osaka Folk Tunes*
Vaughan Williams, Ralph (Hunsberger)
Variations for Wind Band
Sousa, John Philip *Corcoran Cadets March*
Alonso, Francisco *¡Viva Grana!*
Sontullo, R. *Puenteares*
Hanssen, Johannes (Bainum) *Valdres March*
Ginastera, Alberto (John)
"Danza Final" from *Estancia*
DONALD HUNSBERGER, CONDUCTOR

December 11, 1989, Eastman Theatre

Adler, Samuel *Double Visions*
Welcher, Dan *The Yellowstone Fires*
Liptak, David *Threads*
Mailman, Martin
For precious friends hid in death's dateless night
ELISABETH WEIGLE, SOPRANO
DONALD HUNSBERGER, CONDUCTOR

February 7, 1990, Kilbourn Hall

Dvorak, Antonin Serenade in D Minor, op. 44
JEFFREY RENSHAW, CONDUCTOR

Hill Song Trilogy:

Grainger, Percy (Stout) *Hill Song* No. 1
Grainger, Percy (Rogers) *Hill Song* No. 1
Grainger, Percy *Hill Song* No. 2

INTERMISSION

Morris, Robert Concerto for Piano and Winds
JAMES AVERY, PIANO
DONALD HUNSBERGER, CONDUCTOR

February 13, 1990, Eastman Theatre

Percussive Arts Workshop

Childs, William
Concerto for Percussion and Concert Band
STEVE HOUGHTON, PERCUSSION
DONALD HUNSBERGER, CONDUCTOR

March 4, 1990, Eastman Theatre

Schuman, William	*Chester*
Tomasi, Henri	Concerto for Trumpet

PAUL MERKELO, TRUMPET

Husa, Karel	*Music for Prague 1968*

INTERMISSION

Holst, Gustav	First Suite in E-Flat
Schwantner, Joseph	
	". . . and the mountains rising nowhere"

MARIE ALATALO, PIANO

Grainger, Percy	*Lincolnshire Posy*

DONALD HUNSBERGER, CONDUCTOR

May 9, 1990, Eastman Theatre

Shostakovich, Dmitri (Hunsberger)	
	Festive Overture, op. 96
Bach, J. S. (Renshaw)	
	Chorale Prelude—"Jesu, Joy of Man's Desiring"
Bach, J. S. (Hunsberger)	
	Toccata and Fugue in D Minor, BWV 565
Holst, Gustav	First Suite in E-Flat
Grainger, Percy	*Lads of Wamphray*

INTERMISSION

Grøndahl, Larry (Møller)	Concerto for Trombone

MARK KELLOGG, TROMBONE

Williams, John (Hunsberger)	
	Suite from *The Star Wars* Trilogy
Ives, Charles	*Country Band March*
Mamiya, Michio	*Glory of Catalonia March*
Sousa, John Philip	*Semper Fidelis*

DONALD HUNSBERGER, CONDUCTOR

May 28–June 17, 1990

Concert Tour of Japan (Sony Corporation; Eastman Kodak, Japan; Hirayama Arts Office)

Program A:

Bach, J. S. (Hunsberger)	
	Toccata and Fugue in D Minor, BWV 565
Holst, Gustav	First Suite in E-Flat
Husa, Karel	*Music for Prague 1968*
Grainger, Percy	*Lads of Wamphray*
Bach, J. S. (Renshaw)	
	Chorale Prelude—"Jesu, Joy of Man's Desiring"

Rimsky-Korsakoff, Nicolai (Hunsberger)	
	Flight of the Bumblebee
Ives, Charles	*Country Band March*
Williams, John (Hunsberger)	
	Suite from *The Star Wars* Trilogy

Program B:

Shostakovich, Dmitri (Hunsberger)	
	Festive Overture, op. 96
Grainger, Percy	*Lincolnshire Posy*
Schwantner, Joseph	
	". . . and the mountains rising nowhere"
Strauss, Richard (Hunsberger)	
	Dance of the Seven Veils from *Salome*
Sousa, John Philip	*Semper Fidelis*
Walton, William	*Crown Imperial*
Grøndahl, Larry (Møller)	Concerto for Trombone

MARK KELLOGG, TROMBONE

Churchill, Frank (Schmidt)	
	When You Wish Upon A Star

Encores:

Sousa, John Philip	*Hands Across the Sea*
Sousa, John Philip	*The Stars and Stripes Forever*
Ravel, Maurice (Renshaw)	
	Pavane pour une infante defunte

DONALD HUNSBERGER, CONDUCTOR

JEFFREY RENSHAW, ASSOCIATE CONDUCTOR

39th SEASON: 1990–91

September 26, 1990, Eastman Theatre

Handel, G. F. (Baines and Mackerras)	
	Music for the Royal Fireworks
Bach, J. S. (Wright)	
	Chorale and Chorale Prelude—"Herzlich tut mich verlangen"
Diamond, David	*Elegy in Memory of Ravel*
Ito, Yasuhiro	*Festal Scenes*

INTERMISSION

Dahl, Ingolf	*Sinfonietta* for Concert Band
Fucik, Julius	*Florentiner March*
Delle Cese, Davide	*Inglesina*
Fillmore, Henry	*His Honor*

FREDERICK FENNELL, GUEST CONDUCTOR

October 31, 1990, Eastman Theatre

Adler, Samuel

Ultralight, a Fanfare for Wind Ensemble

Ravel, Maurice (Renshaw)

Pavane pour une infante defunte

Hindemith, Paul   *Der Schwanendreher*

GEORGE TAYLOR, VIOLA

INTERMISSION

Penderecki, Krzysztof   *Pittsburgh Overture*

Schramm, Betsy   *The Quickening of a Summer's Morn*

JEFFREY RENSHAW, CONDUCTOR

December 5, 1990, Eastman Theatre

Diamond, David   *Heart's Music*

Tantivy

Messiaen, Olivier   *Oiseaux exotiques*

ANTON NEL, PIANO

INTERMISSION

Stravinsky, Igor

Concerto for Piano and Wind Instruments

ANTON NEL, PIANO

Reed, H. Owen   *La Fiesta Mexicana*

JEFFREY RENSHAW, CONDUCTOR

February 6, 1991, Kilbourn Hall

Bonneau, Paul   Fanfare

Poulenc, Francis   *Suite Française*

Mozart, W. A.(Tribensee)

Suite from *La Clemenza di Tito*

INTERMISSION

Torke, Michael   *Adjustable Wrench*

Badings, Henk

Concerto for Harp and Wind Orchestra

KATHLEEN BRIDE, HARP

DONALD HUNSBERGER, CONDUCTOR

February 16, 1991, Eastman Theatre

PRISM: In Celebration of the Life of Rayburn Wright

Wright, Rayburn   *Japanese Folk Song Fantasy*

DONALD HUNSBERGER, CONDUCTOR

February 24, 1991, Eastman Theatre

Sousa Spectacular VIII

Sousa, John Philip   *El Capitan*

Gomez, A. Carlo (Clarke)   *Il Guarany* Overture

Gounod, Charles

"Je veux vivre" from *Romeo and Juliet*

KRISTI TRIMBLE, SOPRANO

Lehar, Franz (Hunsberger)

"Vilia" from *The Merry Widow*

KRISTI TRIMBLE, SOPRANO

Wright, Rayburn   *Japanese Folk Song Fantasy*

INTERMISSION

Sousa, John Philip   *The Rifle Regiment March*

At The Movies

Fillmore, Henry   *Lassus Trombone*

Bernstein, Leonard (Hunsberger)

Symphonic Dances from *West Side Story*

DONALD HUNSBERGER, CONDUCTOR

April 3, 1991, Eastman Theatre

An evening of soloists and ensembles

Three Canzonas:

Gabrieli, Giovanni (King)   *Canzona a 12*

Gabrieli, Giovanni (Hunsberger)

Canzona quarti toni a 15

Gabrieli, Giovanni (Fennell)   *Canzona noni toni a 12*

Brant, Henry   *Angels and Devils*

RICHARD SHERMAN, FLUTE

Reynolds, Verne

Last Scenes for Solo Horn and Wind Ensemble

PETER KURAU, HORN

Torke, Michael   *Rust* for Piano and Chamber Winds

MARIE ALATALO, PIANO

DONALD HUNSBERGER, CONDUCTOR

May 8, 1991, Eastman Theatre

Bach, J. S. (Knox)

Toccata, Adagio and Fugue in C Major

Dahl, Ingolf   Concerto for Alto Saxophone

JAMES KALYN, ALTO SAXOPHONE

Persichetti, Vincent   *Masquerade*

INTERMISSION

Hindemith, Paul   Symphony in B-Flat

DONALD HUNSBERGER, CONDUCTOR

40th Season: 1991–92

October 11, 1991, Kilbourn Hall
Schoenberg, Arnold (Hunsberger)
    Theme and Variations [op. 43c]
Keuris, Tristan   *Catena*
Wagner, Richard (Votta) *Trauermusik (Trauersinfonie)*
Woolfenden, Guy   *Illyrian Dances*
   LOIS FERRARI, CONDUCTOR

INTERMISSION

Kennan, Kent   *Night Soliloquy*
  ANNE LINDBLOM HARROW, FLUTE
Bourgeois, Derek   *Symphony of Winds*
  DONALD HUNSBERGER, CONDUCTOR

October 12, 1991, Eastman Theatre
PRISM XVI: Musical Waterworks
Thorne, Nicholas   *Adagio Music*
  DONALD HUNSBERGER, CONDUCTOR

November 13, 1991, Eastman Theatre
Koetsier, Jan   *Brass Symphony*
Berio, Luciano (Marciniak) *Petite Suite*
   LOIS FERRARI, CONDUCTOR
Skalkottas, Nikos (Schuller) *Nine Greek Dances*

INTERMISSION

Ranki, Gyorgy   *Tales of Father Goose*
  JOHN MARCELLUS, TROMBONE
Giannini, Vittorio Symphony No. 3 for Band
   LOIS FERRARI, CONDUCTOR
  DONALD HUNSBERGER, CONDUCTOR

February 7–9, 1992, Eastman School of Music
Celebration of the Fortieth Anniversary of the Eastman Wind Ensemble
February 7, 1992
"Winds Are Wonderful" PRISM Concert
Holst, Gustav Chaconne from First Suite in E-flat
  DAVID WALLACE, CONDUCTOR
Street, William *Swinging Down the Street*
  EASTMAN PERCUSSION ENSEMBLE
Hindemith, Paul Symphony in B-flat, mvt. 1
  MALLORY THOMPSON, CONDUCTOR

Strauss, Richard Serenade in E-flat, op. 7
   LOIS FERRARI, CONDUCTOR
Stravinsky, Igor *Ragtime* for Eleven Instruments
  CARL ATKINS, CONDUCTOR
Riegger, Wallingford Nonet for Brass Instruments
  RODNEY WINTHER, CONDUCTOR
Dahl, Ingolf   *Sinfonietta*, mvt. 2
  MICHAEL VOTTA, CONDUCTOR
Mozart, W. A. Serenade in B-flat, K.361, *Adagio*
  WAYNE JEFFREY, CONDUCTOR
Gabrieli, Giovanni (Hunsberger)
     Canzon quarti toni a 15
  MARK SCATTERDAY, CONDUCTOR
Weill, Kurt   *Little Threepenny Music*
  JEFFREY RENSHAW, CONDUCTOR
Nagano, Mitsuhiro
  Matrix for Euphonium and Electronic Tape
  TORU MIURA, EUPHONIUM
Copland, Aaron   *Emblems*
  DONALD HUNSBERGER, CONDUCTOR

February 8, 1992
New Composition Readings
Muncy, Thomas   *Variegations*
Gallagher, Jack *The Persistence of Memory*
Carbon, James   *Angel*
  JAMIE KALYN, ALTO SAXOPHONE
Stern, Robert   *Ultima Fantasia*
  SYDNEY HODKINSON, CONDUCTOR

February 9, 1992
New Composition Readings
Mobberley, James   *Ascension*
Crockett, Donald Concerto for Piano
   DAVID BURGE, PIANO
  SYDNEY HODKINSON, CONDUCTOR
Keuris, Tristan   *Catena*
  DONALD HUNSBERGER, CONDUCTOR

February 9, 1992
Gala Fortieth Anniversary Concert
Copland, Aaron *Fanfare for the Common Man*
  DONALD HUNSBERGER, CONDUCTOR
Vaughan Williams, Ralph *English Folk Song Suite*
  FREDERICK FENNELL, CONDUCTOR

February 9, 1992 (cont.)

Horowitz, Joseph (Konagaya)
     Concerto for Euphonium
  TORU MIURA, EUPHONIUM
 DONALD HUNSBERGER, CONDUCTOR
Giannini, Vittorio   Symphony for Band
  A. CLYDE ROLLER, CONDUCTOR
Shephard, Wiley   *EWE Variations*
McCabe, John   *Canyons*
Williams, John T.   *A Nostalgic Jazz Odyssey*
 DONALD HUNSBERGER, CONDUCTOR

March 30, 1992, Kilbourn Hall

Beethoven, L. van   Rondino in E-flat
Kurka, Robert Suite from *The Good Soldier Schweik*
  LOIS FERRARI, CONDUCTOR
Mozart, W. A. Divertimento No. 3 in E-flat
Starer, Robert   Serenade for Brass
 DONALD HUNSBERGER, CONDUCTOR

May 3, 1992, Eastman Theatre
Sousa Spectacular IX

Sousa, John Philip   *The Liberty Bell*
Suppé, Franz von (Moses-Tobani)
  Overture to *Morning, Noon and Night in Vienna*
Mantia, Simone
 Believe Me, If All Those Endearing Young Charms:
     Fantasia for Euphonium
 JOHN MARCELLUS, EUPHONIUM
Sousa, John Philip
  "By the Light of the Polar Star" from the Suite
      Looking Upward
Tchaikovsky, Peter I. (Winterbottom) *Capriccio Italien*

INTERMISSION

Sousa, John Philip
   George Washington Bicentennial March
Sullivan, Arthur (Mackerras/Duthoit) *Pineapple Poll*
Hunsberger, Donald
 Salute to John Philip Sousa (on the 100th Anniversary
  of the founding of the Sousa Band, 1892)
  JOHN C. BRAUND, NARRATOR
 DONALD HUNSBERGER, CONDUCTOR

June 11–29, 1992
Concert Tour of Japan (Sony Corporation, Eastman Kodak,
and the Shirakawa Arts Office)

Program A:
Bach, J. S. (Boyd) Fantasia and Fugue in G Minor
McCabe, John   *Canyons*
Vizzutti, Allen   *Emerald*
  ALLEN VIZZUTTI, TRUMPET
Traditional (Hunsberger)
    Amazing Grace ("New Britain")
Copland, Aaron   *Emblems*
Grafulla, Claudio   *Washington Greys*
Rachmaninoff, Sergei (Hunsberger) *Vocalise*
Strauss, Richard   Serenade, op. 7
Bernstein, Leonard (Hunsberger)
  Symphonic Suite from *West Side Story*
Program B:
Hanson, Howard   *Dies Natalis*
Persichetti, Vincent   *Masquerade*
Hindemith, Paul Symphony for Band
Susato, Tilman (Iveson)
  "La Mourisque" from *The Danserye*
Gabrieli, Giovanni (Block) *Canzon duodecimi toni a 10*
      Canzon quarti toni a 15
      Canzon duodecimi toni a 10
Strauss, Richard (Hunsberger)
  "Dance of the Seven Veils" from *Salome*
Wagner, Richard (Votta)
  Elsa's Procession to the Cathedral from *Lohengrin*
Vizzutti, Allen
  American Jazz Suite for Trumpet and Winds
  ALLEN VIZZUTTI, TRUMPET
Vaughan Williams, Ralph   *Sea Songs*
Weill, Kurt Three Pieces from *The Threepenny Opera*
Hunsberger, Donald *Salute to John Philip Sousa*
  MICHINOBU IIMORI, NARRATOR
Japan Band Association Contest Composition:
Abe, Yuichi   *Futurism* for Wind Orchestra
Encores:
Sousa, John Philip   *The Liberty Bell*
Balfe (Hunsberger) *The Last Rose of Summer*
Sousa, John Philip *The Stars and Stripes Forever*
      Peaches and Cream
 DONALD HUNSBERGER, CONDUCTOR
 MARK SCATTERDAY, ASSOCIATE CONDUCTOR

APPENDIX A2B

Complete Repertoire of the Eastman Wind Ensemble
1952–1992

CATALOGUE OF PERFORMANCES BY COMPOSER AND TITLE

Month and year of performance(s) are indicated after each item. Parentheses ( ) denote multiple performances within a single month.

A

Abe, Yuichi: *Futurism* for Wind Orchestra 6/92

Adler, Samuel: *A Little Night and Day Music* 12/77

Adler, Samuel: Concerto for Brass, Winds and Percussion 12/69

Adler, Samuel: *Double Visions* for Large Wind Ensemble 10/87; 12/89

Adler, Samuel: *Festive Prelude* 4/71

Adler, Samuel: *Snow Tracks* 4/82; 4/83

Adler, Samuel: *Southwestern Sketches* 2/67; 11/79; 10/84

Adler, Samuel: Symphony No. 3, "Diptych" 1/81

Adler, Samuel: *Ultralight, A Fanfare* for Wind Ensemble 10/90

Adolphe, Bruce: *Chiaroscuro* for Double Wind Quintet 12/73

Albert, Thomas: B-flat Piece for Winds and Percussion 2/81

Alexander, Russell: *Rival Rovers* 3/62

Alford, Harry L.: *Glory of the Gridiron* 11/53; 2/54

Alford, Harry L.: *Law and Order* 1/61

Alford, Kenneth J.: *Colonel Bogey* 1/56

Alford, Kenneth J.: *Dunedin* 2/67

Alford, Kenneth J.: *Mad Major* 10/57; 2/66; 1/83

Alford, Kenneth J.: *Old Panama* 2/66

Alonso, Francisco: *¡Viva Grana!* 10/89

Altenburg, Johann: Concerto for Clarini and Timpani 11/81

Amram, David: *King Lear Variations* 1/69; 2/69; 12/71; 10/74

Anderson, Leroy: *Suite of Carols* 1/59

Anderson, Leroy: Two excerpts from the *Irish Suite* 5/55

Andrews, Ray: *March MKT* 4/73

Angelini, Louis: *Evocation* 2/62

Anonymous: *Congo's Quickstep* 11/75; 10/78 (2)

Arban, J. B. (Goldman): *Carnival of Venice* 1/83

Arban, J. B. (Hunsberger): *Fantasie Brillante* 3/87 (11)

Arban, J. B. (Hunsberger): Variations on le *Carnaval de Venise* 3/87 (11)

Arnold, Malcolm (Johnstone): *English Dances* 2/66; 4/69; 2/81

Arutiunian, Alexandre (Duker): Concerto for Trumpet 4/82

Asenjo, Gunzalez: Concerto for Wind Instruments 4/64

Attaignant, Pierre (Randolph): *Renaissance Dance Set* 3/73

Auric, Georges: *Divertimento* 10/69

Auric, Georges: *La Palais Royale* 11/68; 10/79

B

Baaren, Kees van: *Partita* 10/65; 4/71

Baban, Gracian (Reynolds): *Voce mea ad Dominum* 4/73

Bach, C. P. E.: Six Sonatas for Two Horns, Two Flutes, Two Clarinets and Bassoon, W. 184 4/80

Bach, J. S. (Abert/Weiss): Chorale and Fugue in G Minor 2/54

Back, J. S. (arr. unknown): Fugue in F Major 2/54

Bach, J. S. (Boyd): Fantasia and Fugue in G Minor 2/71; 3/71; 12/85; 6/92 (3)

Bach, J. S. (Cailliet): Prelude and Fugue in G Minor 2/53

Bach, J. S. (Hunsberger) Passacaglia and Fugue in C Minor 2/63; 4/64; 11/66; 11/70; 4/74; 3/76; 5–6/78 (14); 10/81; 4/83; 10/88

Bach, J. S. (Hunsberger): Prelude in E-Flat ("St. Anne") 2/65; 9/77

Bach, J. S. (Hunsberger): Toccata and Fugue in D Minor 11/62; 5/90 (8)

Bach, J. S. (Knox): Toccata, Adagio and Fugue in C Major 5/91

Bach, J. S. (Lake): Chorale—"Jesu, Who in Sorrow Dying" 1/53

Bach, J. S. (Lake): Chorale—"Thou Prince of Life, O Christ, O Lord" 1/54

Bach, J. S. (Leidzen): Chorale—"Come Sweet Death" 1/53; 10/63; 11/67

Bach, J. S. (Leidzen): Chorale—"Jesu, Joy of Man's Desiring" 10/62

Bach, J. S. (Leidzen): Toccata and Fugue in D Minor 11/62

Bach, J. S. (Moehlmann): Chorale—"If Thou be Near" 2/53; 2/69 (2)

Bach, J. S. (Paynter): Toccata, Adagio and Fugue in C Major 10/80

Bach, J. S. (Renshaw): Chorale Prelude—"Jesu, Joy of Man's Desiring" 5/90 (8)

Bach, J. S. (Richardson): Chorale—"Sheep May Safely Graze" 1/54; 11/63

Bach, J. S. (Whitwell): Capriccio "On the Departure of a Friend" 3/79

Bach, J. S. (Wright): Chorale and Chorale Prelude— "Herzlich thut mich verlangen" 9/90

Bach, Vincent: *Hungarian Melodies* 2/85

Badings, Henk: Concerto for Flute and Wind Symphony Orchestra 2/71; 3/71; 10/71

Badings, Henk: Concerto for Harp and Wind Orchestra 2/91

Badings, Henk: *Greensleeves* 10/80

Badings, Henk: Symphony for Wind Orchestra 10/75

Bagley, Edwin E.: *National Emblem* 11/53; 3/60 (2); 11/61 (3)

Baker, Claude: *Capriccio* for Concert Wind Band 2/76

Balassa, Sándor: *Lupercalia* 11/79

Balfe, Michael (Hunsberger): *The Last Rose of Summer* 3/89; 6/92

Ball, Michael: *Omaggio* 12/87

Barber, Samuel: *Commando March* 5/53; 1/54; 2/77

Barlow, Wayne: *Frontiers* 12/87

Barlow, Wayne: *Intrada, Fugue, and Postlude* for Brass Ensemble 1/61; 12/70

Bassett, Leslie: *Designs, Images and Textures* 10/73

Bassett, Leslie: *Sounds, Shapes and Symbols in Four Movements* 2/81

Bassett, Leslie: *Symphonic Sketch* 12/53

Basta, James: Concerto for Marimba and Orchestra 4/84

Beall, John: Concerto for Piano and Wind Orchestra 2/74

Beethoven, L. van: *Ecossaise* 1/69

Beethoven, L. van (Winterbottom): Overture to *Egmont* 1/54

Beethoven, L. van: March in C 1/69

Beethoven, L. van: March in F 1/69; 10/75; 10/87

Beethoven, L. van: Polonaise 1/69

Beethoven, L. van: Rondino in E-flat 3/92

Beethoven, L. van: *Siegessinfonie* 3/79

Beglarian, Grant: *Sinfonia* for Band, adapted from *Sinfonia* for Orchestra 12/69

Bennett, Richard Rodney: *Morning Music* 12/87; 5/88 (4)

Bennett, Robert Russell: Concerto for Woodwind Quintet and Wind Symphony 4/64 (2)

Bennett, Robert Russell: *Suite of Old American Dances* 2/53; 5/53; 12/54 (3); 1/61; 6/61; 10/63; 2/66; 10/77

Bennett, Robert Russell: *Symphonic Songs* 12/57; 10/58; 4/59; 10/81

Benson, Warren: *The Beaded Leaf* 4/81

Benson, Warren: Concerto for Alto Saxophone and Wind Band 2/76; 3/76

Benson, Warren: *The Leaves Are Falling* 4/64 (2); 2/78; 5–6/78 (13); 12/78; 2/80; 10/83

Benson, Warren: *The Mask of Night* 12/72

Benson, Warren: *The Passing Bell* 11/77

Benson, Warren: *Remembrance* 12/68

Benson, Warren: *Shadow Wood* 11/71; 12/71; 4/72; 2/77

Benson, Warren: *The Solitary Dancer* 12/69; 2/73; 4/81

Benson, Warren: Symphony for Drums and Wind Orchestra 2/65; 4/65; 3/69; 9/74; 2/80; 10/84

Benson, Warren: Symphony II: *Lost Songs* 5/89

Benson, Warren: *Wings* 9/84; 10/84

Berg, Alban: *Kammerkonzert* for Piano and Violin with Thirteen Winds 3/83

Berger, Theodor: *Rondo Ostinato on a Spanish Motive* 11/59; 3/71; 10/71

Bergsma, William: March with Trumpets 11/70

Berio, Luciano (Marciniak): *Petite Suite* 12/81; 11/91

Berlioz, Hector: Recitative and Prayer from *Grand Symphony Funébre et Triomphal* 10/87

Berlioz, Hector (Boyd): Royal Hunt and Storm Scene from *The Trojans* 10/62

Bernard, Emile: Divertissement pour instrumens à vent 10/75

Bernstein, Leonard (Hunsberger): "Glitter and Be Gay" from *Candide* 2/87

Bernstein, Leonard (Beeler): Overture to *Candide* 3/62; 10/82

Bernstein, Leonard (Hunsberger): Symphonic Dances from *West Side Story* 10/86; 2/91; 6/92 (6)

Bernstein, Leonard: Latin Choruses from *The Lark* 3/73

Beversdorf, Thomas: Serenade 12/57

Beversdorf, Thomas: Symphony for Band and Percussion 11/56

Bielawa, Herbert: *Spectrums* 12/68; 2/69 (2)

Bigelow, F. E.: *Our Director* 11/53

Bilik, Jerry: *Block M* 2/77

Binkerd, Gordon: *Noble Numbers* 11/76

Binkerd, Gordon: *The Battle* (based on Frescobaldi's *Capriccio sopra la Battaglia*) 10/72

Bizet, Georges: *Agnos Dei* 1/54

Blackwood, Easley: *Chamber Symphony for Fourteen Winds*, op. 2 10/60

Blankenburg, H. L.: *Action Front* 3/62; 10/69

Blomdahl, Karl-Birger: *Kammerkonzert* for Piano, Woodwinds, and Percussion 12/61

Boccalari, E.: *Il Bersaglieri* 10/87

Boismortier, Joseph Bodin de: Concerto no. 3 1/72

Boismortier, Joseph Bodin de (Paubon): *Concerto à Cinque* 2/88

Bonneau, Paul: *Fanfare* 2/91

Bottesini, Giovanni: *Grand Duo* for Violin and Contrabass 4/80

Bottje, Will Gay: Concerto for Trumpet, Trombone, and Winds 5/61

Bottje, Will Gay: *Contrasts* 5/54; 10/73

Bottje, Will Gay: *Symphonic Allegro* 12/53; 12/83

Bottje, Will Gay: Symphony No. 4 5/56

Bottje, Will Gay: Theme and Variations 5/58

Bourgeois, Derek: *Symphony of Winds* 10/91

Bozza, Eugène: *Andante et Scherzo pour Quatuor des Saxophones* 3/71; 10/71

Bozza, Eugène: *Children's Overture* 10/79

Brant, Henry: *Angels and Devils* 10/78; 4/91

Breydert, Frederick M.: Suite in E-flat 12/53

Bricetti, Thomas: *Turkey Creek March* 11/65

Bright, Houston: Prelude and Fugue in F Minor 11/62

Britten, Benjamin (Brown): *Soirées Musicales* 1/65

Bruckner, Anton: Mass in E Minor 4/61

Buck, Larry: *Freckles Rag* 2/86

Buhr, Glenn: *Epigrams* 3/84

Bulow, Harry: *Textures* 11/85; 12/85

Buxtehude, Dietrich (D. Ross [Hunsberger]): *Benedicam Dominum* 12/61

C

Carbon, James: *Angel* 2/92

Casella, Alfredo: *Introduction, Chorale, and March* 12/56

Castérède, Jacque: *Divertissement d'Eté* 2/73

Catel, Charles Simon: Overture in C 1/65

Chabrier, Emmanuel (Safranek): *España* 2/53; 3/89

Chambers, W. Paris: *Alhambra* 10/69

Chambers, W. Paris: *The Chicago Tribune* 10/60; 10/87

Chance, John Barnes: *Elegy* 2/76; 3/76; 1/83; 10/85

Chance, John Barnes: Symphony No. 2 12/77

Childs, William: Concerto for Percussion and Concert Band 2/90

Chow, Wen-Chung: *Metaphors* 10/71; 11/71

Chow, Wen-Chung: *Soliloquy of a Bhiksuni* 3/71; 10/71

Clarke, Herbert L.: *The Three Aces* 2/84; 2/87

Clarke, Jeremiah (Iveson): *Trumpet Voluntary* 10/81

Coates, Eric: *Knightsbridge March* 11/58

Coates, Eric (Williams): *London Every Day Suite* 10/87

Codina, Genaro: *Marcha Zacatecas* 10/65; 10/87

Copland, Aaron: *Emblems* 4/65; 3/68 (6); 1/75; 6/78; 12/82; 2/92; 6/92

Copland, Aaron: *Fanfare for the Common Man* 1/61; 4/76; 2/92

Copland, Aaron: *Lincoln Portrait* 2/88

Copland, Aaron: *An Outdoor Overture* 2/71; 3/71; 5–6/78 (16); 10/80; 10/86

Copland, Aaron: *The Red Pony* 2/74; 12/78

Corigliano, John: *Gazebo Dances* 11/77; 1/82

Costa, P. M. (Seredy): *A Frangesa* 10/65; 10/69

Cowell, Henry: *Celtic Set* 11/70; 3/71; 10/71

Cowell, Henry: *Shoontree* 2/53

Crane, Robert: *Five Baroque Chorale Preludes* 1/61

Fučik, Julius: *The Florentiner March*, op. 214 2/62; 12/77; 1/83; 2/86; 9/90

Fuerstner, Carl: Overture 12/53

G

Gabrieli, Andrea (Ghedini): *Aria della battaglia* 3/59; 3/63; 3/83

Gabrieli, Giovanni: *Canzon in double echo* 2/85

Gabrieli, Giovanni: *Sonata pian' e forte* 11/53; 2/85

Gabrieli, Giovanni: *Two Motets* 4/61

Gabrieli, Giovanni (Block): *Canzon duodecimi toni a 10* 6/92 (6)

Gabrieli, Giovanni (Block): *Canzon quarti toni a 15* 6/92 (6)

Gabrieli, Giovanni (Damrosch): *Jubilate Deo* 3/73; 4/79

Gabrieli, Giovanni (Fennell): *Canzon noni toni a 12* 11/53; 12/73; 10/81; 2/85; 4/91

Gabrieli, Giovanni (Hudson): *In ecclesiis* 11/66

Gabrieli, Giovanni (Hunsberger): *Canzona duodecimi toni* 12/67

Gabrieli, Giovanni (Hunsberger): *Canzona quarti toni a 15* 11/64; 10/75; 4/91; 2/92 (6)

Gabrieli, Giovanni (King): *Canzon primi toni a 10* 10/66; 11/69

Gabrieli, Giovanni (King): *Canzon quarti toni a 15* 12/73

Gabrieli, Giovanni (King): *Canzona a 12* 4/91

Gabrieli, Giovanni (King): *Sonata octavi toni* 11/64; 10/66

Gabrieli, Giovanni (Reynolds): *Benedicam Dominum* 3/73

Gabrieli, Giovanni (Reynolds): *Canzon per sonar duodecimi toni* 3/73

Gabrieli, Giovanni (Reynolds): *Quis est iste qui venit* (from *Sacre Symphoniae*) 10/72

Gabrieli, Giovanni (Smith): Sonata XIX 1/81

Gabrieli, Giovanni (Winter): *Canzon* 2/85

Gallagher, Jack: *The Persistence of Memory* 2/92

Gallus, Jacobus (Kandel): *In resurrectione tuae Christe* 1/81

Ganne, Louis Gaston (Roberts): *Father of Victory* 11/58; 2/77

Ganne, Louis Gaston: *Marche Lorraine* 10/65

Garriguenc, Pierre: *Synthesis* 4/70

Gates, Everett: *Declamation and Dance* 10/72

Gauldin, Robert: *Three Symphonic Sketches* 5/58

Gauldin, Robert: Variations on a Theme by Bartók for Wind Ensemble 11/56; 11/59

George, Thom Ritter: *Symphonic Variations* for Wind and Percussion Instruments 4/65

Gershwin, George (Bennett): Selections from *Porgy and Bess* 2/85

Giannini, Vittorio: Praeludium and Allegro 12/62; 4/86

Giannini, Vittorio: Symphony No. 3 for Band 3/63; 3/81; 9/89; 11/91; 2/92

Gilmore, Bernard: *Five Folk Songs* for Soprano and Wind Band 5/67; 11/82

Ginastera, Alberto (John): "Danza Final" from the ballet *Estancia* 3/66; 2/71; 2/74; 9/82; 10/89

Gluck (DeLamarter): Dance of the Blessed Spirits from *Orpheus* 2/53

Goldman, Edwin Franko: *Boy Scouts of America* 10/57

Goldman, Edwin Franko: *Bugles and Drums* 10/57

Goldman, Edwin Franko: *Cheerio* 11/53; 12/54 (3)

Goldman, Edwin Franko: *Children's March* 10/57

Goldman, Edwin Franko: *Illinois March* 10/57

Goldman, Edwin Franko: *Interlochen Bowl* 10/57; 6/61

Goldman, Edwin Franko: *March Illinois* 6/61

Goldman, Edwin Franko: *On the Mall* 1/56; 2/87

Goldman, Edwin Franko: *Onward-Upward* 10/57; 2/77; 1/82

Goldstaub, Paul: *Festival Prelude* 10/83

Gomez, Antonio Carlos (Clarke): *Il Guarany* Overture 2/85; 2/91

Gossec, François-Joseph: Symphony in F Major 11/67

Gotkovsky, Ida: *Poéme du Feu* 10/79; 12/82

Gould, Morton: *Ballad* for Band 1/53; 2/53; 5/53; 12/54 (3); 3/59; 10/60; 3/62

Gould, Morton: Symphony for Band (*West Point*) 5/53; 4/59; 3/63; 2/76; 12/78; 1/82

Gounod, Charles (Hunsberger): "Je veux vivre" from *Romeo and Juliet* 2/91

Gounod, Charles: *Petite Symphonie* 10/79

Grafulla, Claudio: *Washington Greys* 12/62; 11/67; 10/80; 6/92 (8)

Grainger, Percy (Rogers): *Hill Song* No. 1 2/90

Grainger, Percy (Stout): *Hill Song* No. 1 2/90

Grainger, Percy: *Hill Song* No. 2 5/55; 10/55; 3/59; 1/65; 2/77; 10/80; 10/86; 2/90

Grainger, Percy: *Irish Tune from County Derry* 2/54; 3/69; 10/85; 2/87

Grainger, Percy: *Lads of Wamphray* 2/87; 3/87 (11); 5/90 (8)

Holloway, John: *Wood-up Quickstep* 11/81

Holst, Gustav (Smith): "Jupiter" from *The Planets* 10/82

Holst, Gustav: *Hammersmith* 12/56; 10/58; 11/58; 2/64; 2/72; 10/75; 9/84

Holst, Gustav: First Suite in E-Flat 2/53; 12/54 (3); 5/55; 11/59; 2/60; 3/60 (2); 12/62; 3/66; 5–6/78 (15); 12/78; 4/86; 2/87; 10/88; 3/90; 5/90 (8); 2/92

Holst, Gustav: Second Suite in F 5/55; 3/61; 2/67; 3/70; 4/73; 10/77; 3/81; 10/83; 2/87; 3/87 (11)

Honegger, Arthur: *La Marche sur la Bastille* 11/68; 10/79

Horowitz, Joseph (Konagaya): Concerto for Euphonium 2/92

Hovhaness, Alan: *Return and Rebuild the Desolate Places* 1/69; 2/69; 11/73; 11/83

Hovhaness, Alan: Suite for Band 3/70

Hovhaness, Alan: Symphony No. 4 4/63; 5/63; 12/68

Humel, Gerald: *Five Quotations from a Czech Fairy Tale* 1/61

Hummel, Johann Nepomuk (Corley): Concerto for Trumpet 10/80

Humperdinck Engelbert (Maddy): Prayer and Dream Pantomime from *Hansel and Gretel* 1/53

Hunsberger, Donald: *Salute to John Philip Sousa* 5/92; 6/92 (6)

Husa, Karel: *Al Fresco* 10/75

Husa, Karel: *An American Te Deum* 4/79

Husa, Karel: *Apotheosis of this Earth* 4/72; 4/89

Husa, Karel: Concerto for Percussion and Wind Ensemble 12/72; 11/80; 4/84

Husa, Karel: Concerto for Wind Ensemble 5/85

Husa, Karel: Fanfare for Brass Ensemble 4/89

Husa, Karel: *Music for Prague 1968* 10/69; 5/88 (4); 4/89; 4/90; 5/90 (8)

I

Iannaccone, Anthony: *Apparitions* 10/88

Iannaccone, Anthony: *Of Fire and Ice* 10/86

Ibert, Jacques: Concerto for Violoncello and Wind Orchestra, op. 74 3/61; 4/65

Israel, Brian: Concerto for Clarinet and Wind Ensemble 2/86

Ito, Yasuhide: *Festal Scenes* 9/90

Ives, Charles (Brion): Variations on "Jerusalem The Golden" 1/75

Ives, Charles (Rhoads): Variations on "America" 10/72; 3/84; 4/84

Ives, Charles (Sinclair): Overture and March 1776 11/75; 2/76; 3/76; 2/78; 3/84

Ives, Charles: *Country Band March* 2/77; 5/90 (8)

Ives, Charles: *Omega Lambda Chi March* 1/75

J

Jacob, Gordon: *The Battell* 4/65

Jacob, Gordon: *An Original Suite* 3/62; 10/67; 11/67; 4/82

Jacob, Gordon: *Flag of Stars* 11/63

Jacob, Gordon: *William Byrd Suite* 12/57; 10/58; 11/58; 6/61; 11/61 (3); 10/65; 10/70; 12/72; 12/74; 10/81; 10/82

Jankowsky, Loretta: *Todesband* 2/76

Jenkins, Joseph Wilcox: *Cumberland Gap* 12/62

Jenkins, Joseph Wilcox (Neff): *Pieces of Eight* 11/53; 12/54 (3); 10/77

Jenkins, Joseph Wilcox: *American Overture* for Band 11/59; 3/84; 4/84 (2)

Johnston, Donald: *Montage* 5/70; 9/74; 2/85

Johnston, Donald: Symphony No. 4 5/66

Jolas, Betsy: *Lassus Ricercare* 12/76; 4/81

K

Kabalevsky, Dmitri (Hunsberger): *Colas Breugnon* Overture 3/66; 10/67; 11/67; 11/77; 2/91

Kamioka, Yoichi: *In Autumn Skies* 5–6/78 (18); 12/78

Kane, Irving: *Fourth Stream* 4/72

Kay, Ulysses: *Forever Free: A Lincoln Chronicle* 2/76

Kelterborn, Rudolf: *Miroirs* 12/73; 12/81; 2/87; 11/83

Kennan, Kent: *Concertino* for Piano and Wind Ensemble 4/72

Kennan, Kent: *Night Soliloquy* 2/64; 12/69; 10/91

Kessner, Daniel: *Variations* 3/79

Kessner, Daniel: *Wind Sculptures* 12/77

Ketting, Otto: *Intrada Festiva* 12/68

Keuris, Tristan: *Catena* 10/91; 2/92

Key, Francis Scott: *The Star Spangled Banner* 5/55; 10/69

Keyes, Christopher: *East-Wind Music* 12/87

Khatchaturian, Aram (Hunsberger): Three Dance Episodes from the ballet *Spartacus* 10/69

Kineda, Bin: *Symphonic Movement* 5/78 (2)

King, Karl: *Barnum and Bailey's Favorite* 1/56; 1/61

King, Karl: *Pride of Illini* 11/53

Klein, Lothar: *Symphonic Etudes* 11/73

Klohr, John N.: *The Billboard* 1/56

Koch, Frederick (Nelson): *Composites* 2/71

Meacham, Margaret: *Moon Shadows* for Flute Octet 11/85

Mellers, Wilfred: *Samson Agonistes* 10/60

Mendelssohn, Felix (Boyd): Overture for Band, op. 24 3/64

Mendelssohn, Felix: Overture in C, op. 24 3/81; 10/85; 12/86

Mennin, Peter: *Canzona* 5/54; 3/61; 3/62; 4/69; 12/84

Menotti, Gian Carlo: Excerpts from ballet *Sebastian* 2/63

Messiaen, Olivier: *Oiseaux exotiques* 12/90

Messiaen, Olivier: *Et expecto resurrectionem mortuorum* 10/75; 11/75; 11/80; 11/86; 12/88; 1/89

Miaskovsky, Nicholas: Symphony No. 19 for Wind Orchestra, op. 46 1/60

Michalsky, Donal: *Fanfare after Seventeenth Century Dances* 12/76; 1/84

Miller, Dennis: *Piece in Three Parts* 11/85

Miller, Eric: *Serenade for Eleven Instruments* 11/85

Milhaud, Darius: "Dixtout d'instruments à vent" from *Cinq symphonies pour petit orchestre* 12/67

Milhaud, Darius: *Suite Française* 2/53; 12/56; 12/57; 2/58; 10/60; 2/62; 11/64; 3/69; 10/77

Milhaud, Darius: *West Point Suite* 10/62

Mobberley, James: *Ascension* 2/92

Moore, John: *Quaker Medley Set Quadrille* 11/75

Morawetz, Oscar: *Memorial to Martin Luther King* for Solo Violoncello and Winds, Percussion and Piano 1/84

Morawetz, Oskar: *Sinfonietta* 2/70

Morris, Robert: Concerto for Piano and Winds 2/90

Morris, Robert: *Cuts* for Large Wind Ensemble 4/86

Mozart, W. A. (Tribensee): Suite from *La Clemenza di Tito* 2/91

Mozart, W. A.: Divertimento No. 3 in E-Flat, K. 166 1/72; 4/72; 2/78; 3/92

Mozart, W. A.: Serenade No. 10 in B-Flat Major, K. 361 2/53; 2/58; 12/76; 3/60 (2); 3/65; 4/79; 1/81; 12/83; 2/86; 12/88; 1/89; 2/92

Mozart, W. A.: Serenade No. 11 in E-Flat Major, K. 375 2/55; 1/61; 1/69; 3/73

Mozart, W. A.: Serenade No. 12 in C Minor, K. 388 10/55; 10/60; 10/66; 3/68 (4); 11/69

Muncy, Thomas: *Variegations* 2/92

Myers, Robert: *Enigma Virginia* for Percussion and Wind Ensemble 11/85

Mygatt, Louise: *Windchanges* 11/85

N

Nelson, Ron: *Medieval Suite* 3/84; 11/86

Nelson, Ron: *Rocky Point Holiday* 11/79

Nelson, Ron: *Savannah River Holiday* 12/77; 10/83

Nielson, Carl (Boyd): Overture to *Maskarade* 3/70

Nixon, Roger: *Fiesta del Pacifico* 5/67; 11/67; 2/68; 3/68 (7); 4/68; 3/78

Nixon, Roger: *In Memoriam—Adlai Stevenson* 10/65

Noon, David: *Sweelinck Variations,* Set III 1/84

O

Oettinger, Alan: *Fanfare* 10/71; 11/71

Ohguri, Hiroshi: *Fantasy on Osaka Folk Tunes* 10/89

Orff, Carl (Moerenhout): *Carmina Burana* 3/64

Otterloo, Willem van: *Sinfonietta* for Wind Instruments 12/65; 10/75; 12/85

P

Pace, Pat: *Music for Winds* 3/64

Padovano, Annible (Schmitt): *Aria della battaglia* 12/70

Palestrina, Giovanni (Harvey): *Adoramus te* and *Sanctus* 2/53

Palestrina, Giovanni (Harvey): *Missa Brevis* 11/66

Peeters, Flor: *Modale Suite* 11/65

Penderecki, Krzysztof: *Pittsburgh Overture* 4/68; 3/69; 10/90

Penderecki, Krzysztof: *Prelude für Bläser, Schlagzeug und Kontrabässe* 12/76

Penn, William: *Designs* (for Orchestral Winds, Jazz Quartet, and Percussion) 3/74

Penn, William: *Niagara* 1/75

Perilhou, A.: *Divertissement* 12/73

Perkins, Frank: *Fandango* 5/55

Persichetti, Vincent: *A Lincoln Address,* op. 124a 10/74

Persichetti, Vincent: *Celebrations* for Chorus and Wind Ensemble 3/73; 11/79

Persichetti, Vincent: Chorale Prelude—"O Cool Is The Valley" 2/74

Persichetti, Vincent: Chorale Prelude—"So Pure The Star" 4/71

Persichetti, Vincent: Chorale Prelude—"Turn Not Thy Face," op. 105 10/74; 12/74

Persichetti, Vincent: *Divertimento* for Band, op. 42 2/53; 5/53; 12/54 (3); 10/77

Persichetti, Vincent: *Masquerade* 5/67; 2/68; 3/68 (6); 4/68; 2/80; 10/88; 5/91; 6/92 (6)

S

Sacco, Peter: *Four Sketches on Emerson Essays* 5/66; 3/78; 9/89

Saint-Saëns, Camille (Whitwell): *Occident and Orient*, op. 25 2/82

San Miguel, Mariano: *The Golden Ear* 11/58

Satie, Erik (Ricker): Fourth Nocturne (For Woodwind Choir) 2/75

Scheidt, Samuel (Reynolds): *Centone* No. 5 12/67

Schmidt, Russell (arr.): *When You Wish Upon A Star* 6/90 (7)

Schmitt, Florent (Duker): *Dionysiaques* 11/59; 3/79

Schmitt, Florent: *Lied and Scherzo* for Double Wind Quintet and Solo Horn, op. 54 12/56

Schober, Brian: *Sunflower Splendour* 10/78

Schoenberg, Arnold: Theme and Variations, op. 43a 3/57; 1/60; 11/61 (3); 3/74; 2/76; 10/80; 10/88

Schoenberg, Arnold (Hunsberger): Theme and Variations, [op. 43c] 10/91

Schramm, Betsy: *The Quickening of a Summer's Morn* 10/90

Schreiner, Adolph (Osterling): *The Worried Drummers* 2/63

Schubert, Franz (Reynolds): *Cantos V* 11/74

Schuller, Gunther: *Study in Texture* 4/72

Schuller, Gunther: Symphony for Brass and Percussion 12/81

Schuman, William (Owen): *Circus Overture* 2/74

Schuman, William: *Chester* 11/59; 11/65; 11/75; 3/90

Schuman, William: *Dedication Fanfare* 3/70

Schuman, William: *George Washington Bridge* 2/53; 5/53; 10/60; 2/66; 10/77

Schuman, William: *New England Triptych* 11/79; 10/89

Schuman, William: *When Jesus Wept* 3/61; 11/65; 11/75

Schütz, Heinrich: *Absalom, fili mi* 4/81

Schwantner, Joseph: ". . . and the mountains rising nowhere" 2/77; 3/77; 6/78; 3/87 (11); 5/89; 3/90; 5/90 (7)

Schwantner, Joseph: *From A Dark Millennium* 4/82

Schwartz, Elliott: *Voyage* 4/72

Scianni, Joseph: *Court Square—An Impression* 12/56; 12/62

Seitz, Roland F.: *Grandioso* 10/57

Seitz, Roland F.: *University of Pennsylvania Band* 10/60

Seltzer, M.: *Trombone Solidity* 3/62

Serly, Tibor: Symphony for Wind Instruments 5/66

Shahan, Paul Willard: *Leipzig Towers* for Brass and Percussion 2/55

Shanan, Paul: *Spring Festival in Five Scenes* 5/56

Shanley, Frank: *Concertino* 12/53

Shephard, Wiley: *EWE Variations* 2/92

Shostakovich, Dmitri (Hunsberger): Contradance (*The Gadfly*) 3/71; 10/71

Shostakovich, Dmitri (Hunsberger): *Festive Overture*, op. 96 2/64; 10/65; 2/68; 3/68 (7); 4/68; 3/71; 4/82; 10/85; 5/90 (7)

Shostakovich, Dmitri (Hunsberger): Folk Festival (*The Gadfly*) 3/71; 10/71; 11/73; 10/87

Shostakovich, Dmitri (Hunsberger): Galop (*Moscow Cheremoushky*) 3/71; 10/71; 11/71; 11/73; 10/87

Shostakovich, Dmitri (Hunsberger): Nocturne (*The Gadfly*) 3/71; 10/71

Shostakovich, Dmitri (Hunsberger): Polka (*The Bolt*) 3/71; 10/71; 11/73; 10/87

Sibelius, Jean (Goldman): Three Movements from *Karelia Suite* 2/65

Silliman, Cutler: *Variations* for Band 11/63

Skalkottas, Nikos (Schuller): *Nine Greek Dances* 11/91

Sliker, Harold: *So Proudly We Hail* 10/61

Snow, David: *Sinfonia Concertante* for Piano, Horn, Percussion And Wind Ensemble 11/85

Sontullo, R.: *Puenteares* 10/89

Sousa, John Philip: *Anchor and Star* 4/82

Sousa, John Philip: *Ancient and Honorable Artillery Company* 4/61

Sousa, John Philip: *At The Movies* 2/91

Sousa, John Philip: *The Belle of Chicago* 4/60; 4/61; 1/82

Sousa, John Philip: *The Black Horse Troop* 11/53; 1/60; 3/61; 4/61; 5/61; 11/61 (3)

Sousa, John Philip: *The Bride Elect* 5/70

Sousa, John Philip: *Bullets and Bayonets* 4/60; 4/61

Sousa, John Philip: "By the Light of the Polar Star" from the Suite *Looking Upward* 5/92

Sousa, John Philip: *Comrades of the Legion* 4/82; 2/88

Sousa, John Philip: *Corcoran Cadets* 2/53; 11/53; 12/54 (3); 2/67; 10/77; 4/82; 10/89

Sousa, John Philip: *Daughters of Texas* 11/53

Sousa, John Philip: *The Diplomat* 10/87

Sousa, John Philip: *The Directorate* 5/70

Sousa, John Philip: *Easter Morning on the White House Lawn* 2/88

Sousa, John Philip: *El Capitan* 1/56; 4/82; 2/91

Sousa, John Philip: *The Fairest of the Fair* 11/53

Sousa, John Philip: *The Gallant Seventh* 4/60; 4/61; 2/85

Sousa, John Philip: *George Washington Bicentennial* 2/75; 5/92

Sousa, John Philip: *The Gladiator* 5/70

Sousa, John Philip: *The Glory of the Yankee Navy* 4/61

Sousa, John Philip: *Golden Jubilee* 4/61

Sousa, John Philip: *The Gridiron Club* 4/61

Sousa, John Philip: *Guide Right* 5/70; 11/75; 2/88

Sousa, John Philip: *Hail to the Spirit of Liberty* 4/82; 3/89

Sousa, John Philip: *Hands Across the Sea* 11/53; 11/58 (2); 2/77; 1/83; 10/89

Sousa, John Philip: *The High School Cadets* 4/60; 4/61; 4/82

Sousa, John Philip: *The Invincible Eagle* 4/60; 4/61; 2/84

Sousa, John Philip: *Jack Tar* 2/82; 4/82

Sousa, John Philip: *Kansas Wildcats* 4/61

Sousa, John Philip: *King Cotton* 1/56; 4/82

Sousa, John Philip: *The Legionnaires* 1/61

Sousa, John Philip: *Liberty Bell* 4/60; 4/61; 10/80; 4/82; 5/92; 6/92

Sousa, John Philip: *The Loyal Legion* 4/82

Sousa, John Philip: *The Man Behind the Gun* 4/82

Sousa, John Philip: *Manhattan Beach* 11/53; 3/61; 4/61

Sousa, John Philip: *Marching Along* 10/89

Sousa, John Philip: *The National Game* 4/61

Sousa, John Philip: *New Mexico March* 4/61

Sousa, John Philip: *The New York Hippodrome* 2/82

Sousa, John Philip: *Nobles of the Mystic Shrine* 4/60; 4/61

Sousa, John Philip: *On Parade* 12/77

Sousa, John Philip: *Peaches and Cream* 6/92

Sousa, John Philip: *The Picadore* 4/60; 4/61

Sousa, John Philip: *Presidential Polonaise* 2/88

Sousa, John Philip: *The Pride of the Wolverines* 4/61

Sousa, John Philip: *Riders for the Flag* 4/60; 4/61

Sousa, John Philip: *The Rifle Regiment* 11/53; 3/61; 4/61; 2/91

Sousa, John Philip: *Sabre and Spurs* 4/60; 4/61

Sousa, John Philip: *Semper Fidelis* 11/53; 5/70; 11/81; 4/82; 5/90

Sousa, John Philip: *Sesquicentennial Exposition March* 4/61

Sousa, John Philip: *Solid Men to the Front* 4/60; 4/61

Sousa, John Philip: *Sound Off* 4/60; 4/61

Sousa, John Philip: *The Stars and Stripes Forever* 1/56; 10/67; 10/69; 10/71; 10/77; 5/78 (26); 4/82; 2/86; 5/90 (15); 6/92 (12)

Sousa, John Philip: *The Thunderer* 1/56; 4/82

Sousa, John Philip: *The U.S. Field Artillery* 1/56

Sousa, John Philip: *The Washington Post* 1/56; 4/82; 2/88

Sousa, John Philip: *Who's Who in Navy Blue* 4/82

Sparke, Philip: *Gaudium, A Concert Piece* for Wind Symphony Orchestra 2/82

Speck, Frederick: Concerto for Wind Orchestra 11/85

Stamitz, Karl (Reynolds): Concerto for Horn and Winds 4/81

Starer, Robert: Concerto for Piano and Winds, No. 2 4/72

Starer, Robert: *Dirge for Band* 4/64

Starer, Robert: Serenade for Brass 10/66; 11/69; 3/92

Stevens, Bernard: Adagio and Fugue, op. 31 1/60

Stevens, Noel Scott: *Cameos* 2/64

Stevens, Noel Scott: *Etching* 5/70

Still, William Grant: *From the Delta* 2/54

Stock, David: *Evensong* for English Horn and Wind Orchestra 11/85

Stokes, Eric: *Hennepin Avenue Marches, Struts!* 2/75

Stout, Gordon: Concerto for Marimba and Wind Ensemble 4/74

Strauss, Johann (Godfrey): Overture to *Die Fledermaus* 2/88

Strauss, Johann, Sr.: *Radetzky March*, op. 228 1/60

Strauss, Richard (Harding): Excerpt from *Death and Transfiguration* 1/54

Strauss, Richard (Hunsberger): "Dance of the Seven Veils" from *Salome* 6/92 (7)

Strauss, Richard: Serenade in E-Flat Major, op. 7 11/56; 12/57; 2/58; 10/60; 6/61; 11/64; 10/81; 12/86; 1/84; 2/92; 6/92 (6)

Strauss, Richard: *Fanfare Stadt Wien* 5/87

Strauss, Richard: Suite in B-Flat, op. 4 3/59; 1/60; 1/61; 12/65; 11/74 (2); 2/79

Strauss, Richard: Symphony for Wind Instruments op. posth. 11/53; 2/86

Stravinsky, Igor: Concerto for Piano and Wind Instruments 3/65; 3/71; 10/71; 4/72; 2/75; 1/81; 3/81; 5/88; 12/90

Stravinsky, Igor: *Circus Polka* 3/61

Stravinsky, Igor: *The Firebird* (Berceuse and Finale) 10/63

Stravinsky, Igor: Octet for Wind Instruments 3/65; 10/77; 5/88

Stravinsky, Igor: *Ragtime* for Eleven Instruments 2/92

Stravinsky, Igor: Suite from *L'Histoire du Soldat* 2/89

Stravinsky, Igor: *Symphonies of Wind Instruments* 2/55; 3/57; 3/60 (2); 11/61 (2); 4/73; 11/76; 2/78; 11/82; 10/88

Stravinsky, Igor: *Symphony of Psalms* 4/83; 5/88

Stern, Robert: *Ultima Fantasia* 2/92

Sullivan, Arthur: "I, too, was born in Arcadia" from *Three Quotations* 2/88

Sullivan, Arthur (Sousa): *The Pirates of Penzance* 1/83

Sullivan, Arthur (Mackerras/Duthoit): *Pineapple Poll* 11/61 (3); 2/86; 5/92

Sullivan, Arthur: *The Lost Chord* 2/88; 3/89

Suma, Yosaku: *Blue Skies* 10/67

Suppé, Franz von (Tobani): Overture to *Morning, Noon and Night in Vienna* 2/84; 5/92

Suppé, Franz von: *Poet and Peasant Overture* 2/87

Surinach, Carlos: *Paeans and Dances of Heathen Iberia* 1/65; 10/67; 5/68; 12/78

Surinach, Carlos: *Sinfonietta Flamenca* 4/73; 2/78

Susato, Tilman (Iveson): "La Mourisque" from *The Danserye* 6/92 (6)

Susato, Tilman: Suite from *The Danserye* 4/81   .

Sweelinck, Jan Pieterszoon (Ricker): *Mein junges Leben hat ein End* 10/72

Sweelinck, Jan Pieterszoon (Walters): *Ballo del Granduca* 2/76; 12/81

T

Taub, Bruce: *Band Piece (Chromatic Essay)* 12/84

Tchaikovsky, Piotr Ilyich (Winterbottom): *Cappricio Italien*, op. 45 2/84; 5/92

Tchaikovsky, Piotr Ilyich (Boyd): *Coronation March* 2/88

Tchaikovsky, Piotr Ilyich (Laurendeau): *Marche Slav* 2/86

Texidor, J. (Winter): *Amparito Roca* 2/77; 2/87

Thiere, Charles Le: *L'Oiseau du Bois* 2/85

Thomas, Ambrose (Safranek): Raymond Overture (*The Queen's Secret*) 2/86

Thomson, Virgil: *A Solemn Music* 3/53; 2/54; 5/54

Thorne, Nicholas: *Adagio Music* "After a Fallen Rain" 11/85; 5/89; 10/91

Ticheli, Frank: *Concertino* for Trombone 12/85

Tieke, Carl: *The Conqueror* 2/67

Tieke, Carl: *Old Comrades* 11/58; 12/62; 2/77

Toch, Ernst: *Spiel für Blasorchester* 3/61; 12/65; 11/73

Toensin, Richard: Concerto for Flutes and Wind Orchestra 11/85

Tohno, Shigeo: *Dance of the Japanese Youth* 11/62

Tomasi, Henri: Concerto for Trombone 4/86

Tomasi, Henri: Concerto for Trumpet 3/90

Tomasi, Henry: *Fanfares Liturgiques* 1/59

Torke, Michael: *Adjustable Wrench* 2/91

Torke, Michael: *Rust* for Piano and Chamber Winds 4/91

Traditional (Hunsberger): *Amazing Grace* ("New Britain") 6/92

Traditional (Hunsberger): *Believe Me, If All Those Endearing Young Charms* 3/89

Traditional (Hunsberger): *Sometimes I Feel Like a Motherless Child* 3/87

Traditional (Koff): *La Virgen de la Macarena* 2/79

Tull, Fisher: *Sketches on a Tudor Psalm* 9/74

Tull, Fisher: *Toccata* 12/83

Tull, Fisher: *Variations on an Advent Tune* for Brass Ensemble 2/76

Turina, Josquin (Krance): *Five Miniatures* 1/75

Turina, Josquin (Reed): *La Procession du Rocio* 11/63

Tuthill, Burnet: Concerto for String Bass and Wind Orchestra 11/74 (2)

Tuthill, Burnet: *Rowdy Dance* 3/62

Tveitt, Geirr (Haugland): *Folk Tunes from Hardanger* 2/66

V

Van Blon, Franz: *Under the Banner of Victory* 10/65

Varèse, Edgard: *Intégrales* 3/61

Vaughan Williams, Ralph (Hunsberger): Variations for Wind Band 5/88 (4); 10/89

Vaughan Williams, Ralph: *Folk Song Suite* 2/54; 5/55; 1/59; 1/61; 3/62; 3/68 (6); 4/68; 10/71; 9/74; 10/85; 2/87; 2/92

Vaughan Williams, Ralph: *Sea Songs* 6/92 (7)

Vaughan Williams, Ralph: *Scherzo alla marcia* from Symphony No. 8 in D Minor 1/60; 3/63

Vaughan Williams, Ralph: *Toccata Marziale* 2/53; 12/54 (3); 5/55; 11/61 (3); 2/67; 10/70; 10/80

Velke, Fritz: *Concertino* for Band 4/63

Verdi, Giuseppe (Mollenhauer): *Manzoni Requiem* 11/62

Verdi, Giuseppe (Rogers): Overture to *La Forza del Destino* 3/89

Villa-Lobos, Heitor: *Fantasy in the Form of a Chôros* 10/67

Complete Discography of the Eastman Wind Ensemble
1952–1993

1. **American Concert Band Masterpieces**
Frederick Fennell, conductor
Recorded May 1953, Eastman Theatre
  Mercury MG40006/MG50079
  Mercury Golden Import Series SRI 75086
  Philips PC-1621 (Japan)
Schuman, William: *George Washington Bridge*
Persichetti, Vincent: *Divertimento* for Band
Gould, Morton: *Ballad* for Band
Bennett, Robert Russell: *Suite of Old American Dances*
Piston, Walter: *Tunbridge Fair*
Barber, Samuel: *Commando March*

2. **Marches by Sousa and Others**
Frederick Fennell, conductor
Recorded November 1953, Eastman Theatre
  Mercury MG40007/MG50080
  Philips PC-1628 (Japan)
Reissued on:
  Marches for Twirling (see No. 37)
    Mercury MG50113
  Fairest of the Fair
  Manhattan Beach
  Black Horse Troop
  Daughters of Texas
  Rifle Regiment
  Corcoran Cadets
  Hands Across the Sea
  Semper Fidelis
Jenkins, Joseph, and Jerome Neff: *Pieces of Eight*
Hanson, Howard: *March Carillon*
Goldman, Edwin Franko: *Cheerio*
Fillmore, Henry: *His Honor*
Bigelow, F. E.: *Our Director*
Alford, Harry L.: *Glory of the Gridiron*
King, Karl: *Pride of the Illini*
Bagley, E. E.: *National Emblem*

3. **La Fiesta Mexicana**
Frederick Fennell, conductor
Recorded May 1954, Eastman Theatre
  Mercury MG40011/MG50084
  Philips PC-1622 (Japan)
Mennin, Peter: *Canzona*
Persichetti, Vincent: *Psalm*
Thompson, Virgil: *A Solemn Music*
Hanson, Howard: *Chorale and Alleluia*
Reed, H. Owen: *La Fiesta Mexicana*

4. **Folksong Suites and Other British Band Classics**
Frederick Fennell, conductor
Recorded May 1955, Eastman Theatre
  Mercury MG40015/MG50088
  Mercury MG50388/SR90388
  Mercury Golden Import Series SRI 75011
  Philips PC-1601 (Japan)
Reissued on:
  Frederick Fennell Conducts (see No. 39)
    Mercury MG50388/SR90388
Holst, Gustav: Suite in E-flat
Holst, Gustav: Suite in F
Vaughan Williams, Ralph: *Folk Song Suite*
Vaughan Williams, Ralph: *Toccata Marziale*
Grainger, Percy: *Hill Song* No. 2

5. **Marching Along**
Frederick Fennell, conductor
Recorded January 1956, Eastman Theatre
  Mercury MG50105/MWS5–14/SR90105
  Mercury Golden Import Series SRI 75004
  Philips PC-1612 (Japan)
Reissued on:
  Hands Across the Sea & Marching Along: Marches From
    Around the World (see No. 50)
    Mercury Living Presence CD 434 334–2

Selections reissued on:

Marches for Twirling (see No. 37)

Mercury MG50113

The Heart of the March (two-record set; see No. 38)

Mercury SR2–9131

Curtain Up! John Philip Sousa Favorites (see No. 40)

Mercury MG50291/SR90291

Music of John Philip Sousa (two record set; see No. 42)

Mercury Golden Import Series SRI 77010

Sousa, John Philip: *The U.S. Field Artillery*

The Thunderer

Washington Post

King Cotton

El Capitan

Stars and Stripes Forever

Meacham, F. W.: *American Patrol*

Goldman, Edwin Franko: *On The Mall*

McCoy, Earl E.: *Lights Out*

King, Karl: *Barnum and Bailey's Favorite*

Alford, K. J.: *Colonel Bogey*

Klohr, John N.: *The Billboard*

6. The Spirit of '76: Music for Fifes and Drums

Frederick Fennell, conductor

Recorded May 1956, Eastman Theatre

Mercury MG50111/SR90111

Mercury Golden Import Series SRI 75018

Traditional Marching Tunes for Fifes and Drums

Yankee Doodle

Sergeant O'Leary

The Belle of the Mohawk Vale

Garry Owen

Sentry Box

Rally 'round the Flag

Bonnie Blue Flag

The White Cockade

The Camp Duty of the U.S. Army

The Three Camps

The Slow Scotch

The Austrian

Dawning of the Day

The Hessian

Dusky Night

The Prussian

The Dutch

The Quick Scotch

The Three Camps

Traditional Music for Fifes and Drums

The Breakfast Call: "Peas Upon a Trencher"

The Dinner Call: "Roast Beef"

Wrecker's Daughter—Quickstep

Hell on the Wabash

Downfall of Paris

Drum Solos

Connecticut Half-time

Fancy 6/8

7. Ruffles and Flourishes: Music for Trumpets and Drums

Frederick Fennell, conductor

Recorded May 1956, Eastman Theatre

Mercury MG50112/MS5–13/SR90112

Mercury Golden Import Series SRI 75034

Music for Rendering Honors

Ruffles and Flourishes

General's March

To The Colors

Funeral March

Sound Off: General Dooley and the Old Guard

The American Flag

The Cavaliers

Old Six-Eight

I've Got Three Years To Do This In

So Slum Today

Carry On: Swinging Down the Street

Sound Off: Holy Joe

Soapsuds Row

The Colonel's Daughter

The Prisoner

Rip Van Winkle

The Garrison Belle

General Burt

Bugle Calls of the U.S. Army

Ruffles and Flourishes

Assembly

Adjutant's Call

Church Call

Drill Call

General's Call

Mail Call

Mess Call

Retreat

Call to Quarters

Reveille

Tattoo: Taps

Carry On: Connecticut Half-time
Sound Off: You're In The Army Now
Spanish Guard Mount
The Red Hussars
A-Hunting We Will Go
Pay Day and Double Time
The President's March
The Star Spangled Banner

8. Hindemith/Schoenberg/Stravinsky
Frederick Fennell, conductor
Recorded March 1957, Eastman Theatre
   Mercury MG50143/SR90143
   Mercury Golden Import Series SRI 75057
   Philips PC-1607 (Japan)
Hindemith, Paul: *Symphony in B-flat*
Schoenberg, Arnold: *Theme and Variations*, op. 43a
Stravinsky, Igor: *Symphonies of Wind Instruments*

9. March Time: Marches of Goldman and Others
Frederick Fennell, conductor
Recorded October 1957, Eastman Theatre
   Mercury MG50170/MWS5–29/SR90170
   Mercury Golden Import Series SRI 75055
   Philips PC-1614 (Japan)
Reissued on:
   Screamers! (Circus Marches) & March Time (see No.
      44)
      Mercury Living Presence CD 432 019–2
Selections reissued on:
   The Heart of the March (two-record set; see No. 38)
      Mercury SR2–9131
   Curtain Up! Bravos in Brass (see No. 41)
      Mercury MG50360/SR90360
Goldman, Edwin Franko: *Bugles and Drums*
   Illinois March
   Children's March
   The Interlochen Bowl
   Onward-Upward
   Boy Scouts of America
Fillmore, Henry: *Americans We*
Hall, R. B.: *Officer of the Day*
Seitz, Roland: *March "Grandioso"*
Reeves, D. W.: *2nd Regiment Connecticut National
   Guard March*
Alford, K. J. (F. Ricketts): *The Mad Major*
Rogers, Richard: *Guadalcanal March*

10. Winds in Hi-Fi
Frederick Fennell, conductor
Recorded March 1958, Eastman Theatre
   Mercury MG50173/SR90173
   Mercury Golden Import Series SRI 75093
   Philips PC-1604 (Japan)
Selections reissued on:
   Fennell Conducts Grainger, Persichetti & Others (see
      No. 45)
      Mercury Living Presence CD 432 754–2
Grainger, Percy: *Lincolnshire Posy*
Milhaud, Darius: *Suite Française*
Strauss, Richard: Serenade in E-flat, op. 7
Rogers, Bernard: *Three Japanese Dances*

11. Mozart: Serenade in B-Flat, K. 361
Frederick Fennell, conductor
Recorded March 1958, Eastman Theatre
   Mercury MG50176/SR90176
Reissued on Mercury MG50412/SR90412 with W. A.
      Mozart, *Eine kleine Nachtmusik.*

12. British Band Classics, Vol. 2
Frederick Fennell, conductor
Recorded November 1958, Eastman Theatre
   Mercury MG50197/SR90197
   Mercury Golden Import Series SRI 75028
Reissued on:
   British and American Band Classics (see No. 43)
      Mercury Living Presence CD 432 009–2
Jacob, Gordon: *William Byrd Suite*
Holst, Gustav: *Hammersmith*, Prelude and Scherzo, op.
   52
Walton, William (Duthoit): *Crown Imperial—A
   Coronation March*

13. Hands Across the Sea
Frederick Fennell, conductor
Recorded November 1958, Eastman Theatre
   Mercury MG50207/SR90207
   Mercury Golden Import Series SRI 75099
   Philips PC-1615 (Japan)
Reissued on:
   *Hands Across the Sea & Marching Along: Marches From
      Around the World* (see No. 50)
      Mercury Living Presence CD 434 334–2
Selections reissued on *Curtain Up! Bravos in Brass* (see
   No. 41)

Mercury MG50360/SR90360
Sousa, John Philip: *Hands Across the Sea*
Ganne, Gustav Luis: *Father of Victory*
San Miguel, Mariano: *The Golden Ear*
Tieke, Carl: *Old Comrades*
Prokofiev, Serge: March, op. 99
Hanssen, Johannes: *Valdres March*
Delle Cese, Davide: *L'Inglesina*
Coates, Eric: *Knightsbridge March*

14. **American Masterpieces for Concert Band,** Vol. 2
Frederick Fennell, conductor
Recorded May 1959, Eastman Theatre
   Mercury MG50220/SR90220
   Mercury Golden Import Series SRI 75094
Selections reissued on:
   British and American Band Classics (see No. 43)
      Mercury Living Presence CD 432 009–2
   Gould/Giannini/Hovhaness (see No. 48)
      Mercury Living Presence CD 434 320–2
Williams, Clifton: *Fanfare and Allegro*
Gould, Morton: *West Point Symphony*
Work, Julian: *Autumn Walk*
Bennett, Robert Russell: *Symphonic Songs*

15. **Diverse Winds**
Frederick Fennell, conductor
Recorded May 1959, Eastman Theatre
   Mercury MG50221/SR90221
   Philips PC-1603 (Japan)
Reissued on:
   Fennell Conducts Grainger, Persichetti & Others (see No. 45)
      Mercury Living Presence CD 432 754–2
Selection reissued on:
   Frederick Fennell Conducts (see No. 39)
      Mercury MG50388/SR90388
Persichetti, Vincent: Symphony No. 6
Khachaturian, Aram: *Armenian Dances*
Grainger, Percy: *Hill Song* No. 2
Hartley, Walter: Concerto for Twenty-three Winds

16. **Ballet for Band**
Frederick Fennell, conductor
Recorded October 1959, Eastman Theatre
   Mercury MG50256/SR90256
   Mercury Golden Import Series SRI 75138
   Philips PC-1606 (Japan)

Reissued from different master on:
   Ballet for Band/Wagner (see No. 49)
      Mercury Living Presence CD 434 322–2
Gounod, Charles (Winterbottom): Ballet music from the opera *Faust*
Rossini, Gioacchino (Respighi/Godfrey/Leidzen): Suite from the ballet *La Boutique Fantasque*
Sullivan, Arthur (MacKerras/Duthoit): Suite from the ballet *Pineapple Poll*

17. **Wagner for Band**
Frederick Fennell, conductor
Recorded October 1959, Eastman Theatre
   Mercury MG50276/SR90276
   Mercury Golden Import Series SRI 75096
   Philips PC-1605 (Japan)
Selections reissued on:
   Ballet for Band/Wagner (see No. 49)
      Mercury Living Presence CD 434 322–2
Wagner, Richard:
   Prelude to Act III and Bridal Chorus from *Lohengrin* (Winterbottom)
   Overture to *Rienzi* (Grabel)
   Good Friday Spell from *Parsifal* (Godfrey)
   Elsa's Procession to the Cathedral from *Lohengrin* (Caillet)
   Entry of the Gods into Valhalla from *Das Rheingold* (Godfrey)

18. **Sound Off! (Marches by John Philip Sousa)**
Frederick Fennell, conductor
Recorded May 1960, Eastman Theatre
   Mercury MG50264/SR90264
   Mercury Golden Import Series SRI 75047
Reissued on:
   Sound Off! & Sousa on Review (see No. 47)
      Mercury Living Presence CD 434 300–2
Selections reissued on:
   Curtain Up! John Philip Sousa Favorites (see No. 40)
      Mercury MG50291/SR90291
   Music of John Philip Sousa (two-record set; see No. 42)
      Mercury Golden Import Series SRI 77010
Sousa, John Philip:
   High School Cadets
   The Picadore
   Our Flirtation
   Bullets and Bayonets

Nobles of the Mystic Shrine
The Gallant Seventh
The Invincible Eagle
Sound Off!
Riders for the Flag
Sabre and Spurs
Solid Men to the Front
Liberty Bell

19. **Civil War** (2 vols., two records each)
Frederick Fennell, conductor
Recorded December 1960, Eastman Theatre
   Mercury LPS2–501/502 and LPS2–901/902
   Mercury Golden Import Series SRI 77011
Reissued as:
   The Civil War, Its Music and Its Sounds (December
     1990)
     Mercury Living Presence CD 432 591–2 (two
     disks)
   Hail to the Chief
   Cape May Polka
   Tenting Tonight
   Easter Galop
   Tramp, Tramp,Tramp
   Come Where My Love Lies Dreaming
   When Johnny Comes Marching Home
   Listen to the Mocking Bird
   Old Hundreth
   Dixie and Bonnie Blue Flag
   Come Dearest the Daylight is Gone
   Marching Thru Georgia
   Lulu's Quickstep
   Palmyra Schottische
   Goober Peas
   Carry Me Back
   Old Kentucky, Kentucky
   Garry Owen
   St. Patrick's Day in the Morning
   Port Royal Galop
   We Are Coming Father Abra'am
   Hail Columbia
   Freischütz Quickstep
   Cheer Boys Cheer
   Nightingale Waltz
   The Star Spangled Banner
Field Music of Union and Confederate Troops
   Cavalry Bugle Signals
   Camp and Field Calls for Fifes and Drums

Cavalry Quickstep
Lulu's Gone
Tramp, Tramp, Tramp
Waltz
Storm Galop
Maryland, My Maryland
The Battle Hymn of The Republic

20. **Music of Gabrieli (Andrea & Giovanni Gabrieli)**
Frederick Fennell, conductor
Recorded May 1961, Christ Church, Rochester, New
   York
   Mercury MG50245/SR90245
   Mercury Golden Import Series SRI 75130
Gabrieli, Andrea (Ghedini): *Aria della battaglia*
Gabrieli, Giovanni:
   Sonata octavi toni
   Sonata pian' e forte
   Canzon duodecimi toni
   Canzon noni toni
   Canzon septimi toni
   Canzon quarti toni
   Canzon quarti toni

21. **Sousa on Review (Marches by John Philip Sousa)**
Frederick Fennell, conductor
Recorded May 1961, Eastman Theatre
   Mercury MG50284/SR90284
   Mercury Golden Import Series SRI 75064
Reissued on:
   Sound Off! & Sousa on Review (see No. 47)
     Mercury Living Presence CD 434 300–2
Selections reissued on:
   Curtain Up! Bravos in Brass (see No. 41)
     Mercury MG50360/SR90360
   Music of John Philip Sousa (two-record set; see No.
     42)
     Mercury Golden Import Series SRI 77010
Sousa, John Philip:
   Ancient and Honorable Artillery Company
   Sesqui-Centennial Exposition March
   Golden Jubilee
   The National Game
   Kansas Wildcats
   The Rifle Regiment
   The Pride of the Wolverines
   The Black Horse Troop
   The Glory of the Yankee Navy

New Mexico March
The Gridiron Club March
Manhattan Beach

22. Screamers! (Circus Marches)
Frederick Fennell, conductor
Recorded May 1962, Eastman Theatre
    Mercury MG50314/SR90314
    Mercury Golden Import Series SRI 75087
    Philips PC-1616 (Japan)
Reissued on:
    Screamers! (Circus Marches) & March Time (see No. 44)
    Mercury Living Presence CD 432 019–2
Selections reissued on:
    The Heart of the March (two-record set; see No. 38)
        Mercury SR2–9131
    Curtain Up! Bravos in Brass (see No. 41)
        Mercury MG50360/SR90360
Heed, J. C.: *In Storm and Sunshine*
Allen, T. S.: *Whip and Spur*
King, Karl: *Invictus*
King, Karl: *The Big Cage*
Fillmore, Henry: *Bones Trombone*
Huffine: *Them Basses*
Fillmore, Henry: *The Circus Bee*
Jewell, Fred: *The Screamer*
Fucik, Julius: *Thunder and Blazes*
King, Karl: *Robinson's Grand Entree*
King, Karl: *Circus Days*
Farrar, O. R.: *Bombasto*
Huff, Will: *The Squealer*
Fillmore, Henry: *Rolling Thunder*
Ribble, M. H.: *Bennett's Triumphal*
Duble, C. E.: *Bravura*

23. Giannini and Hovhaness
A. Clyde Roller, conductor
Recorded May 1963, Eastman Theatre
    Mercury MG50366/SR90366
    Mercury Golden Import SRI 75010
Reissued on:
    Gould/Giannini/Hovhaness (see No. 48)
        Mercury Living Presence CD 434 320–2
Hovhaness, Alan: Symphony No. 4
Giannini, Vittorio: Symphony No. 3

24. American Music for Symphonic Winds
Donald Hunsberger, conductor
Recorded May 1968, Eastman Theatre
    Decca DL 710163
Dahl, Ingolf: *Sinfonietta* for Concert Band
Hartley, Walter: *Sinfonia No. 4*
Persichetti, Vincent: *Masquerade*

25. Fiesta!
Donald Hunsberger, conductor
Recorded April 1969, Eastman Theatre
    Decca DL 710157
    Westminster MCA 1409 (reissue)
Reed, H. Owen: *La Fiesta Mexicana*
Surinach, Carlos: *Paeans and Dances of Heathen Iberia*
Nixon, Roger: *Fiesta del Pacifico*

26. Penderecki/Mayuzumi/Williams
Donald Hunsberger, conductor
Recorded May 1969, Eastman Theatre
    Deutsche Grammophon 2530 063
Penderecki, Krystof: *Pittsburgh Overture*
Mayuzumi, Toshiro: *Music with Sculpture*
Williams, John T.: *Sinfonietta*

27. The Children's Plea for Peace
Milford Fargo, conductor
Eastman Children's Chorus
Recorded April 1971, Eastman Theatre
    Turnabout TV-S 34413
Wilder, Alec: *The Children's Plea for Peace*

28. Homespun America (three-record set)
Donald Hunsberger, conductor
Recorded April 1976, Eastman Theatre
    Vox Box SVBX 5309
Reissued as: **Homespun America** (The American Composers Series) Vox Box CDX 5088 (2 CDs)
Music for the Manchester (N.H.) Brass Band, c. 1854–1858:
    Easton's Grand March
    "Giorno d'Orrore" (Semiramide)
    Free and Easy
    Les Rendezvous Waltzes
    Galop
    Serenade—Departed Days
    Quickstep-Blues
    Waltz

Congo's Quickstep

The Fireman's Polka

Hope Told a Flattering Tale (air varie)

Peter's Quickstep

The Fourth of July Overture

My Heaven's Graces

Hail to the Chief

Album also contains music for the Social Orchestra
and for the Hutchinson Family Singers.

29. Strike Up the Band (Marches of John Philip Sousa)

Donald Hunsberger, conductor

Recorded April 1970, Eastman Theatre; issued 1976
Philips 9500 151

Reissued as: **Strike Up the Band** Philips PHCP 10063

Sousa, John Philip:

Semper Fidelis

Belle of Chicago

The Crusader

The Diplomat

The Beau Ideal

On Parade

The Stars and Stripes Forever

Bride-Elect

The Directorate

The Gladiator

Guide Right

National Fencibles

The Occidental

30. Hanson/Schwantner/Copland

Donald Hunsberger, conductor

Recorded November 1978, Eastman Theatre
Mercury Golden Import Series SRI 75132

Hanson, Howard: *Young Person's Guide to the Six-Tone Scale*

Barry Snyder, piano soloist

Schwantner, Joseph: "*. . . and the mountains rising nowhere*"

Copland, Aaron: *Emblems*

31. Eastman Wind Ensemble in Japan (2 vols.)

Donald Hunsberger, conductor

Recorded June 1978, Kosei Nenkin Kaikan Hall,
Tokyo, Japan
Toshiba EMI TA 72043 and 72044

Vol. 1:

Kineda, Bin: *Symphonic Movement*

Benson, Warren: *The Leaves are Falling*

Vaughan Williams, Ralph: *English Folk Song Suite*

Kennan, Kent: *Night Soliloquy*

Delle Cese, Davide: *L'Inglesina*

Fucik, Julius: *The Florentiner*

Kamioka, Yoichi: *In Autumn Skies*

Wright, Rayburn: *Japanese Folk Song Fantasy*
(Rayburn Wright, guest conductor)

Vol. 2:

Copland, Aaron: *An Outdoor Overture*

Bach, J. S. (Hunsberger): Passacaglia and Fugue in
C minor

McBeth, Francis: *Kaddish*

Persichetti, Vincent: Symphony No. 6

Alford, Kenneth: *Colonel Bogey*

Dan, Ikuma: *Grand March*

Sousa, John Philip: *Stars and Stripes Forever*

32. Benson/Brant/Hanson

Donald Hunsberger, conductor

Recorded January 1980, Eastman Theatre
Centaur CD CRC 2014

Benson, Warren: *The Leaves Are Falling*

Brant, Henry: *Angels and Devils*
Bonita Boyd, flute soloist

Hanson, Howard: *Dies Natalis*

33. Sousa Spectacular

Donald Hunsberger, conductor

Recorded April 1982, Eastman Theatre
Tioch Digital TD 1007

Reissued as:

Famous Marches

Tioch KEM-DISC 1004

Peter's Music Factory CD 90 523–2
(Discuro, 9 Gillingham St., London SW1V 1HN,
England)

Sousa, John Philip:

Semper Fidelis

The High School Cadets

Washington Post

Jack Tar

The Loyal Legion

Anchor and Star

Stars and Stripes Forever

El Capitan

Liberty Bell
Comrades of the Legion
The Corcoran Cadets
King Cotton
Hail to the Spirit of Liberty
The Thunderer

34. Carnaval

Donald Hunsberger, conductor/arranger
Wynton Marsalis, cornet soloist
Recorded September 1986, Eastman Theatre
    CBS Masterworks IM421137
Selections (Levy, Rimsky-Korsakov, and "Sometimes
    I Feel") reissued on: *Portrait of Wynton Marsalis*
    CBS MK-44726 (September 1988)
Arban, Jean-Baptiste (Hunsberger): *Variations sur "Le
    Carnaval de Venise"*
Clarke, Herbert L. (Hunsberger): *The Debutante*
    ("Caprice Brillante")
Traditional (Hunsberger): *Believe Me, If All Those
    Endearing Young Charms*
Levy, Jules (Hunsberger): *Grand Russian Fantasia*
Paganini, Niccolò (Hunsberger): *Moto Perpetuo*, op. 11
Traditional (Hunsberger): *'Tis the Last Rose of Summer*
Rimsky-Korsakov, Nicolai (Hunsberger): "The Flight
    of the Bumblebee" from *Tsar Sultan*
Bellstedt, Hermann (Hunsberger): *Napoli—Variations
    on a Neapolitan Song*
Arban, Jean-Baptiste (Hunsberger): *Fantasie Brillante*
Traditional Spiritual (Hunsberger): *Sometimes I Feel
    Like a Motherless Child*
Clarke, Herbert L. (Hunsberger): *Valse Brillante*
    ("Sounds from the Hudson")

35. Vaughan Williams/Hindemith/Copland/Husa

Donald Hunsberger, conductor
Recorded March 1988, Eastman Theatre
    CBS Masterworks MK-44916
Reissued on:
    CBS Masterworks CD 7464–44916–2
Vaughan Williams, Ralph: *Toccata Marziale*
Vaughan Williams, Ralph (Hunsberger): Variations
    for Wind Band
Hindemith, Paul: *Konzertmusik für Blasorchester*, op. 41
Copland, Aaron (Hunsberger): *Quiet City*
    Wynton Marsalis, trumpet; Phillip Koch, English
    horn
Husa, Karel: *Music for Prague 1968*

36. Live in Osaka

Donald Hunsberger, conductor
Recorded June 1990, Symphony Hall, Osaka, Japan
    Sony Music SK 47198
Bach, J. S. (Hunsberger): Toccata and Fugue in D
    Minor
Holst, Gustav: First Suite in E-flat
Schwantner, Joseph: "*. . . and the mountains rising
    nowhere*"
Bach, J. S. (Renshaw): *Jesu, Joy of Man's Desiring*
Grainger, Percy: *Lincolnshire Posy*
Ives, Charles: *Country Band March*
Rimsky-Korsakov, Nicolai (Hunsberger): *Flight of the
    Bumblebee*
Shostakovich, Dmitri (Hunsberger): *Festive Overture*
Grainger, Percy: *Lads of Wamphray*
Mamiya, Michio: *Glory of Catalonia*
Sousa, John Philip: *Stars and Stripes Forever*

Reissues

37. Marches for Twirling

Frederick Fennell, conductor
Reissue compiled from MG50080 and MG50105/
    SR90105
    Mercury MG50113
Sousa, John Philip: *The U.S. Field Artillery*
    Semper Fidelis
    Manhattan Beach
    The Stars and Stripes Forever
Fillmore, Henry: *His Honor*
Goldman, Edwin Franko: *On The Mall*
Alford, K. J.: *Glory of the Gridiron*
King, Karl: *Pride of the Illini*
King, Karl: *Barnum and Bailey's Favorite*
Bigelow, F. E.: *Our Director*
Klohr, John N.: *The Billboard*
Bagley, E. E.: *National Emblem*

38. The Heart of the March (two-record set)

Frederick Fennell, conductor
Reissue compiled from MG50105/MWS5–14/
    SR90105, MG50170/MWS5–29/SR90170, and
    MG50314/SR90314
    Mercury SR2–9131
Sousa, John Philip: *Stars and Stripes Forever*
    El Capitan
    Washington Post

King Cotton
The Picadore
Hands Across the Sea
The Thunderer
Our Flirtations
Meacham, F. W.: *American Patrol*
Klohr, John: *The Billboard*
Heed, J. C.: *In Storm and Sunshine*
Fillmore, Henry: *Circus Bee*
Goldman, Edwin Franko: *On the Mall*
Reeves, D. W.: *2nd Regiment Connecticut National Guard March*
Tieke, Carl: *Old Comrades*
Jewell, Fred: *The Screamer*
Fucik, Julius: *Thunder and Blazes*

39. **Frederick Fennell Conducts**
Reissue compiled from MG50088/SR90388 and MG50221/SR90221
Mercury MG50388/SR90388
Vaughan Williams, Ralph: *Folk Song Suite*
Holst, Gustav: Suite in E-Flat
Holst, Gustav: Suite No. 2 in F
Grainger, Percy: *Hill Song* No. 2
Vaughan Williams, Ralph: *Toccata Marziale*

40. **Curtain Up! John Philip Sousa Favorites**
Frederick Fennell, conductor
Reissue of Mercury MG50105/MWS5–14/SR90105 and MG50264/SR90264
Mercury MG50291/SR90291
Sousa, John Philip:
The U.S. Field Artillery
The Liberty Bell
El Capitan
Manhattan Beach
Hands Across the Sea
Bullets and Bayonets
Washington Post
Sabre and Spurs
King Cotton
Black Horse Troop
Riders for the Flag
Kansas Wildcats

41. **Curtain Up! Bravos in Brass**
Frederick Fennell, conductor
Reissue compiled from Mercury MG50170/SR90170,

MG50207/SR90207, MG50264/SR90264, and MG50284/SR90284
Mercury MG50360/SR90360
Sousa, John Philip: *Solid Men to the Front*
Sesqui-Centennial Exposition
The Picadore
The National Game
Alford, K. J.: *Colonel Bogey*
Alford, K. J.: *The Mad Major*
Fucik, Julius: *Thunder and Blazes*
Reeves, D. W.: *2nd Regiment Connecticut National Guard March*
Delle Cese, Davide: *L'Inglesina*
Goldman, Edwin Franko: *Onward-Upward*
Heed, J. C.: *In Storm and Sunshine*
Tieke, Carl: *Old Comrades*

42. **Music of John Philip Sousa** (two-record set)
Frederick Fennell, conductor
Reissue compiled from Mercury MG50105/SR90105, MG50264/SR90264, and MG50284/SR90284
Mercury Golden Import Series SRI 77010
Sousa, John Philip:
Stars And Stripes Forever
Washington Post
The Thunderer
King Cotton
U.S. Field Artillery
El Capitan
Nobles of the Mystic Shrine
The Gallant Seventh
The Liberty Bell
Solid Men to the Front
Golden Jubilee
Ancient and Honorable Artillery Company
The Rifle Regiment
The Pride of the Wolverines
Sesqui-Centennial Exposition
The National Game
The Gridiron Club
The Glory of the Yankee Navy
Manhattan Beach
The Black Horse Troop
New Mexico
The Kansas Wildcats
Hands Across the Sea
The Invincible Eagle
Riders for the Flag

The High School Cadets
Sabre and Spurs
Bullets and Bayonets
Our Flirtations
The Picadore
Sound Off!

43. British and American Band Classics
Frederick Fennell, conductor
Reissue compiled from Mercury SR90197 and
     SR90220
  Mercury Living Presence CD 432 009–2
Jacob, Gordon: *William Byrd Suite*
Walton, William: *Crown Imperial March*
Holst, Gustav: *Hammersmith*, Prelude and Scherzo
Bennett, R. Russell: *Symphonic Songs for Band*
Williams, Clifton: *Fanfare and Allegro*

44. Screamers! (Circus Marches) & March Time
Frederick Fennell, conductor
Reissue compiled from Mercury MG50314/SR90314
     and MG50170/MWS5–29/SR90170
  Mercury Living Presence CD 432 019–2

45. Fennell Conducts Grainger, Persichetti & Others
Frederick Fennell, conductor
Reissue compiled from MG50173/SR90173 and
     MG50221/SR90221
  Mercury Living Presence CD 432 754–2
Grainger, Percy: *Lincolnshire Posy*
Grainger, Percy: *Hill Song* No. 2
Persichetti, Vincent: Symphony No. 6 for Band
Khachaturian, Aram: *Armenian Dances*
Hartley, Walter: Concerto for Twenty-three Winds
Rogers, Bernard: *Three Japanese Dances*

46. Fennell/Sousa
Frederick Fennell, conductor
Reissue
  Mercury Living Presence CD 434 134–2

47. Sound Off! & Sousa on Review
Frederick Fennell, conductor
Reissue compiled from Mercury MG50264/SR90264
     and MG50284/SR90284
  Mercury Living Presence CD 434 300–2

48. Gould/Giannini/Hovhaness
Reissue compiled from Mercury MG50220/SR90220
     and MG50366/SR90366
  Mercury Living Presence CD 434 320–2
Gould, Morton: *West Point Symphony* (Frederick
     Fennell, conductor)
Giannini, Vittorio: Symphony No. 3 (A. Clyde Roller,
     conductor)
Hovhaness, Alan: Symphony No. 4 (A. Clyde Roller,
     conductor)

49. Ballet for Band/Wagner
Frederick Fennel, conductor
Reissue compiled from Mercury MG50256/SR90256
     and MG50276/SR90276
  Mercury Living Presence CD 434 322–2

50. Hands Across the Sea & Marching Along: Marches From Around the World
Frederick Fennell, conductor
Reissue compiled from Mercury MG50105/MWS5–
     14/SR90105 and MG50207/SR90207
  Mercury Living Presence CD 434 334–2

Single Releases

Caves, Franesco: *Tamboo*
Frederick Fennell, conductor
Recorded May 1954, Eastman Theatre
  Mercury MG70678 45 rpm

Hermann, Ralph: *Prom Night*
Osser, Glenn: *Beguine for Band*
On *Curtain-up! Fennell and the Pops*
Frederick Fennell, conductor
Recorded May 1957, Eastman Theatre
  Mercury MG50340/SR90340
Also includes selections performed by the Eastman-
     Rochester POPS Orchestra and the Frederick
     Fennell Orchestra.

Anderson, Leroy: *A Christmas Festival*
Frederick Fennell, conductor
Recorded October 1957, Eastman Theatre
  Mercury MG71238 45 rpm/YW16161

Epstein, David: *Vent-Ures*
On *The Music of David Epstein*
Donald Hunsberger, conducting
Recorded April 1972, Eastman Theatre
    Desco DC 7148

Walton, William: *Crown Imperial Coronation March*
On *Curtain-up! More March Favorites*
Frederick Fennell, conductor
Reissue
    Mercury MG50325/SR90325

Holst, Gustav: Suite in E-Flat
Mercury Living Presence Sampler
Frederick Fennell, conductor
Reissue
    Mercury Old-6

Goldman, Edwin Franko: *On the Mall*
On *Curtain-up! Musical Almanac*
Frederick Fennell, conductor
Reissue
    Mercury MG50337/SR90337

Khachaturian, Aram: *Armenian Dances*
On *Great Music by Russian Composers*
Frederick Fennell, conductor
    Mercury MG50346/SR90346

Anderson, Leroy: *A Christmas Festival*
Bennett, Robert Russell: "Celebration" from
    Symphonic Songs
On *Curtain-up! Holidays around the World*
Frederick Fennell, conductor
Reissue
    Mercury MG50361/SR90361

Special Issues

Eastmontage
Donald Hunsberger, conductor
Recorded April 1969, Eastman Theatre
    ES 72001

*The Eastman Wind Ensemble—CBDNA 19th National
    Conference* (two-record set)
Donald Hunsberger, conductor; Frederick Fennell,
    guest conductor
Recorded March 1977, University of Maryland
    Crest CBDNA 77-4
Conducted by Donald Hunsberger:
    Mayuzumi, Toshiro: *Music with Sculpture*
    Foley, Keith: *Evosträta*
    Reed, H. Owen: *La Fiesta Mexicana*
    Schwantner, Joseph: ". . . and the mountains rising
        nowhere"
Conducted by Frederick Fennell:
    Krenek, Ernst: *Drei lustige Märsche*
    Grainger, Percy: *Hill Song* No. 2

APPENDIX B

Eastman Wind Ensemble 40th Anniversary Celebration

incorporating presentations by

The Conductors' Guild
The Sonneck Society for American Music

February 7–8–9, 1992

**EASTMAN THEATRE
KILBOURN HALL**

	Thursday, February 6, 1992	
3:45 – 5:00 p.m.	Euphonium Master Class	Room 120
	Toru Miura, Tokyo Kosei Wind Orchestra	

* * * * *

	Friday, February 7, 1992	
9:00 – 5:00 p.m.	*Registration*	Main Hall
1:00 p.m.	*Conductors' Guild Conducting Fellows*	
	Eastman Theatre stage	
	The Conductors' Guild	
1:30 – 4:30 p.m.	*Conducting Session I*	Eastman Theatre
	Faculty	
	Frederick Fennell	
	A. Clyde Roller	
	Donald Hunsberger	
	Michael Charry, President, Conductors' Guild	
	Repertoire	
	Music for Prague, Movement I	Karel Husa
	From a Dark Millenium	Joseph Schwantner
3:45 p.m.	*Welcome:*	Kilbourn Hall
	Dr. Jon Engberg, Associate Director for Academic Affairs	

The Sonneck Society Presents:

3:45 – 5:15 p.m.   *Research Papers I*   Kilbourn Hall
Frank Cipolla, Coordinator
Raoul Camus, Queensboro College, NYC
Robert Sheldon, Curator, Instrument Collection – Library of Congress
Jon Newsom, Assistant Chief Librarian, Music Division –
Library of Congress

5:15 – 5:45 p.m.   *Performance & Theatrical*   Eastman Theatre
Preparation Demonstration
"Developing and Producing a PRISM concert"
Donald Hunsberger and Merritt Torrey, Jr., Stage Manager,
Eastman Theatre

8:00 p.m.   *PRISM CONCERT*   Eastman Theatre
"Winds Are Wonderful"
Presented by the Conducting and Ensembles Department
in Commemoration of the
Fortieth Anniversary of the Eastman Wind Ensemble

Suite in E-flat   Gustav Holst
Movement I – Chaconne

David Wallace, conducting

Narrative commemorating the Eastman Wind Ensemble
by Kenneth Neidig, Editor, BD Guide

Swinging Down the Street   William Street
Eastman Percussion Ensemble

Symphony in B-flat*   Paul Hindemith
Movement I

Mallory Thompson, conducting

Serenade in E-flat, Op. 7   Richard Strauss
Lois Ferrari, conducting

Ragtime for Eleven Instruments   Igor Stravinsky
Carl Atkins, conducting

Nonet for brass instruments*   Wallingford Reigger
Rodney Winther, conducting

Sinfonietta for concert band   Ingolf Dahl
Movement II – Pastoral Nocturne

Michael Votta, conducting

Serenade in B-flat, K.361*   Wolfgang Amadeus Mozart
Adagio

Wayne Jeffrey, conducting

Canzon Quarti toni a 15   Giovanni Gabrieli
instrumentation by Donald Hunsberger

Mark Scatterday, conducting

Little Three Penny Music   Kurt Weill
    Tango-Ballad
    Cannon Song
                    Jeffrey Renshaw, conducting

Matrix for Euphonium and electronic tape   Mitsuhiro Nagano
                    Toru Miura, euphonium

Emblems (excerpted)   Aaron Copland
                    Donald Hunsberger, conducting

CONDUCTORS

Carl Atkins – CEO, Rochester Philharmonic Orchestra, Rochester, New York
Lois Ferari – Doctoral candidate, Eastman School of Music, Rochester, NY
Wayne Jeffrey – University of Western Ontario, London, Ontario, Canada
Jeffrey Renshaw – Western Michigan University, Kalamazoo, Michigan
Mark Scatterday – Cornell University, Ithaca, New York
Munro Sherrill – Emeritus, Fairport High School, Fairport, New York
Mallory Thompson – University of South Florida, Tampa, Florida
Michael Votta – Duke University, Durham, North Carolina
David Wallace – Western Washington University, Bellingham, Washington
Rodney Winter – Ithaca College, Ithaca, New York

*Repertoire performed on the Premiere Concert of the Eastman Wind Ensemble, Frederick Fennell conducting, Kilbourn Hall, Sunday, February 8, 1953.

Saturday, February 8, 1992

9:00 – 12:00 p.m.	*Conducting Session II*	Eastman Theatre
	Repertoire	
	Serenade in B, K.361/370a	Mozart
11:15 – 12:15 p.m.	*Research Papers II*	Kilbourn Hall
	Jon Mitchell, University of Georgia	
	David Whitwell, California State University at Northridge	
	James Croft, Florida State University	
1:15 – 2:30 p.m.	*Composition Readings I*	Eastman Theatre
	New (and recent)	
	Sidney Hodkinson	
	Variegations	Thomas Muncy
	The Persistence of Memory (1989)	Jack Gallagher
	Angel (1989)	James Carbon
	Jamie Kalyn, alto saxophone	
	Ultima Fantasia (1990)	Robert Stern
2:45 – 5:00 p.m.	*Conducting Session II*	Eastman Theatre
	Repertoire	
	Fanfare for the Common Man	Copland
	Music for Prague, Movement 3	Husa
	Serenade in B, K.361/370a	Mozart
5:00 – 6:00 p.m.	*CBDNA – Eastern Division Meeting*	Formal Lounge –
	Thomas Duffy, President	Eastman Commons

7:30 – 10:00 p.m.   *Research Papers III*   Kilbourn Hall
(with musical illustration by the Eastman Wind Ensemble)

"Newly Discovered Approaches to Older Works"

"Trauermusik (1847) by Richard Wagner – A Contemporary
Performance Edition"
Michael Votta, Duke University

*The installation of Frederick Fennell into the
Sonneck Society as an Honorary Member*
Deane Roote, President, Sonneck Society

"Stravinsky's Composition Method in the
Symphonies of Wind Instruments: A Report from the
Paul Sacher Institute"
Robert Wason, Associate Professor of Theory
Eastman School of Music

"Sousa Marches: *Principles for Historically Informed Performance*"
MGSgt. Frank Byrne
U.S. Marine Band
Washington, D.C.

Musical examples conducted by Major Timothy Foley,
Assistant Director, U.S. Marine Band, Washington, D.C.

*   *   *   *   *

Sunday, February 9, 1992

9:00 – 12:00 a.m.   *Conductor Conferences with Faculty*   Room 120

9:45 – 10:45 a.m.   *Research Papers IV*   Kilbourn Hall
Historical band recordings & photographs
Fred Williams, Philadelphia, Pennsylvania

12 noon – 1:00 p.m. – Noon   *New Composition Readings II*   Eastman Theatre
Sydney Hodkinson, conducting
Ascension (1988)   James C. Mobberley
Concerto for Piano (1988)   Donald Crockett
David Burge, piano
Catena (1988)   Tristan Keuris
Donald Hunsberger, conductor

1:00 – 3:00 p.m.   *Conducting Session IV*   Room 120

Repertoire
Serenade in B, K.361/370a   Mozart

1:30 – 2:30 p.m.   *Composition for Winds*   Kilbourn Hall
Roundtable
Warren Benson, Moderator

Panelists:

Samuel Adler	Verne Reynolds
Sydney Hodkinson	Christopher Rouse
David Liptak	Allan Schindler
Robert Morris	Joseph Schwantner

5.00 p.m.

PROGRAM
Gala 40th Anniversary Concert

Fanfare for the Common Man   Aaron Copland

Folk Song Suite   Ralph Vaughan Williams
   March
   Intermezzo
   March

Frederick Fennell, conducting

Concerto for Euphonium   Joseph Horowitz
   Transcribed by Noichi Konagaya

Toru Miura, Euphonium

Symphony for Band   Vittorio Giannini
   Adagio
   Allegro

A. Clyde Roller, conducting

EWE Variations   Premiere Performance   Wiley Shephard

INTERMISSION
Presentation of the National Band Association
Academy of Wind and Percussive Arts Society Award
to Donald Hunsberger
by Edward Lisk, President, National Band Association

*Canyons*** (1991)   John McCabe
   Lento Moderato-Vivo-Lento-Allegro Vivace-Adagio

A Nostalgic Jazz Odyssey (1970)   John T. Williams
**Premiere Performance – Western Hemisphere

Donald Hunsberger, conductor

PROGRAM NOTES

For the 1942–43 season of the Cincinnati Symphony Orchestra, ten composers, among them **Aaron Copland**, were asked to write fanfares. Copland remembered that because those wartime fanfares were intended as "a kind of patriotic gesture," he decided to attempt "a certain nobility of tone, which suggested slow rather than fast music." **Fanfare for the Common Man** was premiered by the Cincinnati Symphony under its conductor Eugene Goosens on March 14, 1943. Unlike the other commissioned fanfares, Copland's gained popularity that lasted long beyond the World War II period; today it is one of his most frequently programmed scores. "When I wrote the Fanfare," Copland said, "I had no idea that it would serve any particular purpose other than that for which it was originally intended. However, I did use it in the Finale of my Third Symphony, which indicates that I thought it was worth further development."

Folk Song Suite reveals Vaughan Williams' interest in and association with the folk song movement which swept through England toward the close of the nineteenth century. His wife, Ursula, wrote: "Folk music weaves in and out of his work all through his life, sometimes adapted for some particular occasion, sometimes growing into the fabric of orchestral writing." The suite, *English Folk Songs,* was written for the Royal Military School of Music at Kneller Hall. After the first performance on July 4, 1923, *The Musical Times* reviewer commented, "The good composer has the ordinary monger of light stuff so hopelessly beaten." Vaughan Williams had been particularly happy to undertake the *Suite,* according to his wife, as he enjoyed working in a medium new to him.

"A military band was a change from an orchestra, and in his not-so-far off army days he had heard enough of the 'ordinary monger's light stuff' to feel that a chance to play real tunes would be an agreeable and salutary experience for Bandsmen."

At the head of his condensed score the composer gave the following credits, not printed in the full score: "The tune, 'My Bonny Boy,' is taken from 'English Country Songs' by kind permission of Miss L.E. Broadwood, J. A. Fuller-Maitland, Esq., and the Leadenhall Press. The tunes of 'Folk Songs from Somerset' are introduced by kind permission of Cecil Sharp, Esq."

– Frederick Fennell

The **Concerto for Euphonium** (1972) by **Joseph Horowitz** was originally written for brass band. The euphonium and wind ensemble arrangement heard today was created by Soigichi Konagaya. This versatile composition was also rewritten in 1974 as a bassoon concerto with orchestra. The Tokyo Kosei Wind Orchestra, Frederick Fennell, conductor, has recently commissioned a new work, "Dance Suite," from Mr. Horowitz and recorded this work.

Vittorio Giannini composed his **Symphony No. 3** for a commission by the Duke University Band, Paul Bryan, conductor, during the summer of 1958 in Rome, Italy, where he was spending his vacation. Of this composition the composer writes: "I can give no other reason for choosing to write a symphony to fulfill this commission than that I 'felt like it' and the thought of doing it interested me a great deal." He continues: "...in our family, music was as much a part of our everyday life as our daily bread. This perhaps explains why when I am asked the question: 'You have written mostly operas, orchestral, chamber and vocal music, how do you feel when writing for band?,' I can only answer, 'There is no difference. The band is simply another medium for which I try to make music'."

The Symphony was recorded in 1963 by the Eastman Wind Ensemble with this afternoon's conductor, **A. Clyde Roller**, for Mercury Living Presence records.

Wiley Shepard (B. 1952) was educated in upstate New York, attending the Herkimer County School of Veterinary Science and Musical Arts. His primary interests were large drums, oboes and long trombones. Archivist of the Epigrammatic Union and a supplier of fodder known to local dairymen as Shepard's Hay, Wiley's father was an avid and considerably skilled performer at country dances where he played the iced tea spoons (having foresworn the usual spoons when his voice changed). Wiley's mother, Dolores Mai, a coloratura contralto, practically monopolized the singing of *Because* at Herkimer County weddings for some three score and seven years, until she began to devote all of her attention to her son's development.

At the age of seven, Shepard composed his first music, a birthday song for his mother entitled, "Because Why! That's Why!," musical examples from which may still be found in the school textbooks of New York's southern tier.

His more mature work consists largely of varietal forms. A veritable tyranny of variety seemed to reign quite plainly, one might say, in the main. The present work, **EWE Variations** was written during a rather stressful period in the composer's life when the warm security of his family oval (an unusual family, not having a circle) came rising into his consciousness, bringing to mind such old favorite melodies as: "That Shapely Sheep May Graze," "Mary Mare, Au Contraire," "Little Beaucoup Has Lost Her Shoe." So the choice of subject for the **EWE Variations**, so closely related to that of Herr Beethoven's Ninth Symphony finale, should not surprise true music lovers.

But such familial security availed young Wiley naught as his scherzophrenic inner-ear flailed about the eight deep-seated hidden egos of these eight great variations.

Upon its completion, it seems he set out on a stroll to clear his turbulent mind. While crossing a large pasture, he came to a crooked fence in which he found a crooked stile (for his very convenience, ironically enough) upon which he slipped and fell a crooked mile, it seemed, until he hit a crooked tile at which point (you smile, and say indulgently, "get on with it!") all his guile departed him. Failing to right himself, he crumpled into a pile for quite some while, too long, at any rate, to be revived. Not even the National Endowment for the Arts could have saved him.

Luckily, the work survives and admirers need not hang their heads sheepishly on his behalf. For even upon the beginning of first rehearsals, the variations were pronounced "a shear delight!" (Several dozen performances have already been scheduled for late spring in New Zealand.)

Even a casual perusal of the autograph reveals a schizophrenic personality vividly evident in each variation. One would have to classify this work as perhaps the most completely, even inherently variant ever written. Surely, there could be no other set of variations in which the reach of the imagination is given such splendid latitude as these eight elements display: the general point of view of each, the gamut of complexity encompassed, the brilliant derivations of fresh material unearthed in each, the economy and rigor of discipline in each, and the delightful play that he enjoyed at the feet of his revered father, suggesting the old Orkney carol, "I Got Plenty O' Mutton," and finally of course, the techniques of Adbescho Schmoroli, his only teacher and fount of recommendations for the various fellowships and teaching positions he sought. Finally, and most astoundingly, even the autography changes from one variation to another: signatore, one might infer, to the alter egos of his most various self. No other music exists such as this!

The work was discovered by Elyea Relaine, who found it in a stack of now obsolete orchestration exercises that had been preserved by the HCSVSMA Composition Department. A fine judge of talent, Relaine snatched this rather uncommon bulk out of the stack and rushed off a FAX notification of her discovery to the capital city of Andorra in the far-off Pyrenees where she had learned that Dr. Donald Hunsberger, conductor of the famous Eastman Wind Ensemble, was conducting a concert with the National Wind and Mountain Bells Orchestra of that bastion of tranquility. Upon receiving this news, and foreseeing special events in 1992...., the rest is his story.

We have so much yet to discover in and of these **EWE Variations**!

Notes by Singh Titwillow

[It may now be stated that further intensive musicological research has uncovered the fact that Singh Titwillow is actually the *nom-de-plume* of none other than composer Warren Benson, whose interests in the EWE (ewe), and in wind bands at large, caused him to create the above aberration. The theme *Mary Had a Little Lamb* is frequently difficult to uncover in the variations which were created by the following composers in honor of the EWE and its conductor:

Samuel Adler
Warren Benson
Sydney Hodkinson
David Liptak
Robert Morris
Christopher Rouse
Allan Schindler
Joseph Schwantner]

Commissioned by the Guildhall School of Music with funds provided by Greater London Arts, **Canyons** is a response to the imposing landscapes of the American South West. Of this composition, composer **John McCabe** writes: "It is not an attempt to match in music the indescribable, but simply an exploration of musical ideas which, in themselves, derive from a personal response to this area. It should be stressed that the canyon scenery is not merely grandiose — it is bursting with an inner energy as well as obvious massiveness, and there is a sense of distance which is important, too."

A Nostalgic Jazz Odyssey was commissioned by the Eastman School of Music on the occasion of its 50th anniversary and premiered during the 1971–72 season. **John Williams** had composed his "Sinfonietta" for wind orchestra earlier and this work was recorded in 1969 by Donald Hunsberger and the **Eastman Wind Ensemble** on the Deutsche Grammophone label.

In contrast to the "Sinfonietta," which is somewhat harsh and massive in tonal texture, **Jazz Odyssey** was written as a fond recollection of the Big Dance Band era of the 1940s and 1950s. While using contemporary improvisational techniques in various sections, the whole work is an exciting view of a wonderful period in America's popular culture.

John Williams is best known to audiences as conductor of the Boston Pops Orchestra and composer of such film scores as the "Star Wars" Trilogy, "Raiders of the Lost Ark," and "E.T."

MEET THE ARTISTS

Toru Miura is the solo euphoniumist with the Tokyo Kosei Wind Orchestra. He is also an instructor of euphonium at Kunitachi College of Music, Tamagawa University, Shobi University and the Tokyo Conservatory Shobi. He directs the Tokyo Bari-Tuba Ensemble and the Euphonium Company as their founder, and also joined the faculty of Soai College of Music in Osaka.

Professor Miura was a performing artist at the 2nd International Euphonium and Tuba Conference, University of Maryland, 1983, to which he brought the members of the Tokyo Bari-Tuba Ensemble for a major performance. Appearing as a performing artist at the 2nd International Brass Congress, University of Indiana, he brought a quartet of players for a general session in 1984. He has also appeared as a solo recitalist at the 3rd International Tuba Euphonium Conference, University of Texas in 1986. In 1990, he was invited as a guest artist at the 4th International Tuba Euphonium Conference in Sapporo.

Other appearances outside of Japan also include clinic and solo performances in Hong Kong, Indonesia, Taiwan, Hawaii and China. Two solo recordings for CBS/Sony include "Invitation to Playing Trombone and Euphonium" and a performance of Gordon Jacob's *Fantasia for Euphonium and Band*. A new solo CD, "Euphonium for Columbia/Japan" has recently been released. His *Euphonium Method* is published by Doremi Publishing Company and three solo books have been published by the Tao Music Company. Toru Miura is also active as a writer for various professional magazines, including *Band People, Band Journal* and *Pipers*.

Mr. Miura was born in Osaka, Japan in 1948. In 1971, he earned the B.M. degree from Tokyo National University of Fine Arts and Music where he studied under Professor Kiyoshi Ohishi, distinguished vice president of the Japan Euphonium Tuba Association. In 1973, Mr. Miura graduated with the master of music degree from the University of Southern Mississippi, where he studied with Raymond Young. In 1973–74 he attended the Eastman School of Music and performed in the Eastman Wind Ensemble, Dr. Donald Hunsberger, conductor. He serves as a T.U.B.A. International Representative for Japan and is the vice president of the Japan Euphonium Tuba Association.

Frederick Fennell

"I grew up in three rooms of the Eastman School — the former Theatre rehearsal room, Kilbourn Hall, and the Eastman Theatre. But my training and career as a conductor began on the football field of Fauver Stadium when, as a freshman I organized and led the first University of Rochester Marching Band. Ninety percent of the marchers were from Eastman, so the next move was to the warm indoors, leading to what became the Symphony Band.

School was tough even then, but the chance to learn was everywhere. Graduation with a Performer's Certificate in 1937 as the School's first major in percussion kept me on with the Symphony Band as a graduate assistant. Theory was the major. At this time I inherited the Little Symphony which greatly enlarged my musical horizon; full faculty status came in 1939, granting continued individual study with all instrumental faculty colleagues.

Returning to School in 1945, I abandoned Fauver Stadium, forgave my life as a percussionist and declared for the profession of conductor when Howard Hanson appointed me to the orchestral faculty.

Then came the Eastman Wind Ensemble, the obvious result of all that had gone before and from the music that led me to it. We played our first rehearsal on 20 September 1952 and made our first recording in this fabulous room [the Eastman Theatre] eight months later. One decade of music making and recording, the operas I conducted in that Theatre — and a full-time residency in Sibley Music Library made life at Eastman unique and extraordinary. I simply consider that I went to school here for thirty years, which ended with the sudden invitation to join the Minneapolis Symphony Orchestra as Associate Music Director. Departure was painful but appropriate."

– Frederick Fennell

Conductor **A. Clyde Roller** has had an impressive background in both professional and academic music fields. For many years he was Resident Conductor of the Houston Symphony, Musical Director and Conductor of the Lansing (Michigan) and Amarillo Symphonies, in addition to appearances as guest conductor of orchestras internationally from Portugal to New Zealand. He has been a favorite in New Zealand, having appeared there six times to take the New Zealand Symphony on tour, recording with them for TV and Radio, and also performing with the Royal Christchurch Society in an all-Beethoven concert. His numerous engagements in the U.S. have included guest conducting the Boston Symphony in Esplanade concerts, appearing at the Alaskan Festival in Anchorage, serving as Principal Guest Conductor of the Oklahoma Symphony, conducting tours with the Arkansas Symphony, directing operas with the Arkansas Opera Company, conducting concerts with the Inland-Empire Symphony in California and the Texas orchestras of Ft. Worth, Corpus Christi, San Antonio and others.

Dr. Roller's academic associations have included his service as Professor of Ensembles at the Eastman School of Music, the University of Houston, the University of Texas-Austin, the University of Wisconsin at Madison, and the University of Michigan. He has been conductor and faculty member at Interlochen Center of the Arts for 40 years. He has also made numerous appearances throughout the U.S. as conductor of 38 All-State Orchestras, MENC and regional orchestras and with the Congress of Strings on both East and West coasts as well as with many other string festivals and projects.

Dr. Roller's career began as an oboist, which led to positions as principal oboist of the Tulsa Philharmonic, the Oklahoma Symphony and the Birmingham (Alabama) Symphony.

A. Clyde Roller has been the recipient of many honors, including the Amarillo "Man of the Year Award," Texas Orchestra Director of the Year 1979, Sigma Alpha Iota's National Artists Affiliate, the Eastman School of Music Alumni Achievement Award in 1981, Outstanding Educator of America Award and listing in the International *Who's Who*. Last season he received the American String

Teachers Award for "outstanding leadership in promoting strings" and also conducted two concerts in Mexico City with the Orquesta Filarmonica de la UNAM.

Donald Hunsberger's attention to musical expression and detail have long been a trademark in his approach not only to music in America's cultural past but to music of today as well. He has premiered more than one hundred new compositions with the Eastman Wind Ensemble in addition to maintaining a large repertoire ranging from the Venetian works of the sixteenth century through contemporary compositions by Joseph Schwantner, Michael Colgress, Brian Israel, and Karel Husa among others. He has recorded with the Eastman Wind Ensemble on Sony Classical, CBS Masterworks, Philips, DDG, Decca, Vox, Mercury Golden Imports, Tioch, Arabesque, CRI, and Centaur Records. More recently, CBS released a Masterwork CD with Dr. Hunsberger and trumpeter Wynton Marsalis. Toshiba-EMI produced two recordings from live concerts presented in Tokyo during the Eastman Wind Ensemble's 1978 tour of Japan and Southeast Asia under the auspices of the Kambara Agency, Tokyo, and the U.S. State Department. Dr. Hunsberger's work with Wynton Marsalis on CBS Masterworks/Sony in the recording of late nineteenth- and early twentieth-century cornet solos involved researching more than one hundred different solo compositions. He created the arrangements, orchestration, and cadenzas for Marsalis' use and recorded them with the Eastman Wind Ensemble. Their album *Carnaval* was nominated for a Grammy Award in 1987 in the category of "best solo performance with orchestra." In March 1988 Dr. Hunsberger recorded a second CBS Masterworks album, "Quiet City", with the Eastman Wind Ensemble, released in spring 1989.

Dr. Hunsberger also has been engaged in the research and recording of early American music for the theater orchestra and brass band. He is music director of the Eastman-Dryden Orchestra, an ensemble that specializes in performing live accompaniments for silent films made in the early 1900s currently in the permanent collection at the International Museum of Photography at the George Eastman House in Rochester. The orchestra has released five recordings on Arabesque of music by Victor Herbert, Rudolph Friml, and Sigmund Romberg. An excerpt of the Eastman-Dryden Orchestra's recording of Victor Herbert's *Mmes. Modiste* was included in the soundtrack of the Merchant-Ivory film *A Room With a View*. Dr. Hunsberger and the orchestra have been the resident ensemble at the Sound of Summer Festival on Hilton Head Island for the past few years.

Dr. Hunsberger has been very active internationally, having conducted and lectured throughout Japan and Southeast Asia, England, Norway, Belgium and Israel. He led the Eastman Wind Ensemble on critically acclaimed tours of Japan in 1978 (under the sponsorship of the Kambara Arts Office) and 1990 (under the sponsorship of Sony Music Communications Inc.) They are scheduled to return in June 1992 and June 1994, again under the Sony sponsorship. He has performed silent film accompaniments with the Pittsburgh, Houston National, Vancouver, Honolulu, Tampa, Orlando, Buffalo, Syracuse, Denver Chamber, and Columbus symphony orchestras. His initial appearance with the Milwaukee Symphony in 1989 led to a return engagement producing and conducting a three-film silent festival. He has been offered return engagements with each orchestra he has conducted.

Eastman Wind Ensemble

FLUTE
Susanna Self
Jennifer Hambrick
Gina Kutkowski
Danielle Rangel, piccolo

OBOE
Sarah Pool
Yuki Kanayama
Michinobu Iimori

CLARINET
Christian Ellenwood
Kathleen Gardiner
Tamara Raatz
Sandra Erickson
Dannene Drummond
Akiho Hattori
Dean LeBlanc
Kevin Morton
Nancy Boone, BB
Carmen Creel, bass clarinet
Michael Manning E

BASSOON
Susan Loegering
William Jobert
Pheobe Peterson

SAXOPHONE
James Kalyn, alto 1
Jeffrey MacKechnie, alto 2
Matthew Sintchak, tenor
Michael Titlebaum, baritone

HORN
Ilene Chanon
Caroline Whiddon
Robert Craven
Julia Pilant
Kane Gillespie

TRUMPET
Larry Knopp
Gregory Jones
Kyle Goldne
Susan Sievert
Brenda Clay
Barbara Hull

TROMBONE
Steven Vlad
Robert Holland
Ohad Wand
David Springfield

EUPHONIUM
Alan Spicciati
Steven Vlad
Robert Holland

TUBA
Paul Erion
Eric Bubacz

PIANO
Christopher Foley

STRING BASS
Gaelen McCormick

HARP
Heidi Krutzen

PERCUSSION
David Hagedorn – timpani
Peter Coutsouridis
David Carlisle
Kenneth McGrath
Michelle Humphreys

David Murray – timpani
Julia Hillbrick
Douglas Wallace
Michael Werner
David Hagedorn

Contributors

Toshio Akiyama received his music education at Musashino School of Music, the University of Tokyo School of Fine Arts, and the Eastman School of Music. He is president of the Japanese Band Directors Association and the Asia and Pacific Band Directors Association and is active in the World Association of Symphonic Bands and Ensembles. He is also an honorary member of the American Bandmasters Association. His publications include "March Music Index 218," "Band Music Index 552," and several band method books. In 1992 he received the International Award for his contributions to bands from the Midwest Band and Orchestra Clinic (Chicago). Currently Akiyama conducts the Sony Concert Band and teaches music education classes at the Musashino School of Music in Tokyo.

Leon J. Bly received a Bachelor of Arts degree from the College of William and Mary, Williamsburg, Virginia, studied conducting with Frederick Fennell, and in 1977 was granted the degree of Doctor of Philosophy by the University of Miami. He was Commander of the 110th Military Police Platoon in Stuttgart, Germany for two years, then returned to the United States and assumed the position of band director in Fredericksburg, Virginia. From 1974 to 1981, he was Director of Bands and Assistant Professor of Music Education at Concord College, Athens, West Virginia. Since September 1981 he has been Chairman of the Wind Department and Director of the Symphonic Wind Orchestra at the Stuttgart Music School, Stuttgart, Germany.

Frank P. Byrne was accepted to "The President's Own" United States Marine Band in Washington, D.C. as a member of the music library staff in 1973. He was appointed Assistant Chief Librarian and then Chief Librarian before assuming his present position of Administrative Assistant to the Director in 1988. In addition to his official duties with the Marine Band, Byrne is active in many professional organizations. His publications include "A Practical Guide to the Music Library" and modern performance editions of Sousa marches. He was music editor and consultant for "A Grand Sousa Concert" and other commercial recordings and also participated in the PBS documentary, "If You Knew Sousa," in which he was interviewed on camera and read excerpts from Sousa's autobiography. In 1993 he received the Sudler Medal of Honor from the John Philip Sousa Foundation for his service to bands on a national level.

Raoul F. Camus is Professor of Music at Queensborough Community College of the City University of New York and Director of the Queens Symphonic Band. For many years he was Director of New York's famed Forty-second (Rainbow) Division Band, and is a retired Army Reserve bandmaster. A past president of the Sonneck Society for American Music, he is an active musicologist specializing in American music. He is the author of *Military Music of the American Revolution*; part two of *The National Tune Index*, entitled *Early American Wind and Ceremonial Music 1636–1836*; *American Wind and Percussion Music* for the twelve-volume series *Three Centuries of American Music*; and numerous articles on bands and their repertoire, including the main article on bands and forty other brief entries for the *New Grove Dictionary of American Music*.

Frank J. Cipolla is Emeritus Professor of Music and former Director of Bands, State University of New York at Buffalo. After receiving his degrees from the Eastman School of Music, he began his professional career as a trumpet player in the Kansas City Philharmonic and later was Instructor of Brass Instruments at the University of Missouri at Columbia. Active in professional organizations, he has served as president of the New York State Band Directors Association and the Eastern Division of the College Band Directors National Association. He has been on the editorial boards of two scholarly journals, *American Music* and the *College Band Directors National Association Journal*, and has published numerous articles, record notes, and reviews focusing on nineteenth-century American bands and bandmasters, including a series of biographical sketches for the *New Grove Dictionary of American Music.*

Donald R. Hunsberger is Professor of Conducting and Ensembles at the Eastman School of Music, where he received his undergraduate and graduate degrees and where since 1965 he has been the Conductor of the Eastman Wind Ensemble. Under his leadership, the Eastman Wind Ensemble has performed on tour in Japan, the United States, and Canada, and has made fifteen recordings, including *Carnaval* with Wynton Marsalis, which was nominated for a Grammy award in 1987. His many arrangements, transcriptions, and editions for various forms of the wind band have been performed worldwide. He has lectured and conducted throughout the United States, Europe, and Pacific Rim countries, co-authored the *Art of Conducting*, and contributed articles to numerous journals. As a leader in researching, restoring, and performing live musical accompaniments for classic silent movie films of the 1915–1930 era, he has conducted over two dozen major symphony orchestras in the United States and Canada.

Jon C. Mitchell serves on the faculty of the University of Massachusetts at Boston, where he is Coordinator of Music Education and Conductor of the Chamber Orchestra. Prior faculty positions were at the University of Georgia, Carnegie Mellon University, and Hanover College, as well as appointments as high school band director in both Illinois and Puerto Rico. As a conductor, he has aided in securing new works for the band repertoire from several composers and has given the American premieres of pieces by Gustav Holst and Ralph Vaughan Williams. Mitchell has published over twenty-five scholarly articles and a book, *From Kneller Hall to Hammersmith: the Band Works of Gustav Holst.* He is assistant editor of the *Journal of the Conductor's Guild* and is principal editor of the *WASBE Journal* for the World Association of Symphonic Bands and Ensembles.

Jon Newsom is Assistant Chief of the Music Division of the Library of Congress, where he combines administrative duties with participation in professional music associations and writing on various musical subjects. He has organized lectures and concerts by Frederick Fennell dealing with the development of American band music; produced an annotated two-record set, "Our Musical Past: A Concert of Nineteenth Century Brass and Vocal Music"; supplied record notes for "American Brass Band Journal Revisited"; penned "The American Brass Band Movement" and several other articles in *The Quarterly Journal of the Library of Congress*; edited *Perspectives on John Philip Sousa*; and contributed numerous articles, record notes, book lists, and reviews for publications such as *The New Grove Dictionary of Music and Musicians, The Musical Quarterly*, and the Music Library Association *Notes.*

Timothy Reynish studied the French horn and was a music scholar at Cambridge University. He held principal horn positions with Northern Sinfonia, Sadlers Wells Opera, and the City of Birmingham Symphony Orchestra before taking up the post of Tutor in the Postgraduate Conducting Course at the Royal Northern College of Music, Manchester, in

1975. He has conducted concerts with several major symphony orchestras in England, as well as in other countries. In 1981, he was the resident host for the first international wind band conference held at the Royal Northern College of Music, a conference that resulted in the formation of the World Association of Symphonic Bands and Ensembles (WASBE) and the British Association of Symphonic Bands and Wind Ensembles (BASBWE). For over ten years he has been the editor of a series of wind band and ensemble publications for Novello & Co. He has also commissioned or given the world premieres of a number of important contemporary compositions for wind instruments.

Robert E. Sheldon, a graduate of the Eastman School of Music, served as museum specialist with the Smithsonian Institution Division of Musical Instruments for twenty-three years, where his duties included performance and restoration/conservation of instruments in the collections. He is currently curator of the instrument collections in the Music Division of the Library of Congress. As a free-lance musician, he has performed on various period wind instruments with organizations such as Aston Magna, Concert Royal, Ensemble for Early Music, and the Amadeus Winds. He has also performed on the French horn and other modern brass instruments with the Theater Chamber Players of the Kennedy Center, the National Gallery Orchestra, the Washington Chamber Orchestra, and his own Saxhorn Ensemble. He has recorded for the Library of Congress, Mercury, Erato, Decca, Nonesuch, and New World Records.

Michael Votta, Jr. graduated from the Eastman School of Music and is currently on the faculty of Duke University, where he serves as Director of the Wind Symphony and teaches courses in conducting and the performance of twentieth century music. Under his direction, the Wind Symphony has performed in Vienna, Budapest, Prague, and other European cities, and in broadcast concerts in Europe and the United States. He has authored numerous articles on wind literature and conducting and is particularly recognized for his writings on the wind music of Mozart, Wagner, and Berg. He maintains an active schedule as a guest conductor and clinician, having appeared with the National Youth Band of Israel and at conferences of music organizations throughout the United States. As a clarinetist, he has performed in the United States and Europe; his solo and chamber music recordings are available on the Partridge and Albany labels.

Robert W. Wason is Associate Professor of Music Theory at the Eastman School of Music. A recipient of Fulbright, National Endowment of the Humanities, and Guggenheim fellowships, Wason has been Visiting Professor at the University of Basel, Switzerland, the University of British Columbia at Vancouver, and the State University of New York at Buffalo. Aside from his work on Stravinsky in the present volume, he has lectured on the history of music theory in the nineteenth and early twentieth centuries and on the analysis of twentieth-century music. He is the author of *Viennese Harmonic Theory from Albrechtsberger to Schenker and Schoenberg* and articles in the *Journal of Music Theory*, *Perspectives of New Music*, *Music Theory Spectrum*, and other journals. Having studied the Anton Webern manuscripts at the Paul Sacher Foundation in Basel, he is now writing a book on Webern's music.